rampage

Also by Katherine S. Newman

A Different Shade of Gray: Mid-life and Beyond in the Inner City

No Shame in My Game: The Working Poor in the Inner City

Declining Fortunes: The Withering of the American Dream

Falling from Grace: Downward Mobility in the Age of Affluence

Law and Economic Organization

rampage

THE SOCIAL ROOTS OF SCHOOL SHOOTINGS

Katherine S. Newman

Cybelle Fox, David Harding,
Jal Mehta, and Wendy Roth

BASIC
BOOKS

A Member of the Perseus Books Group
New York

Books published by Basic Books are available at special discounts for bulk purchases in
the United States by corporations, institutions, and other organizations. For more
information, please contact the Special Markets Department at the Perseus Books
Group, 11 Cambridge Center, Cambridge, MA 02142, or call (617) 252-5298, (800)
255-1514, or e-mail specialmarkets@perseusbooks.com.

Designed by Trish Wilkinson

Library of Congress Cataloging-in-Publication Data
    Rampage : the social roots of school shootings / Katherine S. Newman [et al.].
        p.   cm.
    ISBN 0-465-05103-0 (alk. paper)
    1. School violence—Social aspects—Kentucky—Health—Case studies.
2. School violence—Social aspects—Arkansas—Coal Hill—Case studies. 3.
Youth and violence—United States—Case studies. I. Title: Social roots
of school shootings. II. Newman, Katherine S., 1953–.

LB3013.33.K46R36 2004
371.7'82—dc22   2003018980

04 05 06 / 10 9 8 7 6 5 4 3 2 1

Dedicated to the people of
Westside, Arkansas, and Heath, Kentucky

CONTENTS

PREFACE

In the late 1990s, Americans watched in horror as a wave of mass shootings on middle and high school campuses swept across the country. Banner headlines and terrifying photos screamed from the front pages of the nation's dailies. Round-the-clock television coverage broadcast images of distraught teenagers huddled in the hallways, anguished parents weeping behind police lines, ambulance gurneys wheeling the dead and injured from playgrounds to emergency rooms, and grave stones rising. Columbine High School, in the Denver suburb of Littleton, Colorado, leaped into the public imagination as the nightmare image of the 1990s: children running for cover, police barricaded behind their cars, and a teenage "Trench Coat Mafia" killing themselves after gunning down twelve students and a teacher and wounding two dozen others.

Congress responded to these events as responsible legislators should have: They tried to uncover the source of this unwelcome trend in order to determine what kind of policies might put an end to it. In 1999 the House of Representatives added a provision to the "Missing, Runaway, and Exploited Children's Act" requiring the U.S. Department of Education to study rampage shootings in schools. Representative James Greenwood, a Republican from eastern Pennsylvania who had previously been a social worker, asked the department for research that would explain why such tragedies were occurring in American communities that appeared to be so safe. Greenwood was not after a raft of numbers. What he wanted was a set of in-depth community studies. The Department of Education in turn contacted the National Academy of Sciences, the most prestigious research organization in the country, which has provided scientific advisers to every administration since Abraham Lincoln's.

I (KSN) was surprised to get a call from the Academy asking for my help in this effort. As a professor at Harvard University's Kennedy School of Government and Dean of Social Science at the Radcliffe Institute of Advanced Study, I have authored a number of books on urban poverty and the consequences of economic stress for American families but knew little about the sociological study of crime. However, as the mother of teenagers, and as a social scientist as perplexed as anyone by the sudden eruption of violence in such unlikely places, this study seemed a useful opportunity to put years of training to good use.

I had another reason for answering the congressional call. As director of a new doctoral program in government, sociology, and social policy, I wanted to find ways to demonstrate the program's commitment to scholarship in the public interest. I approached four doctoral candidates in the program and persuaded them to devote the next two years to the question of rampage shootings. Joining the team were Cybelle Fox, a graduate of the University of California at San Diego who studies race, immigration, and the politics of redistribution; David J. Harding, a Princeton graduate whose research focuses on the consequences of concentrated poverty in the inner city; Jal Mehta, a Harvard College graduate who is studying the relationship between education reform and broader social, economic, and cultural changes in American life; and Wendy Roth, a Yale graduate whose work is devoted to understanding the racial identities of Latino immigrants.

In the summer of 2000, Harding and Mehta moved to Heath, Kentucky, and Fox and Roth to Westside, Arkansas, the two communities we studied at close range about three years after each had gone through the ordeal of a rampage shooting. I spent time in both communities. This book is based on interviews with 163 people in Heath and Westside along with neighboring communities, including families of the victims, students who were in the schools at the time of the shootings as well as current students who were not, teachers, administrators, lawyers, officials of the court, psychologists, newspaper and television reporters, and friends, family members, and fellow congregation members of the shooters. We reviewed the national and local news coverage of these two cases as well as the other rampage school shootings that have taken place in the past thirty years. The five of us used up many yellow legal pads sketching out and then refining the analyses we present here. This volume is the product of a complete team effort, from the early days of planning the research, to collecting and analyzing the data, all the way through the writing and rewriting of numerous drafts. Although I wrote the final draft so that the book would have a single voice, each coauthor contributed chapters, and we discussed them as an ensemble. This kind of partnership is rare in academic settings, and we are privileged to have been able to work together in this fashion.

The topics covered here are sensitive ones for the survivors and the families of victims. We asked people who sent their children off to school one morning only to have to identify their bodies at the morgue in the afternoon to revisit terrible images and painful memories. Heath and Westside are still traumatized by what they endured and are struggling to put the experience behind them. Some people, quite understandably, will never be able to do so. Family members of the shooters carry an unbearable burden of guilt and shame. They still love their boys, and they want them to be able to do some good in this world. Everyone we talked to in our interviews had to relive a tragedy they have been trying to get over.

We would like to have been able to acknowledge them all by name, but we must abide by our promise to protect their anonymity and refrain from naming most of them. As we explained to our interview subjects, this was not possible in all cases. The shooters, their families, and many other key characters were subjected to national media exposure, and because it would have been impossible to disguise their identities, we did not attempt to do so. Likewise, we felt it would dishonor the dead and the wounded to camouflage their identities. Hence we have used the real names of those who died and members of their families; the children and teachers who were wounded; and some of the local government officials, officers of the court, psychiatrists, and school officials whose names were already well known from the media coverage.

In all other instances, however, we have changed the names and minor biographical details of the people we interviewed. In many cases we were the first people, other than their immediate family members, they had talked to about the shooting. It was an ordeal for them to discuss the event, and confidentiality was essential in making them feel comfortable enough to break their silence. Because civil suits were still on appeal during our research, many people felt they could not participate in this project. Although those close to the scene may be able to figure out who is speaking on these pages, pseudonyms help shield members of these communities from further scrutiny, which made it more comfortable for them to speak their minds. The resulting text will be difficult for many of these people to read, and they will not agree with everything we have written, but we know that they share our desire to get to the bottom of rampage shootings and our hope that something constructive will come of their ordeal.

There are a few people we can thank publicly here. In Heath, we are especially grateful to the families of the victims—Wayne, Sabrina, and Becky Steger;

Gwen, Chuck, and Christina Hadley; and Joe and Judith James—as well as the families of the wounded, including Mark, Julie, Shelley, and Becky Schaberg. Although we were never able to speak with Michael Carneal, who is incarcerated for the shooting, he and his parents, John and Ann Carneal, gave us permission to contact his psychologist, Dr. Kathleen O'Connor, and his sister, Kelly Carneal. We learned a great deal from them as well as from the attorneys who handled the criminal and civil cases, and we thank them all for their gracious cooperation. Because the appeals of the civil suits were still in progress during our fieldwork, Michael Carneal's parents could not be interviewed for this project. Nonetheless, they did what they could to assist us, mainly by assuring others— lawyers, doctors, and family friends—that they were comfortable with the prospect of their cooperation.

Many public officials went out of their way to offer us support and assistance in the Paducah area. Lewis Carr, a resource officer in the McCracken County Public Schools, Judge Jeffrey Hines, Judge-Executive Daniel Orazine, attorneys Daniel Boaz and Tim Kaltenbach, and Paducah Mayor Bill Paxton were very generous with their time and expertise. We are greatly indebted to Bill Bond, the former principal of Heath High School, and Barbara McGinty, the current principal, for opening their offices and schools to this study. Their counterparts at Heath Middle School were equally open and helpful. Members of the police department, the county librarians, the Sheriff's Department, local journalists and academics, members of the Heartland Worship Center, and the Paducah Area Chamber of Commerce helped us learn about the history of the area and the events that unfolded in the course of the shooting.

Above all, we appreciate the welcome we received from the students, teachers, staff, and parents of Heath High School. They permitted us to visit their homes, classrooms, and churches and spoke openly about the difficulties of navigating adolescence. Libby and Alisha Bobo were particularly kind to us.

Many individuals, families, and institutions gave us a helping hand in the towns of Cash, Bono, and Egypt, Arkansas, the communities that together constitute the Westside School District. Similarly, their neighbors in Jonesboro were generous with their time and expertise. We would particularly like to thank Judge Ralph Wilson, who supported this project from the outset and contacted others in the community on our behalf. Brent Davis, the prosecuting attorney in the Westside case, and his deputy, Mike Walden, were invaluable resources. So were William Howard and Val Price in the office of the public defender. Karen Costello, director of the Victims/Witness Assistance program, and Stacey Worthington, the ombudsman in the Department of Youth Services, have our profound thanks for speaking with us about this very difficult case. Mayor L. M. Duncan in Bono, Mayor Leroy Burdin in Cash, and Mayor Hubert Brodell in Jonesboro went to great lengths to facilitate our research. Diane Holmes, a local counselor, opened many doors for us. Ron Deal, the Family Life Minister from the Southwest Church of Christ, contributed important insights on recovery from tragedy. While in Jonesboro, we were fortunate to make our home in the lovely West Washington Guest House, where Pat and Joe Simpson and Ken Stack not only made us comfortable but shared with us their knowledge of the history of the area and suggested helpful individuals for us to contact.

We are indebted to the Craighead County Sheriff's Office, the Arkansas Department of Youth Services, the staff of the Alexander Youth Services Center, the Public Defender Commission, and the State Police of Arkansas. A number of health care providers helped us understand the crisis management aspects of the Westside shooting, including the Craighead County Crisis Response Team and Mid-South Health Systems. The Westside community and neighboring Jonesboro are rich in religious institutions, many of which we visited during our stay, both to get a feel for the community and to speak with ministers and members of their congregations. We include here Trinity Church, Blessed Sacrament Catholic Church, South West Church of Christ, the Bono Church of Christ, Central Baptist Church, First United Methodist, and the Fullness of Joy Church. The management and staff of the *Jonesboro Sun* opened their archives to us and contributed personal reflections on the tragedy.

We would like to thank the families of the victims in Westside, although most preferred not to speak with us. Their losses were beyond measure. We respect their desire for privacy and hope that this volume will be of value to them. Similarly, the staff and teachers of Westside Elementary, Middle, and High Schools deserve our gratitude for spending time with us, even though it was exceedingly difficult for them to discuss the shooting. Lynette Thetford, a former Westside teacher who was wounded in the shooting, was particularly helpful. Students and parents at all three schools came forward to provide their recollections, and we thank them for this. Finally, we must mention Gretchen Woodard, the mother of Mitchell Johnson, one of the two shooters in Westside. Ms. Woodard was unfailingly honest and willing to confront the terrible consequences of her son's actions, knowing all the while that some people place the blame for this tragedy on her shoulders.

Offenders in juvenile facilities are shielded from contact with the outside world. Although we spoke to the staff at the Alexander facility, where Andrew Golden and Mitchell Johnson were incarcerated, we were not permitted to interview the two boys, nor could we talk with Scott Johnson (Mitchell's father) or anyone in the Golden family. We regret that this volume cannot draw upon these perspectives, which surely would have been informative.

Our work benefited a great deal from the opportunity to exchange ideas with the members of the National Academy of Sciences/National Research Council's Committee on Case Studies of Lethal School Violence, especially the chair of the panel, Mark Moore, and his associates, Anthony Braga and Carol Petrie. Bill Modzeleski, the associate deputy undersecretary in the U.S. Department of Education Office of Safe and Drug-Free Schools, was a valuable resource. Experts who volunteered their services as the National Research Council (NRC) case studies developed included committee members Phil Cook (Duke University), Tom Dishion (University of Oregon), Denise Gottfredson (University of Maryland), Phillip Heymann (Harvard University), Jim Short (Washington State University), Stephen Small (University of Wisconsin, Madison), Lewis Spence (Department of Social Services, Massachusetts), and Linda Teplin (Northwestern University).

The NRC study, published under the title *Deadly Lessons: Understanding Lethal School Violence,* contains a set of case studies of rampage shootings to which we contributed two (the Heath and Westside cases). The other four were directed by a distinguished group of senior colleagues whose insights are reflected in our own work. We are particularly grateful to William DeJong (Boston University), Mindy Fullilove (Columbia University), John Hagan (Northwestern University), Mercer Sullivan (Rutgers University), and their collaborators. From the beginning, we realized that we would probably have more to say than could be summarized in the brief case studies we contributed to the National Academy of Sciences effort. The decision to write this book in addition was stimulated by groundbreaking efforts of our fellow case study authors, and we thank them for listening to our ideas and sharing theirs.

In chapter 10 of this book, we discuss our theory of rampage shootings, drawing on the original fieldwork we did in Heath and Westside and testing it against a data set collected by the Violence Prevention Division of the National Center for Injury Prevention and Control at the Centers for Disease Control and Prevention under the able leadership of Drs. Rodney Hammond and Mark Anderson. These two colleagues generously shared their data and their wisdom with us, out of a common commitment to understanding lethal violence on campus. We are grateful to them for contributing these materials to our study and underline the fact that we alone are responsible for the interpretations offered here, especially for any mistakes we may have made.

Our colleagues at Harvard University, both faculty and students, have heard us talk about this research for several years now and have given us the benefit of their constructive criticism. Professor Chris Winship, in the Sociology Department, invited us to craft a special issue of the journal *Sociological Methods and Research,* which was a great opportunity to think through some of the more vexing problems that attended the execution and interpretation of this research. We are grateful to him and to Professor Charles Rangin (University of Arizona), who reviewed our work and gave us extensive, insightful criticism.

At a critical moment in our writing, several colleagues responded to the call to read what was then a monstrously long draft. Harold Boverman, Howie Becker, Mitch Duneier, Kathryn Dudley, and Ziad Munson deserve medals for taking on this task; the resulting book is far better for their critical input. Drs. Steven Schlozman and Jeffrey Bostic, at Massachusetts General Hospital, helped us learn more about mental health policy in schools. Cheri Minton taught us to use the Atlas coding software. Margot Minardi, Ricardo Mora, and Kevin Psonak came to our rescue in the midst of many a logistical and editorial snafu.

A number of Harvard students assisted us with difficult research tasks that proved essential. Martin West synthesized components of the theoretical literature that helped us form our analytical framework. Naomi Calvo and Miguel Salazar summarized media materials on rampage shootings and near-miss cases beyond those we studied firsthand. Audrey Alforque devoted a summer to transcribing interviews, and Victor Chen tracked down most of the photos that appear here, summarized important media materials, and contributed background research that rounded out our understanding of Mitchell Johnson's past. Special mention must be made of two outstanding Harvard undergraduates, Tory Wobber and Vera Makarov, who worked with the team for almost a year, transcribing and coding interviews. Their work, supported by the Radcliffe Research Partners program, was critical in managing the hundreds of pages of transcripts that form the database for this project. Our weekly discussions with Vera and Tory yielded many ideas that found their way into this book.

The Radcliffe Institute for Advanced Study provided funding for a national conference to unveil the National Academy of Sciences report, which gave us an opportunity to make some of our ideas public and to hear the reactions of the expert audience. Thanks go to the Linda S. Wilson Fund for helping to underwrite this conference. A generous grant from the National Academy of Sciences (Grant No. S184U000010 from the Department of Education to the National Academy of Sciences) provided the resources we needed to complete this work. We also want to acknowledge the vital financial support of the William T. Grant

Foundation and the encouragement of its recently retired President, Dr. Karen Hein, as well as her successor, Dr. Robert Granger. Members of the research team have been supported by the National Science Foundation's Integrated Research, Education, and Training grant awarded to Harvard University's program on Inequality and Social Policy (which I chair) as well as individual graduate fellowships from NSF. This national investment in graduate education makes studies of critical social issues possible, and we are grateful for it.

Literary agent Lisa Adams supported this book from its inception and made many insightful contributions to the manuscript. Jo Ann Miller, editor extraordinaire at Basic Books, saw the book's potential and pushed us to streamline the account. We are grateful for her patience, skill, and devotion to this project. Ellen Garrison, editorial assistant at Basic, provided key insights of her own. The production and marketing staff at Basic applied their customary high-quality craftsmanship, which all authors appreciate. We all have countless family members and friends to thank for putting up with our preoccupation over the past several years. We hope they will feel the sacrifice was worth it. We certainly do.

Finally, we note that the authors' royalties from the sale of this volume are being donated to Heath High School and Westside Middle School for the teachers and administrators to use as they see fit. We hope this gift will go some distance toward returning the kindness extended to us during our stay in their communities.

—Cambridge, Massachusetts

PART ONE

1

EXPLOSIONS

The morning of December 1, 1997, began as most days did at Heath High School on the outskirts of West Paducah, Kentucky. Clusters of students slowly made their way into the school's entrance, reluctant to return to class after the Thanksgiving break. Cheerleaders compared notes on the season's games and pep rallies. Members of the prize-winning school band shifted their instruments around to make space for their backpacks, chatting about the Thanksgiving weekend that had just ended. Hanging back in the corner of the lobby, as was their custom, was the small coterie of Heath's Goths, clad in hard-rock T-shirts and the occasional black trench coat.

Kelly Carneal, a popular senior at Heath, and her brother Michael, a short, slender freshman with dark hair and glasses, pulled into the high school parking lot around 8:00 a.m. The two had been commuting to school together since Kelly got her driver's license. "We drove to school," Kelly remembered four years later, "listening to Mariah Carey's 'Butterfly.'"

Kelly took her backpack out of the trunk while Michael retrieved a bundle wrapped in blankets. The pair walked off toward the band room. Michael got there first, and Kelly followed after chatting with friends. Mr. Samms, the band teacher, strolled through the room and bumped into Michael. "Mike, what have you got there?" he asked, pointing to the bundle. "This? Oh, it's just my English project," Michael replied.

Michael clutched his "English project" and strolled into the main lobby, where he sought out his new friends in the Goth group: Brian Mather, David Maxwell, Cory Giles, and a couple of other boys. Brian heard Michael's bundle hit the floor and asked what was inside. Before Mike could reply, Brian commented to his friends, "Sounds like guns to me." Someone in the group changed the subject and no further attention was paid to Michael. A freshman "dweeb," Michael did not yet "rate" in Goth circles.

Michael opened his backpack and pulled out a pair of bright orange ear plugs, the kind that hunters wear to protect their hearing from the blasts of gunfire. He pulled a pistol from a pouch, reached into his backpack for an ammunition clip, and loaded the gun. Nobody noticed, or even looked in his direction.

Completely unaware of Michael's lethal preparations, the Heath High School prayer group, an unofficial gathering of twenty or thirty Christian students, joined hands in a circle and waited for their leader, Luke Fallon, to call them to prayer. Athletes, band members, "brainy" students bound for college, and the less academically inclined, bowed their heads to thank the Lord and ask for a good day in the name of Jesus. The last "Amens" echoed around the circle as Michael assumed a firing stance—slightly crouched, with both hands stretched straight out in front of him—released the safety catch, cocked the firing pin, and fired three shots in rapid succession. With a loud boom, the percussion bounced off the walls, stunning the crowd. Five more shots followed, as Michael swung his arms in an arc before the students, who were now falling down inside the worship circle.

Kelly Carneal stood just a few feet away from the prayer group, looking at her brother in complete amazement:

> I heard what sounded like firecrackers. . . . They make the little popping sound. . . . And then I saw people turn and start to run. It was like a flower: There was a group of people and it just kind of folded away. . . . And my brother was standing there. He had the gun in his hands . . . and was looking straight ahead. His face looked different, and his body posture[1] was different. . . . He looked like a completely different person. I would not have recognized him had he not had on the same clothes as he had on that morning.
>
> I started to walk towards him, and he turned his head and he looked at me. And I realized he didn't know who I was. I thought, "My brother is going to shoot me!" So I turned around and ran.

A freshman student in the prayer group, Linda Feeney, kept thinking that everything was so normal and so surreal at the same time. She watched the wounded girls slump to the floor, barely recognizing they had been shot:

> I looked down at Nicole, and I was like, "How on Earth is she playing this joke, this is horrible." . . . And then I looked at Jessica and she was like, "Get down!" . . . From that point on I was in total shock, because then I realized

it was for real. . . . Michael's really doing this. I will never forget that stare on Michael's face in a million years. . . . It was just blank, nothingness. It's like there was nothing in him.

Bedlam broke out in the hallways as students ran down the corridors. Screaming, shaking, gasping for air, they arrived in their classrooms to find their teachers unaware of the carnage in the lobby.

Jessica James, a senior who played flute in the school band, a devoted member of Agape (a Christian fellowship group), and a strong student, died on the lobby floor, despite the frantic efforts of teachers to administer CPR to her for over an hour. Kayce Steger, a fifteen-year-old softball enthusiast, an active participant in the Twelfth Street Baptist Church, and a future police officer, died in the emergency room. She had refused a date with Michael only a month before. Nicole Hadley, a fourteen-year-old member of the school band and the freshman basketball team, was kept on life support for the rest of the day as her distraught family waited for her father to return from a business trip out West. Although the Hadleys had only lived in the Paducah area for a little over a year, Nicole had become a good friend of Michael's and a frequent visitor to the Carneal family home. Nicole and Michael "walked together" at their eighth grade graduation, a custom of some importance in the community. At her family's request, Nicole's doctors turned the ventilators off shortly after 10 p.m.; she died almost immediately.

Melissa "Missy" Jenkins, president of the Future Homemakers of America and another devoted Christian, was hit in the spine, hospitalized, and left paraplegic—at the age of fifteen. Shelley Schaberg, described by the school's principal as the best female athlete at Heath and later voted homecoming queen by the senior class, was left with bullet fragments in her arms that required months of physical therapy and put an end to any hopes of a career in basketball.[2] Kelly Hard (age sixteen), Craig Keene (fifteen), and Hollan Holm (fourteen) were all hospitalized with minor wounds and then released. Three years later, when Holm became the valedictorian, he reminded the student body that they had lost two members of their class in December of 1997:[3] Nicole Hadley and Michael Carneal.

How did this awful crime come to pass? On Thanksgiving Day, after feasting with his family and grandparents, Michael rode his bike to the home of his buddy, Jered Parker. When the Parker family left to have their own holiday meal with relatives, Michael climbed through an open window in their garage, found the hidden key to the gun case, and stuffed a 30-30 rifle and four .22 rifles into his duffel bag, along with the earplugs and boxes of ammunition.

Affecting a nonchalant air when he arrived at home, Michael parked the duffel bag by some pine trees outside his bedroom window, and went in to greet his parents. "I'm fine," he said, when they asked about his day. Once upstairs, he locked his door, climbed out the window, and retrieved the bag, stashing it under his bed. Michael carefully screened the weapons from view by moving Lego boxes in front of the bag. He went downstairs to watch TV for a while but was too excited to sit still for long. Lying awake on his bed later that evening, Michael felt a satisfaction that had eluded him for a long time.

"I was feeling proud, strong, good, and more respected. I had accomplished something. I'm not the kind of kid who accomplishes anything. This is the only adventure I've ever had."[4]

Over the weekend, Michael put the guns back into his duffel bag and rode over to the home of his good friend, Craig Holt. He showed Holt and his older brother Danny, a senior at Heath, the collection of rifles. They took turns shooting at a pink rubber ball in the backyard. Danny admonished the boys not to get into trouble with the weapons but said nothing to anyone else about the guns.[5]

On Sunday afternoon of the Thanksgiving weekend, Michael did his homework and played chess with his father. In the evening, he stole two old shotguns from his father's closet and hid them under his bed. He told the prosecution psychiatrists that he was out to impress:

"More guns is better. You have more power. You look better if you have a lot of guns. A kid would say one gun is good, but that Michael had a lot of guns."[6]

Monday morning was a completely normal beginning to the school week. Michael came downstairs with the rifles bound together in duct tape, covered by blankets. On top of the blankets he piled the sheets from his bed and, when asked, told his mother that the cat had thrown up on them and that he was taking them to the laundry room. Michael went into the laundry room and deposited the sheets, but then went directly outside and put the bundle of guns into the trunk of Kelly's car. The pistol and ammunition were stuffed into his backpack. He got into the car with his sister and rode off to Heath High, eager with anticipation. Michael was expecting a triumph.

———

When Bill Bond, the principal of Heath High School, heard the first shots ring out, he ran from his office to the lobby, just in time to see the leader of the prayer group, Luke Fallon, confront Michael, demanding to be told why he was shooting at people. By that time, Michael had put the handgun down on the floor. Michael turned to Luke and pleaded, "Please, just shoot me!" Instead, Bond hustled Michael into his office and turned him over to Ron Kilgore, his academic adviser at Heath. Teachers came running to help the injured, and those who knew what to do began to pump chests and blow into the mouths of students who had stopped breathing.

Moments later, word leaked out of the school that a shooting had occurred. Terrified parents began streaming in from all over the community as the local radio and television stations started to broadcast the news. John Carneal, Michael's father, heard the news at work; his wife Ann got the word at home. They jumped into their cars, Ann bringing all the blankets she could carry. Neither parent knew the details of what had happened or that Michael was involved; they simply rushed to the scene to see if they could help. When they arrived, Bill Bond and Michael's sister Kelly pulled the Carneals into a private office to break the bad news.

Initial accounts of the shooting were confusing, and chaos reigned at Heath as a consequence. No one knew which hospital the injured had been taken to or what their condition was. Distraught parents ran from one emergency room to another. Lacking identification, the hospitals often didn't know exactly whom they had in their care. Shaken parents such as Gwen Hadley, Nicole's mother, were placed in the terrible position of having to identify their children's bodies.

> They said that there was a girl in surgery and a girl coming out of the MRI. . . . They said the girls looked so much alike, they didn't know who was who. So [they] came and got Jessica's picture . . . and . . . Nicole's picture. The pictures were both taken into the operating room. They . . . still weren't sure who was who.
>
> I remember a doctor running and screaming, "A mom's coming, a mom's coming, get her ready." And we went into a trauma room. And Nicole was lying there on a gurney in the middle of the room. . . .
>
> It was definitely Nicole, and I immediately knew she was gone. . . . I [prayed] with her a little bit, but they were bagging her. She still had a smile on her face.

A DEADLY PARTNERSHIP

Students at Westside Middle School near Jonesboro, Arkansas, were trying to buckle down after spring vacation on the afternoon of March 24, 1998. Lunch recess had just ended, and Ron Harris was running late to his class. Scurrying down the hallway, Ron ran into fellow sixth grader Andrew Golden, who was dressed in blue jeans and a camouflage jacket and cap. Ordinarily, Ron wouldn't have even noticed Andrew, but that day he remembered that Andrew had been absent from the morning class they shared. Katie Powell emerged from her science class on an errand for her teacher and ran into Andrew as well. Ron and Katie watched in amazement as Andrew walked calmly toward the fire alarm box mounted on the wall, grabbed the hammer from its side, smashed the glass cover, pulled the alarm handle, and then walked out the exit leading to the playground.

Alarm horns sounded throughout the school, jolting the students and teachers from their desks. Knowing that no drills had been scheduled, Lynnette Thetford, a sixth grade English teacher, poked her head outside the classroom to see what was going on and ran into Katie, headed back to her science room. "Andrew Golden pulled the alarm," Katie reported, "and then ran out the door!" Amazed at Andrew's breach of school rules, Thetford considered ignoring the alarm. But she dismissed the idea, because the school had taught students over and over again that they had to treat every drill seriously. "I felt we had to go outside anyway," she later told police investigators, "and I thought to myself that Andrew was going to get into a lot of trouble for pulling that alarm." Following the rules to the letter, Mrs. Thetford gathered her grade book, instructed her students to put their pencils down, and formed a line to march down the corridor and out the exit door that leads to the playground in front of the school gym.

Thetford's class emerged onto the playground, which was bounded at the back by a wooded hillside only 100 yards from the front of the gym. The "drill" was going by the book, Thetford thought, until she heard explosions coming from behind her. "This is some kind of crazy drill and someone has pushed it too far," she said to herself, "because this is starting to scare the kids." Seconds later, she felt a sharp pain in her right leg and fell to the pavement. The playground seemed to grow huge before her as panic set in. "I was screaming, 'Get down! Get down!'" she recalled later, but in a state of shock, she thought that the kids could not hear her.

A hail of gunfire ricocheted off the pavement and the walls. Students now realized they were exposed to the gunmen and began to scream and tug hard on the door that led back into the classroom building, in a desperate attempt to take shelter. Because the door was locked from the inside, it would not budge. Thetford struggled to stand up so that she could protect the children, but found she couldn't move her leg. She applied pressure to staunch the bleeding until the gym teacher, Coach Thomas, dragged her to a covered walkway behind the class-room building.

Shannon Wright, a popular English teacher at Westside, emerged with her class onto the sidewalk area just behind Thetford's students. Wright walked straight into the firestorm of bullets blasting from the wooded hillside. Sixth grader Whitney Irving heard Wright yell "Run!" and took off in the direction of the gym with her friend, Britthney, running behind her, screaming in fear. Within seconds, a bullet tore into Britthney and she crumpled to the ground. Attempting to shield other students from the onslaught, Shannon Wright launched herself over a young girl and took a bullet in the chest.

Dragging children out of the line of fire, teachers who could get to them stripped their clothing in search of the wounds and applied pressure to stop the bleeding. Those who were trained in CPR tried to remember their marching orders, but they knew more about handling choking victims than gunshot wounds. Seventh grade teacher Mary Curtis kept thinking to herself, "What do I need to do? What can I do?" and tried to follow directions coming at her in staccato: "Wrap that wound . . . try to get a pulse . . . find bandages . . ." Curtis's heart was pounding as she grabbed towels and wrapped wounds, trying to remember what she had seen on TV shows like *ER*.

Most of the wounded were carried into the gym, the closest accessible building out of the line of fire, but not all the teachers could get there. Some ended up isolated in the classroom building, unable to let go of wounded kids long enough to alert emergency personnel or fellow teachers to their whereabouts. Sixth grade teacher Liz Carleton was one of those left to tend wounded students inside. "All I knew was that I was in that building alone with a child who was dying. I was afraid she was going to die on me, and there was no help." Carleton remembered that the school kept big blue barrels full of emergency supplies in the classrooms and somehow had the presence of mind to get some.

> I got [the earthquake kit] open. . . . I was throwing everything back over my shoulder 'cause . . . I didn't know what I needed. . . . But I just got wash-cloths . . . and got on the floor and just put them on her leg. . . . Those cloths were just soaked in a matter of seconds. Britthney asked me, 'Will I lose my leg? Will I lose my leg?'

Within ten minutes of the shooting, police and emergency personnel converged on the middle school. Virtually everyone who arrived on the scene to help had a child or a neighbor in potential danger, and they were frantic about finding out whether they were safe. "Once I got down there and saw how bad it was," remembered Emily Levitt, an elementary school teacher, "all I could think about was my niece." The scene was the stuff of nightmares, with injured kids jumbled on the floor of the gym bleeding and crying, and desperate teachers bent over them trying to staunch the blood and reassure their terrified students.

Attending to the victims was all the harder because no one knew exactly where the shots were coming from or whether the shooting had stopped for good. Children and teachers got the impression that there were at least two shooters and that the assault was coming from the hillside. But they had no way of determining the extent of the danger. Were there other shooters in the building? Were the hillside shooters done? Or were more attacks on the way? One teacher recalled, "The Sheriff's Department came by [while I was holding an IV line on a dying child] and said, 'Do *not* put your back to the woods. Watch those woods because the shooters were right up there. We haven't located them.' So here I am, thinking, I'm the lookout? I'm holding this IV thing, I'm the lookout for the shooters?"[7]

Construction workers tiling the roof of new classrooms even closer to the hillside found themselves targets of the assault as well. Pete Hanson was working on the roof on the north side of the campus. He heard shots coming from the hill and looked up to see two white males in the woods, both wearing camouflage shirts.

> They were standing two feet apart, both firing down the back side of the school area. . . . It was fierce there for a few seconds. . . . This one guy pointed the gun at me and fired three shots. That was the one with the smaller caliber . . . I could hear [the shooters] talking, but . . . I couldn't tell what they was saying. Then they took off back up that hill.

Police radios barked the news that two suspects were headed into the woods, and the Sheriff's Department moved to "throw a net" over the entire area. Investigators Jon Varner, John Moore, and Sheriff's Deputy Marty Boyd heard the distress calls and turned their police cars in the direction of the school at top speed. The officers skidded onto the gravel road behind the school and pulled into the front yard of a house at the top of the hill just in time to see two young boys dressed in camouflage emerge from the woods, rifles in hand. Jumping out of the squad car, they shouted, "Sheriff's Department! Drop your weapons! Get on the ground!" but neither boy made a move to comply. Instead their guns were drawn and pointed right at the police, who would have been well within procedural guidelines to shoot both kids. The police hesitated, stunned by how young the shooters were, and ordered them again to drop their weapons.

Finally, hands in the air, the boys surrendered and held still on the ground as police officers began to go through their pockets. The contents added up to a small armory: Remington .30 caliber rifles, Smith & Wesson pistols, two-shot derringers, semiautomatics, and hundreds of rounds of ammunition. Even in a community accustomed to guns, it was a shocking arsenal. More stunning still was to find it in the hands of eleven-year-old Andrew Golden and his thirteen-year-old buddy, Mitchell Johnson.

The officers could hardly believe their eyes: How could two such young boys inflict such massive damage? Yet before them was evidence of careful, if somewhat juvenile, planning: a van full of provisions, including sleeping bags and pillows covered with Warner Bros. "Looney Toon" characters, a load of junk food, and a map to a remote hunting area where the boys planned to hide out. More chilling still was the hillside location where the boys were caught. Looking down, the officers could see a clear and unobstructed view of the playground. A trained sharpshooter could not have picked a better position from which to cause such carnage.

———

How, exactly, did this plot unfold? Many details are still unknown, but the basic outlines are clear enough. The morning of the shooting, Mitchell Johnson and Andrew Golden skipped school. Mitchell missed the school bus and told his mother that his stepfather, Terry Woodard, who had actually already left for work, would give him a ride to Westside. He sailed out the door after saying good-bye. Gretchen Woodard, Mitchell's mother, was busy taking care of her youngest child and didn't give much thought to Mitchell's account. When she looked outside and saw that the van was gone, she assumed all was well: Mitchell was on his way to school with his step-Dad.

What Mitchell actually did was steal the keys to his stepfather's van and drive it—with great difficulty, since he didn't really know how to drive—to Andrew Golden's house. Andrew was home alone; his parents had left for work, expecting that he would get himself to the school bus. Andrew was waiting in the bushes when Mitchell drove up. The two boys set about trying to pry open the locked safe that held the ample supply of guns belonging to Andrew's father. They pulled hard on the door but couldn't budge it. Next they took a blowtorch to the safe. That didn't work either. In frustration, they scooped up a .38 caliber derringer, a .38 caliber snub-nose, and a .357 magnum that had been left unsecured in the house, along with ammunition.

They stowed the guns and ammunition in the back of the van along with the supplies they planned to use after escaping into the woods. But since the pistols they had stolen would not suffice as long-range weapons, they drove to Andrew's grandparents' house. Using a crowbar, they broke into the house and in short order found exactly what they came for: a wall covered with rifles, secured only by a cable running across through their trigger guards. Rummaging around the tool shed behind the house, the boys found a pair of garden shears. Minutes later, they clipped the cable and added four handguns and three rifles to their arsenal.

Mitchell and Andrew drove toward the school, parked the van in a cul-de-sac about a half mile from Westside, and made their way to the wooded hillside. The boys may have intended to unleash the onslaught outdoors during the lunch recess, but the ground was rain-soaked and muddy, so the students stayed indoors. How were they going to lure the kids out of the building? Apparently, Andrew had considered this potential snafu nearly nine weeks before the shooting: Andrew left Mitchell behind on the hillside and ran to pull the fire alarm. With the horn sounding, he charged back up the hill and got into firing position only a few feet from Mitchell, who was already set to shoot. They set up an enfilade, creating a cross-fire that made escape from the volley almost impossible.

Within minutes of the alarm bell sounding, the boys unleashed thirty shots and hit fifteen people. Stephanie Johnson, age twelve, a math whiz and a devoted member of the Full Gospel Pentecostal Church, was pronounced dead on the scene. Eleven-year-old Natalie Brooks, a straight-A student who planned to become an astronomer, died at St. Bernard's Hospital. So did Paige Ann Herring, a hazel-eyed sixth grader whom teachers and fellow students called "the peacemaker," and Britthney Varner, described by her family as dainty, fragile, and wildly in love with her eight-month-old baby brother. Teacher Shannon Wright died in the same hospital. Nine other children and a teacher were treated and released.[8]

Ballistics reports and the police investigation revealed that Mitchell fired five shots from Andrew's grandfather's semiautomatic rifle, equipped with a scope, killing at least one, but probably two people, and wounding at least three. Andrew, the more skilled marksman, fired twenty-five shots, killing three people and wounding at least two others. The entire rampage took less than five minutes.

———

While Varner and Moore hustled Mitchell and Andrew off to the Craighead County Jail, emergency personnel worked feverishly inside the school gym to treat the wounded, and radio stations in the Jonesboro area began broadcasting news of the crisis. Within minutes of the first radio spots, cars began to converge on the school. Roads are long and narrow in this part of the country and traffic jams are rare, but that afternoon a two-mile backup clogged the only route to the middle school.

Parents abandoned their cars along the road and began running through the fields to get to the campus. What they found when they finally arrived was blood all over the playground and hundreds of terrified children huddled in the gym crying. Children whose parents did not come to the school right away were anxious to reach their families. Teachers ran to find their cell phones, but attempts to make calls produced mainly busy signals. Some distraught parents waited for several hours before they heard anything about their children.

Sixth grade teacher Liz Carleton was standing in the gym with two cell phones in hand, trying to figure out whose parents were out of town and whose were at home, when her eyes turned toward the doorway. In walked Dennis Golden, Andrew's father and her former high school classmate. "Liz, Liz," he asked anxiously, "is Andrew okay?" By then Liz had been told by several students that Andrew was one of the shooters, but from the look on Dennis Golden's face, she surmised that he was completely in the dark about it. Liz pulled Dennis aside and assured him that Andrew was safe but explained calmly that he would need to accompany her to the principal's office. They crossed paths with a group of shell-shocked students who gasped when they saw Andrew's father. Dennis realized something was very wrong and insisted that Liz come clean. "Liz," he pleaded, "you have got to be the one to tell me!" Reluctantly, she relented. "They say that Andrew was the one who pulled the fire alarm and started shooting." Dennis went limp and took Liz's cell phone to call his wife.

Susan Miller, the principal of Westside Middle School, was as stunned as anyone else. She came out of her office, where police officers were huddled, to find Dennis and Liz on the way in. "Dennis," she said, "I think you need to step into the office and talk to some of these officers."

They took him straight to my office and shut all the doors and told him, "Your son is in custody." He couldn't believe it. He was devastated . . . shocked. He came to get his kid and found out his kid was the one who had done it. You can't imagine the look on that man's face. The fear!

Gretchen Woodard, Mitchell Johnson's mother, was stuck at home because her son had stolen the only functioning car in the family. A phone call from a family friend brought the stunning news that Mitchell had shot his classmates. Hours later, when Gretchen was finally able to reach her husband, Mitchell's stepfather, she arranged a ride. By that time there was no point going to Westside School. Mitchell and Andrew had been booked into the Craighead County Jail, charged with five counts of capital murder and ten counts of first-degree battery.

It took the shooters' parents weeks to unravel the sequence of events that led to this end point. Mitchell and Andrew's classmates needed about five seconds. At least a dozen of them knew the identities of the shooters without so much as a word from the police. Even Monte, Mitchell's younger brother, knew who was responsible.

HOW COULD IT HAPPEN HERE?

The tragedies that tore apart the communities of Heath and Westside shook the whole nation as well. Young boys not yet old enough to shave had murdered, maimed, and terrified whole towns. Brothers and sisters lost their siblings; parents who expected their children to bury them in ripe old age, instead are tending their children's graves. Empty bedrooms covered with posters of movie stars and stuffed animals are all that is left. Some of those rooms stand untouched to this day, silent memorials to children who will never come home from school.

Teachers dedicated to a life in the classroom and the respectful affection of their students had to contend with the blame that came with accusations that they should have known these boys were troubled. Suffering from their own posttraumatic stresses, they had to tend their wounds in private. Attention naturally flowed to the children who survived and the families who lost their loved ones.

For the country as a whole, school shootings opened up a searching self-examination as only a total shock can. Have we lost our grip on our children? Do we no longer understand what makes them tick? Are parents too involved in their own lives to pay attention to what their children are doing? Have guns become so ubiquitous that we are hardly even surprised when a postal worker or a disgruntled student fires a few rounds into a terrified crowd of coworkers or classmates? Are we no longer able to judge when a community is safe and when it just looks that way? Or do we need to fear what is bubbling beneath the surface in crime-free suburbs?

What the Heath and Westside communities experienced was a relatively new kind of violence: a rampage school shooting. These are a special kind of attack, quite unlike the more familiar revenge killings we hear so much about. Rampage shootings are defined by the fact that they involve attacks on multiple parties, selected almost at random. The shooters may have a specific target to begin with, but they let loose with a fusillade that hits others, and it is not unusual for the perpetrator to be unaware of who has been shot until long after the fact. These explosions are attacks on whole institutions—schools, teenage pecking orders, or communities. Shooters choose schools as the site for a rampage because they are the heart and soul of public life in small towns. Rampages tend to take place in rural and suburban settings—they rarely occur in urban areas—and rampage shooters are predominantly white boys.[9]

These attacks are frightening and perplexing not because they are common—they are rare—or because they conform to our image of violent crime—which we associate far more often with urban communities, where violence is far more common. Rampage school shootings terrify us because they contradict our most firmly held beliefs about childhood, home, and community. They expose the vulnerable underbelly of ordinary life and tell us that malevolence can be brewing in places where we least expect it, that our fail-safe methods (parental involvement in children's lives, close-knit neighborhoods) do not identify nascent pathologies as well as we thought.

None of these sociological considerations were a focus of attention for the grieving parents, students, clergy, teachers, and public officials in the Heath and Westside communities when they suffered these losses. They had no idea that they were at the leading edge of a storm of rampage school shootings that gathered force across the country in the late 1990s. Known far and wide as wonderful places to raise a family, tight-knit towns where everyone really does know your name, these communities had to face some serious self-examination. Answers were not easy to come by, for the usual signs of impending disaster—high levels of background violence, dysfunctional families, chaotic schools, distracted adults too busy with their own lives to pay attention to the local teens—were strikingly low in both places.

Heath, Kentucky, is located a few miles west of Paducah, a small city of about 25,000 people that sits at the confluence of the Ohio and Tennessee Rivers in the southwestern part of the state. Long a transportation hub, Paducah has had its share of ups and downs since the end of World War II. Barges and tugboats once plied the rivers, and farming was a mainstay of the local economy. Today there are only a handful of farms left in McCracken County, and the main employers are in medical services, shipping, railroad manufacture, chemicals, paper mills, and the nation's only uranium enrichment plant.

Once a prosperous town, Paducah has fallen on hard times, and many of the storefronts on Main Street are vacant. Strip malls of chain stores and restaurants near the interstate highway have pulled customers away from the town center. The pride of Paducah, an "Information Age Park" that was supposed to lure high-tech industries, is only about 10 percent occupied. Even so, the uranium plant (United States Enrichment Corporation) is doing well and has brought a steady stream of engineers and professionals to the area since the 1950s. The newer residents are the kind of folks that didn't used to settle in farming country. Yet they nestled in alongside the rural working class—the original "Heatherans," as they call themselves—now displaced from farming into manufacturing. Locals and outsiders have been joined in recent years by families moving out of Paducah, lured mainly by the new subdivisions springing up in the middle of what was once a farmer's world.

While families have been moving steadily to these outskirts, their arrival has not stimulated much growth in the number of gathering spots. Leigh's Barbecue, where old-timers enjoy pulled pork and potato salad at the lunch counter surrounded by memorabilia from Heath High football victories, is a favorite local hangout. When residents want to shop, they drive in to a well-endowed strip between Heath and downtown Paducah. They also patronize a few chain restaurants, gas stations, and car dealerships, a mall, a Wal-Mart, and some entertainment facilities such as bowling alleys and a movie theater. Many families with children attending Heath High School live closer to this strip than to the school, and kids frequent the mall and movie theater; some have after-school jobs in the restaurants and stores. Nonetheless, the social world of most Heath adolescents revolves around high school and church.

The residents of Heath are mixed in every way except race. Large mansion-style houses with Greek pillars and circular drives in front give way eventually to modest tract houses typical of the 1950s. Farther outside of town are the two-bedroom trailer homes. But the faces inside these homes are almost all white, whether in mansions or trailers. Whites on the periphery think of central Paducah as a bit dangerous, an enclave of drugs and gangs (albeit on a small scale by big-city standards) and would not have been surprised if a rampage shooting had happened in the high schools attended by "inner-city" students. But in Heath itself, where violence is rare, where the biggest discipline problems are tardiness, skipping class, and the occasional temper tantrum, a mass murder was inconceivable.

Had they contemplated such a prospect, Michael Carneal would never have come to mind as a potential rampage shooter. The product of a happy, stable, comfortable home, a churchgoing boy of above-average intelligence with no serious disciplinary record and no known history of psychiatric problems, Michael did not strike anyone in town as a killer.

Yet all was not well with Michael Carneal. Warning signs of an unraveling character were overlooked, and the very virtues that made residents of Heath proud to be part of this quiet, civic-minded town also left them vulnerable to trouble, unable to communicate amongst themselves about problems brewing in their midst.

———

Much the same might be said of the Westside community, whose residents swear that it is the most unlikely setting for any kind of violence, let alone a mass school shooting. Nearby Jonesboro is a small but growing city of 55,000 people in northeastern Arkansas, about 130 miles from the capital, Little Rock. Bible Belt to the core and proud of it, Jonesboro has more than seventy-five churches within its city limits. Flat farmland surrounds the city, long a center of cotton, rice, and soybeans—the familiar crops of the Mississippi Delta. Jonesboro is blessed with a thriving economy, small-town solidarity, and a low crime rate. Its downtown district boasts a lovely bed-and-breakfast hotel with a wide veranda lined with rocking chairs from which one can watch the world go by. Dozens of churches—some grand and ornate, others the essence of Christian simplicity— are interspersed with coffeehouses, dress shops, and antique stores. Outside of Jonesboro, the winding roads of the Westside area cross green hills and lead down into little valleys where houses are tucked away from the traffic.

Until the shootings at Westside Middle School, the worst this community had to fear was natural disasters, especially tornadoes that rip through the region in the spring and early summer, leaving behind a trail of destruction. Disaster preparedness is a necessity in Jonesboro, a resource everyone had to draw on in the wake of the rampage shootings.

Like Heath, the Westside school district lies outside of town and is populated almost exclusively by white, Christian families. Serving the tiny communities of Bono, Cash, and Egypt,[10] the entire school district, from kindergarten through twelfth grade, has only 1,600 students, with the middle school accounting for 250 of them. There are richer people (owners of large farms, managers of white-collar firms who commute into Jonesboro) and poorer people (inhabitants of the mobile home parks who work on farms or in construction). The students are well aware of these differences, but they haven't hardened into oppositional camps of haves and have-nots. Everyone loves the football team—win or lose—and kids do "cross the tracks" and befriend each other across class lines.

It is a tranquil place, with little experience of crime, although like the residents of Heath, they look toward the city as a potential exporter of trouble. Gangs are rumored to be a problem in the center of Jonesboro, and Westside's ex-urban residents are relieved to be distant from troublemakers. Until the shooting erupted at the middle school, their main concern was whether the school buses would arrive on time every morning.

Cash and Egypt are mostly rural, with large expanses of farmland between the houses. A post office and a café are the only public buildings in the Cash town center, and a single store (officially called "The Store") marks the town crossroads of Egypt. Bono is a little larger and less agricultural, but residents complain that there is still only one place to eat—a modest burger joint at the main intersection. A small grocery store, a convenience store with a gas station, a pawnshop, a Laundromat, and an auto body shop can be found in the center of Bono, but a serious shopper has to make the 30-minute drive into Jonesboro. Cash and Egypt are even farther out of town.

Young people feel the community's remove most keenly. Their parents may work in Jonesboro, and thus "escape" during the day, but teenagers, especially those who can't drive, spend virtually all their time in these small, outlying places. When kids get home from school, they are stuck. The geographic isolation leads them to have few contacts outside of their own school district. Their communities, as one lawyer we met explained, are "isolated and closed, a world unto itself."

People tell themselves that this is a virtue, that being far away from the rest of the world wards off the crime and delinquency growing in larger communities like Jonesboro. Those who have exited the urban centers—even the small ones—are often certain that they have left behind the wellspring of trouble.

As with the residents of Heath, though, the very story residents tell themselves about the bucolic virtues of small-town life obscures recognition of the seeds of trouble. In retrospect, there were reasons to worry about Andrew Golden and Mitchell Johnson, but at the time of the shooting, the near-universal response to their arrests was, "What? Them?" Golden's parents had grown up in the community; his father had attended the same schools Andrew was passing through, and his mother came from the next county over. Both postal workers, they were the kind of solid, hard-working citizens everyone wants as a neighbor. "Salt of the Earth," we were told, time and again.

Gretchen and Terry Woodard came from the lower end of the class spectrum, and Terry had a checkered past, but nobody dwelled on it. Terry was a Jonesboro native in a place where being a native counts for a lot. By the time he settled back in Bono, after spending time out of state in prison on a drug charge, Terry was a married man with a steady blue-collar job. He had matured into a responsible father and left his problems behind. Gretchen and her children, on the other hand, were outsiders who had seen their share of family turmoil. By all accounts, though, they were in the happiest condition ever when they moved to Bono. Beloved by their neighbors in the mobile-home park where they lived the Woodard family was considered dependable, churchgoing, and responsible. These were not the kind of people who produce killers, and no one thought Mitchell Johnson capable of anything worse than an occasional outburst of bad manners, for which he generally apologized with remorse.

The mysteries have only deepened with time. How could these low-crime, family-centered communities have spawned such murderous violence? How did these particular families, known and respected by neighbors, teachers, and preachers, produce rampage killers? That is precisely what we wanted to know when we arrived in these two communities in June 2000. Our efforts were initially part of the National Academy of Sciences study of lethal school violence mandated by Congress as part of the 1999 "Missing, Runaway, and Exploited Children's Act." The Academy had contacted Katherine Newman about contributing to a comparative study of six communities around the country that had experienced rampage school shootings, and she in turn assembled a team of doctoral students to join her in doing fieldwork in Heath and Westside. The project soon turned from a set of modest case studies to a full-blown scholarly obsession as we dug deeper into the events that led up to these tragedies. We became a team of coauthors on a mission to understand how mass murder erupts in the midst of communities that seem like the last places in the world that would experience such terror.

Ours was not a simple task. First, the communities themselves were not exactly overjoyed to be under the research microscope. Having survived a terrible ordeal, first on account of the shooting and then at the hands of an intrusive national media, many were ready for the subject to fade away. Some suffered a kind of secondary trauma because their neighbors wanted them to "move beyond" the catastrophe when they simply couldn't. These victims had no one to talk to about the one event that now defined their social identities, and they were reluctant to come out of the protective shell they built around themselves as a consequence. In both instances, we met understandable resistance to talking about what led to the rampages. Second, the events in question had occurred three years before our arrival, and the conflicting accounts we gathered from people who had different vantage points at the time of the shootings, as well as different histories afterward, were difficult to reconcile. In the end, we concluded that the divergent accounts offered valuable clues to the underlying conflicts, cleavages, and social interests at play in these two communities.[11]

We were fortunate that the imprimatur of Congress and the reputation of Harvard University helped to reassure those we sought to interview of our legitimacy and sincerity. Although some people continued to wish that we would just go away, the vast majority of residents in Heath and Westside embraced our purpose, opened their homes and hearts, and told the story as they saw it, determined to help other communities avoid their fate.

NEW IDEAS

Very little has been written about school shootings to date.[12] What we find in the popular press tends to take the lens down to the pathologies of individuals or pulls it all the way back to global laments about the way our society is changing, with worries about increasing rootlessness, family disintegration, or cultural decline as underlying narratives. These perspectives deserve their due and we explore the evidence for them in chapter 3. But in this book we offer a different take, one that owes itself to the insights of sociology over psychology, of the social dynamics that led to the tragedies at Heath and Westside.

Drawing on our own fieldwork in both Heath and Westside—some 163 interviews in all—and a special data set we created to capture the patterns of rampage school shootings since the 1970s, we home in on new dimensions of these attacks. In particular, we focus on the organizational structure of schools, which leads teachers and administrators to overlook the scattered evidence of rage building up inside those who become shooters. We look as well at the dark side of small towns that become blind to the problems festering among teens, where the social networks and friendships that make them "wonderful places to raise the kids" stifle the flow of information about the marginal and the troubled. It turns out that in towns where "everyone knows your name," there are reasons why people who observe menacing behavior keep it to themselves.

Several succeeding chapters take a close look at the underside of adolescent life, at the pressures teenagers generate in one another to climb atop the social pecking order and stay there, policing the boundaries of popularity against "wannabes." The internal pyramid of the popular and the untouchable, sustained by exclusion and harassment, pushes the vulnerable, the unsuccessful to the margins. There are reasons why the shooters don't go out quietly when they decide to address their social dilemmas. They arrive at these tragic solutions after a period of small trials and big errors. There is nothing spontaneous about a rampage school shooting.

A great deal has been written in newspapers and magazines about individual shooters. Virtually nothing in the media or the scholarly literature examines what happens to the towns they have devastated. The last few chapters in this book dwell at length on what happened to both communities, on the dynamics of blame and responsibility and the role that faith played in assigning both; on the divisions that erupted as the victims split off from the bystanders; on the changes the schools made to try to reassure the families, protect the kids, and develop a greater sensitivity to outcasts. Finally, in part 3, we look carefully at how well the theories we derive from the close study of Heath and Westside fit the rest of the nation's school shootings as well as "near miss" plots.

No book on this topic would be complete if the topic of "what we should do now" were omitted. The lessons we learned from our immersion in the world of rampage shootings are offered at the end of the book. We take a hard look at the options for intervention and conclude that the best bet we have for prevention lies not in trying to identify the people who are going to shoot their teachers and classmates—though preventative mental health measures are good policy across the board—but rather on intercepting the flow of information when the threats fly. This is a challenge, given the fiercely private world of adolescents, but it is not an impossible task.

2

THE SHOOTERS

THE THREE BOYS RESPONSIBLE FOR THESE TRAGEDIES WERE NOT KNOWN troublemakers. Other kids came more readily to mind as the violent types. These boys were not high on the list of problem cases—not by a mile. What drove them to murder their classmates? What was lurking below the placid surface? The answers are embedded in two places: the psychological troubles that were brewing on the inside and the sociological bruises that were collecting as the boys engaged with peer groups, schools, and neighborhoods. The relationship between these psychological and sociological factors is a combustible one: The personalities emerging within the adolescent boys magnified the social dilemmas they faced into what felt like crushing burdens, and the pressures that typically build up in teenage society exacerbated their individual psychological problems. But we begin here with interior portraits of the boys, for we need to know the intimate details of their emotional lives if we are to understand the fears, furies, and hopes that were driving them toward mayhem.

MICHAEL CARNEAL

Michael Carneal had lived in the area all his life, but had been enrolled at Heath High School for less than a semester when the shooting occurred. A small, slight, bespectacled fourteen-year-old boy known for his socially awkward behavior, Michael was three years younger than his sister Kelly, one of the star students at Heath. A section leader of the school band, reporter for the school newspaper, singer in the Kentucky all-state choir, Kelly had achieved virtually everything that was possible. Indeed, the year of the shooting, Kelly graduated as valedictorian of her class and went on to college out of town, a mark of distinction claimed by very few of her classmates.

The Carneal parents, John and Ann, were respected members of the Paducah community. John is a longtime workmen's compensation and injury lawyer who is admired for his work on behalf of the less fortunate. Ann earned a teaching degree at nearby Murray State University but stayed home to take care of her children. Third-generation residents of Paducah, the Carneals were devoted members of the Lutheran Church, reliable volunteers in local charities, and among the most active parents at Heath High School. They never missed a band competition, and they manned the concession stands during football games. The Carneals made a point to let their children's friends know they were welcome in their home, and they developed bonds of mutual affection with many of them. Ann Carneal had befriended Nicole Hadley, who died at Michael's hands. Devoutly Christian, Nicole had hoped to influence Michael to increase his commitment to Christ; she had "witnessed" her own faith to him on many occasions.

The Carneals had been married for twenty-six years at the time of the shooting. Psychiatrists who interviewed all members of the Carneal family in the aftermath of the shooting are unanimous in their view that John and Ann were good parents. Their perspective was echoed by virtually everyone we met in town: friends, fellow churchgoers, and mere acquaintances alike. "We had dinner together almost every night," Kelly recalled, "usually with one or two of either my or Michael's friends there too, because they didn't eat dinner in their houses."

> We went to church together and then they helped with a lot of our school activities, so that kind of turned into family time. . . .
>
> They always had tried to keep our family close and always tried to keep the lines of communication open. . . . I was an 18-year-old senior . . . I wanted to get in my car and go drive and hang out at the mall and cruise like everybody else did. They always tried to keep us spending time with each other and letting us know that we could talk to them and they would still love us no matter what we did.

Yet all was not well. A high-performing daughter and an insecure, socially immature younger son is a recipe for sibling tension known to millions of American families. Dr. Kathleen O'Connor, a psychologist on the staff of the Northern Kentucky Youth Correctional Facility, counseled Michael for the four years he was incarcerated there. A slight, blond woman in her fifties, O'Connor heard an earful from Michael about how hard it was for him to be the younger brother of a star:

> Michael . . . decided quite early, I think about at age seven . . . that he was probably not ever going to be as . . . successful as [Kelly] was. So he kind of started going on a diversion path. "Well, I'm not going to be able to compete with her, so I'm not going to. I'm just going to become different." . . . He had some of the same teachers and always [heard] the same song: your sister this, your sister that. Why can't you be more like your sister?

Despite the invidious comparison, Michael did reasonably well in school until seventh grade. At that point, he began a steep slide that bottomed out with a grade point average of 1.8 in the eighth grade. Despite an IQ of 120, which placed Michael in the 91st percentile for his age group,[1] he was in trouble academically.

He had other problems to cope with as well. Kelly was a stand-out musician, whereas Michael was one of only two (out of 62) band members who were asked to sit out the beginning of the season because the band had too few uniforms. He was added back in when two others dropped out, but it rankled him that he was first chosen to stand down. Kelly had boyfriends and seemed able to navigate the shoals of adolescence. Michael was a social misfit. John and Ann worked hard to avoid comparisons, but the contrasts were clear to everyone in the family, including Kelly. "He tries to be as good as me," she told prosecution psychiatrists, "and he can never size up."[2]

Millions of American families experience sibling rivalry. Michael's reaction to his weak stature relative to Kelly reflected something darker and more disturbing. Strange fears began to dwell in him, anxieties he could not shake. Michael's behavior at home began to reflect some of these pressures, although the family did not know how to interpret what they saw. He was afraid of sleeping alone in his room, fearing strangers or monsters hiding under the bed or climbing through the windows. He thought these demons were going to hurt him and then go after his family. Michael often spent the night on the living room couch, where he felt less vulnerable. He started smuggling weapons—mainly kitchen knives—into his room and hiding them under his mattress, so that he could defend himself from attack. When he had to go into his bedroom, Michael would often open the door and yell, "I know you're in there!" before entering. His fears often grew so insistent that he would not let his feet touch the floor, but instead skipped from one piece of furniture to another, hoping that the monsters would not be able to get to him.

When Michael took a shower, he would cover the vents in the bathroom. "He would . . . go from the bathroom to his room with maybe like six towels wrapped around various parts of his body," Kelly recalled. At the time, she thought Michael was just a modest fourteen-year old who didn't want his sister to see his body. Instead, he was covering himself in a desperate attempt to ward off would-be assaults from imaginary enemies, like the snakes that were poised to slither in through the vents.

"Michael's fears were always there," Dr. O'Connor explained. But as he got older, they generalized toward the world outside his home. He was convinced that someone was going to do something horrible to his family, and this made him feel shaky and unsafe everywhere he went. Michael told his mother about bullying in school, about kids who threw his science experiments out the window, about boys who pushed him into lockers. Why not divulge these hideous fears? "He was very embarrassed," Dr. O'Connor explained. "He didn't want to bother people."

Something else held Michael back. He had come to believe that anyone who came to his aid would be targeted by the same demons that were after him. It is quite possible that the monster Michael was worried about, at least subconsciously, was himself. His growing recognition that he was spiraling out of control, that he might do dangerous things, may have begun to make him worry that he might harm the people he loved most. The magnified fears were increasingly placing Michael in a "no exit" situation: no one to whom he could turn who wouldn't be victimized, and no way to ward off the terrors by himself.

Surprisingly, throughout this period of psychological disintegration, Michael did manage to maintain something of a social life. Indeed, he had had one girlfriend already, and there were several boys who counted him as part of their inner circle. He visited various boys at home, stayed overnight with their families, and saw quite a bit of them at his own home. Michael was free to ride his bike to visit them, and they were invited along on his family outings. At least from this superficial point of view, Michael seemed to be doing fairly well in his social world.

Beneath the surface, though, Michael was unraveling psychologically and struggling to prevent others from seeing just how disturbed he was. Had anyone looked at the contents of the hard drive on Michael's computer—often compiled late at night in the family living room, where he slept—they would have gotten a glimpse of the angry, violent impulses brewing beneath his awkward exterior.[3] One piece on the computer describes the torture and degradation inflicted on the Smurf cartoon characters by an evil mastermind.[4] The ten-page story depicts the innocent cartoon characters being shot, burned, microwaved, and driven into a sexual frenzy until they violate their own kind. Michael downloaded from the Internet instructional material on the "Raping of a Dead Corpse," and the many ways that innocent visitors can die in Disneyland.

One story Michael wrote himself, "The Lone Grunger," focuses on a young man who is shunned by people who pretend to be friends. The main character in the story is excluded from a party thrown by his closest buddies; the story breaks off midstream with the claim that "it's no big deal." These stories all revolve around fantasy worlds full of harmless, sunny people (or cartoon characters) who are suddenly wrenched into pain and degradation or forced to violate those they love. They feature an omnipotent and evil protagonist, usually a young man who revels in violent revenge.

"The Secret," a short story Michael wrote in his freshman year of high school, contains a passage that makes it clear that his thought patterns were starting to take on paranoid dimensions:

> I have been lead to believe that there is a secret in my family that my parents and my sister know. . . . I am always excluded from things. . . . I overheard my parents debating "whether they should tell me or not." I still don't know what they were talking about. I think I'm an alien but I'm not sure.

Michael's hard drive is frightening testimony to an interior life that bore little resemblance to the outward Michael, who was known for his sympathy toward the homeless, his joking (if odd) banter, and his subordinate, shrinking response to challenges from stronger boys. He was spinning into depression, a path that is reflected in his handwriting. As the shooting drew near, his letters began to bleed into a jumbled string of undecipherable blocks.

The defense psychiatrist hired to assess Michael's psychological condition, Dr. Dewey Cornell, interviewed Michael for nearly fifteen hours over a period of six months after the shooting. Cornell also talked with Michael's parents and grandparents, his pediatrician, and numerous friends and teachers, and he painstakingly assembled a portrait of the hidden Michael. Cornell's portrait is one of a young man who couldn't function socially, who attracted aggressive bullies because he was awkward and never fought back, who tried to curry favor with kids whose attention he craved, and who imploded in school because these social failures deepened his clinical depression.

> Michael had repeated experiences of being harassed and humiliated by peers at school. He had the impression that everyone felt they could take advan-

tage of him. He usually did not challenge kids who harassed him and passively accepted the abuse. He found it hard to stand up for himself and did not want to get into a fight. Nevertheless, Michael deeply resented these experiences and could not put them out of his mind. He stated, "I get mad, but I won't do anything. When I'm mad, I do nothing but think about things people have done to me, and it makes me real mad."

In eighth grade, he started to feel isolated and unpopular with his peers. Students made fun of his clothing and glasses and called him a "nerd." In the school washroom, larger boys would pick on him by flicking water on him and threatening him. Michael stated that two older boys in particular who had been held back a grade . . . would spit on him and then dare him to hit them.[5]

Michael had a particularly rocky time in eighth grade, as these tales of bullying suggest. But he was the victim of one very public incident of teasing that haunted him for months to come:

A gossip column, "Rumor Has It," in a school newspaper . . . implied that he had a homosexual relationship with another boy, one of the Grady brothers. . . . Michael was humiliated by the allegation, particularly when other students began to tease him and call him "gay" and "faggot."

This very public teasing—which somehow escaped the attention of the staff that was supposed to supervise school publications—felt like character assassination to Michael and did indeed have lasting consequences.[6] It precipitated an avalanche of bullying, teasing, and humiliation that followed Michael for the rest of middle school. Michael was unable to escape and unwilling to fight back or enlist the help of adults. Instead, he buried his rage, expressing himself only on paper in an essay he wrote for an eighth grade teacher. Michael's writing, reproduced here verbatim, lapses into incoherence at various points, a symptom of his increasingly disordered thought process. He details incidents that were clearly imaginary, but the text makes it clear just how wounded he was by the middle school gossip column:

They *ALL* mocked and slaughtered my self esteem it got so bad i turned to drugs sad to say but yes. After a crummy day at [Heath Middle School] when someone put into the school news paper that i was gay. I went home and cried yes I admit it i cried. I sat and thought about everything that had happened that day the day before that. So I snorted 7 Tylenol 3's made me puke alot and faint.

So as the preachings of my friend [friend's name] against drugs I got off drugs. And I live hapily ever after.
not.

I still am emotional about this subject but I have been clean for a year now.[7]

Few people realized what the one-liner in the school paper cost Michael emotionally. This is not to say he never told anyone about his frustrations. Michael did confide in his mother, to whom he had always been very close. Hence, Ann was aware that Michael was suffering in his social relations and occasionally down about his reputation. Yet when she offered to intervene, Michael rebuffed her, fearing that her input would make matters worse. This too is a common dilemma in early adolescence, an issue we discuss at length in chapter 7.

Given his incapacity to defend himself, it stands to reason that Michael would try to avoid situations in which his enemies would have opportunities to harass him. Yet those occasions seemed to multiply as he got older and tried to enter new social groups. When Michael became a freshman at Heath, he wanted to follow Kelly's lead and join the school band. It was common knowledge that new band members were hazed by the older, senior musicians, although the harassment was regarded as mild and mostly in fun. Since the band traveled to other cities, the opportunities for hazing blossomed—in hotel rooms, in practice rooms, on the bus, and in the bathrooms. The older boys in the band caught Michael and wrapped him up in a blanket, letting him go only when a chaperone happened by. One bigger boy put Michael into a headlock and rubbed his head so hard with his knuckles that it started to bleed. Michael told the psychiatrists that he was harassed, verbally or physically, almost every day in band class. Just as soon as the band director left the room, students would descend upon him, hitting him and pushing him to the ground. On the good days he was called names or threatened with beatings that didn't actually occur. On the bad days, his antagonists made good on their threats, or so he saw it. Yet our own interviews make it clear that Michael often gave as good as he got, instigating his own share of pranks—putting gum in girls' hair, for example. He had the reputation among the band chaperones for being a "royal pain" to manage on a field trip.

Michael appears, from this vantage point, to have fallen into step with adolescent culture, but on the inside, school felt more like a minefield, and his psychological resources for navigating the trouble spots were weak. Some days he acted the clown and tried to slough off his troubles by being goofy. He wore capes to school, drank "white out" correction fluid, set off stink bombs and tried to enlist others in a round of horseplay. Some kids laughed in a good-natured way about Michael's antics; others thought he was pathetic. One boy was so enraged by Michael's immature behavior that he threatened to hurt Michael and "followed him around, glaring at him and intimidating him."[8]

Over time, however, Michael moved toward a different solution to his dilemmas, one that led almost inexorably to the shooting. He began to seek the attention and approval of the one oppositional peer group available: the Goths. In this loose collection of older boys who dressed in black, listened to dark, grunge rock music, and affected an attractive, dangerous aura, Michael found the antithesis of Kelly's friends, those high-achieving, churchgoing, popular kids. He was desperate to claim a place among the "freaks" who had rejected the very same people who were busily rejecting Michael.

The Goths were not a club or a group with clearly defined boundaries. They were more like a fluid clique with a charismatic figure at the center: Brian Mather. His hair fell down to the middle of his back; he wore studs in his ears; he wore a black trench coat and painted his nails black. In the midst of the devout, Bible Belt town of West Paducah, Mather urged the group to reject Christianity and embrace the religion of Wicca. The Goths followed his lead in striking a disdainful pose and saw themselves as morally superior to other cliques. High on their list of hypocrites was the prayer group, whose more popular members the Goths claimed preached one line (virginity before marriage) and enacted another (sexual relations). Mather's unconventional style and defiant attitude made him magnetic and powerful in Michael's eyes.

The feeling was not mutual. Michael was tolerated, but not exactly embraced, by the Goths. To remedy this uncomfortable situation, Michael began to engage in his own form of deviant behavior, hoping this would convince the Goths that he was one of them in spirit. He stole money from his father and gave it to members of the group. He ripped off a fax machine and handed it over. He began shoplifting and gave the merchandise he stole to boys in the group. CDs from Michael's own collection were passed off as booty from shoplifting escapades, gifts designed to impress a group composed of self-styled rebels. Some success seemed to follow from his efforts, but it was never enough to secure these alliances. Michael was trying to bribe the Goths into associating with him, but the strategy did not work.

The plot to take over the school at gunpoint emerged in part from this sticking point. We do not know exactly who suggested the shooting at the outset. We do know that Michael was trying to shock the Goths into seeing him as worthy. He wanted to transform his public image—that of a failure and a misfit—into one that was notorious and dangerous. At the same time, Michael understood that shooting up the school would result in removing him altogether from the scene of his discomfort, out of range of those who bullied him. Both purposes—the intention to improve his reputation and the desire to extract himself altogether from the social torment he experienced—fused in Michael's mind, spurring the plot forward.

"On several occasions during the Fall of 1997," Dewey Cornell wrote in his psychiatric report, "the boys discussed various schemes for using guns to take over the school."

> One of the plans involved taking over the school office and another plan involved firing at students in the hallways. During one of the conversations, Michael volunteered to obtain guns for the boys. . . . Brian Mather accepted Michael's offer and on several occasions reminded him that he was supposed to obtain guns for them.[9]

Michael was determined to follow through. He made a down payment on the plan by stealing a gun from his father's closet, an old one that had been handed down in the family. Mather spurned this offering, telling Michael that his dad's pistol was not good enough: "[Brian] . . . wanted a shotgun."[10] Feeling somewhat humiliated by this rejection of his first attempt, Michael began to think about where he could get shotguns.

Jered Parker, a neighbor of Michael's, had guns at his house. Michael often went to visit Jered after school; the two were friends. "One day at Jered Parker's house, Jered tapped on his father's gun case and said to Michael that these guns were the kind they needed to 'do the school thing'."[11] Some time after that, Jered's father and the boys used the guns for target practice in the backyard. Michael returned to the Parker household and stole guns from them on two occasions, building the arsenal he turned on the prayer group.

Did the Goth group participate in a conspiracy?[12] Or was Michael overinterpreting their encouragement for offers of assistance? Deputy Mark Hayden transported Michael from the state police station after his arrest to the detention facility where he was held before his trial. In the course of the ride, Michael claimed that the rampage was indeed planned by the entire group during that lunch-hour conversation, and each boy laid claim to a particular kind of weapon.[13] They understood that Michael would be stealing the guns over the Thanksgiving break, and by common consent gave their approval when he told them, "Monday is the day."

We know that Michael's capacity to read the subtleties of other people's intentions was limited. He might well have imagined that they were planning to join in when they were merely contributing to hypothetical scenarios and fanciful projections. Under the duress of potential indictment, the Goths claimed that nothing was ever planned at all; they engaged in idle chatter that was never taken seriously by anyone, save perhaps Michael.

Police reports of interrogations of the Goths provide some evidence for this perspective. The Wednesday before the Thanksgiving break, Michael sat with the Goth kids during lunch, when the subject of the "big event" on Monday came up. The police interrogated all of the participants about what was discussed in preparation for possible conspiracy charges to be lodged against several of the Goths. Brian Mather claimed that he could not remember what was discussed. David Maxwell was more forthcoming, but during an interrogation at police headquarters,[14] he told Officer Baker that what Michael saw as an offer of participation, he understood to be a joke:

> MAXWELL: . . . I might have said, like, comments jokingly . . . simply because that's what I thought it was. I think I said, ah, something along the lines of, "Well, is there going to be blood and guts" and stuff like that?
>
> BAKER: What was the response?
>
> MAXWELL: [Michael] said, "Yeah, sure," you know . . . just kind of laughed about it. So I, you know, I . . . I naturally assumed he was joking about it.
>
> BAKER: . . . We have direct information that you specified . . . out of the weapons that were described, what, you know, that what [weapons] you might like to have. . . .
>
> MAXWELL: No, no, no, no, no, no, no. No, I can promise you that, no. I didn't have any idea he was going to use [weapons].

Whatever the truth of the conspiracy charge, it is very clear that a lot of people heard Michael talk in vague terms about how Monday would be a big day. The week before the Thanksgiving break, he warned a number of his closer friends, including some members of the prayer group, to stay away from the school that day. Michael even told some kids to avoid the lobby.[15] As it turns out, this is a typical pattern of warning behavior in school shootings. (In chapter 7, we explore why kids do not take these outbursts seriously and why they fail to come forward with information about threats.)

Michael expected that Monday morning to be a mixture of triumph and release from persecution. As he explained the plan to the prosecution psychiatrists, he thought he would be widely admired just for bringing the guns to school.

> Michael imagined that when he took the guns to school, his friends would say, "Wow!" or "Cool!" . . . He thought that . . . "everyone would be calling me and they would come over to my house or I would go to their house. I would be popular. I didn't think I would get into trouble. I didn't think I would get expelled or put on probation or go to jail. . . ." However, Michael then added spontaneously, "People who go to jail in our school have lots of friends, and all the kids say 'Wow!'"[16]

He thought the Goths would accept him as a gutsy guy, or as his Goth friend Cory Giles put it on seeing the guns, "You've got the biggest balls here."

In fact, however, when Michael showed the boys the guns that morning in the school lobby, they were not particularly interested. In fact, their very lack of attention spurred Michael to push beyond his own ambivalence:

> Brian said . . . "I know what's in there [in the backpack], I heard the sound. It sounded like a gun to me." Another boy said, "Those aren't guns," and another said, "Yeah, right." Michael said that at that point Brian Mather said, "He's going to do it!" One other boy said, "There aren't guns in there."[17]

They then changed the subject altogether and started talking about their new CDs. "No one talked to me," Michael recalled. He interpreted this as a personal slight and a betrayal. If he was going to accomplish his main mission—improving his image in their eyes—he was going to have to do something dramatic:

> I was thinking that if I didn't pull out a gun and take over the school, they wouldn't like me. If I didn't take out the guns, they would be mad at me.

The defense psychiatrist agreed:

> Michael perceived that the boys were disavowing their involvement in the shooting, and this made him angry and determined to show them that he

could go through with it. Michael also felt that the boys would laugh at him for bringing the guns if he did not go ahead with their plans.

But it wasn't easy for him to summon the courage. Michael began talking to himself, repeating in his mind over and over, "I have to do this for myself."[18]

Only after the fact did he realize how twisted his priorities were, how he focused on his own desire for approval and disregarded entirely the rights and feelings of others. Under the pressure of questions from the prosecution's psychiatric team, he broke down crying and volunteered his self-criticism:

> I regret what I did. I know I killed people. It wasn't right. I took people's lives. Their family cares for them. I have no explanation for what I did . . . I don't know why I did it. I don't know why I wasn't bluffing this time. I guess it was because they ignored me. I had guns, I brought them to school. I showed them to [the Goths], and they were still ignoring me. I didn't expect to kill anyone. I was just going to shoot. I thought maybe they would be scared and then no one would mess with Michael.

MITCHELL JOHNSON AND ANDREW GOLDEN

The shooters at the center of the Westside tragedy were younger than Michael Carneal, still in middle school. Separated by two years, at the stage in life where a year can make a huge difference, Mitchell Johnson and Andrew Golden were not known to be friends. Indeed, Westside classmates had no idea that they even knew each other on anything more than a casual basis.

Mitchell Johnson was new to Westside, having arrived in town only two years before the shooting. His family was from Minnesota, and his mother (Gretchen) and father (Scott) met and married while she was working as a correctional officer in a state prison and he had a job in a meat packing plant. Scott was Gretchen's second husband and the father of her two sons, Mitchell and Monte.[19] Both Gretchen and Scott come from working-class backgrounds, but they were making enough money to provide for their growing family in small-town Minnesota.

Financial stability did not ensure emotional peace, though. Scott Johnson was a hard drinker, a tough disciplinarian, and had a mean-tempered, explosive character, as Gretchen told us:

> Anybody can father a child, but when it comes to being a Dad, Scott lacked, and not . . . for lack of loving a child, but he just—he's a screamer, I guess.

He will scream and yell. Of course to me [as an adult], that's the nature of the beast; I don't care. After he'd scream and yell at Mitch for 15 minutes . . . it was real tough. As far as discipline and things like that, a very ugly character. Scott has his very dark side to him and I'm sure I haven't unfolded all the layers yet.

Scott would come home from work and punch holes through the walls, losing his temper so badly that Mitchell and Monte would be left shaking like leaves. As the older brother, Mitchell tried to protect Monte to the extent he could, but there was little he could do to shield him.

The atmosphere at home deteriorated when Gretchen's job shifted to afternoons and nights. By this time, Scott had landed a new position as a long-distance trucker and was often gone overnight. What to do with the children? Gretchen's mother lived about twenty minutes away in a trailer park and was willing to keep the boys on the days when their parents couldn't manage. At the age of eight, Mitchell found himself spending quite a few hours at his grandmother's house, an arrangement his father disapproved of in loud and uncompromising terms. He would come to collect the boys and let loose with a tirade that left Mitchell physically ill.

The best way to deal with Scott Johnson, it seemed, was to lie low. As it happened, though, Mitchell needed help badly. During the summer he turned eight, an older boy in his grandmother's neighborhood took to forcibly raping Mitchell, repeatedly and violently. He threatened to kill Mitchell's grandmother if he ever told anyone about it. Mitchell was deeply ashamed about these sexual assaults, afraid of endangering his grandmother, and terrified about the reaction he would provoke from Scott if he turned to him for help. Gretchen was completely in the dark about it; indeed, she knew nothing of this history until after the shooting. Instead, Mitchell buried his shame, only to discover that the neighbor boy had turned his violent attention to Monte. Having always tried to act the protective older brother, the trauma Monte endured added to Mitchell's despair.

Scott and Gretchen eventually separated in a difficult divorce. He was belligerent about the breakup and periodically threatened to take the children away. Gretchen moved in with her mother after her marriage broke up and witnessed firsthand how Scott's threats sent Mitchell into a tailspin:

Scott was screaming, calling me, good Lord, and Ma, every name in the book. It was awful and ugly. He'd come busting through the door and he'd say, . . . "I'm going to keep these kids. It ain't a proper home for them here

. . . I'll put them in a fucking foster home before they stay here with you," and he slammed the door. Mitchell [began] throwing up. It took me and Mom over an hour [to calm him down].

Gretchen was not sorry to leave this stress behind when she landed a promotion that took the family to Kentucky, where she began working in a federal prison. By this time, Mitchell was ten years old. Not long after they arrived in their new community, Gretchen met the man who would become her third husband, Terry Woodard. A native of Arkansas from the outskirts of Jonesboro, Woodard was serving time in the federal facility where Gretchen worked. He had been convicted on felony charges for selling drugs but was nearing the end of his sentence.

When Terry got out of prison, he married Gretchen and moved the family to Bono, on the outskirts of Jonesboro. He got a steady job with a firm that hauls heavy equipment, found a home in a small trailer park that belonged to the company, and settled down to a stable life. By all accounts this was the happiest time in the family's life. Terry was a caring, loving, stepfather, almost the opposite of Scott Johnson. Mitchell got along famously with him. Terry and Gretchen had a baby together. Terry's job paid well enough so that Gretchen didn't have to work.

Mitchell seemed to adjust well to his role as the new kid at Westside Middle School, where he made friends, joined the sports teams, and began singing with his church choir for elderly residents of nursing homes. Musically inclined, Mitchell developed a taste for barbershop quartets and started singing in the school choir as well. "Yes, Ma'am" and "No, Sir," the kind of boy who holds open a door for a lady—that was the Mitchell Johnson that most Westside teachers recalled. Only a year before the shooting, one of his seventh grade teachers took the unusual step of sending a note home to Gretchen and Terry praising Mitchell for his conduct. The beautifully decorated card is carefully preserved among Gretchen's mementos from better days.

To the parents of Mitchell Johnson: You can be very proud of your son. He is always so honest and polite to me. I want you and him to know I appreciate him.

There was a different Mitchell in the mix, however. Angry, belligerent, boastful, and bullying—this was the Mitchell known to those who had seen his dark side. Only a few Westside teachers caught a glimpse of this Mitchell; his peers saw the full-blown version on many occasions. The mean Mitchell landed himself in a disciplinary "time out" at Westside called "in-school suspension" or "ISS" on at least three occasions. In sixth grade, Mitchell lost his temper and slammed his fist into a thermostat in the hallway, breaking the glass case. Shannon Wright, the teacher who died in the rampage, put him into suspension for that infraction. The next year, he got angry and cursed at a teacher.

The worst episode took place only a few weeks before the shooting. Mitchell wore a baseball cap to school even though he knew this was against school rules. The ISS teacher, Beverly Ashford, ordered Mitchell to take the hat off. He refused. She insisted, called another teacher for help, and the two of them wrested the hat from Mitchell. Ashford reprimanded Mitchell harshly, and sent him to ISS, which she supervised.

Mitchell was humiliated, furious, and unrepentant. He made no secret of his anger. In an essay he was ordered to write during detention he seemed to be threatening retribution. Ashford read the paper in which Mitchell said, "He had some squirrels he needed to kill" and that when he was done, "There would be no more ISS." She was so unnerved by what she read that she brought the paper to the school principal and worried out loud about what Mitchell was planning. No action followed. However, Mitchell fumed over the humiliation, so much so that some people speculated after the fact that he had deliberately set out to kill Beverly Ashford. Mitchell denied this charge.

Apart from these incidents, the only record of misbehavior on Mitchell Johnson's part involved cursing on the school bus, an infraction for which he was paddled on the rear end, a punishment still legal in Arkansas. In retrospect, this steady but fairly low-level misconduct was a warning flag that all was not well in Mitchell's world. Yet none of the adults at the school considered Mitchell a serious disciplinary problem or a troubled child. Indeed, they were glad that Gretchen and Terry supported the school when it did have to punish him. Parents tend to assume their children can do no wrong and blame the school when their kids get in trouble. By contrast, the Woodard family backed the school up 100 percent, lecturing Mitchell in front of teachers about how he would have to "swallow his medicine." Since Mitchell usually apologized profusely after he was reprimanded, and was known for the most part as a "real pleaser," a Bible believer, a faithful choirboy in the Central Baptist Church, and an A and B student, it is not hard to understand why he was admired by most grown-ups.

His peers were another matter. Even Mitchell's friends were wary of his moodiness. "He did have a temper," one boy recalled. "I remember that definitely. At lunch . . . there were guys he didn't want to deal with, and he'd like hit the table."

Mitchell had a habit of pushing kids around, picking on kids, and bragging or swaggering. Mitchell tried to persuade his classmates that he was worldly, sophisticated, and a little bit dangerous. He claimed he had been inducted into the Westside Bloods, a gang in Jonesboro. Mitchell flashed gang signs and wore colors to prove it, and he occasionally told tales of initiation rites he had endured to gain entry. No one believed his stories. Instead, they dubbed him a gang "wannabe," dismissing him as a braggart. The rebuke cut deeply and Mitchell brooded over every rejection.

Chris Jackson thought of himself as one of Mitchell's closest friends. The two boys had sleepovers together and, as Chris remembered, "talked all the time," sitting on Chris's bed into the early morning hours. During spring break, just a week before the rampage, they went off on a typical Saturday escapade to the railroad tracks, where they took turns shooting their BB guns. Later that evening, Mitchell showed Chris a "death list" that included teachers, students, and administrators at Westside.

Why, we wondered, were these particular people on Mitchell's hit list? "They upset him," Chris explained.

He was just getting sick and tired of everything and so he asked one of his friends to help him do [the shooting].[20] He came to school Monday and we talked. He showed me that list and I was [telling him], "Man, dude, uh-uh." And then he didn't come to school the next day. I was worried.

What, exactly, was Mitchell getting "sick and tired" of? Girls, among other things. Although he had competitive, contentious relations with boys, girls seemed to gravitate toward Mitchell, but not as fast or as firmly as he wanted. Unusual among thirteen-year-olds, Mitchell was very interested in "going steady," and talked a lot about getting married. Westside girls remember that he wanted several of them to wear his ring for formal pictures taken at a school dance, evidence of his budding success as a ladies' man. When Candace Porter, an eleven-year-old who was wounded in the shooting, broke up with Mitchell only a few weeks before the rampage, he took it very hard, moping around and denouncing her. He was apprehensive about the impact of this breakup on his reputation, worried that Candace would tell other girls that she had dumped him. Chris Johnson remembered that "two of the girls that were shot would not go out with [Mitchell]." Mitchell has always maintained that he never aimed at anyone in particular and that he was beside himself when he discovered that Candace was among the wounded. The townspeople were not convinced: it did not escape their notice that all of the dead students were girls.[21]

The ups and downs of adolescent romance are familiar enough. Yet psychiatrists might see something more troubling underlying Mitchell's story. The boy's history of sexual abuse may have come back to haunt him that year. He may well have suffered insecurity and anxiety about his own masculinity and taken rejection by girls as a sign that there *was* something wrong with him. One thing we know for sure: small southern towns are not comfortable places for young boys who are worried about their sexual identity. We asked teenagers who are currently enrolled at Westside Middle School to tell us what the worst epithet they could imagine might be; almost to a person they responded that it would be a catastrophe to be called gay.[22] Mitchell's swagger, his extreme sensitivity to girls' rejections of his romantic intentions, and his unusual interest in marriage may reflect this anxiety.

One other piece of evidence fits this profile and also helps us understand the tensions that brought Mitchell to the brink. The summer before the shooting, he was caught with his pants down while changing the diaper of a two-year-old girl in Minnesota. Mitchell was charged with molesting the child in juvenile court, although it appears that the case did not result in a hearing.[23]

Scott was furious about Mitchell's transgressions. Gretchen was stunned to learn of the charge and recognized immediately that her son needed help. She took Mitchell to a psychologist when he returned home to Bono. The psychologist concluded that it was an isolated incident (and did not discover Mitchell's history of being sexually assaulted). Clearly, something was going wrong in this boy's life, but no one around him recognized the depth of the problem.

At Christmas that year, only a few months before the shooting, Mitchell and Monte went back to Minnesota to visit their father. They took the bus by themselves and on the way home were left stranded at the Chicago bus terminal for two days because of heavy snowstorms before any adult realized where they were. The boys were falling through the cracks that had opened up between Scott and Gretchen. Mitchell was starting to unravel. Teachers noticed a distinct change in him when he came back from that vacation. Where Mitchell had once been rather attentive and almost affectionate in his politesse, he now seemed a bit withdrawn and uninterested.

In truth, Mitchell desperately needed an adult he could confide in. He sought out one teacher he was particularly close to and told her that he was tired of being bullied. She listened attentively and suggested that she might try to mediate the tension, but privately thought that Mitchell was overly sensitive and thin-skinned. It turns out that Mitchell had some major worries, verging on desperation. He had been kicked off of the basketball team for carving a kind of tattoo into his arm, and he had been caught calling phone sex lines, charging the costs to his father's credit card. Scott was livid. He threatened to call the police in Minnesota to report his son and proclaimed that he would take Mitchell away from his mother on the grounds that she was unfit to raise him. He stormed over the phone from Minnesota that he was going to teach his son a lesson. And when Scott called, he did not mince words. The prospect of having to leave Westside to live with his father was nothing short of terrifying for Mitchell. But it was a terror well hidden. Gretchen was aware that he was upset, but Mitchell did not reveal to her his growing sense of hopelessness.

Only after he was incarcerated did he tell his mother that he felt his whole life was being sucked down into a bleak, black hole. Mitchell's reluctance to confide in his mother remains a source of enormous sorrow for her. "What probably hurts the most in my heart," she said with great sadness, "is that he couldn't come to me and tell me this hate that was within him."

Instead, the hate built up. The sense of rejection—by girls, by peers who didn't accept his self-image as a gang tough, by his threatening father—deepened inside. On the outside, though, all was macho. And when he did get in trouble, Mitchell was invariably remorseful and contrite. Westside administrators recall his apologies verbatim because they were unusually heartfelt. This was the Mitchell that adults knew, enjoyed, and felt a special kinship with. But the Mitchell known to his Westside schoolmates was a boy looking to claim some stature in the social pecking order. And the Mitchell that no one knew was the boy roiling inside with anger, fear, and confusion to the point of despair.

Since older kids usually rule over younger ones, one might imagine that Mitchell took the lead in concocting the plot to shoot up the school. Yet at least half of the people we interviewed concluded that Andrew Golden was the more likely ringleader, despite his junior status.

There were several reasons for people to think the rampage might have been the younger boy's idea. First, Andrew came from a family of gun enthusiasts and even at age eleven was a skilled marksman. He had been given his own rifle at the age of six and had won awards in shooting contests. His parents, Pat and Dennis, were officers of the Jonesboro Practical Pistol Shooters Association and had many guns in their home, most of which were behind lock and key. Andrew's grandfather, Doug Golden, who worked for the Arkansas Fish and Game Commission, was an avid hunter with a large arsenal in his home as well—the cache of weapons from which Andrew and Mitchell stole the guns they used in the shooting.

Second, although Andrew seemed to melt into the background at school, in his neighborhood he had a reputation for belligerence. Andrew's neighbors described him as the kind of boy they didn't want playing with their children. "Andrew was a sweet child whenever his parents were around," one neighbor commented. But "whenever he was away from his parents he was a little demon. . . . I feared that child." Other parents on the block evidently shared her feelings about the boy because he had a "filthy mouth," occasionally hit little girls on the arms, and rode his bicycle around with a knife strapped to his side.[24]

Cats had a way of dying on Andrew and at least one person we interviewed claimed that he had starved some to death in a barrel in his backyard. Another witness saw the boy push the heads of kittens through a chain-link fence. Two children in the neighborhood, later victims of Andrew's high-powered rifle, were banned from playing with him after they told their parents that they witnessed him shooting a cat. Natalie Brooks, who died in the rampage, was so frightened of Andrew that her father told her never to play with him again.

None of this seems to have registered with Andrew's parents, who seemed to feel that he could do no wrong. They were defensive when he got in trouble and actively intervened to prevent Westside Middle School from using what administrators regarded as appropriate punishment.[25] Teachers were of the opinion that Andrew was given too much latitude in his young life, partly because Andrew was a "latchkey" child of two working parents, but also because Andrew was a much-beloved only child and the lone grandchild of Dennis's parents.[26]

For this reason, or so community opinion would have it, he was overindulged and rarely subject to discipline. If Andrew did poorly in a particular class, or got in trouble with one teacher, his family just arranged for him to be moved to another. If he "cursed like a sailor," his father and grandfather laughed it off and encouraged him, saying it was cute and would make a man out of him. Pat Golden would throw her hands up in mock disgust and claim she couldn't do anything to restrain him. "Andrew's parents and grandparents," one teacher remarked, "always made sure he had things his way."

Andrew never made his way into detention and was not regarded by anyone as a problem child. School officials could remember only one incident that was troubling. In first grade, the boy brought a toy gun to school, which was strictly forbidden. The gun was confiscated immediately, and the teacher told him he would get into big, big trouble if he touched it. Andrew promptly convinced a classmate to retrieve it for him, and during recess he filled it with mud and gravel and fired it at a fellow first grader, hitting her in the eye. He was paddled for this infraction on a day when his grandmother was at Westside. She confronted Andrew's teacher in the hallway when it was time for children to be picked up from school, screaming at her in front of her students. At that time, Pat and Dennis Golden instructed the school to place their son on the "no paddle" list.

This incident aside, Andrew was rarely in trouble, and no one at Westside described him as badly behaved. He occasionally delivered "one-liners" in class or walked around hitting boys in the back of the head and messing up girls' hair, but this was minor stuff. His kindergarten teacher described Andrew as "cute as a button," and "happy, smiling." He was something of a class clown and often talked out of turn, but teachers often thought of him as a "chip off the old block," because his father, Dennis Golden, had a reputation as a cut-up during his years at Westside High School. Andrew was not one of the popular boys, but he was not friendless either. He seemed to be getting along reasonably well in sixth grade, the year of the shooting.

Yet there were some warning signs that year. Denise Simpson, an administrator at the Westside Middle School, remembered a troubling incident that seemed on the surface to have been resolved but might have been a missed signal. A school counselor reported that a friend of Andrew's had alerted her to the fact that Andrew was threatening to hurt himself. The counselor called Pat and Dennis Golden, following standard procedure, as an administrator later recalled:

> [Pat] said something to the effect of "Well, if we need to pursue this, I'll be glad to get him some help. [His Dad and I] work all the time, and this is the first time we've ever heard of it." His mom was very cooperative, very nice, and said that she would take him out to our service center where we get extra help and she would kind of see what was going on.

Other accounts of this episode do not quite square with this one. The kid who relayed the story insisted that Andrew said he was going to hurt kids at the school, not himself. The boy told his father, who in turn claims that he contacted the school about the threat. There is a factual dispute here and one that proved emotionally difficult in the aftermath of the shooting, when fingers of blame were pointing in all directions. Denise Simpson was hurt by the suggestion that they had ignored a warning of the catastrophe to come:

> The counselor was as surprised as anybody . . . [that Andrew was one of the shooters]. . . . Then all these other people made these accusations that . . . we should have known he was going to do what he did. . . .

Andrew's behavior after the shooting contributed to the view that he was the more troubled of the two. Andrew said nothing, showed no emotion, clammed up tight. In some circles, this was taken as evidence that Andrew had sustained a mental or emotional breakdown. We were unable to see the psychiatric evaluations of Andrew because they are sealed, but we interviewed a number of people who saw the reports on both boys, and they were unanimous in viewing Andrew as the more troubled of the two. Andrew's attorney concluded that an insanity plea made sense, but his motion was rejected.[27] The legal move added to local gossip that Andrew was the one who was psychologically unbalanced, while Mitchell perhaps craved attention but was not so disturbed that he would take the lead in plotting to shoot his classmates. We do know that Andrew was instructed by his family not to talk to anyone about what he had done, and it may be that his withdrawn countenance reflected this and nothing more.

Yet appearances can be deceiving, even for those who had a close vantage point of the two boys after their arrest. Several people had the opportunity to observe and interact with Mitchell and Andrew over the months that followed the rampage, including Michelle Collins, an employee of the juvenile corrections system who monitored the conditions of their incarceration,[28] and Frances Perkins, an employee of the Craighead County Jail, where they were housed for four months while awaiting trial. Neither is an expert in child development, and their accounts cannot be corroborated, because no one else had the opportunity to observe Mitchell and Andrew as they did. Hence we must approach their interpretations with caution. Nonetheless, their unique vantage point, so soon after the shooting makes these accounts worthy of notice.

Michelle Collins is certain that Mitchell was, and remains to this day, full of remorse for his actions. He has taken every opportunity to reach out from the juvenile facility where he has been held since his conviction to express his contrition.

> Mitchell told me that [if it were] possible for [him] to give [his] life right this minute to bring back those little girls and Ms. Wright, so she could be with her son and with her family. He said, "Lord, take me right now. [But it's not] possible so I just have to keep praying for forgiveness and pray for them."

Mitchell spent as much time as he could with pastors assigned to the juvenile facility, studied his Bible, and continued to tell his mother and Michelle Collins that he hoped he would have a chance to do some good in the world when he is released. From his apparent sincerity, Michelle deduces that the shooting was not his idea. She is less certain of what to say about Andrew Golden, although she did describe him as the "darker of the two." The younger boy has never confided in her and she does not know what goes on in his mind.

Frances Perkins, who works in the jail, reached a very different conclusion. A ten-year veteran of the jail staff, she was working the day shift when Andrew and Mitchell were arrested. As the weeks passed, she observed closely the relationship between Mitchell and Andrew and formed her own views on just how much they regretted their actions. The answer, she surmised, was not much. "I talked to them once [about it]," she recalled, "and asked them why they had done [it]. Never once seen any remorse. Never once seen any emotion." After a few months, she decided to put the question to them directly. "Andrew," she said, "I got to ask you something that's really eating at me." "What?" [he asked]. "Why?" Andrew's eyes dropped to the ground. He didn't have a response.

Mitchell stood in that kind of cocky act and he just said, "Because I wanted to." "Is that your answer?" [I asked], "that you wanted to?"

Frances was stunned. Even a hardened killer would be less cold-blooded. She decided to test Mitchell, figuring the best way past the tough-guy façade was to remind him of the one person she had ever seen bring him to tears: his little sister Jesse. "Mitchell," she pressed, "I don't want to sound like a fool, but I want you to think about something . . .

> What would you do if your little sister that you love so much went to school one day and didn't come back home anymore, ever, because some kid like you walked into school and shot her? How would you feel?" "I'd feel awful," [Mitchell responded]. "I hope that someday I'd kill him."

"Is that your answer?" "Well, he wouldn't live to tell about it." [All through this Andrew was just crying.] "Andrew, can you give me an answer?" He shook his head no.

Andrew seemed forever anxious to impress Mitchell; he may well have been the one to suggest the rampage, hoping that this would cement his status in the older boy's eyes. At one point he confessed to Frances that it had indeed been his idea. But she wasn't convinced. Observing their behavior, Mitchell seemed the most excited by their notoriety, especially when television accounts of the shooting were aired.

What disturbed her the most, though, was not the thought that Mitchell had masterminded the shooting but that, contrary to public appearances, he was utterly unmoved by the consequences of his murderous acts.

He put on a show for visitations. . . . He would cry, he would do all the fake alligator tears I call them . . . Remorseful and all this garbage. . . . The only person that Mitchell was able to visit by himself was [his] mother . . . If she didn't come, forget it. We're talking concrete walls. No tears.

As Frances saw it, Mitchell seemed more concerned about stage-managing their impending judicial hearing, telling Andrew that they had nothing to fear. Months after the shooting, when the trial was about to get under way, Mitchell tried to shore up Andrew's flagging resolve.

[Mitchell] said [to Andrew], "I got your back. " 'Man, don't sweat it . . . They ain't got nothing on us." . . . I got you covered. Just back me up on this. They can't prove anything.' . . . Andrew did say something about how he liked that teacher [Shannon Wright] . . . and that it was an accident. Mitchell said, "Man, don't be messed up about it."

Mitchell did not like authority figures of any kind but was particularly rebellious in the face of women in charge. The female workers in the jail dreaded his father's visits for the way they catalyzed eruptions in Mitchell:

Mitchell didn't seem to recognize any kind of supervision. He hated authority, he hated cops. . . . He would come back [from visits with Scott] and slam his cell and start cursing and acting really bullish and hateful and arrogant, real arrogant. He really didn't like women. . . .

While the staff genuinely cared for Gretchen and recognized how much she grieved for her son, there was no love lost between Scott Johnson and the jail staff. He accused the staff of mistreating Mitchell, insisted on celebrity status, and encouraged a defiant attitude in his son, which made him harder to manage. "Mitchell's father," Michelle remembered, "I don't think he gave a hoot about the boy."

He never had any contact with him until it started to get into the trial and court time. He never wrote, he never came to check on him, he never came down to see him until just prior to the court ordeal. . . . His mother seemed to be a very loving mother, but I can definitely tell where [Mitchell] got his arrogant attitude . . . from his father, good Lord. He is a test for a saint.

Mitchell's contrition and apologies simply rang false to Frances. She was convinced that the boy was more of a charmer than his father but that underneath lay a master manipulator. Andrew, she thought, was not clever enough to put on a show. He was just a scared little boy who sought approval from more authoritarian types:

[Mitchell] is a dominating type of personality and he's demanding . . . very demanding. He was a schemer, manipulating. He might cry and then turn around because [his mother] bought it. Andrew wouldn't cry at all. Andrew would be quiet or else he would be acting silly. Andrew never threatened or challenged us.

Even so, Frances had to admit that there were extremely troubling aspects of Andrew's personality that suggested he was capable of violence.

[Andrew] hated cats. And I said, "What did you do with this cat?" He said, "I've done several things to cats. . . . I shot bottle rockets at them. I tied one to the clothesline and I shot [BBs] at them. . . . I've shot them full of BBs." He said, "They would just be lying there scrawling and hollering . . .
. . . [Andrew] was talking about nothing else and how he would slit their throats and wring their necks and stuff like that. He thought he was so cool that he just grab that head and cut that throat. Good Lord!

It is tempting, given this evidence, to conclude that Mitchell was a manipulative boy, with a deep hatred and anger festering below the polite surface he showed in the church choir, and that Andrew was "cute and smiling" but also pathologically attracted to violence. These conclusions may be warranted. At the same time, even those who observed them during the long months they were in the Craighead County Jail were looking at two boys who were "on stage." The audience was no longer the kids in Westside classrooms, but a potentially more threatening cast of characters: other teenagers (mainly older juveniles) who were locked up as well. We cannot discount the fear they may have felt in this situation or the blustering they might have put on to fit in with a more hardened crowd.

Their true colors may have been more visible in the Alexander Juvenile facility, where they ended up for several years after the trial. There Mitchell was known as one of the most cooperative, repentant, religious, studious, and helpful of the inmates. The staff feel warmly toward him, believe he will do good once he is released, and have done their best to give him special privileges to reward his good behavior. Scott Johnson has never visited Mitchell at Alexander, which may be one reason he has been calmer and more positive than he was in the jailhouse. Andrew, on the other hand, retreated into himself at Alexander. He was, by all accounts, the most silent of eleven-year-old boys. Unlike Mitchell, who expressed remorse almost continuously, Andrew never spoke about the shooting at all.

———

How are we to draw meaning out of these two sad episodes? Journalists and psychologists have put forward a variety of explanations for school shootings, focusing for the most part, as we have here, on the shooters themselves and the individual pressures that led them to kill. However, we believe greater insight can be obtained from focusing attention on the sociological level of the community— on how the social structure of small-town life contributed to the shootings, in particular how it obscured the warning signs that a shooting would occur. We turn now to the competing theories of school shootings, exploring their virtues and shortcomings against the background of the two cases we know best.

3

EXPLAINING RAMPAGE
SCHOOL SHOOTINGS

THE 1997–1998 ACADEMIC YEAR LEFT A BLOODY TRAIL OF MULTIPLE-VICTIM homicides in communities that imagined themselves violence free. Rampage school shootings had actually erupted before,[1] but in the late 1990s, a string of six incidents created a sense that an epidemic was under way. On October 1, 1997, sixteen-year-old Luke Woodham of Pearl, Mississippi, killed his mother, came to school, and shot nine students, killing two. One month later, Michael Carneal killed three and wounded five. Fourteen-year-old Joseph Todd shot two students in Stamps, Arkansas, two weeks after Michael's rampage. Mitchell Johnson and Andrew Golden left four students and a teacher dead and wounded ten others. A few weeks later, fourteen-year-old Andrew Wurst of Edinboro, Pennsylvania, killed a teacher and wounded three students at a school dance. The killing season for that year ended on May 21 when fifteen-year-old Kip Kinkel murdered his parents and then went on a shooting spree in his Springfield, Oregon, school cafeteria, killing two students and wounding twenty-five.

The next year brought us "Columbine." The sheer scale of the Littleton, Colorado, rampage was so enormous that this one word will, for years to come, conjure up horrific images of dead and wounded children. Eric Harris, age seventeen, and Dylan Klebold, eighteen, invaded the school with an arsenal of guns and bombs, killing twelve students and a teacher, wounding twenty-three others, and finally ending their own lives. One month later, T. J. Solomon injured six students in a school shooting in Conyers, Georgia.

For those who have "been there," each new rampage shooting resurrects terrible memories. Christine Olson, an eighteen-year-old honors student who graduated from Westside High School, had a sister in the middle school at the time of the rampage. She remembered well how the Columbine shooting propelled her own community backward:

> When I heard about Columbine, I spent most of the day crying at school just because it brought back so much. It was just strange how it really affected the community again because we thought we . . . were doing so much better. . . . It took about a year for us to [start healing], and then . . . almost exactly a year after, [Columbine] happened.

Ironically, Michael Carneal felt much the same way. He attempted suicide twice during his incarceration at Northern Kentucky Youth Correctional Center after learning of the events in Littleton. In some way, Michael felt responsible for the shootings that followed his own. "When will it ever end?" he asked his therapist.

The answer, sadly, was no time soon. After a brief respite, the shootings continued. On March 5, 2001, fifteen-year-old Charles Andrew (Andy) Williams killed two students and wounded eleven more as well as a campus security guard, and a student teacher at Santana High School in suburban Santee, California. Two weeks later, eighteen-year-old Jason Hoffman wounded three students and two teachers at Granite Hills High School in nearby El Cajon, California.

To many, it seemed that suddenly, mysteriously, the scourge of deadly youth violence had burst free of poor and minority neighborhoods and came calling in the kinds of comfortable communities that residents believe are perfect places to raise kids. If the shooting had happened at Paducah Tilghman High School, located in the city, residents like Marjorie Eagen would not have been surprised.

> Tilghman is at least 50 percent lower socioeconomic, you've got a greater mix of races at Tilghman. Those are the kids from the projects. . . . That's the city school. You've got the kids that have access to guns, that see drugs sold on a daily basis. . . . If it happened [there], everybody would have said, "Did you hear what happened?" It would have been a big thing, but it wouldn't have been an attorney's son from Heath. People move out to Heath to put their kids in school so they don't go to the city school.

Media pundits weighed in on the causes of deadly school shootings, and academic studies, government commissions, congressional working groups, and presidential summits soon followed—too many, some argued, given how seldom school shootings happen. Indeed, critics such as Orlando Patterson, a sociologist, and Michael Eric Dyson, a professor of African-American studies, argued that the only reason these rare events generated the attention they did was that the shooters and most of the victims were white.[2] Had they been black, the attention would have been minimal and the need to explain the pathology less pronounced.

There are good reasons to dwell on rampage school shootings even though they are rare. They are an unprecedented kind of adolescent violence. We do not understand why they happen and have barely begun to consider their long-term consequences. Models derived from the study of urban violence have minimal value in deciphering the causes of rampage school shootings. Understanding what leads to these attacks does not free anyone of the obligation to think just as hard about the far more common incidence of urban shootings, something social scientists and policymakers have been working on for decades.

A steady stream of explanations came forth when rampage school shootings emerged, ranging from bullying to a southern culture of violence, from mental illness to lack of discipline, from violent media to the availability of guns.[3] Do these theories hold water? We address this question by looking first at whether the phenomenon is new, epidemic, and worthy of a policy response, and then at how school rampages differ from other kinds of mass murders. Finally, we look at the ways in which received wisdom falls short of the kind of explanation we need.

EPIDEMIC OR "SCHOOL HOUSE HYPE"?

In the year following the massacre at Columbine High School, the nation's fifty largest newspapers printed nearly 10,000 stories related to the event and its aftermath, averaging about one story per newspaper every other day.[4] No wonder parents worried about their children. A Gallup poll conducted in August 2000 found that 26 percent of American parents feared for their children's safety at school.[5] Twenty-nine percent of the high school students polled by ABC News in March 2001 said that they saw some risk of an attack at their school, but immediately after the Columbine attack, 40 percent saw some risk.[6]

The intense media coverage and renewed fear generated by the string of shootings around the country led some observers to claim that we are in the midst of an epidemic.[7] This view has not gone unchallenged. Critics, such as the Justice Policy Institute, have argued that the widespread "panic" over school shootings is unjustified. In reports issued in July 1998 and April 2000, the institute reminded the nation that school is still the safest place for a child to be. Even during the seemingly deadly 1998–1999 school year, the chances of dying in school from homicide or suicide were less than one in 2 million. The rate of *out-of-school* homicides alone was about forty times higher.[8]

What worried opponents of the epidemic hypothesis was not just the hype but the responses emerging from policymakers.[9] Resources that might be spent on addressing more deadly problems facing America's youth, especially abuse, neglect, and inner-city youth violence, could be wasted on the statistically minor threat of school shootings. In the rush to take action, critics warned, educators might adopt measures that could backfire, including zero-tolerance policies, profiling, or security measures that induce or aggravate a climate of fear or shunt more troubled youths into the criminal justice system. Finally, they feared that intense media coverage of school shootings would spark more violence as copycats swung into action.

Both perspectives, the epidemic view and the hype view, have some merit. Schools are indeed the safest place for our children to be, statistically. Yet if parents and children fear school violence, the schools' primary mission will be profoundly impaired. Parents' concerns cannot be dismissed as irrelevant just because they are not entirely rational.

Moreover, their fears are not unfounded. Attacks of the kind we discuss in this book *did* increase in the 1990s. They are assaults of a very specific kind, and it pays to bear their characteristics in mind. As we define them, rampage school shootings must:

- take place on a school-related public stage before an audience;
- involve multiple victims, some of whom are shot simply for their symbolic significance or at random; and
- involve one or more shooters who are students or former students of the school.

This definition excludes many kinds of shootings that are cause for worry as well. For example, a student who comes to school looking to shoot a particular antagonist, or the school principal, but does not fire at others would not be counted here. Gang violence, revenge killings following drug deals that go bad—these kinds of mayhem are not included in our definition. Rampage school shootings, then, are a subset of a much larger category of murders or attempted murders and are closer in form to workplace or "postal" attacks than they are to single-victim homicides on or off campus.

Bearing this definition in mind, we can now turn our attention to the patterns that have emerged in recent years. The solid line in Figure 3.1 charts the

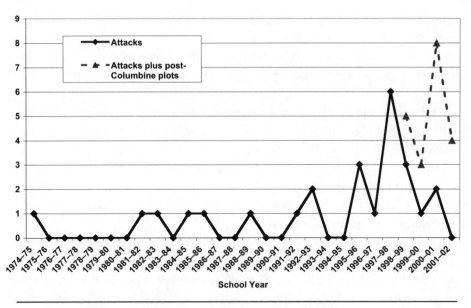

Figure 3.1   Number of School Shootings by School Year

number of school shootings in the United States since the 1974–1975 school year, including only shootings in which the offender targeted the school per se (excluding shootings related to gangs, drug activity, or disputes that spill over onto school property).[10] The numbers are very low until the early 1990s. They began to increase in the 1992–1993 school year, peaking in 1997–1998 and falling again to zero in 2001–2002. Do these data reflect a short-term epidemic, squashed—as so many patterns were—by the enormous wound of the terrorist attacks on September 11, 2001? Possibly, but the story is not a simple one, because although the number of actual attacks declined, police and school officials foiled a number of plots in 2001–2002. The dashed line in Figure 3.1 tracks plots discovered by police and school officials after the rampage at Columbine.[11] There is no way to know whether these plots would have culminated in shootings and deaths or would have stopped short, remaining nothing more than adolescent fantasies. Either way, they are not particularly reassuring: students are still thinking about, planning, and moving to execute rampage shootings.

Rampage shootings are not unique to the United States. At least five multiple-victim, student-perpetrated incidents of school violence have taken place in other nations since 1975—two in Canada, one in Germany, one in the Netherlands, and one in Kenya.[12] Erfurt, Germany, was the unhappy scene of a sixth deadly attack in April 2002, in which a student who had been expelled from his high school returned in a fury and murdered sixteen people and wounded six. And although no rampage shootings occurred on middle or high school campuses after the September 11 terrorist attacks, several very similar shootings erupted on university campuses.[13]

Curiously, the peak in school shootings came at a time when other trend lines for violence were headed in the opposite direction. Decreases were recorded in adult homicides, youth homicides, drug- and gang-related youth homicide in the inner cities, and nonlethal violence in schools for the same period when school shootings spiked.[14] Of course, it must be remembered that this sharp uptick still represents a small number of deaths and that the incidence of homicide on school campuses remains low.

Media coverage does contribute to a school violence panic and certainly aggravates the difficulties for communities in which rampage episodes have occurred. But the press should also be credited with helping to avert some potential rampages. Articles pointing to the unwillingness of students to come forward when they heard warnings of impending violence trained attention on the need for teenagers to speak out and helped foil some near-miss plots. For example, in November 2001 a plot to shoot up a New Bedford, Massachusetts, high school was uncovered solely because one seventeen-year-old participant came forward.

Unfortunately, relaying threats to adults is not the norm. A poll taken in November 2001 revealed that 61 percent of high school students who knew of someone bringing a gun to school did not report it; 56 percent of those who heard another student make a weapons-related threat said nothing.[15] Even so, between 1999 and 2001, at least seven school shootings were prevented when peers reported the plans to school or law enforcement authorities.[16] The media coverage helped to shift the balance, at least in these cases.

RAMPAGE SCHOOL SHOOTINGS AND INNER-CITY VIOLENCE

Deadly violence among youths is indeed concentrated in poor areas of our nation's inner cities. For example, in 1989 the homicide rate for black males of ages fifteen through nineteen in urban areas was almost thirteen times higher than the national average for that age group.[17] Accordingly, researchers concerned about youth violence have concentrated primarily on explaining urban conditions; the results are both heartening and depressing.

Youth violence increased dramatically in the late 1980s and early 1990s, a period in which rates of crime and violence among other age groups actually went down. The increase was concentrated among, but not limited to, black males. Countless studies have tried to explain this trend. Some of them point to the size of the "at-risk" population, but this appears not to be a very influential factor: violence increased in the 1980s across all age categories, regardless of their size, simultaneously. And we are not likely to "age out" of this problem. Youth violence is not simply "kids killing kids." The majority of people who kill adolescents are adults, and most victims of adolescent killers are adults. Kids and guns do not mix well. The increase in homicides committed by youths came entirely in the form of murders involving firearms.[18]

Given these patterns, social scientists want to know two things: First, *which* youths are violent? Boys are more likely to commit violent acts than girls, and almost all violent offenders first manifest their tendencies between the ages of fourteen and eighteen. Violence peaks in the midteens for black and white males, although the rates for black males rise sharply again in their late twenties.[19] Beyond race, gender, and age, other risk factors for violence among youths include domestic violence and abuse, weak family bonding and ineffective supervision, lack of opportunities for education and employment, peers who engage in or accept violence, drug and alcohol use, gun possession, and individual temperament.[20] Finally, public perceptions notwithstanding, violent youths actually seem to be trying to accomplish goals where conventional means to achieve them are out of reach. They look to elevate their status among peers, cement an identity, acquire material goods or power over others, or find justice or retribution. Defiance of authority and the satisfaction that comes from risk taking and impulsivity also figure among the purposes to which violence is put.[21]

The second basic question social scientists ask about youth violence is why it increased in the late 1980s and early 1990s. Major culprits include the increased availability of guns, the crack cocaine epidemic, and a culture of violence, but none of these factors works by itself. Criminologist Mark Moore has suggested a synthesis that starts with the deteriorating social and economic conditions of inner-city neighborhoods in the late 1970s and early 1980s and adds responses of neighborhood residents that produced steadily increasing violence, fear, and breakdown of social control. As sociologist William Julius Wilson has argued, during the 1970s, joblessness increased in inner-city communities because of the outmigration of the middle class and the movement of blue-collar jobs away from U.S. cities. Economic and social stress contributed to the breakdown of families and other community supports for children and adolescents.[22] In search of support, identity, and meaning in the face of declining opportunity, more youths became involved in gangs, and with the introduction of crack cocaine, gangs turned to this volatile end of the drug market, where violence is the only available mode of protection and social control. Guns are readily available and proliferate. The streets become considerably more dangerous, and an environment develops in which victimization of the weak is commonplace.[23]

Despite the high rates of violent death among inner-city minority youths, relatively little of this violence occurs in city schools. For example, as of 2002, the last gun homicide in New York City's schools occurred in East New York's Jefferson High School on February 26, 1992. The city of Chicago has not had a gun homicide in a school since November 20, 1992.[24] National statistics paint a similar picture. In the nine school years between 1992 and 2001, on average only 8.7 students and slightly less than one school staff member per year were killed in violent attacks in urban schools. Student deaths from violent attacks in cities declined steadily over this period from eighteen in 1992–1993 to four in 2000–2001.[25]

Urban schools do have considerably higher rates of nonlethal violence. Thirty percent of males and 16 percent of females reported being assaulted at inner-city schools or while traveling to and from school.[26] Even so, urban schools are far safer than urban streets or homes. Students are three times more likely to be assaulted by a weapon in the neighborhoods where they live than in the schools they attend.[27]

Can the lessons learned from the study of inner-city youth violence be applied to suburban and rural school shootings? James Garbarino thinks so. Garbarino, a professor of psychology at Cornell University, is the author of a widely cited book, *Lost Boys: Why Our Sons Turn Violent and How We Can Save Them*.[28] He has interviewed and treated hundreds of violent boys from inner-city neighborhoods. In *Lost Boys*, he applies insights garnered from those encounters to children like Mitchell Johnson and concludes that the same constellation of psychological problems is responsible. He argues that the roots of youth violence begin at an early age with rejection, neglect, and other forms of abuse. These problems are then magnified by toxic social environments, such as inner-city neighborhoods and dysfunctional families, leading to muddled emotional and moral thinking.

Garbarino assumes that all types of youth homicide have similar causes and that urban youths who turn violent experience problems similar to those of suburban and rural rampage school shooters. In doing so he relies on a questionable "social epidemic model," which views violence as a health problem among the nation's youth.[29] In his view, youth violence works like a contagious disease, first afflicting the most susceptible population, which is urban minority youths, and then spreading to other populations—suburban and rural youths.[30] By what mechanisms does the contagion spread? *Lost Boys* does not say.

Epidemiological patterns, however, are strikingly divergent. Criminologists Diane Wilkinson and Jeffrey Fagan observe that suburban and rural shootings occurred in three clusters: the fall 1997, the spring of 1998, and the spring of 1999.[31] Urban youth homicides do *not* cluster but are continuous for over a decade between 1985 and 1996.[32] A copycat effect seems to have been in play in the Columbine shooting, but not in the big cities. Moreover, shootings in suburbia are rare. If there were a direct link between the two types of violence, with city violence spilling over into surrounding areas, we would expect to see a lot more of it than we do.[33]

Suburban and rural shootings almost always happen on school grounds, whereas this is rarely the case in the cities. In rural communities, school is one of the few "public stages" where an attention-seeking shooter can create a spectacle.[34] In the city, there are many other (potentially more meaningful) stages available. In chapter 6, we take this notion even further, arguing that the school plays a central role in the social life of adults and children in suburban and rural settings. The school itself is a highly symbolic target of the attack.

There are some striking differences between urban youth who become violent and rampage shooters in suburban and rural schools. The former are usually labeled early as "problem kids." They are deemed troubled, and then their actions confirm the label. Murder represents the culmination of escalating problem behaviors. In contrast, school shooters are almost always kids no one would have expected to turn violent. They are often stigmatized as geeks or nerds. They act to *defy* their labels.

Finally, urban shootings "unfold through stages of decision making and escalation . . . the culmination of lengthy ongoing disputes," whereas shootings in rural and suburban communities are "mass shootings, often with strangers as the victims if not the targets, and no acute ongoing dispute between victims and offenders."[35] Generally, no one is a stranger in the small, close-knit communities where these shootings have occurred. Nonetheless, rampage shooters often cast a wide net beyond individual targets, and some have no specific targets at all. Michael Carneal was surprised to learn the identity of his victims; Mitchell Johnson and Andrew Golden also were unaware of whom they killed. When urban violence erupts because of ongoing conflicts between individuals or groups that have a "beef" with one another, the identities of the opponents are almost always known.[36] Rampage school shooters plan their attacks well in advance; urban shootings are more spontaneous, erupting at the tail end of a dispute.

Rampage school shootings unfold in places where residents say they trust their neighbors so much that they leave their doors unlocked and regularly watch out for each other. Urban youth violence happens in communities where residents are often afraid to leave their houses for fear of the drug dealers who rule the corners and addicts who rob and steal to support a habit. Sociologist Elijah Anderson describes how drugs and poverty create an environment in which the only way to avoid victimization is to maintain one's reputation and presentation as tough and willing to defend oneself at any cost.[37] When a young man lives with mortal fear, he may react quickly, almost spontaneously, to threats as a form of self-protection. Rampage school shooters are not spontaneous at all. Michael Carneal planned his assault over a period of weeks, as did Mitchell and Andrew.[38]

Urban and rural people live in different worlds where murder is concerned. The communities of Heath, Kentucky, and Westside, Arkansas, were stunned and shocked by the school shootings. When Khalil Sumpter shot two students in East New York City's Jefferson High School in 1992, everyone was horrified by the deaths, but hardly surprised that violence had entered the schools. Kids and guns mix depressingly often in East New York. The shocking element was that the schools had joined a long list of unsafe places in the community.[39]

Despite the differences, there are important similarities between the two kinds of violence that should not be ignored. One is the potential link between violence against others and violence against oneself—between homicide and suicide. Some school shooters are suicidal or deeply depressed. Eric Harris and Dylan Klebold killed themselves after the Columbine massacre. T. J. Solomon put a pistol in his mouth, but didn't pull the trigger, after he fired into the lobby of his Conyers, Georgia, high school. Friends of Andrew Wurst, the rampage shooter from Edinboro, Pennsylvania, feared that he might kill himself the night he killed his science teacher and wounded two students at a school dance.

For these youths, a violent attack may be a way to "go down in flames" or to commit suicide by forcing others, especially police, to shoot them. Law enforcement personnel, criminologists, and psychiatrists have a term for this situation: "victim-precipitated homicide" or "suicide by cop." It is an "exit strategy" favored by those who seek a spectacular—and particularly masculine—suicidal end, and it is surprisingly common. One study of shootings involving officers of the Los Angeles County Sheriff's Department found that more than 10 percent of the incidents over a ten-year period met this criteria.[40]

Psychiatrist Alvin Poussaint and journalist Amy Alexander suggest in their book *Lay My Burden Down: Unraveling Suicide and the Mental Health Crisis Among African-Americans* that victim-precipitated homicide may be an important aspect of inner-city youth violence. The hopelessness and isolation of life in poor inner-city communities may lead some youths to engage in fatalistic life-threatening behaviors ranging from the slow death of smoking, obesity, and drug abuse to violent confrontations with others or the police. Even if inner-city youths are not explicitly suicidal, despair may lead to a willingness to put one's life on the line when one is "disrespected."[41]

Summing up the evidence, we conclude that there are significant differences between the rampage school shootings, which are mostly committed by youth in rural or suburban settings, and the kind of youth violence associated with inner-city settings. The random nature of victimization, the degree of advance planning, and the locations and public nature of the events all separate rampage shootings from urban shootings. We are looking at a separate genre of youth violence.

COMPARING ADULT AND YOUTH MASS MURDERS

Mass murders by adults bear some resemblance to rampage school shootings. In the twenty years between 1976 and 1995, 483 mass murder incidents took place in the United States (by offenders of any age)—on average about two per month.[42] Although we tend to imagine that the victims of such rampages were killed by strangers, in fact only about 20 percent of mass murders involve victims whom the offender did not know. Almost 40 percent of the victims are family members.[43] Some characteristics of mass murders resemble rampage school shootings. For example, compared with single-victim murders, a larger proportion of mass murders occur in small towns or rural areas (43.3 percent compared with 24.1 percent). Mass murderers are also predominantly white (62.9 percent) and male (94.4 percent), and slightly over 40 percent of such crimes are committed by young adults, aged twenty to twenty-nine.[44]

The *New York Times* conducted a study of 100 rampage attacks that occurred between 1949 and 2000, including twenty that took place in schools.[45] The authors point to a critical difference between adult and youth rampage killers: youths were far more likely to have peer support for their attacks. In two cases, the Columbine and Westside shootings, young killers acted in pairs. In other cases, friends knew a shooting was going to happen and helped the shooter prepare by driving him to school, actively encouraging him in his plans, or help-ing him learn to use a gun. Occasionally such friends crossed the line from being helpful to being coconspirators; in Bethel, Alaska, and Pearl, Mississippi, stu-dents other than the shooter were prosecuted. In virtually all of the school shootings, other students were warned of the impending attack. These circum-stances almost never obtain in adult rampage shootings: adult shooters do not act in groups, and they are less likely to have warned anyone.[46]

One form of adult rampage shooting that may be especially similar to school shootings is workplace homicide, particularly in instances in which an employee or former employee attacks his boss or coworkers. Disgruntled employees shoot their supervisors and colleagues depressingly often in the United States, and the number of such incidents has doubled since the 1970s, to about two attacks per month.[47]

Two similarities between workplace attacks and school shootings are note-worthy. First, like school shooters, workplace shooters are arguably attacking not just individuals but the institution itself. School shooters may be angry at the entire social system of the school and the community. The same kind of general-ized fury may be present in so-called "postal" rampages.[48] Second, like school shooters, workplace shooters often suffer from painful marginalization. They are the oddballs in the office, the guys that others make fun of behind their backs, the ostracized and harassed. For school shooters, relations with peers at the school may deny them status and security. For workplace shooters, being fired may be the last straw in part because it drops their status to zero, especially for middle-aged men—the typical workplace shooter—for whom unemployment is particularly difficult. Shooting asserts power.[49]

From our point of view, workplace shootings and school rampages have some profound and unfortunate similarities. They represent the tips of similar icebergs, where those who feel ostracized, marginalized, and threatened with emasculation react with murderous violence. Obviously, they are more similar in motivation than in design, but if we want to understand why they happen, it is useful to focus on those commonalities.

POPULAR EXPLANATIONS OF
SCHOOL SHOOTINGS: HOW DO THEY FARE?

Academics, government working groups, and think tank researchers have tried to account for the patterns we find in school shootings. Perhaps as many as a dozen explanations have emerged in the process. It is important to consider just how well they do the job of explaining the problem we address in this book and to identify where they fall short. In chapter 10 we propose a new theory of school shootings, drawn from the original research laid out in detail in part 2. For now, though, we need to hold received wisdom up to the light of what we learned in Westside and Heath and what we know about other cases. The examination tells us that there is more work to be done.

Mental Illness

Few school shooters are diagnosed with mental illnesses before their crimes. Yet many are discovered afterward to be mentally ill. Depression and schizophrenia or one of its variants are particularly common. Only a small minority of these children are under treatment.[50] Rampage shooters on campus do share troubling mental conditions with other killers. In a study of 102 adult and juvenile rampage killers conducted by The *New York Times,* "33 of the offenders killed themselves after their crimes. Nine tried or wanted to commit suicide, and four killed themselves later. Nine were killed by police officers or others, perhaps committing what some refer to as 'suicide by cop.'"[51] In more than half of the cases, friends, family, and even the offenders themselves tried to get help or warn others about the impending violence.

The complexity of mental illness as a causal factor in school shootings is illustrated by the case of Michael Carneal. Michael had no known history of mental illness before the shooting. After the shooting, a history of mental illness on his father's side of the family was uncovered. When he was evaluated by forensic psychiatrists, two separate defense experts found him to be able to understand the consequences of his actions but to have been mentally ill at the time of the shooting; the prosecution's psychiatric team disagreed.[52] Michael eventually developed full-blown schizophrenia and manages in prison today because he is taking antipsychotic medication; hence, we tend to agree with the defense in this dispute.

Unfortunately, we have little information about the mental health of either Mitchell Johnson or Andrew Golden. Because they were convicted in juvenile court, their psychological evaluations are sealed. According to some who have read them, however, there was no conclusive evidence of mental illness.[53] Andrew's lawyer sought to have him declared both insane and incompetent, but the court set this concern aside as inapplicable in juvenile court. In addition, the behavior of these two shooters does not suggest that they planned or hoped the shooting would result in their own deaths. Indeed, they were among the few school shooters who attempted to flee after their crimes. They even had an elaborate getaway plan.

We might expect adults who routinely deal with adolescents, such as school personnel, to be able to spot mental illness. It turns out to be exceptionally difficult, largely because problems like clinical depression or schizophrenia may be in their early stages, lacking some of the symptoms that manifest themselves later in life. At the onset of the disease, kids are often aware of how different they are from others and, feeling the stigma that comes with this territory, work hard to conceal their troubles. Michael Carneal fits this description well. In chapter 4, we delve deeper into the difficulties that schools and other organizations have in identifying troubled youths like him. It is not that teachers don't care about their students. Instead, as we will show later, the organization and culture of schools make it extremely difficult to spot troubled adolescents before they lash out.

Given the number of adolescents who are depressed and suicidal, mental illness cannot be viewed as a straightforward predictor of rampage school shootings. According to the National Institute of Mental Health, up to 8.3 percent of adolescents suffer from depression, and in 1996 suicide was the third leading cause of death for people aged fifteen to twenty-four. More than 2 million Americans are affected by schizophrenia, which usually develops in the late teens or early twenties. Ten percent of schizophrenia patients eventually commit suicide.[54] These trends dwarf the number of rampage shootings in schools, and for this reason we must treat the relationship of mental illness to these attacks with caution.

"He Just Snapped"

When we are at a loss to explain something, we look for the most proximate or immediate potential cause. We note that a shooter was just rejected by a girl, punished by a parent or a school official, insulted or assaulted by peers. Timing leads to the assumption that the incident caused the boy to "snap." Our legal system supports this kind of logic—though probably more in popular myth, television, and movies than in reality. We allow defendants to plead "temporary insanity," in which a person is briefly unable to tell right from wrong, given the overpowering influence of his surroundings.

We reject the notion that proximate events explain much about school shootings. They may be the straw that broke the camel's back, but at most they help explain *when* a shooting happens rather than *why*. Events that seem to be precipitators usually turn out on closer inspection not to be. For example, Luke

Woodham, who killed two students and wounded seven in Pearl, Mississippi, in 1997, broke up with Christina Menefee, the first person he shot. The end of their relationship was widely assumed to be the catalyst for Luke's rampage. Yet the breakup occurred months before the shooting. Woodham planned his attack carefully rather than acting impulsively after the breakup.

Nicole Hadley politely rejected Michael Carneal's awkward advances, leading many people in the Heath community to believe that this defeat caused Michael's rampage. But Nicole was one of the people Michael warned to stay away from the lobby that Monday; after the fact, he was adamant that he never meant to hurt her. Mitchell Johnson had indeed just been dumped by his girlfriend, kicked off the basketball team, and reportedly was afraid he would have to move back to Minnesota with his father after being caught using his father's credit card to call phone sex lines. Andrew Golden may also have had some girlfriend trouble. However, Michael, Mitchell, and Andrew had an entire holiday break away from school between these events and the shootings. In none of these cases did the shooters "just snap," if by this we mean a spontaneous and immediate reaction to a major disappointment.

To put great weight on immediate precipitating events also ignores an important aspect of most school shootings: they are usually planned well in advance. Michael Carneal had talked about taking over the mall or the school with peers at school for weeks before the shooting. Mitchell Johnson and Andrew Golden evidently planned the shooting for months and finalized the plan during the week of spring break.

Family Problems

No explanation for school shootings has received more attention than family problems. The Final Report of the Congressional Bipartisan Working Group on Youth Violence is a good example of the notion that it all begins in the home: "Although there is no single cause for youth violence," the report concludes, "the most common factor is family dysfunction."[55] But what kinds of families are these? Here the picture gets much murkier. A Secret Service study of forty-one school shooters who committed their crimes between 1974 and 2000 found that the perpetrators come from a variety of family backgrounds, ranging "from intact families with numerous ties to the community to foster homes with histories of neglect."[56]

Problems within the family, such as divorce, domestic or sexual abuse, frequent relocations, and fragile family relationships as well as lack of awareness or involvement in children's lives, were all cited by the people we interviewed in Westside and Heath as reasons that youths turn violent. Penny Nichols, a seventh grade teacher at Westside, was convinced that the home and family are the root of the problem:

> My interpretation is if they put so much emphasis on what goes on at school, how they're bullied and how teachers may not do this and may not do that, or maybe teachers need to do more of this—you know, it's screaming at everybody: "Home life, home life, home life!"

Diminishing adult and parental authority over children is another variant of this theme and was frequently mentioned as a growing problem by community residents we interviewed. Parents are increasingly losing control of their kids, they say, because they work long hours and have little time to spend with them. Moreover, many people in the community feel that parents have relinquished authority for disciplining their children to the school while the school in turn believes that, increasingly, parents are not supportive of the school's disciplinary decisions.

There can be no doubt that some school shooters have difficult family lives.[57] An FBI review of eighteen school shooting cases concluded that potential warning signs of a school shooter include turbulent parent–child relationships, family acceptance of pathological behavior, access to weapons in the home, lack of closeness or intimacy with family members, a child who "rules the roost," and lack of limits or monitoring of television and the Internet.[58] As the FBI correctly warns, many students fit this profile, so distinguishing between shooters and nonshooters solely on the basis of family characteristics is impossible.

The complexity of the role of family problems is illustrated in the Heath and Westside cases. On the outside, the Carneal family was the opposite of the stereotypical "dysfunctional" family.[59] The Commonwealth Attorney hardly knew what to make of Michael's rampage, given the boy's background:

> Michael comes from a very good family. Father's a lawyer here. Mother's a very good person. . . . Most kids that come from homes where they have two loving parents, raised them properly, and present them with all the opportunities they can are less likely to commit crime than those who come from broken homes with little supervision.

The Westside shooting presents a contrasting picture; here family problems were clearly central, at least in Mitchell Johnson's case. His parents were divorced. He had moved frequently. His troubled relationship with his father was a source of enormous anxiety, and the thought of possibly having to live with his father pushed him into a pit of hopelessness. He had suffered repeated sexual abuse at the hands of a neighborhood youth in Minnesota, and although it is not uncommon for children to be afraid of confessing that they have been victimized, Mitchell's fears were aggravated by his concern about his father's temper. Various people close to Mitchell have suggested that the shooting was a displacement of the anger and frustration he felt toward some family members and his abuse.

All of these background facts point toward family history as a harbinger of the eventual rampage. Yet Mitchell's life with his mother and stepfather in Bono was more stable than he had ever known it before. Gretchen and Terry Woodard were, by all accounts, caring and concerned parents.

In contrast to Mitchell's more clearly troubled family history, Andrew Golden's family background was fairly stable. His family was close, and they were well-respected longtime residents of the community. We know that there was tension involving Andrew's stepsiblings (his mother's children by a previous marriage) and that eventually they left the home to move in with other relatives. This may have had an impact on an impressionable young child. Andrew's father and his grandmother were involved in his life at school and wanted him to keep out of trouble.

Yet teachers and administrators at Westside felt that Andrew's parents were overindulgent and generally let him have his way. They pulled him out of a class when he complained that a teacher had spoken harshly to him about not acting up in class and distracting other students. Teachers suspected that Andrew was not disciplined at home for misbehaving. Neighbors were particularly aghast at Andrew's threatening behavior toward their kids and his abusive treatment of animals. Clearly he was a boy with some problems who was given greater latitude than was perhaps healthy, but he certainly suffered no abuse at the hands of his family. They cherished him.

These cases illustrate the complex nature of the relationship between family problems and school shootings. It may well be that problems surfacing behind the closed doors of the home contribute to school shootings, but their role is not straightforward.

Bullying

Bullying at school is probably the most commonly accepted explanation for school shootings, and for good reason. Shooters do express fury at being excluded, teased, and tormented.

Bullying is a nationwide problem. According to the National Association of School Psychologists, about 160,000 children miss school every day for fear of bullying.[60] A 1998 study of almost 16,000 children in grades six though ten found that 10.6 percent are subjected to this kind of torment at least "sometimes," 13 percent bully others at least "sometimes," and an additional 6.3 percent both are bullied and bully others.[61] Victims of harassment tend to exhibit lower levels of social and emotional adjustment. It is harder for them to make friends, and they are lonely. Bullies get involved in delinquency and substances abuse, and they tend to do poorly in school. Kids who both bully and are bullied seem to be at the greatest risk; they are both victims and aggressors.[62]

Did problems of this kind play a role in the Westside and Heath shootings? By all accounts, the answer is yes, but as with all such answers, it must be qualified. When the police asked Michael why he shot his classmates, he told them he was tired of being picked on. Mitchell and Andrew both complained that they were on the receiving end of harassment. Yet there is a significant discrepancy between their accounts and the views expressed by fellow students. The shooters seem to have given as good as they got. All three were described by their peers as kids who teased and bullied others. Maria Walter, a classmate of Michael's, noted that he "got picked on a lot."

> But he also picked on other people. . . . I never saw mental illness in him when I was around him. He was just always annoying. He's always the one who got us in trouble in classes just for pulling pranks all the time. . . . But I never really thought it was a bullying thing. . . . [He was] always the one who teased everyone else. And then when he comes out and says he was picked on, it's like, wait a minute.

Peer Support

In contrast to adult rampage shootings, youth shootings often are committed by groups or with encouragement from peers.[63] In almost half of the thirty-seven school shooting incidents studied by the Secret Service, "attackers were influenced or encouraged by others."[64] The Columbine and Westside shootings were both done by pairs of students, and law enforcement officials and prosecutors have attempted to link other youths to violent plots.[65] Luke Woodham was supposedly part of a satanic cult led by a friend who had recently graduated from his high school. Charges were brought against six students who prosecutors believed were in the group, although charges were eventually dropped against all but one.

The group's alleged leader eventually pleaded guilty to a conspiracy charge and was sentenced to six months in a boot camp and five years' probation.[66]

The importance of influence by peers can be hard to substantiate, however. Even when researchers have access to all records and interview people who have direct knowledge of the individuals involved, the extent of their participation is not easily assessed. Students who are accused of joining a plot or encouraging a shooter keep quiet about their involvement after the fact.[67] Hence, what we know about peer connections derives from the shooters' own perceptions, which are sometimes clouded by mental illness, rage, and their own motivations, including the desire to underplay the contributions of peers to protect them from criminal prosecution or to claim the "credit" for themselves. In Heath, for example, none of the suspected coconspirators would talk to us because of pending lawsuits.

The degree to which shooters receive support from their peers extends beyond the alleged conspiracies to the reactions of those who are forewarned. In over three-quarters of the shootings examined in the Secret Service study, other students were told of the impending attack.[68] Some of these warnings provided acquaintances the opportunity to encourage the shooters, or at least to convey their approval. In other cases, friends may have tried to discourage the shooters or keep them out of trouble. Andrew Wurst's friends knew he had a gun and was suicidal. They took turns watching him to make sure he did not kill himself.[69]

Peer support for a school shooting must be seen in the proper context. In no case does a shooter appear to be overwhelmingly influenced or manipulated by his peers. But in the complex mixture of factors that lead to a school shooting, peer support—often misinterpreted by the socially marginal or psychologically unstable—can lead an individual further down the path toward violence.

However, there are symbolic reasons why communities may be jumping to conclusions about the involvement of friends in rampage school shootings. When kids from middle-class white homes do terrible things, peers from less stable backgrounds are often pulled into the picture as sources of corruption. The first person questioned in Westside was an African-American boy from another school. Two days after the Heath shooting, the McCracken County sheriff told the media that he believed other students conspired with Michael before the shooting because, he reasoned, Michael could not have used the six guns he brought to school that day himself, but must have anticipated having help from others. The Goths they questioned tended to be older, looked suspicious by local dress standards, and were from less elevated backgrounds than Michael.

Changing Communities

We tend to think of small-town life as stable and close—the opposite of the rootlessness that seems to predominate in new suburbs or big cities. Yet change has come to many parts of the United States. Dense social ties have given way to more impersonal relations in rural areas and small towns.[70] Demographic change brought on by migration and population turnover have disrupted tight social ties between families and neighbors. Emile Durkheim, classical social theorist of the nineteenth century, argued that rapid social change produced a condition called "anomie." He worried that it would lead to increases in suicide as the interdependence of "old" societies gave way and eroded the social ties that keep people stable.[71]

In Heath, the growth of new industries in the area has brought an influx of upper-middle-class engineers and other professionals to a formerly rural farming community. New residents simply may not have connections to longtime residents, and their busier professional lives may make forming such attachments more difficult. One Heath father voiced this opinion:

> Paducah has always wanted to grow. . . . Well, it's getting bigger, but you have to realize when it gets bigger, you end up with bigger problems that you never had before. . . . [With new people moving in,] I think the life becomes so much faster. I think it becomes so impersonal. I think everybody feels that if they have a rule [to cover an infraction], that's their only responsibility. That they don't need to have any consciousness about anything.

Related laments about the pace of life in American communities may also bear on school shootings. The amount of time that Americans spend working has increased as a result of new technology, changing gender roles and women's employment, and the increasing importance of consumer goods.[72] The average American spent 163 more hours working per year in the 1990s compared with twenty years earlier.[73] More time working means less time to devote to family and community. This was certainly felt to be a problem in the two communities of Westside and Heath, as one mother from West Paducah noted:

> [We] have a lot more working parents in today's society than we did—I mean, not just [for] material things. But I mean for necessity things. Me and my husband both have to work to make ends meet. . . . We have a lot of parents that don't care what other children do. . . . I think that they put more responsibilities on their children at too early of an age. [My daughter] has a lot of friends that, that their parents don't know half of what goes on in their lives.

Similar complaints issued from the Westside community. The mayor of Bono complained, "Most parents now, they turn the kids loose and say, 'Be back home at twelve o'clock. Don't bother me.' I think that's the big problem. I think it has to start at home." Although dual incomes have become a necessity for many families, the larger problem, according to many Heath and Westside residents, is changes in the nature of what it meant to be a parent.

Laments about parents being less invested in their children's lives do not always square with reality. Heath and Westside are communities that boast a high level of community connectedness and solidarity. Teachers know the parents of their students from neighborhood, family, church, or other connections. People watch out for one another. And although there are newcomers in town, families are deeply rooted: children follow their parents and often their grandparents into the same schools, generation after generation. Indeed, one of the reasons people in both communities gave us for remaining there was just the depth of the connections they enjoyed with their neighbors and fellow church members.

In fact, we argue in chapters 5 and 6 that precisely the opposite problem played a role in both school shootings. It was not the weakness of social ties in Westside and Heath that proved their undoing, but the strength of those bonds. Dense, all-encompassing, interconnected networks of friends and family can make the lives of misfits unbearable and actually stifle the flow of information about potential warning signs.

Culture of Violence

The first few school shootings occurred in southern states, leading some observers to wonder whether a "southern culture of violence" was behind the crisis. According to this view, the South has evolved a distinctive culture that legitimates violence as a way of solving disputes or of guarding and gaining social status. The antebellum South was notorious for the use of intimidation, threats, and the deployment of real violence to control former slaves.[74] Psychologists Richard Nisbett and Dov Cohen coined the phrase "culture of honor" to capture its flavor, arguing that its origins lie in rural societies in which material possessions are at increased risk of theft, making a reputation for toughness important.[75] Creating and maintaining this reputation requires credible threats—and actual acts—of violence.[76]

Rates of violent crime are indeed higher in the South.[77] Nisbett and Cohen think that this social history left its traces in the personalities of contemporary southerners. To demonstrate the point, they created experiments that test responses to insults and found that southern students were more likely to be angered and less likely to be amused. Southern students showed a sharper physical reaction to these stresses, with higher levels of cortisol and testosterone. Finally, southerners tended to become more aggressive, less deferential, and more domineering and were more likely to express concern that someone who had observed the insult would perceive them as less masculine.[78]

Using violence to settle interpersonal disputes is not unheard of in the Heath and Westside schools, and fights do break out between students. Some of the things students would fight over—honor, social status, defending others—do conform to the culture of violence hypothesis. Rick Bowman, a Heath student active in athletics, explained what kinds of troubles would lead students to fight with one another:

> As a general rule, girlfriends, boyfriends, you're cheating on me or I'm cheating on you, I'm going to beat up the person that you're cheating on me with, even though it's your fault. . . . Family members, like sisters, brothers, close cousins, if they get picked on, heard rumors about, then you're always going to have a fight.

Adults are not complete innocents in these matters; some support or tolerate adolescent violence under certain circumstances. Stacy Hunt, a Westside student, described the lessons her father taught her brother about fighting: "My dad's always telling him don't throw the first punch, but don't walk away." Rick Bowman seconded that view, explaining that Heath teachers accept a student's right to defend himself. It's "the person who threw the first punch [who would be] getting into trouble," he said. "The person retaliating will get nothing."

Is there a culture of honor in these communities? Andrew Golden may be the closest exemplar. He stood guard over the periphery of his family's property and warned kids off with a BB gun. Andrew did not have trouble with the idea that guns could settle arguments. But there is nothing particularly southern about his perspective. Mitchell Johnson—whose worst moments even before the shooting reveal a belligerent side—did not grow up in the South. His formative years were spent in Minnesota. Michael Carneal—who did grow up in the South— was not considered particularly violent and did not himself resort to violence to settle disputes. Dr. O'Connor was certainly of this opinion:

> [W]e never saw aggression out of him. In fact the only aggressive thing we ever saw was he pulled a peer off of another [who] started fighting. . . . Michael took him to the ground until staff could get there to hold them. So we never saw him aggressive.

Indeed, one of Michael's brewing problems before the shooting was that he was not really able to stand up for himself. He was known as the kid who just "took" physical abuse without confronting or standing up to anyone.

The "southern culture hypothesis" was dealt a series of setbacks as shootings and near-miss plots occurred in California, Pennsylvania, Washington, Colorado, Oregon, Massachusetts, Kansas, Florida, Michigan, and New York. If a particularly southern culture were responsible for school shootings, we would expect to see a much greater proportion of school shootings occurring in the South. We don't.

Gun Availability

It has not escaped the public's attention that school shootings depend on access to guns. Mass murders tend not to happen—in school or anywhere else—when knives are the only weapon available. Scholars and media pundits have been quick to point out that the increase in the number of firearms has coincided with the recent string of school shootings.[79] Since 1970, the number of guns in the United States has doubled, to about 200 million. One might conclude that access to guns is spreading rapidly, but the increase has actually been fueled by people who are already gun owners acquiring additional firearms. The proportion of adults who own guns has stayed relatively constant since 1980 at about 30 percent. This is not a low number; it is the highest proportion of any industrialized country, but it hasn't changed much over the years.[80]

National surveys tell us that about 20 percent of youths have brought some sort of weapon to school. Far more youths than this claim that they could easily get a gun. But the geographic differences are significant. In rural areas and small towns, where most school shootings have taken place, access to firearms is more assured.[81] Our own interviews with adolescents in Heath and Westside match these survey findings. Almost all of the kids in these communities told us that it would be very easy for them to get a gun.[82]

Mitchell Johnson and Andrew Golden were able to gain access to an arsenal of weapons for their crime. As we noted in chapter 1, most of the Goldens' weapons were secured—either in a safe or by a cable—but Mitchell and Andrew put their hands on more than enough firepower. Michael Carneal amassed an armory of nine weapons and thousands of rounds of ammunition by stealing them from his father and a neighbor. The availability and ubiquity of guns normalized their presence in these communities, which is part of the reason that none of the students who saw Michael with a gun before the shooting said anything about it to adults.

The presence of guns is clearly causally related to the shootings, but it is not clear that their increasing availability accounts for the recent spate of massacres in schools. Hunting communities have always kept guns at the ready, but school shootings began to occur fairly recently.

Violent Media

Americans believe that the country is saturated with bloodthirsty imagery: Video games, television, movies, and music are filled with ugly violence. By all accounts, the situation is getting worse. Exposure to violent media has increased dramatically among our youth over the last decade, pushing media influence forward as a prime explanation for the string of school shootings in the mid- to late 1990s. Indeed, when President Clinton held a presidential summit on youth violence in May 1999, he took great pains to welcome high-level representatives from the entertainment industry.[83] Quite apart from the moral objections people have to these sensational materials, psychologists tell us that violence desensitizes viewers to its consequences. Young people are particularly impressionable or ill-equipped to distinguish between drama and reality.

The available scientific evidence on the contribution violent media makes to violence among youth is inconclusive, although it is suggestive. Exposure to media violence is consistently associated with a variety of antisocial behaviors, from trivial violence against toys to serious criminal violence. Children who are exposed to media violence tend to identify violence as the best solution to a problem or to exhibit hostility and nonviolent but aggressive behavior. Consuming violent media inures viewers to the impact of pain; hence they are less aroused or disturbed—and less likely to intervene—when they witness bloody scenes.[84]

It is difficult, however, to sort out whether exposure leads to violence or kids who are already prone to violent behavior select this kind of media material. Randomized experiments—which avoid this "selection" problem—show that young children exposed to violent television engage in more violent play afterward than children in a control group.[85] To our knowledge, no similar experiments have been performed with adolescents, whose maturity might lead them to be more sophisticated consumers of media violence. Also, there is little evidence on the cumulative effects of consuming violent media over time.

✳ Millions of young people play video games full of fistfights, blazing guns, and body slams. Bodies litter the floor in many of our most popular films. Yet only a minuscule fraction of the consumers become violent. Hence, if there is an effect, children are not all equally susceptible to it. In our own interviews, almost all adolescents scoffed at the idea that they were so easily influenced by television, music, movies, and video games.[86]

Michael Carneal did play violent video games, and he saw the usual run of bloody movies. He had been playing violent video games since he was a child, including "Mortal Kombat" and "MechWarrior," favorites of millions of American teenagers. When asked in a police interview the morning of the shooting whether he had read or seen anything like his shooting spree, he mentioned the movie *Basketball Diaries*.

The protagonist in this film takes revenge on a Catholic school priest who had abused him by shooting the priest and a number of his classmates, to the cheers of some of his friends. Michael later denied that the movie had played any part in the shooting, noting that he mentioned the film only because police officials asked him whether he had seen or read anything reminiscent of what he had done. He volunteered that although he had seen *Basketball Diaries* several years before, it had not made much of an impression on him. He added that it made him angry that people tried to explain his actions in terms of a movie; he did not want to claim any such cover.

While there is clearly no one-to-one correspondence between exposure to violent video games and behavior, we agree with one of his psychiatrists that "Michael's exposure to media violence can be regarded as a factor which contributed to the attitudes, perceptions, and judgment which led to his violent behavior."[87] There is evidence for this perspective earlier in Michael's life. One of his church group leaders remembered that when hypothetical dilemmas were presented to the youth group he participated in, Michael's solutions often involved "shooting someone with a bazooka." Michael and his friends discussed a number of violent fantasies that were in part based on things they had seen in movies and video games. Although it would be far too simplistic to say that Michael's actions were caused by the movies he saw, violent video games and media provided a template for action and images of masculinity that appealed to a boy who felt weak and socially inadequate.

It is harder to assess what role violent media and video games might have played in the Westside shooting. Mitchell Johnson played violent video games, including one that featured shooting, at friends' houses, but he did not have access to them at home; his family couldn't afford the games. A Westside Middle School teacher testified before the Senate Commerce Committee, in a hearing on parental warning labels on albums, that "Mitchell brought [rap] music to school with him, listened to it on the bus, tried listening to it in class, sang lyrics over and over at school and played a cassette in the bathroom about 'coming to school and killing all the kids.'" His mother says he owned only two rap CDs, Tu-Pac Shakur's *All Eyez On Me,* and Bone Thugz n Harmony's *E 1999.* However, these two albums connect fame directly to violence.[88] One friend mentioned that Mitchell often talked about blood and gore, and that he had a penchant for "gory" movies. Gretchen Woodard, Mitchell's mother, disagreed completely:

> All the things that were said about rap music and video games, and we didn't even have Nintendo. Mitch had two rap tapes, but nobody said anything about his six barbershop quartet tapes and all his gospel tapes. . . . Mitchell loved music, just the different sounds.

We know considerably less about Andrew Golden's viewing habits, except that he was a latchkey kid whose frequent time alone at home may have left open the possibility for exposure to violent music or television. According to adults who knew Andrew, he was enamored of *Beavis and Butthead* and *South Park* (as are thousands of other children), and he used to play the clown and mimic the characters in those television shows. Although both shows are fairly violent, the violence does not seem to involve guns. Andrew's grandfather has said in media interviews that Andrew did play video games with guns.

The Copycat Effect

The timing and clustering of school shootings suggests that the later tragedies took their inspiration from the earlier ones. Not all shootings are sparked by copycatting. The rampage in Pearl, Mississippi, happened not long before Michael Carneal's shooting. Michael took his fateful steps a few months before Mitchell and Andrew fired on Westside. Yet there was never any suggestion that they were particularly aware of the events in these other communities.

Research on imitative violence suggests that media coverage affects the form and method of crimes rather than the amount of crime.[89] This may not be the case for individuals who are suicidal, however. There is some evidence, although it is highly contested, that youth suicides spike after highly publicized suicides, especially by celebrities.[90] It seems inconceivable that otherwise healthy and happy adolescents would shoot up their school because others went on rampages before them. Rather, troubled youths may see a model for a solution to their problems in previous school shootings.

Simple explanations cannot account for why some schools, communities, and individuals suffer or perpetrate school shootings. Violent media are part of the picture, but millions of children play "Mortal Kombat," and only a few become murderers. The availability of guns certainly makes the task of mounting a massacre easier, but it does not explain the "epidemic" of school shootings because we have not witnessed an increase in the *number* of people who own guns in the United States. It would be comforting, in some respects, to think that the problem is confined to parts of the country that are more enamored of violence as a way to solve disputes. Yet school shootings have spread to the West, the East, and the North. What, then, are the alternative explanations?

We will come back to this question in chapter 10, where we present our own theory of school shootings. But first, we need to lay out the elements of our alternative perspective. In part 2, we dig deep into background features that researchers have not focused on thus far. In the next chapters, we examine the organizational features of schools and communities that make it hard to identify children who are the verge of breakdown, the pressures that close-knit communities generate for those on the social margins, the ways adolescent culture contributes to depression and despair deep enough to motivate a deadly shooting, and the role of that very same culture in holding other kids back from reporting the threats they hear. These are the keys to understanding rampage shootings.

PART TWO

4

UNDER THE RADAR

There are so many what ifs . . . Had [Mitchell's mother] known the van was stolen, she would have been out looking for him. Had the school called to say Mitchell wasn't at school, she could have done something. Had anyone at the three gas stations called the police, maybe it wouldn't have happened.

—Michelle Collins, Craighead County
Juvenile Corrections employee

Survivors of the rampage shootings have spent years thinking about the opportunities they missed to stop the plots before they took their deadly toll. It is a painful inventory of warnings overlooked, signs misinterpreted, and the difficulty of discerning patterns where most observers can see only a piece of a complex puzzle.

Teachers and other school staff have been placed under the microscope in this regard almost as often as parents have. They are the adults in the best position to see the evidence, so clear in hindsight, that might have alerted authorities to an impending explosion. But attempts to learn through mistakes are often greeted with resentment, bitterness, and anguish. Telling teachers or principals, who were in the line of fire themselves or had to contend with traumatized survivors, that they are to blame for what happened is the last straw. School staff members who spoke with us in Westside and Heath could not hide their dismay at what they regarded as the misplaced attention to the school's role in these shootings.

Well they're wanting to find somebody to blame it on and they blame us. . . . I remember having somebody say, "Well, did you think this would happen?" "No, I never thought it would happen." "Yeah right. That's what they all say when we ask them that." Like I should have known there was something around.

—Penny Nichols, Westside Middle School teacher

In Heath, the victim's families did more than merely suggest culpability. They sued the teachers and administrators throughout the school system.[1] Lawsuits of this kind were never filed at Westside, but it was easy to find parents who interpreted the school's reticence after the shooting as evidence of some sort of responsibility.[2]

Looking back, it seems clear that the boys who committed the shootings were deeply troubled. Yet virtually none of the staff we spoke with at either Westside or Heath could have ever imagined that Michael, Mitchell, or Andrew would become mass murderers. "There's about 150 kids who were in the freshman class when the shooting took place," noted Doug McCafferty, a former administrator at Heath Middle School. "I could probably have listed 100 before I got to Michael that I thought might have done something." Staff at Westside, including teachers who had Mitchell and Andrew in their classes the year of the shooting, were equally shocked to learn who was firing from that hillside.

If you tell me to make a list of all the boys who would do this . . . by no means would [Andrew] have been the top of the list . . . it's been terrifying. To think that you've got this child who did this awful thing where we could tell you twenty more that we wouldn't be surprised at all to do such a thing.

—Westside Middle School teacher

You know, . . . I still cannot believe that Mitchell Johnson did that, because he was . . . the most polite student I've ever had. "Yes ma'am, No ma'am, May I help you do this?" And it wasn't like he was trying to be fake. It was like he wanted to fit in and he wanted to be helpful.

—Westside Middle School teacher

Knowing now how deeply troubled these boys were, why were they so far off the schools' radar screens at the time of the shooting? How could teachers and administrators have had *no inkling* that these boys harbored such resentment and violent impulses?

Our focus is not on the omissions or commissions of teachers or administrators at either school. Indeed, it is a disturbing truth that these two rampages took place in fairly typical American public schools, with teachers, administrators, and staff who care deeply about their students' well-being. Given their dedication, it is heartbreaking for them to realize that an unthinking public may judge them to be cold and callous in the wake of a school shooting. "I hope [nobody] gets the feeling that we're a bunch of monsters down here," worried Warren Matlock, a Westside High physics teacher. "For the most part, we have a good school." The defensive lament is almost a tragedy in its own right and we do not propose to add to it here.

Our task here, rather, is to invoke a sociological perspective to understand why no one knew that these youths were having serious problems. This means shifting the lens away from individuals and personalities and toward the *system,* to look at schools as organizations. We argue that the culture and social structure of American public schools leads to information loss, which in turn obscures the pain and anger inside some students—emotions that, in rare cases, boil over into rampage shootings. The question is not how *individuals* could have missed the warnings signs, but rather how the organization of public schools prevents them from recognizing and processing the information correctly.

Lest anyone assume from the outset that these "design flaws" are the consequence of foolish planning or are easily remedied, we must point out that there are virtuous reasons that schools are designed in such a way as to make gathering data on students difficult. Creating sensible measures for prevention is thus an exceedingly difficult and delicate task. Indeed, an understanding of the causes does not necessarily suggest solutions.

THE DARK SIDE OF ORGANIZATIONS

We like to think of organizations as efficient ways of conducting the daily business of society, and in general they are. But they are not problem free. Indeed, they have a dark side, which sociologists call "organizational deviance."[3] It occurs when events created by or in organizations fail to conform to the goals or expectations of the institution and produce instead unanticipated and harmful outcomes.[4] That may sound like a freak occurrence, but sociologists understand that organizational deviance is more likely to be a by-product of routine ways that bureaucracies function.[5] Activities that are part and parcel of an institution can lead to consequences that no one intends, even though they serve perfectly useful purposes most of the time. These system characteristics are not harmful in and of themselves, but they can create other problems: "the same characteristics that produce the bright side will regularly provoke the dark side from time to time."[6]

Diane Vaughan's sociological analysis of the 1986 *Challenger* space shuttle explosion provides a good example of organizational deviance, and we draw liberally on it here in order to understand school shootings. In her book *The Challenger Launch Decision: Risky Technology, Culture, and Deviance at NASA,* Vaughan applies the organizational deviance perspective to analyze NASA's decision on January 28, 1986, to launch the space shuttle *Challenger*, which exploded 73 seconds after takeoff. The nation watched in horror as the sleek white craft ignited in a ball of flames, killing seven astronauts, including schoolteacher Christy McAuliffe.[7]

The *Challenger* exploded because of the failure of a tiny part called an O-ring, which did not function properly in the cold temperature on the launch pad. Official investigations focused on whether NASA engineers and administrators knew that the O-rings might fail at low temperatures and, if so, why they authorized the launch. Received wisdom held that midlevel managers *realized* there was a risk of O-ring failure but did not inform senior administrators, *deliberately suppressing* this information for fear that further launch delays would reflect poorly on them.

After ten years of research, Vaughan's conclusion was that the prevailing account was wrong. The decision to launch was made not because of malfeasance but because the routine operation of the NASA bureaucracy ensured that information did not flow between key decision makers.

Vaughan's paradigm holds promise for a new perspective on school shootings. In the cases we studied, information about the shooters' troubling behavior was in wide circulation but did not end up in the right hands. To appreciate how the sociological framework changes our view of rampage shootings, we must first explore in some depth the parallel problem as it developed in the *Challenger* case.

Why did the NASA brass not realize that the O-rings would fail? Vaughan has an answer: "structural secrecy," the separation of knowledge that develops because of the way NASA organized its internal hierarchy and division of labor. While some of the working engineers were concerned about the effects of cold temperatures and voiced those concerns to their peers and superiors, that information never made its way to the administrators who were responsible for making the final decision to launch.

NASA engineers and administrators had drastically different opinions about the probability of failure of the launch. The working engineers who had studied the O-rings most closely estimated the "probability of failure with loss of vehicle and of human life" to be 1 in 100. Managers and administrators, not privy to all of the data, tests, and calculations the engineers had, based their estimates mostly on the successful flight rate and thought the probability of failure was closer to 1 in 100,000. With so much at stake in the launch decision, we might have expected these competing estimates of risk to surface on the desk of a NASA leader. They did not.

Sociologist David Bella developed the concept of "systematic distortion" to explain situations of this kind.[8] Information that "does not support the ambitions and survival needs of [an] organization" is "filtered out." This is the rule rather than the exception, Bella tells us. NASA is in the business of launching space-craft; the accumulated delays in the *Challenger* case frustrated this mission; hence, the risk parameters that moved up into the decision-making hierarchy were the ones more favorable to the launch. They were not "corrupt" figures. On the contrary, the administrators' estimates were reasonable. So were the less favorable figures, but they tended to rest with the lower-level engineers.

In short, based on what was later determined to be inadequate information, following conventional rules of decision-making, and impaired by normal human cognitive practices, NASA administrators decided the O-ring failure risk was within an acceptable range and therefore gave a green light to the launch. The engineers' concerns were filtered out as the information made its way up the hierarchy because they were deemed irrelevant: a collective decision had been made that the risk was acceptable. The organizational structure and the environment in which it was located thus determined which critical pieces of information would be taken into account when key decision makers assessed the risk. They acted according to the rules, not against the rules, and thus the *Challenger* launch decision was a case of organizational deviance rather than individual failure or malfeasance.

In this chapter we argue that we can better understand why school shootings occur if we think of them as instances of organizational deviance, as failures of the system itself. Schools, too, practice structural secrecy; they ignore information that does not fit the operating paradigm, and they push toward the goals we ask them to accomplish—which blinds them to problems hiding under the surface.

STRUCTURAL SECRECY

Schools possess a lot of information about students: health records, academic progress records, disciplinary histories, an understanding of their relationships with peers, and sometimes detailed information about their home lives. But because tasks are highly segregated in schools, that information is held by different people. For example, each teacher is responsible for what happens inside his or her own classroom, but there are few formal methods in place for communicating about students across faculty.[9] Administrators handle discipline for serious infractions. Similarly, counseling is the purview of guidance counselors and other mental health professionals, and information revealed in that context does not make its way to others. This is the essence of structural secrecy: the organization's division of labor, hierarchy, and specialization tend to fragment information, because knowledge about goals and tasks is segregated.[10]

As it turns out, various adults at the school and in the community had pieces of information about the shooters. Tables 4.1–4.3 detail the information known about each boy and who, broadly speaking, knew it.[11] Clearly, the school did not have access to all of the relevant information. Teachers were unaware, for example, that Mitchell had been sexually abused as a boy or that he later molested a two-year-old girl. Similarly, teachers at Heath did not know that Michael had brought a gun to school on two separate occasions before the shooting. (Why other students failed to come forward with that information—or any of the threats he and the other shooters issued—is the subject of chapter 7.)

Nonetheless, even though the shooters did not have serious disciplinary problems, the school *was* privy to a number of disturbing facts about each of the boys. When we look systematically at who knew what, we see that information about each of the boys was spread over multiple individuals, and in Michael's and Andrew's cases, across multiple schools. Particular individuals knew pieces of the puzzle, but never the whole picture. Although certainly not predictive of mass murder, together the details about each boy points to serious problems.

Schools have the technology and expertise to collect, integrate, and disseminate information. However, they deliberately refrain from centralizing what they know, and for good reason. They respect their students' privacy. Sociological ideas—such as labeling theory[12]—have made their way into pedagogical science and general morality. We worry about tagging people in ways that prejudice future teachers or bosses. We deliberately "lose" information about students to avoid prejudicing their chances for recovery from a bad year. The notion that adolescents deserve a clean slate runs so deep that schools may not even be made aware of run-ins students have had with the law. The Columbine massacre is a case in point. When the Sheriff's Office investigated a complaint generated by Eric Harris' threatening Web site, they informed the school that they were looking into a student who was trying to build a pipe bomb, but they did not tell the school deans which student was under investigation.[13] We pay a steep a price for maintaining these privacy commitments.

Table 4.1: Information Known About Michael Carneal Prior to the Shooting

School Staff

Information	Location	Individual(s)*
Dip in grades	Middle school	Teachers
Violent writings	Middle school	Teacher A
Fish stomping incident	Middle school	Teacher B
Public humiliation	Middle/high school	Principal, teacher A, teacher C
Not socially skilled	Middle/high school	Some teachers
Jokester/prankster	Middle/high school	Some teachers
Sloppy school work	High school	Teacher C
Disturbing essays	High school	Teacher C
Disciplinary history	High school	
Looked at porn on school Internet		Principal, librarian
Stole can of food from pantry in life skills class		Teacher D
Caught with plastic nunchakus		?
Chipped paint off wall		Teacher E, principal
Scratched boy on neck while they marked each other with pens		Teacher ?, principal

* Identities changed in some cases to protect confidentiality

School Peers

Threats
Fantasies with Goth group about taking over the mall and the school
Brought guns to school twice
Stored rifles at a friend's house
Bullying/teasing
Stole guns, money, fax machine, and CDs and gave to friends
Stink bomb
Fish stomping incident
Told a friend that he shot a cow
Threw bike in bonfire
Sold and gave away pornography and *Anarchist's Cookbook*

Community

Suggested solving problems with extreme violence
Threw bike in bonfire
Abnormal fears

Michael's Family

Odd behaviors
Threw bike in bonfire
Abnormal fears

Table 4.2: Information Known About Mitchell Johnson
Prior to the Shooting

School Staff

Information	Location	Individual(s)*
Written veiled threat	Middle school	Administrator, teacher A
Disciplinary history	Middle school	
Called teacher a bitch		Administrator, teacher B
Broke glass case		Administrator, teacher A
Scuffle over baseball hat		Administrator, teacher A
Called bus driver name		Administrator, bus driver
Kicked off basketball team	Middle school	Coach, administrator?
Self-mutilation	Middle school	Coach, administrator?
Bus terminal incident	Middle school	Staff member D
Bullied/teased	Middle school	Teacher C
Temper	Middle school	Teacher A, staff member D
Signs of withdrawal weeks before shooting	Middle school	Teacher B

* Identities changed in some cases to protect confidentiality

School Peers

Threats
Gang wannabe
Thug/bully
Interest in violent media
Rumored to have brought a knife to school
May have been suicidal

Mitchell's Family

Molested two-year-old
Poor relationship with biological father
Frequent moves
Sex-call credit card incident
Father's threat to involve police and move Mitchell back to Minnesota

Mitchell

Sexually abused

Table 4.3: Information Known About Andrew Golden Prior to the Shooting

School Staff

Information	Location	Individual(s)*
Threat (to self or others?)	Middle school	Administrator, counselor
Strong interest in guns	Elementary school	Teachers
Newly latch-keyed	Middle school	Teacher A
Disciplinary history	Elementary school	
Pellet gun incident		Administrator, teachers C and D
Mistreatment of animals (?)	Elementary school	Staff member E

* Identities changed in some cases to protect confidentiality

School Peers

Threats
Threats to self or others
Mistreatment of animals
Neighborhood menace

Community

Mistreatment of animals
Neighborhood menace
Petulant grandfather, some suggest violent

Andrew's Family

Interest in violent media
Interest in guns

The Clean Slate and Information Loss

The idea that students are entitled to a fresh start is a conviction deeply held among the administrators and teachers we spoke with at Heath and Westside. It is the reason that they never established formal means of communicating with one another about their students and the reason that disciplinary records do not follow students from school to school. Bill Bond, principal of Heath at the time of the shooting, recognized the dilemma. "I'm not going to say that in a small high school teachers don't know [about each other's students]," he explained, "[but] we don't really exchange much information about kids from teacher to teacher."

> You say, "Gosh, you should, because then they would know [about problems]." Well, my thinking is that *if you don't expect much, you won't get much. If you expect behavior problems, you're gonna find behavior problems.*

I really like a clean slate, let's get on with it. Everybody starts from scratch. . . . All kids start—come in with the same record, the same everything. What they do in your classroom is . . . based on performance and not anything on the past. . . . That's the reason that I don't really get heavily involved in what a kid did in the middle school behaviorwise unless there was some severe behavior problem—and I mean severe—that I need to know about (italics added).

Of course, a completely clean slate may be impossible in a small community. Informal gossip does circulate. And many schools have formal record systems for students with disabilities or learning disorders. But the channels are not always particularly informative where ordinary kids are concerned. The only information ninth grade teachers at Heath receive about their incoming freshman class is, according to one teacher, "Mother's and father's name, home phone number, address, and their schedule. That's it." Anything more detailed would have come through informal channels that depend on personal ties between high school and middle school teachers. As a consequence, most of the staff at Heath High School knew nothing about Michael Carneal's rocky experiences in middle school and had no reason to pay him closer heed.

Teachers do talk to one another informally about disciplinary incidents, but they refrain from dwelling on the emotional difficulties their students encounter. "[It's harder to] deal with the emotional problems of the students," Audrey Shaw, a Heath High English teacher explained. "[With] discipline, you can always give advice on how you've handled it. With the emotion part, it's kind of unknown territory."

Yet it would be a mistake to conclude that there is a lot of free-flowing discussion on either subject. There is a strong informal prohibition against gossip, precisely because teachers are trying to avoid biasing one another against incoming students. Cadres of social scientists have studied "teacher expectancy effects" and have shown the problem to be quite real. Robert Rosenthal and Lenore Jacobson, authors of the influential volume *Pygmalion in the Classroom,* showed that when teachers were told in advance which students would excel and which would not, their expectations were fulfilled. The students teachers thought were brighter did better in school—even though the students in that group had been selected at random. Teachers' expectations affected in subtle ways how they interacted with their students, which in turn affected the students' performance. It was what sociologist Robert Merton termed a "self-fulfilling prophecy."[14]

Pygmalion in the Classroom and studies that followed from it continue to generate controversy in academia,[15] but the original conclusion is a basic tenet in the education field: Assuming a student will do poorly or cause trouble in the classroom because of how he or she has done in other schools or with other teachers unfairly handicaps the student before class even begins. The best prophylactic against this practice is to limit access to contaminating information. This is one of the virtuous reasons for the clean-slate mentality and the structural secrecy it sustains.

Institutional Memory Loss

A big part of the problem, then, is that formal records are not passed along from school to school. But even when formal records are transmitted, they are rarely complete. Unless the school has a policy or is required to track specific information about students, the staff tends not to. This too is a way of preserving the clean slate: There is no institutional memory of disciplinary problems. One teacher who has taught for over thirty years explains how he deals with students who misbehave in class: "I don't ever write kids up [in my class]. I just take care of it myself."

A number of incidents involving the three shooters we studied were never recorded anywhere. For example, two students told us that in middle school Michael had stomped on a fish in biology class. School officials were not aware that any fish had been stomped on but acknowledged that such an incident may have been handled by the teacher in the classroom and not reported to the principal. There were other incidents that never made it into disciplinary records. Kara Anchrum, an administrator at Heath, described the process as she tried to recall an interaction with Michael during his three years at the middle school. An incident had occurred in his art class that she was charged to investigate, but no paper trail emerged.

> There was a list of names of the kids in the class, and I had to interview every child. . . . That's the most I can tell you about it. And here's the problem. I keep anecdotal records. If something comes through and it's not a violation, I may not record it. . . . For future reference, I just [keep] a discipline log, just anecdotal records. . . . Because the law says you can't hold this one over a child's head the next year. So I throw [the discipline log] away.[16]

Discarding information that does not violate school code practically ensures that only seriously disruptive students will be identified. The student with a pattern of minor incidents will go unrecorded.

Similarly, when a staff member at Westside heard from a student that a fellow student was mistreating animals, the information was recorded in his personal notes but was not included in his file because the behavior, although certainly troubling, did not occur on school grounds.

> I didn't think of this until maybe six months after the shooting . . . and it, it bothers me a little bit, but I think what she said was that he had put her cat in a trash can. . . . I'm 99 percent sure that it's Andrew. And I probably have it written down somewhere, but I haven't been able to find it.

That information was lost or misplaced and, as a result, we will never know whether the student in question was Andrew. Maintaining a strict boundary between school and community is another virtuous source of information loss. We don't want a Big Brother society, but the consequence is that a kid who mistreats cats may be a completely unknown quantity in school.

Counselor–Student Confidentiality

Counselors and school therapists may have access to a wealth of information that teachers—and sometimes even administrators—are not privy to. If counselors are not required by law or school policy to pass along what they know, they don't. Counselors cannot do their jobs properly unless they can maintain confidentiality, for no one would confide in them if they thought the information would circulate. Administrators may prefer to be in the dark about some aspects of their students lives.[17]

> Well I don't need to know the kid's using drugs unless it's a school issue of using drugs at school. If the counselor is working with them, then I don't need to know that. It's not any purpose me knowing that. Now if he's using drugs at school, then I'd need to know about it.

This is evidence of *systemic distortion:* information that does not relate to an organization's ambitions or survival gets filtered out.[18] Important information "disappears," not because of intentional decisions to ignore it but because "people deliberately do not seek out unfavorable information."

Andrew saw the school counselor about the threat he made to harm himself or other students, but it appears that this news never made it beyond the counselor and a school administrator. Had Andrew's teachers known of these threats, they may have paid more attention to him or interpreted his behavior a bit differently in the months before the shooting. Michael never saw a school counselor, and the only episodes that brought Mitchell to a counselor's door were occasioned by "girl problems."

WEAK OR MIXED SIGNALS

Individual faculty members at Heath and Westside did have *some* information about each of the boys. Why didn't it add up? We argue here that these small pieces of data were routinely misinterpreted because, taken alone, they constituted weak or mixed signals that something was wrong. Why are some signals, such as violent writings, bullying, or being bullied, seen as subtle or questionable signals to insiders when to an outside observer they appear to be glaring?

Teenagers: Masters of Disguise?

Some kids go to great lengths to hide their problems. Michael Carneal did his best to keep emergent signs of mental illness—what was later diagnosed as schizotypal personality disorder—from those around him, including his own family. He held his tongue despite his anger and shame. Similarly, Mitchell told no one, including his own family, about the sexual abuse he had suffered as a child. Kids who wear their suffering on their sleeves are not the ones who become school shooters, as one administrator told us.

> It's going to be one of the ones, just like Michael, who never gave us a clue that something was wrong. The ones that tread by my office last month: "I'm about to explode. If one more person calls me fat, I'm going to go crazy." It won't be him because he's letting out, and we're going to give him some counseling. . . . It's the ones that just slip through and never let anyone know that something is coming. . . . I wish there was a way that you could identify [them].
>
> —Kara Ancrum, Heath administrator

Faculty members at Westside and Heath would agree that one cannot so easily pick out a future shooter. Yet all three of these boys dropped important clues about their pain and anger despite the effort to cover it up, as a school therapist pointed out:

> I think all the shootings could have been prevented if someone would have listened to the kids. You know, kids really aren't that sneaky. . . . They tell

you without using words; some of them are blatant enough to use words. They're going to be heard, one way or another . . . through their actions. . . . The shooting [at Westside] could have been prevented.

To gather that something was terribly wrong in these boys' lives, school staff would have had to correctly interpret these signals. Studies of organizational deviance have found that when those signals are weak or the messages are mixed, this task can be exceedingly difficult.[20]

One factor that complicates efforts to identify seriously troubled students is the Jekyll-and-Hyde aspect of their personalities. All teenagers behave differently before their peers than when they are among adults, particularly teachers and family members, but the gaps were extreme for Michael, Mitchell, and Andrew.[21] It almost seems as if there were six shooters—not three.

Most of Mitchell's teachers considered him to be extremely polite, among the best-behaved boys they had ever known. In contrast, peers described Mitchell as a swaggering bully, with an explosive temper who liked to pretend he was a gangster. Why were most of his teachers oblivious to Mitchell's bad side? In part, his was an example of mixed signals. Mitchell *did* sometimes act up and become belligerent, but when he was sent to the principal's office, he was extremely remorseful and would apologize "ten times over." "It was almost scary to think about how nice he was to me," remembered Denise Simpson, a Westside administrator.

> He did get in trouble occasionally. Not very often. He was not on my trouble list. . . . The times that Mitchell was in trouble would be for things like belligerence. He might say a bad word. . . . He would come to my office and he would be very remorseful . . . "I'm so sorry, I shouldn't have said that." He'd talk to his teacher. Some kids will . . . take a week before they decided they did the wrong thing and the only reason [they confess] is because they got caught.

Mitchell even turned himself in when he did something wrong. Denise knew Mitchell as a sixth and seventh grade student. He stood out, she recalled, because he was so respectful.

Fragmentation

Detecting troublesome patterns is particularly challenging when the information required to see them is fragmented. The daily schedule of middle school, which sees students move from class to class without continuity between teachers or advisers, made it hard for teachers to see how Mitchell was unraveling. Teachers who see students for fifty minutes a day may simply not have enough information to see the patterns.[22] Shifting away from the elementary school system, in which students spend almost the entire day with one teacher, compartmentalizes relationships: no one sees the whole child. The child, in turn, does not have a ready confidante in any adult. "I don't want to appear to be derogatory to any teacher or anything," Emily Levitt, a Westside elementary teacher, told us, "but this middle school situation was a completely new situation for these sixth grade kids."

> We had talked about this before the shooting . . . that there was no connection
> [between the teachers and the students]. The students felt frustrated because
> they couldn't go to their homeroom teacher and say, "this is my problem."

Julia Sampson, one of Mitchell's teachers, noticed a distinct change in the boy a few months before the shooting, after he returned from a visit with his father. Whereas previously he had been rather attentive and almost affectionate in his politesse, he now seemed a bit withdrawn or disinterested. Sampson thought he might just need a little more space:

> I saw a change in my relationship with Mitch. He did not interact with me as
> much, [starting in] January and I didn't know what to do. [I thought] maybe
> I was being too motherly . . . giving him too much advice and he felt un-
> comfortable. . . . I thought maybe I just needed to back off and give him
> space. He was growing up and I respected that.[23]

Mitchell was one of Sampson's favorite students, but she only had him for one period each day. Indeed, the one teacher who spent her entire day with students in in-school suspension (ISS), Beverly Ashford, had a very different view of Mitchell.

> Some of the teachers said Mitchell Johnson was one of the nicest, quietest
> kids they had. Well I'm sure that's the side they saw, because they had him
> fifty minutes a day, five days a week. When I have kids all day long for seven
> hours [for ISS], I see a different side.

It was during this full day together that Ashford realized that Mitchell had a mean streak. When she read the journal entry he wrote for Shannon Wright during ISS, Ashford recognized in it a threat to harm. She got worried enough to take it to the school principal:

It was a threat. Yes, that's the reason I turned it in to my supervisor, because I definitely took it as a threat. You don't kill squirrels and get rid of an in-school suspension forever. It doesn't take a rocket scientist to figure that out.

Beverly Ashford was one of the very few adults who had seen Mitchell's bad side on enough occasions to form a view of him as a troubled child. Although more consistent contact might not have led staff to predict that Mitchell would turn deadly, it would almost certainly have led more people to recognize that he was spiraling downward in the weeks before the shooting.

Michael Carneal also signaled to adults at school that all was not well. Perhaps one of the strongest signs that he was in deep trouble is to be found in a story he turned in to his eighth grade English class, called "The Halloween Surprise." The teacher asked students to write a story about Halloween and many students complied by turning in gory fiction. Carneal approached the teacher to ask if he could use the real names of fellow students in his piece. She told him that he would have to ask their permission. It is not clear whether he followed through on that instruction. What is clear is that Michael's story is graphic, bloody, and far more disturbing than any other submitted, by his own admission. "Halloween Surprise" (see Figure 4.1) depicts an ongoing battle between two groups of students involving various guns and other weapons. The protagonist—named Michael—vanquishes the well-liked "preps" and subjects them to various tortures before making a gift of their bodies to his mother for her birthday.

Teachers are trained to identify what they call "alert papers," those that suggest suicidal tendencies, eating disorders, or physical abuse. They turn alert papers over to guidance counselors or the administration. Michael's eighth grade English instructor was a new teacher, in only her second year on the job. When interrogated by plaintiff's lawyers in the course of a civil suit filed after the shooting, she admitted that she had no memory of Michael submitting the "Halloween Surprise" paper but felt that even if she had seen it, she did not have enough experience to determine whether it might have been a signal of a troubled teen.[24] Moreover, she said that it was not unusual for her to receive violent writings like Michael's story from students, especially given the nature of her assignment. Teens seem perpetually fascinated by blood and gore. How do you tell a creative appropriation of scenes from an Arnold Schwartzenegger film from the fantasies of a potential rampage shooter?

Educators want students to write as a means of self-expression, but if they pen something scary, the teacher is placed in the same awkward position as a priest. Teachers will not be trusted if they divulge secrets. When Michael submitted the school assignment excerpted in chapter 2, explaining how humiliated he felt when

The Halloween Surprise

Many of the people Michael refers to in this story appear to be real students at Heath. We have changed all the names in the story (except Michael's) to ensure their anonymity. The story was originally three single-spaced pages long. We have preserved most of it here to allow readers to see what Michael's teacher saw and judge for themselves how far from a typical creative writing assignment this was.

One day a kid named Mike was on his way home when a gang of about 5 to 10 preps walked up and pulled out tire irons and crow bars. The next thing he knew he was lying on the ground and the preps were hitting him with the weapons. Then the head prep, Jake Streeter, and his girlfriend, Allison, pulled out these huge chrome Berrettas and shot Michael in the leg about 10 or 12 times.

Michael heard a loud squeaking noise. When he looked up he saw his little brother Robert riding an old tricycle, speeding around the corner then he cut the engine and pulled something out of his trench coat. It was a sawed off shotgun! Robert cocked the gun then opened fire on the mob of preps.

Since half of the preps were dead or severely wounded and the other half had no idea what was going on we decided to ambush the girls.

Michael and Robert jumped into their truck that was filled with uranium, and took off for the woods where all the preps were having a Halloween party...

When he finally got there he hid in the bushes and spied on them. Then he gave Robert the signal and they jumped out and went trigger happy with their MAC 10s and hit Tracy in the leg which made Allison very angry. So she picked up a Glock and shot Robert in the shoulder.

Weak but not defenseless Robert picks up a grenade and tosses it at Allison. It explodes and sends fragments flying not only in Allison's neck but also in Natasha's arm. With Natasha's pain over come by adrenaline and anger, she picks up an ax used to make fire wood and cuts Jean's head clean off, But it's still resting on her neck until Natasha flicked it and it fell to the ground...

The next day everybody wondered where the preps were but nobody cared about Michael.

They all marched down the halls with Robert leading on his tricycle. When they turned a corner they saw the preps. The next thing you know there's a big fight...It was like a riot. Lockers ripped up, teachers being drug from their 18 wheelers and beaten and looting.

R.I.P. Robert Wheeler. Died of a pipe bomb. oft his tricycle

But the revolution wasn't over and Jake Streeter was still alive. With both of the revolution leaders dead the followers needed a new leader. Who would it be? . . .

His name was Mark Capstone. He was determined to kill all the preps.

(continued on next page)

Figure 4.1: An Eighth Grade Paper by Michael Carneal

Figure 4.1
(continued from previous page)

The next day Mark gathered up all of his weapons and headed for the preps hang out.

When he got there he grabbed a couple of AK-47s out of his backpack and busted down the door and wasted a whole clip on Ethan. Then Ethan just stood up and his arms fell off. Then he started walking towards Mark so Mark got a rocket launcher out of his backpack and fired at Ethan. There were body parts everywhere. A leg here and a nose there...

Millions of people were dead, dying or had been infected with cancer.

"But at least all of the preps are dead! Along with everybody else." Michael mummered to him self...

Michael's Mom's birthday was the next day so he decided to get a present from the "Your Mom Has a Birthday Only When There's a Riot" store. But it was still Halloween and he wanted to get his Mom a good surprise.

So the next day he found five preps. The first one he crucified on a metal cross that had been heated up to a glowing red temperature.

The second one he tied there hair to a huge bungee cord that just happened to be to long and made them jump off of a bridge.

The third one he heated up a drill bit and drilled it into one of his eyes and then put a pin hole in their wrists and Chinese water tortured them while they bleed to death very slowly.

The fourth one he shot their knee caps four times each. Then do the same to their elbows then make them wrestle an alligator then throw them in the salty ocean to drown.

And the fifth one he will drive a very long pole up their buttox and stick the other end in the ground so they ride the pole. Then hook wires tied from their legs to winches on the ground and make them pull the preps feet.

Then he gave the bodies of the preps to his mom for a good Halloween surprise.

---

he was called gay in the middle school newspaper, he wrote at the top of the page, "Please don't tell anyone. Very Personal." As far as we know, Michael's teacher respected his privacy. That confidentiality comes at a cost when it masks a troubled mind: The cry for help may not be heard by anyone. Apparently, it wasn't.

Michael wrote a number of assignments that, had they been seen together, would have been a fairly clear signal that he was in trouble. For example, when freshman students were asked to write letters to themselves as seniors—a custom in many high schools—Michael's missive began: "Dear Mike, How are you doing. Do you remember this old thing. If you are reading this I am surprised your still alive." Another assignment asked him, "If you could walk in the shoes of any celebrity, who would it be?" To this, Michael responded, "Kurt Cobain because he is famous and he is dead like all the great artists of time. Picasso as an example he was depressed his whole life now 1 painting of his is worth millions."

Taken together, Michael's stories and essays point to a depressed and disturbed youth. But no one teacher had all of these essays. "The Halloween Surprise" was a story Michael said he turned into his eighth grade English teacher (though she had no memory of it); the others were given to the ninth grade English teacher. Although Michael's writings in ninth grade clearly suggested that he was, as former Heath High School Principal Bill Bond admitted in a civil deposition, "a very unhappy and disturbed young man," there was nothing in them to suggest that Michael would lash out against others.[25]

With hindsight, Michael's ninth grade English teacher, Laura Rankin, could see that Michael was shutting down. Three weeks before the shooting, his homework began to veer sharply away from his assignments. She handed the work back to Michael and told him that the paper he turned in had nothing to do with the reading for that week. He just shrugged his shoulders.

> At the time it didn't appear to be anything different from any other student that just for some reason was just tired and didn't want to do the assignment. . . . Seems like there's always a legitimate excuse that I can come up with that explains the behavior in a way that it's not something that I should be concerned about.

Without more information, even an experienced teacher like Rankin did not see the storm brewing. Slacking off before a school vacation is not unusual. Neither are essays about depression, or even suicide, for that matter. "It is not unusual to run across, say out of a hundred and twenty [students], maybe . . . five to ten students who have written about suicide," explained one Heath teacher. "At this age, [there's] a fascination, curiosity with suicide." Michael's essays and overall performance in the weeks before the shooting was a signal, but a weak one.

The fragmented nature of student-teacher contact in middle school may also have led Westside to lose track of Andrew. Andrew was generally well remembered at his elementary school, where teachers spent the entire day with him, but when he moved to the middle school, he all but disappeared.[26]

> Andrew was the back in the corner, nobody really noticed him. He wasn't a popular kid in his class, but he wasn't a not popular. He was just an in-the-middle kind of guy.
>
> —Denise Simpson, Westside administrator

When they do remember him, his teachers think of a shy, docile, and compliant child. This quiet, even sweet, side of Andrew is in marked contrast to the way his neighbors and peers knew him. Still, the school had at least one signal that something was troubling Andrew, which came a few months before the shooting. As the school describes the incident, a friend in Andrew's gym class overheard Andrew threaten to kill himself. (The friend claims Andrew was threatening to hurt others.) In any case, Andrew later recanted—saying he had only been joking—but the school called his parents to let them know. His parents said they'd take care of it, and nothing further came of the incident.

Why didn't the school do more to follow up on what sounds like a serious problem? As we saw with Michael, these sorts of statements are all too common, making it very difficult to distinguish a real threat from an offhand remark.

> Kids say all the time, "I wish I could just kill myself." I wouldn't say it's a sentence you overlook. [Andrew] didn't give any details, and when the counselors talked with him he said, "Oh, I was just kidding. I was just mad at somebody and I said I'm going to hurt myself, trying to get attention."
>
> —Denise Simpson

Approximately one in five adolescents seriously considers suicide each year and around 8 percent of adolescents attempt it.[27] Yet more of them think and talk about suicide than ever make a move to carry it off. Knowing the outcome, it is now painfully clear that the school should have taken Andrew's threat more seriously, but in the context of "suicide talk" that is mainly just talk, his remarks constituted a weak signal.

Bullying

Other potential signals were missed, including bullying. Mitchell, Andrew, and Michael all complained after the shooting that they were teased, bullied, or "put upon," but the teachers were either unaware of or downplayed the significance of their torment.

Many teachers were aware that bullying was an issue at Westside, but others were clueless. Evelyn Michaels, a teacher who had both Andrew and Mitchell in her classes at various times, decided to look into the issue more thoroughly after the shooting. "[I said] to my kids in class, 'Well, at least bullying isn't a problem here,' and someone started laughing. . . . So I decided doing a little survey about every two weeks anonymously." Bullying turned out to be more common than she thought. Yet by far the most common reaction is to conclude that bullying just "goes with the territory." We've all been bullied or teased. Sociologists have a word for this: *normalization*. NASA engineers normalize risk because it is unavoidable in their business. Bullying is so routine in schools, so the reasoning goes, that every child has to come to terms with it, and there is not much that schools can do to prevent it.

Teachers occasionally go one step beyond normalizing teasing. They rely on it strategically as a method of social control. Alice Stearns, a French teacher at Heath, relies on a little needling when it helps her manage the classroom:

> I try to not embarrass kids in front of the class. That's not a good thing. But sometimes I do, just sarcastically, because they keep asking for it, you know. They say sarcasm is the worst way in the world to handle teenagers. I dis-agree wholeheartedly. I think they use it, I think they like it. And I think it's good for the kids. [laughter] Oh, well.

John Marks, an administrator at Westside, has some sympathy for many of the kids who are labeled bullies, because they are reacting to the aggressive or provocative behavior of their victims.[28]

> I talked to a lot of kids that get bullied, they brought it on themselves. . . . Some kids are bullied just because they are just good kids, they are just dif-ferent. But a lot of what I see is the kids that are getting bullied, they have aggravated [others] to death . . . [and] they are getting bullied back, or the other kids are striking back.

Mitchell deserved the teasing he received, according to at least one administra-tor at Westside; the boy provoked his own abuse. "I know that one of the sixth grade teachers said that Mitchell had talked to her about someone picking on him," he said.

> Knowing Mitchell, I'm not sure what he did to get picked on. [laughs] . . . [Mitchell was] known as a whine-bag. I mean in football he was always whining because the other kids were bullying him. . . . In my opinion, [Mitchell] was the bully.

Others agreed. Mitchell, Andrew, and even Michael were as likely to have ha-rassed others as to be victimized themselves. Indeed, all three boys were charac-terized as catalysts.[29]

[Michael] was an instigator. I know that a lot of times [the] media want to make it look like kids that become shooters are picked on until they just can't take it anymore. But he was a picker, not a kid who was picked on. If [Michael] felt inferior, and I'm sure he did, that was something that was going on more in his own mind. It wasn't anything external.

—Dawn Anderson, Heath High music teacher

National studies tell us that it is quite common for the two roles—the bullied and the bullier—to fuse. It is a mistake, then, to dismiss complaints about harassment coming from someone who is "an instigator."[30]

Students who are seen as different or as acting outside of acceptable norms are teased, either by students or by adults at the school, as a way of pulling them back into line with prevailing norms. Whether we accept teasing because it is humorous or functional or because we don't know how to stop it, social harassment is regarded as commonplace by most of the people we interviewed. Consequently, neither teachers nor administrators thought of bullying or teasing as a signal of deep-rooted emotional distress. Repeated class disruption, fighting, a lack of friends, signs of physical or sexual abuse, or poor personal hygiene—these problems are red flags in most school districts. Being the victim of a bully is not.

"Just Laugh It Off"   Whether Michael instigated or not, he was teased and humiliated. He reacted to these bullying incidents precisely as teachers recommended: he laughed it off. In following their instructions, Michael was trying to ensure that his tormentors would be denied the satisfaction of knowing how much their digs hurt. The strategy failed. "Michael was angry [about the harassment]," Dr. O'Connor surmised, "but Michael doesn't show much anger."

> You really never know where Michael is emotionally because [he] doesn't like to express a lot of emotions. And one way that he started coping with bullying was that he would laugh at the things that people were doing to him on the outside . . . when [he] would be pretty much devastated on the inside.

When a child follows reasonable advice—appearing unconcerned about abuse—he inadvertently makes the task of being spotted as a depressed child much harder, because he is producing mixed signals.

Michael was devastated by the ragging that followed the eighth grade newspaper story that labeled him gay, but none of the adults in charge at the time seemed to know it. Doug McCafferty, a middle school administrator at the time of

Michael's rampage, was furious about the fact that the article had slipped through unnoticed, and the paper was discontinued soon after that issue was printed, but not because of its impact on Michael:

> It's odd that [the "Rumor Has It" column] has become a focal point, because it wasn't at the time. No one made a big deal about it. I got upset about it. But not about Michael Carneal. . . . At the time it wasn't a big deal. To anybody else, it wasn't anything.

McCafferty didn't see how Michael reacted to the incident or hear anything from Michael's parents about it. He also didn't ask. Unbeknownst to the school, the teasing and bullying only intensified thereafter.

"They Were Overreacting"   Mitchell was perceived by others as overreacting to mild teasing. He liked to brag, particularly about his exploits on the football field, but he was not a great athlete, and when his peers cut him down to size, he flew off the handle. No one understood why he reacted this way,[31] including teachers he was close to. "[Mitchell] had a quick temper," one teacher recalled, "and when he was in the sixth grade . . . he would come and talk to me about it." He would react sharply to a little teasing, she said, which prompted her to explain to Mitchell that he needed to avoid giving the jokers the satisfaction of seeing him upset by their ragging. Her advice did not make much of an impression, or so it seems. "In his mind, he was being picked on," she noted.

All three shooters "overreacted," but no one recognized their response as a sign of anything deeper. Dr. O'Connor reminded us that kids who can't take it may be letting everyone else know that there are some deep cracks under the surface of their personalities:

> If you have kind of a shaky personality structure to begin with, then [bullying] affects you differently than it does other kids who are more psychologically intact. Michael never wanted people to know he was bothered by what was going on. He never told his parents a lot of this stuff. . . . When you have someone as sensitive as he was and is, it does affect them differently. Is he overreacting? Yeah, probably. Probably so.

Instead of seeing extreme reactions as a sign of emotional distress, we tend to see them as a personality problem, an inability to cope. Overreaction then becomes a signal of social incompetence rather than of psychological trouble.

"Teachers Can't Do Anything About It"   How teachers and administrators handle complaints makes a big difference in whether students bother to report their distress at all. The sad fact is that bureaucratic organizations are not always responsive, even to legitimate complaints. The adults who run schools like to imagine themselves as empathetic, sensitive, and proactive, especially in protecting the vulnerable. But the press of business or the desire to avoid trouble sometimes gets the better of them, as Rebecca Morris, an off-site therapist, noted bluntly:

> We tell kids all the time if something happens or Johnny hurts you again you come and you tell an adult. I can't tell you how many times I've been out . . . [with] one of my kids on the playground and a child will come up to the teacher and say, "Ms. so-and-so, this kid did—" "Oh, just go on and play." . . . They tell them that they will help them if they will just tell an adult. And they do tell an adult and nothing is done.

What do kids conclude when they compare the didactic message ("tell an adult") with adult behavior ("just go and play")? Several messages, none of them very helpful, come through loud and clear: (1) tough it out; (2) I cannot be bothered by your problem—solve it yourself; and (3) adults are ineffective social control agents. Adults, on the other hand, may mean something quite different: (1) you need to learn how to deal with conflict; or (2) you need a tougher side, because there is more of this in store for you.

Teachers and administrators have no unified approach to dealing with bullying when it occurs. Some kids are told to "turn the other cheek"; others may be told to "go tell the principal . . . or [a] counselor. . . . It just depends on who he tells," according to one Westside teacher. Since each situation may be different, it makes sense to give teachers such discretion. Yet it leaves students unsure of how adults will respond to their situation and encourages the belief that they cannot depend on the adults to provide an adequate response.

LOOSELY COUPLED SYSTEMS

Exacerbating the impact of structural secrecy and weak or mixed signals was the "loosely coupled" organizational structure of the school, which allowed problems that did not interfere with its main functions to go unnoticed and fester. The components of an organization are linked to one another and interdependent in their normal operation. But in some bureaucracies, those links are tight and in others they are loose. For example, assembly lines in factories are tightly coupled. As a new car moves through the factory, different parts are added and steps are followed in a precise and well-orchestrated sequence. Cars would not come off the assembly line if a worker decides that he would rather wait until after the wheels are on to install the brakes or to put the oil in before the engine is installed.

Contrast this description with a secondary school, the archetype of a loosely coupled system.[32] The various parts of a school can operate relatively independently. Teachers have a great deal of autonomy in their classrooms. Within a general framework—for example, state mandates governing graduation—teachers decide what the homework is, how it's graded, and who constitutes a discipline problem.[33]

Professional authority lies at the heart of what makes schools loosely coupled systems. Teachers are trusted to work independently, without direct supervision or detailed instructions, relying instead on their training and socialization to achieve their goals.[34] Teachers do face material incentives and constraints, but as they readily point out, they don't go into the business for the money.[35]

Another reason schools are loosely coupled is that there is a significant gap between official mandates and day-to-day operations. Standards of evaluation for teachers and other employees are generally ambiguous and flexible and have often been designed to accomplish competing and sometimes contradictory objectives, such as establishing order, fostering academic achievement, and seeing to the emotional and social development of the child. Even when official goals are explicit, they may be only vaguely related to other pressing concerns the school cannot ignore, such as demands from teachers, parents, and politicians. Schools *are* constrained by the political environment and by legal mandates, but these are boundary conditions rather than blueprints for daily conduct in the classroom.

The distinction between tight and loose coupling is critical to understanding organizational deviance. Traditionally, tight coupling has been identified as a source of problems, and loose coupling has been deemed protective. Sociologist Charles Perrow, in his book *Normal Accidents,* relies on this concept to explain calamities such as airplane crashes and nuclear reactor accidents, including the near meltdown of the Three Mile Island nuclear power plant in 1979.

The accident at Three Mile Island occurred when multiple parts of the nuclear power station failed simultaneously and because the breakdown of some parts caused the malfunction of other connected parts. The failures affected not only the plant's production of electricity but also the automatic safety devices. Communications systems that transmit information and control commands between the plant and the operators in the control room failed as well. Three Mile Island operators had a hard time stopping the accident from occurring, *and* they did not know what was happening in the plant itself. Perrow argues that the complexity of the nuclear power plant system and the tight coupling of its parts made a catastrophic failure much more likely because there was little slack in the system to allow time for small problems to be corrected before they mushroomed into big ones. Once the problems started and began to spread, there was little the human operators could do to keep control. Hence, in highly complex organizations that are also "tightly coupled," disasters (or what Perrow calls "normal accidents") are routinely produced.[36]

Loosely coupled systems, by contrast, "can recover from upsets because sequences are not that inevitable, there is slack in resources, substitutions are possible."[37] For this reason, loose systems are not prone to normal accidents. Or are they? We argue that sociological confidence in loosely coupled systems may be misplaced. School shootings show us why. Problems can go unnoticed in a school precisely because they do not disrupt its basic functioning. Individual student problems often do not interrupt daily routines and may therefore fester unnoticed until a major eruption, such as a shooting, thrusts them into view. The fact that schools are loosely coupled organizations may contribute to rather than protect against organizational deviance.

IDENTIFYING TROUBLED YOUTHS:
THE SQUEAKY WHEEL

Disorder and disruption interfere with the ability of teachers to teach and students to learn. However, unlike business firms, schools cannot use direct economic incentives to maintain control. Schools cannot rely on physical restraint or force as do prisons or asylums. And unlike private schools and colleges, public schools cannot select their students; they must take all comers. Removing troublesome students is bureaucratically complicated, although sometimes necessary, for public schools. Hence, maintaining order becomes a key organizational goal of the school, one to which time and resources must be devoted, even though there is precious little of either.

Schools have developed elaborate and systematic procedures to handle "problem students," from those who question the legitimacy of assigned learning tasks to those who start fights or bring weapons to school. These steps are often detailed in lengthy handbooks that are distributed to students and parents at the start of each school year. Disruptive students are often "managed" with discipline, such as warnings, detentions, in-school suspensions, home suspensions, counseling, and, in states where it is still legal, corporal punishment. They may even be removed from the mainstream system entirely and placed in alternative schools for chronically disruptive youths.

But students who disrupt the main functioning of the school—those who are routinely sent to the principal's office for fighting or disrupting class—are *not* the ones who become school shooters. According to the Secret Service report on targeted school shootings, nearly two-thirds of the attackers in their study had never or rarely been in trouble at school.[38]

Teachers and administrators are expected to handle classroom disturbances and defiance of authority according to rules that are spelled out in the disciplinary handbook. Nevertheless, discretion is exercised even when the code of conduct suggests otherwise. Most of all, teachers reach their own decisions about what offenses they bring to the attention of the administration.

The handbook says nothing about how teachers are to handle students whose behavior does not specifically violate the code—it focuses on the discipline that teachers and administrators are expected to mete out when students are caught fighting, bringing drugs or weapons onto campus, refusing to obey authority, and the like. There are no comparable instructions, procedures, or training on how to identify troubled kids who have not breached the code. Disruptive behavior, which suggests that a child is experiencing emotional distress, is the most important clue a school is likely to catch. Without such a signal, school authorities are likely to be completely in the dark about a kid who is troubled.

Given how serious their personal problems were, why did Michael, Mitchell and Andrew escape closer scrutiny? Embedded as they were in a loosely coupled system, their emotional problems festered because they did not throw a wrench into the gears, causing problems so severe that order was at risk. Nothing in their behavior made it impossible or even difficult to conduct a class or run the cafeteria. Classrooms do not function like an assembly line, where a minor problem in one domain derails another. They are quite disconnected, and the authority figures at the helm of each classroom are largely on their own to decide how deviant conduct will be dealt with.

Of course, even a loosely coupled system can suffer a breakdown. Kids who are extremely disruptive, who make it impossible to conduct the daily business of the school *are* dealt with: they are counseled, punished, sequestered, or put in special schools. Only seriously problematic students warrant this kind of attention. "The squeaky wheel gets the oil," as one counselor explained.

Michael wasn't particularly squeaky, though. He simply didn't give off the signs the school was looking for. "Michael didn't have hostile acts toward other students," said Bill Bond.

He wasn't rebellious with adults. He didn't talk back to adults. . . . He didn't have classroom problems. Teachers didn't send him out of the classroom for being disruptive, you know. He didn't refuse to do his homework. He didn't show up for class tardy. . . . He wasn't a truant. . . . He didn't get caught smoking. He didn't hang out with kids that smoked. . . . He didn't do those things that would have gotten him a lot of disciplinary write-ups. He had never exhibited any aggression towards other students.

School shooters remain off the radar screen because they do not behave in ways that alert schools to their potential for violent behavior. They are not jamming the gears, making the daily operation of the school impossible. And the radar itself is not a uniform instrument; teachers apply their own judgments to disciplinary situations, and decide when they are going to report or even record an incident; they keep the information to themselves much of the time. The loose coupling of the school structure means that information gets lost and, as a consequence, seriously troubled kids go unnoticed. Those loose connections may not be so protective after all; they may just paper over problems that become evident only too late in these rare cases.

THE COSTS OF AMBIVALENCE

Schools are conflicted about whether it is their responsibility to identify and help emotionally troubled youth. We want our schools to produce children who have mastered the skills they need to compete in the economy, achieve the American Dream, and be responsible and upright citizens. However, some argue that schools should play an additional role, that of facilitating the social and emotional development of youth. This new purpose is warranted, they argue, because families are increasingly fractured and burdened by work. Extended kinship networks and close community ties are generally thought to be on the decline, resulting in a decrease in supervision and meaningful interaction between adults and children. Given the breakdown in social and emotional supports for our youth, it seems reasonable to many that schools should assume that role, particularly given that children spend much of their waking lives there. It is not clear, however, that these goals are compatible, if only because the school year is too short to take care of them all.

These multiple purposes of American public schools are evident in the goals the faculty of Heath High School set up in a self-study they conducted five years before the shooting. The aims include traditional goals, such as enhancing communication skills, productivity, and the ability to learn, but they also include more developmental and moral goals, such as promoting maturity, responsibility, tolerance, self-respect, and happiness.[39] This sounds clear enough, but the implications are complicated and potentially contentious, because not all teachers (or parents, for that matter) subscribe to this vision; moreover, teachers don't necessarily mean the same thing when they use the words. These aims pose a challenge to schools as organizations because a complex mix of "production" techniques and personnel is needed to address so many goals in one space.

Teachers: Instructors or Counselors?

Are faculty members solely academic instructors, or are they part-time counselors as well? Teachers and administrators we spoke with at Westside and Heath disagree on this point. An administrator explains the tensions:

> It's real important, though, that your teachers understand that they're not coming to school to teach U.S. history. They're coming to school to teach 120 students, and their subject matter is U.S. history. . . . In elementary school, they know they're teaching students. In high school, though, you might get some teachers that are very, very bright in their subject . . . [but] they don't really like to teach kids. They don't really want to talk to kids about that drug issue or that pregnancy issue or that relationship between people. They don't really want to deal with that. They don't even want to hear it. They're there to teach history. Well, I say that's fine, but you need to be [teaching] in a college, because that's not what we're about here.

Not all of the teachers we spoke with—either at Heath or Westside—want to be counselors, and many resent the expectation, at least in part because they feel underqualified and overwhelmed by the increasing demands of their jobs.

> I think that . . . they ask [us] to . . . solve more . . . social problems that I don't feel that we're qualified to do. . . . Our school is being asked to look for warning signs and build student self-esteem and help problems . . . help in their development more than I feel that I have that training to do. I kind of resent that. I feel like I'm swamped . . . drowning. I don't feel like I can solve everybody's problem or even be aware of everybody.
> —Helen Bancroft, Heath High School history teacher

Nurturing students and encouraging student achievement are competing demands that create a role dilemma for teachers: If they cannot do both, they must choose one.[40] And an increasing emphasis on testing in schools over the past few decades has led teachers to focus—often with great reluctance—on academic skills over personal growth.[41]

In schools with more resources, it is often possible to do it all. For example, in prestigious private schools renowned for academic achievement, significant resources are often devoted to keeping close tabs on students' nonacademic lives. Parents complete lengthy intake forms detailing family history; teachers with fewer students (and fewer difficult students) closely monitor family problems and other barriers to learning and healthy adolescent development.

In public schools, however, those human resources are in shorter supply. Frustration among teachers grows because they are simultaneously asked to perform more of the duties that were once handled at home while meeting higher academic standards in the classroom. The performance pressures reach all the way down into elementary schools:

> We're to the point now where we give a test at the beginning of the year and a test at the end of the year. . . . You have to show [gain] or else you may not have a job. . . . You get so much pressure during the day for academics that when there's a family problem . . . it's hard to handle it yourself. Very hard.
>
> —Eileen Moss, elementary school teacher

If we think about the school as a kind of business for a moment, we can grasp how complex this task is. Teachers are expected to achieve uniform outputs (standardized test scores, college admission, and so on) with highly variable inputs (students). Their success depends heavily on what happens to their students in other contexts that teachers cannot control (particularly the home), and they will be held responsible for outcomes that are powerfully influenced by those environments.

Some school counselors and therapists complained that teachers are reluctant to let a student leave their class in order to speak to the guidance counselor. The pressures teachers face to boost their students' scores is a large part of the problem, according to this Westside counselor:

> [Students] are supposed to be able to see [a counselor] at any time, but then you have the academic teacher saying you can't miss my class or you're go-

ing to be behind in homework. There's a struggle between the structure of the academic process and the needs, the emotional needs, of these kids.

Rebecca Morris, a therapist who is not on the Westside staff but who has provided services to middle school children, argues that ambivalence about the mission of the school and benefits of counseling are also to blame.

There are some teachers that just feel like counselors do not belong on campus . . . and they make it difficult. They say, "OK, you can only have this child between 11:10 and 11:45." . . . Well, if I have a crisis come up [and] I wouldn't be able to get that kid, that was too bad. They just—they would keep putting me off. . . . I tried to put myself in their shoes . . . teachers are asked to do a lot in a short amount of time.

Before the shooting, the little training or professional development teachers received, both at Heath and Westside, was focused almost exclusively on academic issues—on incorporating new technology in the classroom, best practices, team building, or boosting subject areas where standardized tests indicated a need for improvement. Virtually no training was devoted to spotting troubled students. Since the shootings, the illusion that teachers can simply focus on academic achievement has disappeared in both schools, and they have given over at least some of their professional development time to these concerns. Even so, teachers continue to feel poorly equipped to deal with emotionally troubled students.

School Counselors: Too Many Roles to Fill?

Who, then, is prepared to catch the warning signs and handle students' emotional problems? Guidance counselors are formally assigned this task, but they too are saddled with competing responsibilities.

Having to deal with volumes of paperwork makes the situation worse. Government mandates originating from well-intentioned legislation translate into paper trails covering everything from civil rights issues to curriculum, tracking graduates, and ensuring that special education students are receiving a proper education. These are worthy pursuits, but they take time away from working directly with students.

You have the mounds and mounds and mounds of government paperwork that is demanded of these school counselors. . . . They have no time left over to work with kids. . . . Hit-and-miss counseling is all school counselors can do any more because they've got so much paperwork.

—Rebecca Morris

Teachers often refer students who have personal problems to school counselors, but a guidance counselor's primary role is more likely to be academic scheduling. Before the shooting, Heath High School had a single guidance counselor for 600 students. Attending to the emotional health of students is the last priority his principal gave him.

Before the shooting, Westside Middle School had one guidance counselor for its 250 students. Although the counselor was expected to focus a bit more on emotional issues, she had no mental health training to speak of.[42] To be fair, most of the problems counselors are presented with do not require this kind of professional background. The high drama of middle and high school, to which any parent with teenagers can attest, is based mainly on petty squabbles amongst friends.

Students do come to counselors for help that needs professional attention,[43] but it is not always easy to distinguish a serious problem that requires therapy from a less severe one that can be resolved informally. Michael Carneal's peer problems appeared to teachers as petty dramas, but they took on enormous significance in his mind. Westside had access to a school-based therapist before the shooting who could be called in for referrals. However, neither Mitchell nor Andrew was ever referred to the therapist, not even when a fellow student reported that Andrew threatened to hurt himself or others. A guidance counselor explained that the close-knit nature of the school—where many of the teachers were "generational," meaning they had graduated from Westside themselves—fostered a climate hostile to outsiders, including outside counselors or therapists.

Having limited resources means that not all students who need attention receive it. Those who were noticed were the "good kids" from the "good families"—"the kids who got straight A's and were in the plays"—as well as the *really* troubled kids who were "squeaking" so loudly that they couldn't be overlooked. The rest were simply ignored, according to one counselor.

[The counselors] don't even know half the kids any more, and if they tell you they do, they're lying. . . . They don't know the kids, they don't really know the problems. They know the families who have been troublemakers over the years and peg them.

No one heard Andrew because he was not squeaking.

CONCLUSION

I don't know what the solution is. I've thought about it long and hard. I think getting inside their heart and their heads is the only chance you have. . . . If they just have one adult in this building that they can feel like is on their side, then they probably don't need to bring a gun to this school. But it only takes one kid. . . . I know full well that this can happen here again. Even all the things that we've tried to do. . . . A kid can still slip through the cracks.

—Margaret Bledsoe, Heath High science teacher

We have attempted to understand why some kids fall through the cracks, with potentially serious emotional and social problems remaining unidentified. Even when teachers, principals, counselors, and other school staff care deeply about their students, as was the case at both Heath and Westside, the organizational structure and culture of American public schools can lead to information loss.

We have identified four reasons for this deficiency. First, the structure and culture of schools lead to the fragmentation of the information that is available about troubled students. When we examine everything known in the schools about these boys, it appears that there was sufficient evidence that they needed more help and guidance, but because no individual had the whole picture about any of these boys, no one recognized the depth or seriousness of their problems.

Here the cherished American notion of the clean slate comes into conflict with the need to identify troubled students. Structural secrecy and institutional memory loss protect a student's privacy and ensure that the mistakes he made in the past will not become an albatross. These worthy goals are responsible for the persistence of organizational designs that fragment information within a school. We want to avoid any deleterious "expectancy effects," but we don't recognize what a steep price we may be paying for that protection.

Second, even the information school faculty do have is often misinterpreted, blurring the meaning of potentially informative signals. All three boys had Jekyll-and-Hyde personalities, carefully presenting themselves one way to teachers but acting another way with peers, making the interpretation of their behavior even more difficult. Michael's violent writings and the patterns of bullying all three boys experienced and perpetrated might have been understood as signs that they needed help. Yet the normalization of these unfortunate problems—like the normalization of risks on the launch pad of the *Challenger*—led observers to discount their importance.

Third, schools operate in a cultural and social environment in which there is considerable ambivalence about the proper role of schools in students' lives. As a society, we have not come to any consensus on whether school personnel should be responsible for identifying and helping emotionally troubled youth, yet there is a consensus that the main goal of our schools is learning and academic achievement. The result is that resources, both in terms of staff time and staff training, are not directed toward identifying and dealing with social and emotional problems. Teachers are not trained to counsel students but are increasingly expected to do so, even as academic standards and high-stakes testing push them toward devoting more attention to the three R's. Counselors, even when properly trained, are so saddled with responsibilities for scheduling and logistics that often they have little time to spend on students' emotional issues.

Finally, in the context of ambivalence about school goals and loose coupling, the resources available for identifying troubled youths are directed primarily toward the students who interfere in a big way with the maintenance of order. Those who are disruptive in the classroom or are struggling academically are the "squeaky wheels" that get the grease. Schools develop elaborate procedures and codes for dealing with serious troublemakers. Students like Michael, Mitchell, and Andrew, whose academic performance is average or better and whose disciplinary infractions are relatively minor, remain well below radar range.

Can we be certain that greater information sharing would have prevented the shootings at Heath and Westside? There is no way to know for sure. Moreover, there are some serious drawbacks to increasing the surveillance and tightening the reporting structure. Children could easily be saddled with labels ("troubled," "problem student") that they cannot shake, even when they straighten up after one rocky year. These "false positives" can become self-fulfilling prophecies as the system reacts by placing such students under special scrutiny. Indeed, it is precisely because of this threat to the "second chance" philosophy that school systems fail to transmit disciplinary records across their bureaucratic boundaries.

These arguments may be especially disheartening to those who are searching for a way to identify troubled students and prevent future school shootings. With many schools that are already falling behind in meeting tougher academic standards, can we afford to devote more resources to the social and emotional needs of youths? Must we weaken confidentiality and abandon the clean slate principle in order to increase the flow and availability of information? We address the prevention of future school shootings at the end of this book.

5

THE UNDERBELLY
OF SOCIAL CAPITAL

How could it happen *here*? Residents of Heath and Westside had long thought that their communities were impervious to the problems that plague the cities. "This place is just like Mayberry," the mayor of Bono explained. Kids don't shoot their classmates in Mayberry.

Social scientists have recently taken a good look at the characteristics of communities that flourish. High on their list of desirable elements is the degree of social connectedness that neighbors and friends share. *Social capital* is the concept they draw on to explain why these structural features of community life matter so much.[1] High levels of social capital prevail in homogeneous communities, where social networks are interleaved, where parents know one another as well as their children's friends, and where, as a consequence, social trust is high. In communities where social ties are solid, parents participate in the PTA, vote on election day, attend meetings, and have confidence in the institutions that serve them. In affluent and poor communities alike, high levels of social capital lead to lower crime rates.[2]

Outside of small-town USA, the decline of social capital and the corresponding longing for the resurrection of community has proved to be a powerful narrative. Americans believe that rootlessness is rising as people move for new jobs, affordable housing, or winter sunshine and in doing so sunder the ties that bind communities and generations.[3] During the past thirty years, we saw large increases in the number of dual-earner households; divorce rates climbed; and the rise in single-parent families was dramatic.[4] Families complain about the growing isolation of their children, fostered by the spread of television, video games, and the Internet, which keeps them occupied in their rooms. When political scientist

Robert Putnam documented the decline of social capital in his book *Bowling Alone,* his insights were embraced far beyond academia—Putnam was featured in *People* magazine and invited to the White House by both Presidents Clinton and Bush to discuss specific plans for how to increase civic engagement.[5] His research resonates with the concerns of people throughout the country who feel that we have lost something in the rush to take care of business. Both the left and the right support this diagnosis; social critics of all stripes hold individualism in modern American life responsible for a host of social problems and "community," vaguely defined, as the antidote.[6] It is not hard to understand, then, why the media and the millions of Americans who consume it would conclude that the erosion of community must explain rampage school shootings.

But this decline and fall story,[7] powerful as it is, cannot account for the tragedies in Heath and Westside. Putnam would find much to admire in both places, for they epitomize the kind of America he is searching for. They are throwbacks to an idyllic past when neighbors and relatives had close connections. Parents of Heath High School students are very involved in their children's lives and activities. Nobody locks their doors in the Westside area, because the neighbors have known one another for generations. Adults would not hesitate to reprimand an unrelated child whom they saw misbehaving. Heath and Westside are the exceptions that prove Putnam's rule, or so they thought.

And yet the shootings happened there—and in many other small towns: Pearl, Mississippi; Bethel, Alaska; Edinboro, Pennsylvania; Conyers, Georgia; Lynnville, Tennessee; Fort Gibson, Oklahoma; Notus, Idaho; Dekalb, Missouri; and Goddard, Kansas. These, too, are close-knit rural towns. Of course, rampage school shootings also happened in previously anonymous suburbs like Littleton; there is nothing in small-town water supplies that makes them the only possible locales for these tragedies. Yet over the past thirty years, 60 percent of school shootings have taken place in rural areas.

There are actually two parts to the question, "How could it happen here?" First, what is it about small-town life that makes them disproportionately frequent sites for school shootings? We will confront that question in the next chapter. Here, however, we turn to a second question that is perhaps even more puzzling: How is it possible that in towns that everyone described as "tight-knit," information about the shooters' strange and even dangerous behaviors was never passed on to people who could have done something about it? In chapter 4, we argued that schools did not pick up warning signs in part because they are loosely coupled systems. However, in the world beyond the schoolyard, these "tightly knit" towns are no better at gathering information than anonymous cities. How could such serious problems fester unnoticed in towns where gossip is rampant, where everyone seems to know everyone else's business, where word travels so quickly that it is impossible for anyone to throw a surprise party without the birthday girl learning all about it in advance?

THE EVIDENCE FOR SOCIAL CAPITAL

Although there has been a recent influx of new residents in Heath and Westside, there is still a core of old-timers. When they graduate from high school, seniors who have attended Westside schools since kindergarten have their picture taken together; one graduating senior told us that at least half of her class appeared in the photo. Although there are some transient residents in Heath who came to town for employment in the uranium processing plant, most of the adults in the area—70 percent, by some local estimates—have known each other all their lives.[8]

This residential stability over generations means that many Heath and Westside parents attended the same schools and experienced the same adolescent scenes as their children. Parents are former classmates of their children's teachers and have often known one another longer than their children have been friends.

Putnam notes, with regret, that Americans have let go of the communal activities and associational life that made the country the "nation of joiners" that French observer Alexis de Tocqueville remarked on in his book *Democracy in America,* after his 1831 visit to the United States. In these modern times, we tend to express our commitments by putting checks in the mail to the charities and advocacy groups we favor. Long gone are the days of the Masons or the Elks Lodge, where face-to-face contact flourished.[9]

Bucking these national trends, levels of civic engagement soar in Westside and Heath. The Masons, the Lions Club, the Kiwanis Club, and Childwatch are all active in Westside. The Fraternal Order of Police in Paducah has 75–100 members, almost all of whom help out with fund-raisers and programs for disadvantaged children. One such program, Cops and Bobbers, takes disadvantaged kids fishing at a lake with police officers to help build important connections between children and adults. Participation in sporting teams is a popular activity in Westside, and many residents, young and old, are in softball leagues. On one summer evening while we were in town, ten softball fields were in use by different leagues, most with more than one game scheduled for the evening. "You go out here at Southside to the softball complex," Warren Matlock, a Westside teacher, commented, "and you see a thousand little girls out there playing softball." Many leagues were organized through churches or other organizations, and parents and children would often play together.

In Cash, Arkansas, one of the three small communities that make up the Westside School District, the Masons are still active, although they have had to consolidate with a lodge in a nearby community. The town frequently comes together for city hall meetings. Once a year, Cash holds a town reunion for everyone who lives in or came from the community. What began as a school reunion became a townwide gathering, because the boundaries between the school and the larger community are blurry. People come from as far away as California to attend, and some 300 people participated in 2000.

Church is an essential ingredient in the social capital stew.[10] There are five churches in Bono (on average, one for every 300 people), and three in Cash (one for every 100 people). Residents of both communities attend church on Wednesday evenings as well as Sundays. Social life revolves around faith. Churches buzz with activity seven days a week. People gather for singing, suppers, and special revivals. Adults participate in mentoring programs and Sunday school groups, even when their children have grown out of these activities. Churches connect people even in nonreligious contexts, running social groups for mothers of preschool children, picnics and potlucks, sports teams, charity drives, Boy Scout groups, youth groups, and volunteer groups, and the list goes on. Although attending church is somewhat less popular among the teenagers, it is nearly universal among adults and young children in the Westside community.

Associational life is by no means limited to church-related activities. Residents in Westside participate in groups such as the Jaycees, the Boy Scouts and Girl Scouts, and a group called the Foundation for the Arts, which helps children put on performances. There is a shooting club for kids, although many parents independently take their kids hunting and to target practice. As Warren Matlock, a lifelong Bono resident, reminded us, these connections prevent kids from going astray.[11]

> Kids that aren't involved in things are the kids that . . . make trouble, because they want to be noticed. Everybody wants to be noticed. I always try to encourage anybody I can [to get] involved in something. . . . As a dad with two teenage daughters, I spend a lot of nights on the road. I've got ball games, choir concerts, band concerts, plays, this church activity or that church activity. And you can probably count on one hand all the activities of my kids that I've missed in their lifetime.

SOCIAL CAPITAL AND
THE COMMUNITY'S RADAR

Given these extensive social ties, residents of Heath and Westside were stunned to realize after the shootings erupted that they had no idea that anything had been simmering below the surface. Ironically, part of the reason lies in the ways they were convinced by their own master narrative of life in these pastoral communities. The social capital narrative is what anthropologist Clifford Geertz would call a story that people tell themselves about themselves.[12] Like all such tales, it is incomplete. The aspects of community life that are not so rosy do not make it into the master narrative.

Contrasting themselves with troubled neighborhoods in the city centers, residents of Heath and Westside were still dumbfounded that rampage shootings could erupt in their schools. "We have kids that are pretty family oriented," a Westside administrator said. "I don't know anybody in a 'gang.'"

> The family plays a pretty strong role in the lives of most of [our kids]. You might not find that in some of the inner-city places where you have latchkey kids. And I think we're getting more of that all the time with both parents working. But most of the kids I deal with are pretty good kids. I think religion still plays a pretty big role in most of [their lives].

Given this predisposition, it is hardly surprising that most people in Westside thought it was "the last place that anything like this would happen."

This perception was so strong that many Westsiders who initially did not know about Andrew and Mitchell's role in the shooting were sure that the attack had been the work of an outsider. Eileen Moss, a Westside elementary school teacher, likened her thought process at the time to what she went through after the bombing of the federal building in Oklahoma City. She was certain that the bombing was the work of an evil foreigner, because no American could hate his own country that much. "That's the way it was with [this] shooting," she said. "There's . . . some foreign person from another school who must have done this. It just can't be somebody from Westside, because we're all like family." When Eileen discovered the real authors of the shooting, she applied the narrative again:

> I don't want to say anything against anybody, but that Mitchell Johnson, . . .
> I consider him to be an outsider. Andrew, . . . I mean, I went to school with
> [his uncle], . . . thought they were good people and everything.

I feel like that Mitchell Johnson was the one that thought it up and maybe influenced [Andrew]. I know he's got a troubled background with his family and everything. And I just think he's the instigator. . . . Andrew, of course he did some of the shooting too, but I still can't rationalize that someone from Westside, . . . thought of doing that.

If the residents' simple contrast overstates the trouble in other communities, it also provides only a partial picture of what is happening at home. To be sure, much of what they admire about their communities is very real. They are friendly settings full of people who are close to one another. We interviewed one man who agreed to talk only if we promised to spend a day canoeing with him. This was typical of how we were received in two towns that could have been extremely wary of outsiders investigating the worst moments in their histories.

At the same time, Heath and Westside are not as different from the rest of America as they like to think.[13] The rates of single parenthood, for example, were not much lower in these communities than they were in surrounding communities (and were actually higher in Cash, Egypt, and Bono than in nearby Jonesboro).[14] Kids watch the same movies and television shows as their counterparts in Boston and New York, listen to the same CDs, and work in the same fast food and retail outlets that suburban kids do. Adolescents chafe at their lack of independence from their parents, and parents worry about their kids getting the education they needed to succeed in today's economy. These Edens of social capital are not exempt from the familiar adolescent rites of bullying and social exclusion that so scarred Michael Carneal. Nor are they so distant from the urban imagination that Mitchell Johnson couldn't win status by portraying himself as a gang member.

The master narrative obscures routine kinds of illicit activity. As with teenagers everywhere, rampant drinking, sexual promiscuity, and drug use were common among both the more popular and the "burnout" kids—those who focused heavily on drug use. In Westside, drugs—especially crystal methamphetamine—are in evidence throughout the county. Indeed, one county sheriff we interviewed pointed out that rural Arkansas was experiencing an epidemic of drug production, sale, and use and noted that the problem had seeped into Westside High School. One staff member noted that a "drug clique" had been dealing drugs at school, financed in part by one of the town's more notorious families, which then used their ill-gotten gains to purchase a house that now serves as "party central." Ku Klux Klan enthusiasts were rumored to be involved, which explained why some serious tensions were brewing between the party house crowd and the one and only minority student at Westside.[15]

We found no independent evidence that gangs, drugs, or serious violence had ever made its way into Westside Middle School. The levels of violence and drug use in the larger community, or even in Westside High School, are not markedly different from levels in other communities of this size either. Still, when Westside residents say then that their community is the last place one would ever expect violence of any kind, they are engaging in a bit of denial.

Redundant Safety Systems?

Because their incomplete narratives suggested that these communities were addressing the problems of youth better than they actually were, they did not set up the kind of institutions that could have identified, helped, or contained troubled kids like Mitchell, Andrew, and Michael.

In her study of the 1986 *Challenger* explosion, Vaughan argues that confidence in the reliability of redundant safety systems was a strong part of the organizational culture of NASA.[16] Similarly, the close-knit, small-town nature of the communities where these shootings took place led school personnel to believe that social safety systems were in place as well. If the school didn't pick up on a warning sign, it was assumed that others in the community would. "We had all kinds of signs," sighed one Westside teacher. "We just were too innocent."

> We're still a tight community from the old school. . . . If my kid did something, he doesn't worry about if momma's there to see him or not, if somebody else saw him, he knew he was going to get in trouble. We still do that, and if I see a neighbor's kid doing something, I would still get on to him. . . . We were guilty of thinking too much of our kids, I guess. But looking back on it, . . . we had all kinds of signs in Mitchell. . . . We just didn't pick up on it.

A community that routinely catches minor infractions may have fewer mechanisms in place to seek out the larger ones—especially those that are well hidden. "Coming from a great community, it's going to take a lot longer for you to identify some problems," Kevin Wright, a youth program coordinator told us.

> Put you in the Bronx and start seeing these signs, . . . it wouldn't be a secret and nobody would have a hard time admitting it, because you expect

that. . . . You're in a very rough area, rough city, that's going to happen. . . . To make people identify that there's a problem in a great [place] like this is very, very hard. Unfortunately, sometimes it takes an occurrence like [the shooting] . . . for us to see that. I think that's why you [don't] see things like [school shootings] happening in cities. In . . . places that you want to move to get away from it all, . . . it's very easy not to see some of the more negative things, . . . and when you don't see them, they begin to grow and grow and grow.

Misinterpreting Signals

The behavior of the shooters was also filtered through lenses that made it seem less dangerous than it turned out to be. We see the world through frames that help us organize our thoughts.[17] Information that does not relate to an existing frame or contradicts it is poorly processed. When that happens, we have what sociologists call a "disqualification heuristic," a systematic avoidance of unfavorable information.[18] NASA engineers knew that the shuttle was loaded with multiple, redundant safety systems, and they counted on these systems to counteract the problems they knew might develop with erosion around the O-rings.[19] The forces that pushed the organization toward its central goal resulted in a downplaying of the information that would have led in the opposite direction.

Residents framed Heath and Westside as safe places. Evidence to the contrary was likely to be discounted. A Lutheran church group leader who spent a lot of time with Michael Carneal heard him make dozens of "threats" about using weapons, but she did not take them seriously.

> When . . . we would have discussions on how to resolve issues [in confirmation class], Michael's responses would be very violent in nature, very violent. . . . He would make reference to some type of weapon to be used. . . .
>
> [For example,] . . . we would be discussing the eighth commandment, "[Thou shalt] not bear false witness against thy neighbor." And so we would come up with an example, [like] . . . rumors are being spread about you. . . . Michael would come up all the time with suing or, . . . "Oh, me and my buddies would go after them with a bazooka gun."

Michael's answers were so outlandish that she did not credit them. "All right, child, where in the world would you get a bazooka gun or an A-1 missile?" she laughed to herself. Had Michael threatened to stab someone with a pencil, his comments might have been given more credence.

Another important frame had to do with Michael's family. They were so well respected that it never occurred to anyone at the church that they could raise a son who would be dangerous to the community. Three generations of Carneals attended the Lutheran church, and the camaraderie between them and the rest of the community conferred a protective aura around Michael, even when his behavior was peculiar. Knowing the family as well as they did, suspicions that something was wrong were dispelled by internal voices. "He wouldn't do that," or "I can't believe that would go on." Anomalous information was somehow fitted into the frame, defined as a quirk or an aberration rather than a challenge to the master narrative. Michael was therefore quirky or goofy, but not a candidate for extreme violence.[20]

The Golden family had a reputation in Westside for being extremely supportive, even overprotective, of Andrew. Sandra Banks, one of Andrew's elementary school teachers, had known the family for years.

> I graduated with his dad. . . . His grandparents live down the road from my best friend that I grew up with. . . . [Andrew] probably made me think of my son. You could tell he was loved to death and given everything he wanted. . . . He was happy. The family was wonderful. . . . They picked him up every day. They brought him to school. Dad or Grandma was always there.

What could go wrong with a child who was so loved?

The long association between Andrew's family and the Westside school also colored their interpretation of the boy's behavior when he did step out of line. Teachers who knew Andrew's father remembered him as a bit of a goof-off and prankster too. Andrew appeared to be a "chip off the old block." In his day, Dennis Golden had glued the legs of a chair to the floor so a teacher could not move it. When he was in high school, Dennis inserted crayons into the pencil sharpener. Familiarity breeds interpretations of children's behavior that may be wide of the mark, over- or underestimating the importance of the signals they give off. The prankster Dad who turned into a hard-working man and a loving father set the frame for understanding Andrew. He too would make the transition from a cut-up to a solid man. The frame disqualified any evidence of the disturbed child Andrew really was.

THE MYTH OF SOCIAL CONTROL

In such small communities, where people have known each other for generations and mobility is still relatively rare, gossip is a favored pass-time. The mayor of Bono has lived in the area for twenty-four years, and he worked in a neighboring town for twenty-seven years before that. When he finishes Bono's business, the mayor ambles across the street to the used-car lot and second-hand store, both of which belong to him. There, at the crossroads that define "downtown" Bono, he often spends the remainder of the day socializing with a long-standing group of older neighbors who hang out there daily.

Gossip is enhanced by what sociologists call *multiplex relations:* when people are linked to each other in more than one context. A teacher at Westside High School may also be a group leader at a local church, drive the school bus, coach soccer, and help out with the school band. She has likely lived in the Westside district all her life, graduated from Westside High School, and has children who attend the school. This variety of social activity almost ensures that people in Heath and Westside have multistranded relations with one another.[21]

Information known in one sphere is likely to make its way into others and, in no time, to spread to the entire community. "People know everything," Ron Kilgore, a social studies teacher at Heath, pointed out. "And what they don't know, of course, they tend to make up."

> I don't know that this community is any worse or any better than any other [in terms of gossip], but it's—since people do tend to know each other—it's probably more hurtful because it travels to more places or it's more pervasive.

Westside and Heath exemplify a condition sociologist James Coleman called *intergenerational closure*—adults in a community are better able to monitor children's activities because they are friends with the parents of their children's friends.[22] Adults are also more willing to look after unrelated children. Moreover, they share a common set of beliefs about proper conduct—a kind of *normative closure*—which children in the community absorb.[23] Back-channel communication permits adults to find out what their secretive kids are up to.[24] Problem behavior may be identified in exactly this fashion. Gossip has helped school resource officers (SROs—see chapter 10) find out about everything from students smoking marijuana to bringing weapons to school.

These were communities in which it was virtually impossible to get into trouble undetected—or so the residents thought. Eleventh grade student Kirsten Gelfand put her finger on the pros and cons of intergenerational closure:

> "What's good about [Heath] is . . . you know that if you are in trouble or if you know something is wrong, you can always rely [on the fact] that some-

body's going to be there. . . . What is bad about it is . . . everybody knows everybody's business. . . . Especially like just around school. Somebody [gets] caught doing something, by the end of the day, everybody knows about it. . . . People from the school go and tell their parents. . . . Parents tell the teachers. It just gets everywhere.

If this were the full story, we would expect that the troubling aspects of Michael, Mitchell, and Andrew's behavior would be all over town. Yet very little was known about the boys who gunned down their classmates; peers who witnessed troubling behavior never reported it to their parents.

How could such serious problems have gone unreported in a town where gossip is the norm and privacy the exception? If so much social control is exercised, how is it possible that Michael, Mitchell, and Andrew gained enough privacy to commit these crimes?

The Concealment Game

Gossip leads adolescents to hide their actions and become much more secretive. It also dissuades students from confiding in friends and teachers for fear of the way negative gossip can spread uncontrollably through social networks. Jessie Pickins, a student at Heath, told us that some students she knew did talk to a teacher, Ms. Taylor, but that she wouldn't because Ms. Taylor lives nearby and is a friend of her mother's.[25] Anything Jesse confided in Ms. Taylor was likely to get back to her mother in a flash. Students monitor the information that their teachers have access to and try to dam the flow of "data" that could be harmful. Either way, through subterfuge or self-censorship, information that could trigger alarm bells fails to reach adults who might be able to intervene.

Michael Carneal was very sensitive about gossip. He knew how quickly information could spread. But Michael also went to great lengths to hide information about himself altogether. One prosecution psychiatrist claimed that Michael "was intensely private and fearful at home"[26] and tried to hide his mental illness and social problems from his family as well as from others. Michael also tried to conceal from his family how unhappy he was at school and how badly he was teased. He was concerned that his parents might meddle in ways that would make matters worse. Ann Carneal wanted to call the school about the gossip column suggesting that Michael was gay, but Michael insisted that she refrain, telling her that "it wasn't that big of a deal" when in fact it was a terrible ordeal for him.[27]

Grown-ups tell themselves that they maintain a great deal of social control over children in their communities, but in fact there is a great deal of behavior they are unaware of. Adolescents are very good at hiding their actions from the watchful eyes of adults, even in places where such observation is harder to avoid than elsewhere. In small-town America, deviant behavior is sometimes driven further underground; adolescents become even better at self-monitoring and keeping information about themselves to themselves.

Why the Neighbors Don't Tell

Residents of Westside and Heath tell themselves that their communities are protected by the tendency for adults to look out for each other's children, to act as remote sensors on behalf of parents who may not be there to witness objectionable behavior. This friendly surveillance system is one of the most comforting aspects of life in their towns. The mayor of Jonesboro told us earnestly that if our research suggested that the community was in any way responsible for the shooting at Westside, he wanted to know about it so that he could do something.

Yet, like parents everywhere, adults in these communities do not really want to hear that their kids are behaving badly. They care about their families' reputations and may get angry at the messenger and defensive on behalf of their children. Fearing just such a reaction, neighbors often withhold what they know—even when they believe the situation is potentially serious. As one Heath resident put it, "It is always easier to tell someone that you really don't know that, 'Hey, your son really needs some help.'" The dense web of connections between people facilitates information sharing, but it also provides a powerful incentive for neighbors to hold their tongues rather than make enemies. In places where people stay put for generations, such enemies could become like the Hatfields and the McCoys—an outcome no one readily seeks.

In a focus group interview with parents in Heath, we asked if they wanted to hear from others if their child was doing something wrong. Initially, everyone agreed that they did. But after a few moments, one mother spoke up hesitantly about what happens to the bearer of bad news:

> I have yet to see a parent that has gotten a phone call like that from a friend, from a teacher, from someone else, [who] didn't stand up and say, 'I don't believe it, they were being nosy, and they were out of line.' . . . These are the same people that say if you ever see my daughter speeding please call and tell me. . . .

> I know some friends—luckily it wasn't me—that called . . . and [the parents of the misbehaving child] didn't believe it. Things ended up surfacing . . . , the kids ended up getting in trouble, but the parents still held it against the original person that called, because they thought that they were out of line.

Our focus group of Heath parents reported that if a neighbor called them out of honest concern for their children's behavior, that would be fine, but if they were just being nosy, or there were some jealousy or competition involved, the "reports" would be regarded as unwelcome interference.[28] There is a lot of "noise" in a system like this, a great deal of room for misunderstanding. How does one determine what a neighbor's motives really are? How can an adult in possession of news worth telling be sure her report won't be regarded as meddling? One mother felt she had to make her calls to the school anonymously so that no one would get mad at her.

> I had about three different occasions in middle school where I saw things [that] didn't need to be going on, or that [my daughter] . . . witnessed on the school bus or at school. To this day she does not know that I called and let the principal know. I never gave a name, because I don't ever want to call and tell on a student. . . .

As much as parents want to monitor each other's children and to use intergenerational closure to the community's advantage, the possibility of misinterpretation and the anger that follows causes virtually everyone to hold back. The social repercussions of misjudging the situation can range from the loss of a friendship, to hostile relations that complicate the many social occasions when adults are together, to open and public rifts. These problems are compounded when neighbors have multiplex ties and cannot avoid someone who bears a grudge.

Children also play a role in restraining their parents from exercising the civic impulse to report wrongdoing. Children who are the source of their parent's insider knowledge worry about being tagged a tattletale if their own mother comes forward. They will plead with her not to expose their "betrayal" because of the repercussions they face in the adolescent world. In this way, children interfere with the lines of adult communication that operate—in theory, if not always in practice—in tight-knit towns.

When the information in question is truly disturbing and serious, the potential ramifications of reporting it are even greater. In the case of the school shooters, it was enough to prevent adults in the neighborhood who knew of their worrying behavior to avoid telling their parents or the school. The counselor at Michael Carneal's ministry camp who listened to a steady stream of violent responses to her hypothetical questions in confirmation class was understandably reluctant to say anything to the boy's parents, whose families had been members of the church for at least three generations. Instead, she assumed "they knew already," that they could not "not know" about his aberrant behavior. Hers was the understandably cautious response to a potentially embarrassing encounter with a fine family whose son was giving off signs that he was veering out of control.

Similar dilemmas surfaced among neighbors of the Golden family. Many of them knew of Andrew's aggressive rowdiness and threatening language, but no one we spoke with had confronted his parents. The Golden family was known for being overprotective. When a teacher at school had punished Andrew, his grandmother had jumped to his defense and yelled publicly at the teacher who paddled him. Neighbors knew about these incidents. Their decision not to come forward was likely informed by their understanding of the response they might expect to receive: defensiveness, fury, and a breakdown in their social relations. The fact that Doug Golden, Andrew's grandfather, who worked for the Arkansas Fish and Game Commission, was rumored to have killed a dog himself may have given neighbors pause to think that perhaps they did not have the same standards as the Goldens for appropriate behavior.

One neighbor whose daughter saw Andrew shoot cats did not mention it to his family, even in passing. Another neighbor, Patricia Hansworth, told us that Andrew's stepbrother once told her son that Andrew was starving a cat in a barrel in his backyard and that he shot cats. Hansworth was clearly disturbed by this information, yet she did not tell Andrew's parents. Instead she assumed that Andrew's mother must know, since Andrew's stepbrother had told her son about it; she assumed he probably had told his mother as well.

The assumptions that people make—that parents *must* know—could be quickly checked, even in a casual way. Yet the reasons for staying clear of sticky situations are not hard to fathom. The same multiplex ties that promote the spread of gossip throughout a community can also prevent it from reaching the people who might need to hear it.

CONCLUSION

In many respects, Heath and Westside hearken back to a better age that the rest of us fear we may never see again. In the cultural oscillation between individual freedom and a desire for more community, they represent a communal vision that seems to be disappearing from other parts of America. Scholars, journalists, policy experts, and many parents have assumed that adolescent problems—ranging from juvenile delinquency to violence—reflect the decline of family and community that is characteristic of much of modern life. As parents become more occupied with their work and other activities, and as more children grow up in single-parent or divorced households, the connections between parents and children are seen as dwindling rapidly. Even in communities such as Heath and Westside, these explanations are offered, and the solutions put forth claim that we need *more* adolescent social control, *more* enforcement of family values in our communities, *more* social capital.

But this is not the correct diagnosis for rampage shootings. Heath and Westside are amply endowed with these virtues, but that did not help to prevent the shootings. In fact, believing in this very narrative about their communities made it more difficult for residents to see and respond to problems that were festering just below the surface. Michael and Andrew in particular were seen through the lens of their families' community reputations, and their violent or strange behavior was often minimized because of what turned out to be inaccurate assumptions about the lines kids from good families would not cross.

The shootings also revealed gaps in the remote surveillance system that residents believe keeps their children safe from harm. Adult monitoring was not effective in disciplining Andrew Golden for the threats, bullying, or violence to animals that many of his neighbors were aware of, the rowdy behavior and threats that Mitchell Johnson was known to make, or Michael Carneal's stealing or selling pornography downloaded off the Internet.[29]

The very density of community structure can also help us explain why acquaintances and friends who are privy to warning signs do not come forward. It is a big part of the reason grown-ups whose children are "under control" are the last to know about the discord beneath the placid surface of community life. The neighbor who confides that a child is misbehaving out of his parents' sight might expect gratitude but reap hostility instead. And if today's neighbors will still be there thirty years hence—a common occurrence in both Heath and Westside—the repercussions of complaining about a kid's behavior, or warning his mother that he seems depressed, can be serious. Paradoxically, then, there may be less information available to adults in towns with high levels of social capital than in more anomic settings.

6

THE STRANGLEHOLD OF ADOLESCENT CULTURE

A BANNER HEADLINE BLAZED ACROSS THE FRONT PAGE OF THE *PADUCAH SUN* ON the day after the shooting: "Why?" The nagging question still hung in the air when we arrived in Heath and Westside more than three years later. By then, though, confidence that an answer could be found had drained right out of the townspeople. "Everyone who has been through this has looked for a magic bullet," Dan Orazine, the Judge Executive in Paducah, told us, "and I don't think there is one."

In chapter 2 we examined this question narrowly, focusing on the biographical details of the boys' lives. Here we reconsider the question more broadly, trying to understand how the cultural and social milieu in which they lived could have spawned such acts of violence. These explanations may not be the ones we want to hear, for they come close to implicating all of us. The impetus for the shootings did not come from bad parenting or broken families, the Internet or music videos. Rather the rage that fuels school shooters emerges as the last act in a long and bitter drama that is central to the adolescent world they inhabit. American teenagers are ruthless arbiters of one another's social worth. Anyone who falls short will feel it where it hurts as their "friends" let loose with a relentless barrage of put-downs. To fail the "test of cool" is to be subjected to withering attacks on one's self-worth.

If the adolescent world were completely self-contained, a hermetically sealed chapter in the life cycle, it would be hard enough to live through. But it isn't. The teenagers' pressure cooker is created and sustained by youths, but its power derives from the way the surrounding adult society reinforces its central messages. Grown-ups are party to the status-seeking, ridicule-laden social system of youth culture. Their participation, tacit and explicit, in the status games reinforces the worst aspects of teenage life. In homogeneous small towns where adults are heavily invested in the activities of their kids, reputations made in high school can last into adulthood. Under these circumstances, adolescent social failures are magnified and can seem more like a life sentence than a rite of passage.

Although the impetus for such shootings is rooted in adolescent status competition that is reinforced by adults, broader cultural scripts of masculinity also play an important role. Status competition among boys often centers on demonstrating a narrow notion of manliness. Andrew, Mitchell, and Michael not only failed to become respected social actors, they also failed to become powerful *males*. The shootings provided an important way for them to defy the labels they had been assigned and to demonstrate publicly that they were the men-in-the-making that they claimed to be.

When students go to school and shoot randomly at their classmates, they are, more than anything, trying to send a message to everyone about how they want to be seen. In rural and suburban America, school is often the community's most central institution for adults as well as kids. The shootings provided a way for the boys to redefine their identities and assert their masculinity on the community's most public stage. By randomly targeting their classmates, they showed that they were less interested in revenge against particular individuals than in broadcasting their message to the peer and community social structure that had rejected them.

SOCIAL FAILURE IN
ADOLESCENT SOCIETY

"Popular" kids are at the top of the heap in adolescent culture, and any understanding of how the hierarchy is experienced by those who are outside this charmed circle must still begin with them. Although ironically the "popular" kids are often disliked or even disdained by their less trendy classmates, they are the most powerful actors in this social system. People pay attention to the clothes they wear, the activities they value, the kids they favor (and those they despise).

How do young people enter the winners' circle? Looks are paramount; it is virtually impossible to be a popular kid without being physically attractive. Money matters too—partly because it can buy the other things that count, like the right clothes or cars. Unlike physical attributes, the elements of popularity that are tied to consumption link rank ordering among teens to their parents' status. We asked teenagers in Heath and Westside, "What makes people popular?"

A lot of the times it's like basically what your parents do. Well, that's how a lot of kids base it on—if you have money or if you don't or if you just shop at Gap. That's . . . [what] the kids in our school base popularity on.

—Stephanie Holder, Heath High School sophomore

If you're wearing really nice clothes and your mom drops you off in a nice car and you have a lot of money in your pocket, or if you're skinny and pretty and have really good hair. . . . And if you're a guy and you're built or you're popular or whatever, the football players are going to go for you.

—Stacey Hunt, Westside High School sophomore

The in-crowd in these high schools is set apart because its members have more active social lives. They go out on dates and throw wild parties, opportunities made possible by their—or their parents'—greater affluence. The critical factors were similar among middle schoolers. Even for those too young to drive or throw parties, the social hierarchies—based on clothes, looks, and athletic prowess—are much the same. In a small community, cliques and social labels acquired in middle school feed directly into high school social position.

Cultural ideals that rule the rest of society play a key role in this milieu as well. Entire industries are built on (and reinforce) women's desires to "look skinny" or have "good hair" and men's desires to build their biceps or drive luxury cars. Ironically, though, adolescents tend to valorize these superficial qualities at the expense of traits that make a real difference in their fate as adults.[1] This is particularly true where achievement in school is concerned. It is hard to get anywhere important in the adult world without completing college and, increasingly, graduate or professional school.

Yet this plain truth is rarely recognized by youths. At a time when kids are trying to grow up and differentiate themselves from adults, the easiest way to make the difference between the generations clear is to resist what all those adults are pushing: doing well in school. Time horizons matter as well. Getting better grades in ninth grade may result in a higher class rank, which may lead to admission in a better college, which may eventually provide more occupational options. Yet these considerations are abstract in comparison with the more immediate and pressing problem of getting a date or making enough spending money to show a girl a good time.[2] In a postindustrial economy where an ever-lengthening training period is needed before young people can enter the adult world, adolescents spend many years in a kind of status limbo.[3] They cannot forecast whether they will be successful adults until they are well into their twenties, and that is too long a time to wait to establish a meaningful place in the pecking order. They tend to substitute the most superficial values of the broader culture, reinforced by an extensive advertising industry, in the meantime.

By these adolescent standards, all three of the shooters in our cases were "losers." None of them qualified for the kind of respect they craved. This was most obvious in Michael Carneal's case. Small, slender, and burdened by the universal marker of the dweeb (glasses), Michael had been picked on by older, bigger boys for as long as he could remember. Even in eighth grade, where he was technically at the top of the middle school social ladder, he had a miserable year. When he moved to ninth grade, things got much worse; now at the bottom of the age heap, he found himself on the receiving end of hazing rituals and the last in line for dates. At the time of the shooting, seventy days into his freshman year, Michael was at his nadir in terms of social status and respect.

Andrew was closer to the middle of the social ladder, so average as to be almost forgotten. The son of two postal workers, he had enough money to dress well (teachers reported that he always wore Doc Martens shoes), but, like Michael, he was in middling activities such as the band, and he did not play sports. While he was not unpopular with girls (he had "dated" several classmates and some thought his short buzz cut was cute), his small size and average social status kept him from being a more attractive candidate. He was also not terribly personable and was described as being young for his age, somewhat immature socially and emotionally. He was not a "prep" and was described by one teacher "as a good old boy," the equivalent of a Future Farmer of America. But what was most striking was that for a student who would become one of the most notorious in town history, Andrew seemed to have been so ordinary as to be virtually invisible at school.

Of the three shooters profiled here, Mitchell should have been the one with the least to worry about socially, and is thus most difficult to understand. He was bigger than other boys; he often acted as the bully himself. Mitchell was passable at sports and played on the school football and basketball teams. He had had a couple of girlfriends, and other girls seemed to be interested. One teacher said that he wasn't quite in with the "lead dogs," but he was close to it.

Had Mitchell been able to see his own position clearly, he might have been more content. Unfortunately, he hungered for more than he had and undervalued his own social achievements. He worried that girls found him undesirable, although there was evidence to the contrary. Even his teachers knew he was doing well in the adolescent tournament, although they also realized that he didn't know it. "[Mitchell] was perfect, ideal," one teacher remembered. "Girls were really starting to like him."

> He was probably the most eligible bachelor in my [class]. There were probably seven or eight boys, and he was . . . the most eligible. He didn't know it [though]. When he would say something in class, I could see the girls giggling.

Mitchell's reaction to the failings he thought he had suffered was to bluster, brag, and overstate his bona fides.

Sociologist Erving Goffman characterized social interaction as a series of pressured performances, each with a specific meaning intended for a special audience. In Goffman's dramaturgy, audiences are always critical, looking for the cracks that invalidate an actor, showing him to be less than the person he is claiming to be. This is treacherous turf, requiring constant vigilance against those discrediting mistakes.[4] Mitchell is a prime example of Goffman's model. He was always on stage, working overtime to win acceptance, admiration, and a place high on the totem pole. When the stage was set before his peers, the performance was all about being a gang member, wearing colors, and flashing hand signs. When adults were the audience, he shifted to being the most polite, respectful choir boy. Yet discrediting information was leaking out of Mitchell at every turn. His peers didn't buy the gang label and ridiculed him for false claims. And enough teachers heard him swear or experienced his disrespectful outbursts for him to be, at best, incongruous in their eyes. Indeed, Mitchell reserved his real animus for precisely those people—kids and adults—who were privy to these contradictions.

The more glaring the disjuncture, the more vulnerable Mitchell was to losing his public identity altogether. A good actor wants to appear completely natural, to camouflage his artistry. Mitchell was trying too hard; the studied aspects of his performance were becoming too transparent; and the discrediting evidence was becoming harder to hide. Being cut from the basketball team, or moping after being dumped by his girlfriend proved that he wasn't really on top of his game. Mitchell became an attractive target for ridicule precisely because he was just too obvious a performer and the act wasn't completely convincing. Four teachers we gathered together talked about this aspect of Mitchell.

> Mitchell tried to act real macho, but I think that he had a little bit low self-esteem, he was self-conscious.

INTERVIEWER: How could you tell?

He tried to please.

Spoke too much, he talked loud.

Acceptance from other people.

And he'd want to know, "Does this look good on me today?". . . I said, "You look handsome." He looked for acceptance, and he loved to be bragged on.

Mitchell's game was making it inside the winners' circle, but because he did not qualify, his slightly more popular peers slapped him with the ultimate punishment: the label of "wannabe." This experience is not that unusual; popular kids police the boundary between in-crowd and out-crowd with laserlike intensity. The occasional rejection, quite public and intensely humiliating, will come down on the nearly popular (as opposed to the out-and-out reject) if for no other reason than to reinforce the power of the real elites to determine who stays and who goes.[5] Sociologists Patricia and Peter Adler reached a similar conclusion after studying middle school students on the fringes of popular cliques: "On the one hand they were more accepted than the total rejects, yet they experienced the bulk of the rejection behavior, as they were the ones who tried to be included and were alternately welcomed and shunned."[6] It can be more painful to fall just short of success than to be an out-and-out failure from the beginning.

For Mitchell, hanging in a liminal position—not quite in the popular group, but obviously in the running—was maddening. It had the effect of magnifying both his successes and his disappointments, because so much was on the line. Dating is key to being popular, but it exposes one to being dumped. Being on the basketball team is a triumph, but getting cut from it is a very public blow. Hence, although Mitchell was clearly in the top half of the middle school social hierarchy, his precarious position on the edge of popularity made him feel insecure. What's more, he was trapped in a vortex that was pulling him down as all of these sources of rank collapsed at the same time. The desperation motivated Mitchell to look for a way to move himself forcefully into the limelight as notorious.

FINDING A NICHE IN
THE ADOLESCENT WORLD

Andrew, Mitchell, and Michael failed to attain the status and respect they craved. They also lacked what would have been crucial buffers—a sense of personal identity and a like-minded group of peers who valued them for it. Adolescence is not made up solely of rivalries and social tournaments. It is also the period when kids begin to define what they value, what they hope to achieve, and what kind of people they hope to become.[7] Despite the overarching pressures for conformity, teens do manage to differentiate themselves, but only with the help of supportive peer groups. Belonging to cliques and clubs diminishes the need to perform and provides insulation against teasing, bullying, or negative status comparisons from the larger group.

Early adolescence is toughest for those who are not at the top of the status totem pole precisely because they cannot measure themselves in any way other than how they fare in comparison to those who are. The lack of organized groups—clubs, debate teams, theater groups—means that jockeying for position is a lonely, fraught, individual effort, with kids clawing at one another to move up and down the rungs of a single status ladder. The most pointed teasing, the most excruciating attention to flaws in performance, and the most private disappointment cascade on middle school students. The pain is deeper, and the resources, in terms of group support, are weaker than they will be in high school. Our observations are confirmed by research that shows consistently that junior high school students have lower self-esteem and less positive self-evaluations than high school students.[8]

During early adolescence, youths have not yet developed a firmly established sense of their personal identity and hence tend to see themselves through the lenses of their peers.[9] Students are often unable to differentiate their own sense of self from the social identity imputed to them by others. They lack that protective coating that comes with some sense of individual purpose. When Michael Carneal was publicly labeled as gay, he worried a lot that he might actually be homosexual even though—as he told psychiatrists later—he had never experienced sexual feelings for other boys or men. Mitchell was obsessed with winning compliments from teachers or other students to validate his persona. For Mitchell and Michael, lacking an internal way to rebuff their insecurities, the shootings provided a very public way to demonstrate to themselves and others that they were who they wanted to be.

Given his age, Michael at least had the opportunity to find a social group that he could have called home. If middle school is a social ladder, high school is more like a social pyramid. The basic ordering of the hierarchy is unchanged—preps at the top, band kids in the middle, other assorted people at the bottom—but the middle groups have specialized on the basis of their interests and activities and not just where they fall in relation to the top group. Student life becomes differentiated horizontally and vertically as students become involved with more var-

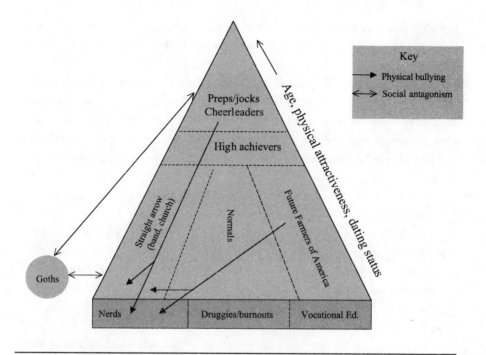

Figure 6.1   The Social Pyramid at Heath High School

ied extracurricular activities such as the student newspaper, the drama club, and the choir and form friendships around these interests (see Figure 6.1). Instead of viewing life as a classwide popularity contest, students become more concerned with defining their own identities and seeking to find a peer group that will support them in these efforts.[10] Jenny Peterson, a Westside senior who seeks her center in the high school band, knows full well that she hasn't made the cut with the inner circle of athletes and cheerleaders.

> My whole goal of high school is not to be popular. It was to have fun and have friends. My good friends were in band with me. . . . I don't feel like I fit in really well with the more popular athletes and the richer people but . . . I have fun going on the church retreats, and the church camp, and all those things. And those are the people I want to hang out with.

Students we got to know in these middling high school groups echoed her sentiments, and they were not just handing us sour grapes. Those who were shut out of the in-crowd still feel a degree of envy and resentment about what they have been denied: social recognition, invitations to parties, and more options for dates. Yet they also embrace an alternative value system that is genuinely, if not always completely, satisfying.

Michael had started down this road, but he had not gone far. The oppositional, contrarian identity he was in the process of crafting might well have insulated him from the adolescent standards by which he had been found wanting (particularly in comparison with his sister). In his school papers, stories, and e-mails, Michael delineated the kind of teenager he wanted to be. For example:

> My name is Michael Carneal. . . . I really hate sports I have low self esteem and I play guitar . . . I have an over achieveing sister Kelly who is a senior. I hate being even compared to her. this explains my respning [?] behind being odd and strange and dressing the same way I act. . . . Sometimes I make buttons . . . expressing my opinions. I don't take stuff from teenagers or parents and I am seriously mad at the world. I like Gwar [a rock band] and Atari Teenage Riot [another band]. . . . [11]

Unfortunately, Michael did not succeed in getting other kids to accept his alternate game. He grasped the basics of adolescence—that kids who were too square were not popular—but his poor intuitions about which minor transgressions would be rewarded and which would mark him as a jerk were faulty. Trying to buy his way into the Goth group did not do the trick. Drinking salad dressing in the cafeteria brought him more mockery than friendly laughs. Wearing a cape to school was another unsuccessful gambit.

Mental illness made it hard for Michael to calibrate the impact of his efforts. For example, he thought he had no friends, even though there were quite a few kids who claimed, even after the fact, that they were his friends. When kids tried to get close to Michael, he would "pull away" in a way that was different from other teens, leaving him psychologically isolated. This loneliness also led to a deep depression, which in turn increased isolation from others.

All in all, Michael had not yet found the social niche that was so sustaining to people like Jenny Peterson, whose status was less than they might have liked. Michael came from a high-achieving family and seems to have remained ambivalent about his middling academic performance. Although he tried to move into the Goth group, he also retained his friends in the band, many of whom fit the goody-goody stereotype that he derided when among the "freaks." He flunked out in all of these contexts: he was not the student his sister was; he was the youngest, newest, and least accepted member of the Goth group; and he was one of two band students asked to sit out because of a shortage of uniforms. Instead of providing him with the security of an identity group, Michael's marginal position in various cliques exacerbated his sense of failure.

PARENTS AND PECKING ORDERS

Although much of the pain that motivated these shootings came at the hands of other teenagers, adolescent social hierarchies gain much of their force by the way they are reinforced by adults. In chapter 5, we illustrated how the intense social capital that made these towns so distinctive made residents blind to much of what was happening among teens just below the surface. Here we illustrate how adult investment in adolescent lives can actually exacerbate the feelings of marginality for those who do not succeed by mainstream standards.

If school were just one of many places adolescents spent their time, social failures within them might not take on such enormous significance. Indeed, in big cities school is less important, because there are other proving grounds: the streets, the clubs, summer camps. In communities like Heath and Westside, by contrast, the school is the undisputed focal point of community life—for everyone. This aspect of school shootings was noted by a former Jonesboro resident who works for the state police.

> In a lot of these small towns, [school] is the center point of the community. It is the one point that draws the community together. While they may all have churches, they're subdivided among Methodists, Presbyterians. This [school] is where moms and dads and children come to participate in sporting events, Parents' Night. It is the focal point of the community. It's almost sacred ground.

Parental involvement in children's activities at the Heath and Westside schools is <u>ubiquitous</u>. Parents run sports teams when the school budgets can't pay for coaches. They help lead the drug-free schools programs. Extracurricular activities could not function without the parents, who accompany teams and performance groups all over the state. The marching band that Michael played in, for example, has trips every Saturday from September until Christmas break. Parents chaperone the buses, haul instruments, and make sets. The former principal, Bill Bond, estimates that there are twenty parents who do nothing else every Saturday for months. But Bond said that after a while it didn't even seem like an obligation:

You can't believe the number of parents that are involved with band. And I mean drive a hundred miles to stand there and hold balloons and give to the kids. It doesn't matter. . . . They don't consider it work when you show up at band contest on Saturday, because they love it, it's part of their lives.

As the focus of community life, the school becomes as central a part of the parents' lives as it is for their kids. Their presence dissolves the boundaries between school and community.

What are the consequences of living in a town where adults are so heavily invested in the social scene of the younger generation? Social capital can be stifling when parental involvement conflicts with the natural teenage desire for independence. "A lot of parents really struggle with letting go," a church pastor remarked.

Kids don't want their parents to be around them at this time, because they want to spread their own wings. . . . [But] they want to have the support of their parents. . . . If it's a school activity, they want their parents in the stands. They want to be cheered or applauded. . . . [It's] a difficult balance.

Community involvement in schools means that successes and failures are magnified beyond school boundaries. Kids who distinguish themselves on the playing field or the stage are well known around town. When Mitchell was cut from the basketball team, he not only lost the opportunity to play, he also lost the chance to shine in a public arena. When Michael was asked to stand down from the marching band, his parents' regular presence in the concession stand compounded his embarrassment. His sister Kelly offered to give up her spot so that her brother could play; her generosity probably did not ease Michael's situation.

A bad reputation sticks, especially in a small community. Multiplex ties may not be an ironclad source of social control, but they do ensure that no one gets a second chance to make a first impression. Under these conditions, a community can resemble a jail or an asylum, what Erving Goffman called a "total institution," in which efforts to craft a particular public identity can easily be foiled. Reputations once established can prove unshakable, because they are telegraphed through overlapping networks. Teenagers from cities or suburbs who fall afoul of school pecking orders may be able to escape to clubs that are off campus. Children at the bottom of the school hierarchy may rest at the top of another social system in summer camp, a welcome refuge from the misery of teasing. But this is typically possible only when there is no one common to both groups who can spread a negative reputation to the new circle. In Heath and Westside, distinct social spheres were nonexistent.

The task of continuously projecting even a minimally respectable front before all of these audiences was overwhelming for Michael, especially in the face of a deepening mental illness. Wherever he went—school, church, or a friend's house—Michael was apt to embarrass his well-respected family and give himself yet another chance to lower his social standing. Goffman reminds us that being an actor on the "front stage"—at work, at church, at a party—is hard work; putting forward a character portrait that is socially acceptable requires energy and attention. Performance is draining, especially for someone who can barely hold his wilder thoughts in check. It is particularly debilitating when the person knows full well that his thoughts are not normal, as Michael did. "He realized he couldn't function in society," Dr. O'Connor remembered. "At one point he told me he thought he'd be safe in jail. He wouldn't have to make a pretext of functioning where he didn't think he could." The shooting provided an exit from what was for him a nearly overwhelming task of constant social performance.

Adults magnify the trials and tribulations of adolescence and reinforce the status metrics that govern it. Football and basketball games are big events in these small towns; they are gathering points for everyone in the community.[12] Upcoming games and those that have just passed are the centerpiece of gossip in the local hangouts. In communities where people stay put through the generations, the fans in the stands are both parents and alumni (and often former players themselves). They care about how the team does on the field and have done for perhaps as long as thirty years. Parents know the players, the local merchants recognize them, and—much to the dismay of those who do not play the glamour sports—they are known and respected around town. "In a small town there's not a whole lot to do," Eddy Gorman, a Westside staff member explained. "[Sports provide] a kind of social center. On Friday night, if there's a home football game, it'll just [be packed]." Eddy thinks that high school athletics even overshadow the much larger sports program at Arkansas State University.

School athletes, especially football players, were also favored within the schools, which led to some resentment among other students.[13] Christine Olson, an academically inclined Westside High School student, looked on with frustration at the privileged world of football players.

> The football team is so glorified. . . . All of our subjects are supposed to be educational. And they get out of class to go eat lunch and go to watch *Remember the Titans* on one of their game days. . . . I mean my schedule was like

physics, college algebra and pre-calc, history, and all this stuff. And we don't get any privileges like that. . . . We bust our tails and we don't get anything for it.

Nonathletes at Heath were particularly upset about the lack of recognition extended to their accomplishments. "The football team was awful," one student complained, "but they got a whole lot of attention."

Our band was good. You know we'd win a competition and nobody would say a thing about it. Our choir was really good. We sent the most people to all state, and higher state, nobody said a word about it. Smart kids, they didn't care about the smart kids. . . But they definitely paid the most attention to the sports kids.

How so? we asked

Well, like, recognizing accomplishment. You know, like pep rallies—they had pep rallies for our constantly losing football team. They would make announcements, "Oh, the football team went and got beat by so and so," or "The basketball team went and got beat by so and so." But they never recognized anything else that anybody [else] did.

Students at Westside High School alleged that the football team was sometimes exempted from the random drug tests that are, in theory, administered to all students. We have no way of independently verifying this charge, nor do we think it should be taken at face value. Yet whether or not it was actually the case, some Westside High students thought it was; for them, this belief provides one more example of responsible adults supporting a key pillar of the social hierarchy among students: athletes rule.

These examples are drawn from Westside High School, but the sorting machine begins to operate in middle school. Middle school students are offered few organized activities, but sports is an exception. Football and cheerleading begin as early as fifth grade in Westside and are an important source of status even for middle school students. Parents who had been through the system before realized that these accomplishments would become important and coached their children about what activities they should join in middle school if they wanted to make the grade down the line.

Columbine High School embroidered this culture of athletic admiration beyond anything we saw in Arkansas or Kentucky. The Colorado state wrestling champion was allowed to park his $100,000 Hummer all day in a fifteen-minute spot, and a football player was allowed to tease a girl about her breasts in class without sanction from his teacher. Sports trophies were the only ones displayed in the front lobby; sports pages in the yearbook were in color, whereas photos of the debate team and other clubs were in black and white.[14] Eric Harris and Dylan Klebold were subjected to unfettered bullying—physical and verbal—at the hands of athletes at Columbine.[15] Not surprisingly, when Harris and Klebold exacted their revenge, they began by barking "All the jocks stand up!" The shooters asked people "if they were jocks. If they were wearing a sports hat, they would shoot them."[16] In a school where athletes were granted special privileges, they were also first in the shooters' gun sights.

Michael had some similar sentiments. According to one of his psychiatrists, he "believed that his school favored 'sports people' and that no one would do anything if he complained and that the kids would just come down harder on him."[17] He was not simply expressing his own anger at jocks or preps. The superior position of athletes was ratified by the school itself, and this bothered Michael as well.

Administrators at Heath were not unaware of the potential for favoritism, and they consciously worked to honor the achievements of students who were artistically or intellectually inclined. A special recognition ceremony for students with the highest academic achievement was held annually. Parents were invited as a matter of course. When the academic team won the state championship in Kentucky, Heath High held a postcompetition pep rally. The team's defiant pride suggests their pleasure at this recognition and their awareness that they were bucking the tide. "This year our academic team won the Kentucky State 1A school tournament," a senior reminded us.

> So we had a big pep rally, and me and the other senior on the team, we were standing with the trophy between us in front of the entire school, heads cocked back defiantly. Come get me. And so from then on, people have actually known my name.

The community at Heath also showed its support for activities other than football and basketball; the band had boosters and a banquet night, just like the football and basketball teams, and participated in interscholastic marching band competitions. Parents put their time where their values lie; by doing so, they give a lot more than lip service to the idea that there is a life beyond football.[18]

These valiant attempts to be more even-handed did not level the playing field: undue favoritism toward athletes and popular kids remained an informal norm. In part, the practice reflects the cultural continuity and normative closure that develops when generations stay put. By some local estimates, 50 to 75 percent of the staff attended the local schools and therefore grew up with the same pecking order. The favoritism cuts deep, according to Westside students like Ralph Montgomery:

> [Popular kids] will [truss] you up more, and physically just push you around, just because they don't stand as big of a chance to get attention, or whatever. School officials are less likely to be hard on them. If somebody like me, that don't have a lot of friends [and wasn't] popular . . . went to the more popular kids and started pushing them around or something, [school authorities] wouldn't have no problem throwing me in detention.

Teachers who gave special treatment to popular kids or kids from "good" families sent the message to the rest that the adolescent pecking order would be reinforced.

Michael Carneal thought that popular kids had special privileges in his school, and he resented the double standard, as he explained in this essay:

> Recently there was a petition going around concerning the expulsion of several students because they were in the possession of alcohol. . . . If I got caught with alcohol would the accused have a petition for me? I don't think they would. . . . [T]he year before last the school incorporated a "zero tolerance policy" meaning you would be expelled. A lot of people have gotten caught since then, and some were put on probation and some were expelled. . . . Normally the people caught are not as popular as they are in this case. So why bend the rules this time? If they do, they better bend the rules for me on down the road.

HIGH SCHOOL NOW AND FOREVER

How does the future appear to a marginalized young adolescent? Matt Stone, creator of the popular cartoon show *South Park* and a 1989 graduate of Columbine High School, appeared in Michael Moore's celebrated film *Bowling for Columbine,* where he offered a blunt account of the lessons he learned as a nonconformist oddball in the middle of Littleton. Stone noted how hard it was for outcasts to realize that high school is not forever, that the losers in adolescence often turn into the more interesting and respected adults while the football heroes sink into obscurity. "You just wish someone could have just have grabbed them and gone, 'Dude, high school is not the end of [life],'" Stone lamented.[19] Harris and Klebold thought it was.[20]

For students at Columbine, this may be more of a perception than a reality. Littleton is a growing suburb with many newcomers moving in and few lifelong residents. In Heath and Westside, where people really *are* rooted for generations, it is common for kids to finish high school with the same cast of characters they knew in kindergarten. Most young people from Heath and Westside ultimately settle down in the same community where they grew up, and some never move away at all. The main avenue of escape is to leave for college, but few pursue it. Even the kids who are bright and highly motivated tend to stay local. Courtney Walsh, a friend of Michael's, saw this inertia plainly. "So many kids will say that they hate Paducah and can't wait till they graduate so they can get out," she remarked, "and they'll end up going to [Paducah Community College]. Just for lack of trying to get into another school."[21] The McCracken County School District estimates that 60 percent of Heath students go to college, and students estimated that less than 5 percent would go to school out of state. Students in the junior college live at home while studying. Heath teachers said that it was rare for students to have a career and goals in mind at a young age or to have serious college ambitions. Most students seem to follow the crowd, and the normative pattern is to stay local, for college and afterward.[22]

Even as adolescents grow into adults, the small-town views, habits, and patterns don't change, and neither do most of the friendship groups. "This is a fairly provincial place . . . in a lot of ways," remarked Ron Kilgore, a Heath social studies teacher.

> We're West Kentucky and damn proud of it is sort of the attitude. A lot of the people, even a lot of the teachers—and I don't mean this critically, although I don't think it's terribly healthy—commute to college and they never leave their home. They never leave their community, and so the ideas . . . that they're exposed to in college are seen still as outsider notions. And there's sort of a safety net or safety screen pulled around.

When people remain in the community for work or school, their high school personas remain with them. Friends made at Heath or Westside High stay with them for life, and the past is hard to escape. Of course, there are countercurrents to this stability. As "smart" kids who might have been in an out-crowd in high school move on to more prestigious white-collar jobs, the pecking order can be inverted. But from the vantage point of a marginalized teen like Michael Carneal, it can appear that the loser tag will stick for life.

ON THE OUTSIDE LOOKING IN

Small-town environments work well for people who are accepted and can participate fully. But for an oddball nonconformist like Michael Carneal, the idea of growing old in Heath must have looked like a fate worse than death. Michael absolutely disdained much of what the town stood for. Consider his views on the quilting festival, an annual celebration that epitomized much of what older residents thought was best about the town. In an e-mail written shortly before he began his freshman year at the high school, Michael wrote:

> . . . Our town really SUCK.
>
> We have this big QUILT FESTIVAL . . . 50,000 old bags in snitty cars that drive . . . an amazing 20 miles an hour come to town for a week and we all go Downtown and freak out the old lady quilters. . . . I asked [one] for some spare change and she said she didn't have any but "good luck." I said "Good luck I've already got your wallet. . . . IT WAS COOL. Ok my point is that there is nothing here.

A point of pride among adults, the quilting festival seemed like an anachronism to a disaffected teen. Michael's band of choice is *Ween,* a group that released an album that parodied the country music that many locals enjoyed.

Michael detested what he saw as hypocrisy, particularly when it revolved around religion. He joined the Goth group in denouncing popular kids who publicly preached abstinence but had sex anyway, and downloaded on his computer a document that points to a series of inconsistencies in the Bible. In an essay ostensibly about gays in the military, Michael argued that one cannot follow the teachings of the Good Book one day and ignore them the next:

> And if your still using the Bible as an excuse than your pitiful. . . . These twins from school. . . are always interpreting the Bible. They say . . . it says that "men are the best" and "women should just stay home. . . .
>
> NO
>
> Some of the women are bungee jumping, record setting, T. V. staring and some are even running our government. . . . These people who interpret the Bible that way look at girls in there bathing suits and look at dirty maga-

zines. Nope. None of that if women had to stay home. So look at the big picture when you interpret the Bible and the consequences.

Michael's resentment at small-town strictures surfaced in his attraction to rebellion. He downloaded material that explicitly called for students to rise up and challenge the conformity imposed on them by the schools. "The School Stopper's Textbook: A Guide to Disruptive Revolutionary Tactics, revised edition for junior high/high school dissidents" offers 100 suggestions for disrupting the classroom and "trash[ing] your school." The text admonishes students to resist the conventional practices forced on them in schools on the grounds that they are being forced into rigid molds that stifle individuality. Ted Kaczynski, the Unabomber, wrote essays that resemble this piece; indeed, Michael may have taken some of his inspiration from Kaczynski, since his work was sitting on Michael's hard drive. Although it is impossible to know how seriously Michael took these writings, they seem at a minimum to capture his own response to small-town life.

Perhaps the most striking, and disturbing, indication of frustration and anger at a close-knit, idyllic community is displayed in "Fall of the Smurfs," the story mentioned briefly in chapter 2. In describing his hatred of the Smurfs, the narrator describes how their innocence, their naïve happiness, and their sanitized world (where even sex is illegal) disgusts him.

The parallels between the utopia of the Smurf community, where everyone is happy and innocent but very much the same, and a close-knit, homogeneous community such as Heath are striking.[23] Social capital works well for those who are included, but those dense social ties seem oppressive or hypocritical to boys like Michael who do not fit in neatly.[24] When the future looks as if it will be no different from the present, a boy like Michael, who feels depressed, unwelcome, and a complete misfit, may conclude there is no exit.

FAILING AT MANHOOD

Seeking status, performing for peers, finding an identity, and dealing with meddlesome adults—these are tasks that face all adolescents. But it is a gendered process too. The challenges play out differently for boys and girls. We will not engage in the fruitless debate over whether it is easier or harder for boys or girls.[25] The point here is simply that the process of finding a workable niche is distinctive along gender lines. All of the rampage shooters are boys. We argue that this is no accident, for in addition to failing at adolescence, they were—at least in their own eyes—failing at manhood.

Masculinity is central to what makes a popular boy the king of the mountain.[26] To be a man is to be physically dominant, competitive, powerful in the eyes of others. Real men exert control and never admit weakness. They act more and talk less. If this sounds like the Marlboro Man, it is because adolescent ideals of manliness are unoriginal. They derive from cultural projections found in film, video, magazines, and the back of comic books. In-your-face basketball players, ruthless Wall Street robber barons, and presidents who revel in being "doers" and not "talkers" all partake of and then reinforce this stereotype. Twenty years ago, action figures like Superman were muscled, but within the range of a normal man's physique. Over time, they have morphed into exaggerated body builders, with extremely thick necks, impossibly puffed out chests, narrow waists, bulging thighs. To the extent that these toys stand as idealized versions of the male body, it seems that something in the culture is pushing toward a vision of manhood that is just about as impossible to achieve as Barbie doll figures are for girls. Evidence that this pressure is having a negative effect on boys is piling up as study after study shows increased steroid use among boys as young as twelve.[27]

Of course, high school boys are not able to claim the mantle of the tycoon, and few of them look like Arnold Schwartzenegger. Their closest approximation focuses on the arena to which they do have access: sports. On the playing field, they live out myths of what men should be like that go back at least as far as the Greek and Roman gods. Girls also play a key role in intramale competition, by serving as trophies that validate a boy's sexual appeal.

Bullying is one violent way that boys try to demonstrate their masculinity. Smaller, physically ineffectual boys are often singled out as targets of bullying by older boys. The captain of the debate team at Heath told us how he had his head knocked into the lockers on one occasion, and was beaten up by a bigger kid on the bus on another. One (not small) freshman told us that for months he would dodge behind a teacher when he saw an older bully coming, to avoid receiving hard punches on the shoulder that "really physically hurt." Another senior told us that he witnessed a group of twelve older boys chase and tackle younger and smaller ones for fun. Students described bullying and harassment as an everyday occurrence in the hallways, in "flex time," and in the bathrooms and said that despite its prevalence, teachers were either unaware of it or unable to stop it.

Bullying makes it possible for more powerful students to call attention to their superiority on grounds that favor them. Scholarly students told us that bullying was often initiated by farm boys who had been held back at least one grade and often two and resented the brighter futures of the college-bound kids. Pushing others around was a means for these kids to draw attention to the ways that they were strong and others weak (literally).

In addition to physical bullying, teasing that degraded the victim's masculinity was also common. Bullying experts have suggested that in recent decades, as teachers have become more aware of the importance of cracking down on physical bullying, teasing with the explicit intention of lowering the victim's self-worth is on the rise, and it has even been given a name: shaming. While the purpose of physical bullying is to control the victim (in the classic case, such as to make him turn over his lunch money), the purpose of shaming is to make the victim feel worse about himself.[28]

There is probably no more powerful source of stigma for an adolescent boy than being labeled gay. The risk to a boy's reputation is immeasurable, and his place on the social ladder is utterly compromised if even a smidgeon of it sticks. Jim Jacobs, a Heath sophomore, has heard these rumblings in the hallway:

> I've heard so many people talking about people that are . . . gay. They call them names and . . . I have heard twice somebody threatened somebody just cause they're that way. And [being labeled gay] . . . would be the worst thing, because everybody would be against you. And some people are cool with it, you know, but most people in this school are not cool with that.

You said people actually threaten [gay students]?

> Yeah. . . . Right after school, outside by the buses there. And they were making fun of [one boy] and then they said they were going to, you know, "We're going to beat you up," for no reason. He wasn't even doing anything to them. He didn't even say anything. And he was like walking by and they said that.

How does being labeled gay compare with other stigmatized identities? We asked students which of the following it would be worst to be socially: gay, poor, not white, not religious, or overweight and unattractive. In Heath, almost uniformly they responded that it would be worst to be gay. In Westside, students were divided about whether it would be worse to be gay or black.[29] The racial tolerance message had penetrated the culture in Paducah, but a similar sentiment did not seem to apply to gays.[30]

Why is being gay such a stain on one's reputation? The most common response was that gays violated traditional standards of what it means to be masculine. Said one student, "Guys aren't supposed to act feminine and stuff like that. They are not supposed to be gay, I guess." Another girl, now one year out of high school, said that gay people were "dirty":

Like me and my boyfriend now we share a lot of those common thoughts about it. We just think it's gross. I mean, we still talk to the people, we still hang out with them. Not so much hang out with them but we talk to them at school and when we see them in public. And now I don't talk to them about it either.

The power of this epithet has grown so much that it now covers a much wider range of behavior than the purely sexual reference that it connoted in the past. The term "gay" is now used as a slang term for any form of social or athletic incompetence. Students routinely say to one another "that's gay" when they are talking about a wide array of mistakes or social failures. If someone fails to make the right move on a soccer field or drops a lunch tray in the cafeteria, the kid behind him is quite likely to say, "That's really gay." Why? One fifteen-year-old girl provided an explanation: "Boys have a fascination with not being gay. They want to be manly, and put each other down by saying 'that's gay.'" Thus for boys, the struggle for status is in large part competition for the rank of alpha male, and any kind of failure by another boy can be an opportunity to insult the other's masculinity and enhance one's own. It is a winner-take-all society, and any loss one boy can inflict on another opens up a new rung on the ladder that he might move into.

For Michael, who already had severe doubts about how well he was navigating these gender waters, being labeled gay, beginning with the "Rumor Has It" column and continuing because of the teasing that followed, was torture. He told the psychologists that this was a primary reason for his academic slide in the second part of eighth grade. Michael said boys would call him gay in part because he refused to be mean to girls. He added that he had always felt more comfortable around girls than boys because girls did not tease him, and because with girls he did not have to compete to demonstrate his masculinity. For a boy who already had an extremely fragile self-esteem, who had repeatedly been picked on and was unwilling or unable to fight back, being labeled "gay" or "pussy" explicitly underscored one key source of his social failure.

Andrew Golden's central experiences with status and power centered on his abilities as a wielder of weapons. As we have noted, starting at a young age, Andrew was fascinated and perhaps obsessed with guns and all they represented, beginning with when he posed for photographs as a little boy dressed in camouflage with a rifle. As a first-rate hunter, he had proved his ability to master nature with a weapon in his hand, and his experiences riding around the neighborhood with a knife strapped to his leg showed that he could similarly make other kids bow before him. Despite his small size, he was described as a menace, someone who cursed and yelled at other children, saying that if they came over to his yard he would shoot them with his BB gun. These sources of status translated poorly to school, where he was so invisible as almost to be forgotten. Not surprisingly, when he sought to rewrite the rules of the adolescent society on his terms, he did so with a gun in his hands.

Mitchell Johnson's social failures were caught up in his attempt to be masculine, although his problems were different. The influence of dominant ideals of masculinity on Mitchell's behavior is even more transparent than it was for Michael and Andrew: he was a tough guy wannabe. He liked lifting weights and, given a choice, would opt to play games that involved guns over other types of games. Mitchell was also a fan of gory and violent movies. While these are interests common to many boys (and some girls), he was particularly invested in living out the macho image of his fictional heroes in real life, as Westside teacher Emily Levitt recalled.

> [Mitchell] thought he was being bad. His image of himself was big and bad, because [his brother] Monte was just a teddy bear. One day, Mitchell, he said, "I feel sorry for [Monte]." "Why do you feel sorry for Monte? Everybody loves Monte." "Yes, but he's not very tough." [Mitchell's] idea of himself was he's got to be big and bad.

Mitchell's excessive concern with masculinity was likely intensified by having been a sexual assault victim earlier. His bravado, faux gang affiliation and his molestation of another child were simultaneously attempts to erase the deep shame of abuse, to assert a masculine identity, and to stave off future attack. To ensure his safety, Mitchell even found himself a protector, making quick friends with the biggest boy in his class. The extreme seriousness with which he took his relationships with girls, the need for a long-term commitment from them, and his inability to handle female rejection could also be interpreted as insecurities derived from past abuse.

Unfortunately, Mitchell could not persuade peers that he really was a hard guy. And if kids at Westside could see through these false claims, Mitchell was positively a laughingstock when he tried his stories of gang exploits in jail in the company of kids who knew the real article. An employee of the county jail where Mitchell was held for four months before his trial remembered his ludicrous performance:

> He tried to talk gang. He tried to flash gang signs. He would take his comb and try to carve gang signs on the paint, on the door, on the bunk, on the table . . .

He would tell the boys that . . . he was originally from Chicago. He was a gang member from such and such a group. These other boys would laugh at him because they *were* gang people. They would ask him [questions] and he wouldn't be able to answer them and that would embarrass him. And that would make him very angry. He did not want to be laughed at.

For Mitchell, image really was everything. One of Mitchell's female friends reported that he threatened to kill her the day before the shooting if she ever told anyone that his girlfriend had dumped him. He was more enraged by the possibility that others would find out that he had been rejected than he was about the end of the relationship. In a period of life where one's "rep" is central, Mitchell was consistently unsuccessful at getting others to believe the manly image that he was trying to project, a failure that helped provoke even more desperate actions.

CULTURAL SCRIPTS

How do socially marginal, psychologically distressed youths manage the cross-pressures they experience? We argue that adolescents have a limited repertoire of "cultural scripts" or "strategies of action" that they can draw on to resolve their social problems.[31]

Cultural scripts do not provide the ends toward which action should be oriented but rather the "tools" that people have at their disposal as they try to solve problems. Consider the television campaign in the late 1990s that advised kids to "squash it" when challenged to a fight. The campaign showed teens walking away from tense encounters by saying "squash it," and by using a hand signal, bringing the palm of a flat hand down onto a vertically clenched fist. These encounters were often combined with a voice-over from a celebrity validating the idea that walking away was the more difficult (and manly) thing to do. The goal here was not to change teen values: The campaign began from the assumption that most kids already wanted to avoid fighting but could not figure out how to get out of the situation when challenged in public arena. By introducing a new script— "squash it"—adults were hoping to give kids a new tool that they could use to extricate themselves without losing face.[32] Where school shootings are concerned, our task is to figure out what scripts the shooters have in their repertoire.

More specifically, we want to know what model of "problem solving" Michael, Andrew, and Mitchell employed to address the fact that they suffered from low social status, flawed social interaction, marginality with respect to social groups, and weak claims to a masculine identity. The moderate, even typical scripts they employed, did not do the trick. That breakdown pushed them in the direction of taking more radical steps, culminating in rampage shootings. They did not "snap" so much as build toward their crimes as the less violent options failed to produce the results they wanted.

The first strategy, which all three employed, was to try to change their social position through performance. Michael and Andrew played class clown. Michael was notorious for his antics (stink bombs, stomping on fish); teachers and students recalled that Andrew liked to imitate characters from *South Park* and *Beavis and Butthead*. It did not work. Playing the class clown might prevent a kid from being labeled a square, but it does nothing to ensure that he will no longer be ignored, or in Michael's case, to insulate him from being teased. While a skilled stand-up comedian can make headway with the in-crowd, an awkward, goofy kid is not going to get anywhere.

Michael also tried desperately to find an identity group that would be willing to take him. He floated between the academic achievers, the band, and the Goths, but he never got beyond the fringe of any of these groups. Mitchell, too, was trying to solve his social problems by trying to "act" his way into higher social status. Whether he was trying to get girls to wear his ring at a party or boasting about his latest gang exploits, Mitchell was always on stage. But because he overstepped, others delighted in skewering his performance. Mitchell would in turn respond with more of the same, which only made matters worse.

Another option might be to ask for adult help in reversing social marginality. Unfortunately, such a move runs headlong into two primary cultural scripts—one about how adolescents should behave and another about how men should act. The adolescent script, described in more detail in chapter 7, requires that teenagers display independence from adults in coping with disputes, failures, and pressures. The masculinity script follows suit, requiring that men solve their problems and avoid appearing weak by turning to others for help.[33]

Michael Carneal did occasionally confide in his mother, the person to whom he was closest, about the harassment he faced. But as he got older, he understood that running to mama is a sign of weakness. Instead, he would hit the steel drum in his backyard to let it out. Mitchell never talked to anyone about his sexual abuse. With the cultural script of masculinity firmly in hand, neither Mitchell nor Michael was able to lean on an adult about problems that were devastating to them.

Mitchell did manage to talk to at least one of his teachers about the fact that he had been bullied. But as we saw in chapter 4, adults are not always responsive to complaints about bullying, since they are inclined to think of it as a normal part of adolescence or something kids should just laugh off. Even if teachers had come to his aid, they would not have been able to solve his real problem: being perceived by other kids as a socially unsuccessful wannabe.

Another option available to Michael, Mitchell, and Andrew was simply to live with it. Millions of adolescents choose this path as a response to social marginality, teasing, and even bullying, convinced that there is nothing they can do to change the situation. Michael took this option for what felt like an eternity. Although he endured bullying from elementary school on, he laughed on the outside, even though he was distraught on the inside. Eventually this strategy became untenable. The teasing got worse, and so did his mental illness. He had to find an exit, a way to end the unrelenting social and psychological pressures. Mitchell was also locked in a downward spiral. Having been caught making sex-talk phone calls, his father was threatening to move him back to Minnesota, a very scary prospect. We know less about Andrew's mental state, but for at least two of the three shooters, simply "taking it" would not work any longer.

At this point, they had a number of more drastic options available to them, including running away or even suicide. Suicide is an idea that many school shooters entertain. Michael considered suicide a number of times during middle school and had thoughts of jumping off a building or slitting his wrists. In the months before the shooting he became, in Dr. O'Connor's words, "seriously suicidal," taking his father's handgun and contemplating killing himself for a week. Immediately after the shooting, he begged the leader of the prayer group to "Please, just kill me." A school official reported that Andrew had threatened to kill himself. A friend of Mitchell's reported to the police that Mitchell had also contemplated suicide.

But suicide is a weak way to die, one at odds with the script of masculinity. School shooters are looking for status-winning, manhood-enhancing departures. Rampage school violence can lead in this direction if desperate individuals enter a public space and threaten others in a way that leaves the police no choice but to shoot.[34] Such shooters prefer to be shot—suicide by cop—than simply to kill themselves, because it is in closer concordance with a machismo code. Bethel, Alaska, school shooter Evan Ramsey said that his original plan was to bring a gun to school "to scare the hell out of everybody and kill myself" but that ultimately he decided, after being egged on by friends, that he wanted to "go out with a bang."[35] The script of masculinity helps us understand why the boys, despite their suicidal tendencies, ultimately decided to turn their anger outward toward others.[36]

Another option the boys explored was to fantasize, by themselves and with like-minded others, about violent things they could do to change their status. Michael began to write elaborate fantasies, drawing in part on available cultural scripts in which boys like himself used weapons to take power over the hated preps. Even if it was only in a fantasy world, for once Michael wouldn't be the weakling who could never fight back but rather the man who caused others to quake in their boots.

Mitchell and Andrew were in much the same boat. Police concluded that the two had fantasized back and forth for months—on the bus and over the phone. In their minds, Andrew would no longer be the small boy "put upon" by bigger boys, and Mitchell would no longer be the one who talked big but could never back it up. In real life, however, their situation was unchanged, and for Mitchell it was getting worse—cut from the basketball team, dumped by his girlfriend. No amount of fantasizing could rearrange what he considered to be an unbearable reality.

The boys were seeking to establish themselves as people to be respected, not excluded, by showing that they were men capable of doing big things if they weren't listened to. Unlike adult assassins, who want to work in secret, Mitchell and Andrew told virtually everyone in sight, hoping to redefine themselves through their threats, which might have obviated the need for the shooting itself.[37] But they were unsuccessful—no one took what they said seriously.

Issuing threats creates intense pressures to follow through. Michael's example is a case in point. When that fateful Monday came, Michael had committed himself to making something big happen. Failing to follow through would have been the ultimate example of "wimping out." Although they weren't sure what he planned to do, several of his friends had gathered at the prayer circle in anticipation of something. When it appeared that he wasn't going to do anything, they went back to ignoring him, increasing his frustration. Perhaps one reason that peer involvement is so common in school shootings is that boys, in particular, escalate from inchoate threats to action in an effort to avoid the loss of face that would come with backing out. Police have speculated that such a dynamic was present between Andrew and Mitchell, with neither willing to be the one to back down from the big talk that they had concocted together. This was clearly the case in the shooting in Bethel, Alaska, where the shooter Evan Ramsey (who was also teased mercilessly about his nerd status by more popular boys) made his plans known and then wavered. Evan's friend James admonished him, "You can't go back, everybody would think you're nothing. Everybody would just have one more reason to mess with you."[38]

ALL THE SCHOOL'S A STAGE

Having exhausted their other options, the boys came up with a dramatic solution: the indiscriminate shooting of their classmates and teachers. This would solve their social problems in a way that the other strategies had not. No longer would they try to accommodate themselves by scraping and bowing before the lords of the adolescent society; instead they would show who was really in charge and stake their claim to a notorious reputation. The performance was a public one, and their prior threats guaranteed that no one would doubt who was responsible for these dramatic actions.

For Mitchell, who was always claiming more than he could actually back up, the shooting provided irrefutable proof that he was the man he always advertised himself to be. No longer would the popular group be able to reject him as someone not quite worthy of inclusion; now they would see that he should have been a "top dog" all along. At the same time, it provided a manly exit from his impending clash with his father. Finally, the shooting provided a highly public way of telling the world that this victim of sexual abuse could no longer be messed with; he would protect himself, violently if necessary.

The shooting was also a statement of Andrew's power; he would be invisible no longer. He would be respected and feared. The shooting allowed him to superimpose this image of himself onto a community that valued strengths that he did not have (size, athletic talent). Andrew was trying to forcibly rewrite the adolescent scorebook, to show that the boy with the best shot rules.[39]

For Michael, the shooting provided a way to invert the social hierarchy—to move himself at once from his position close to the bottom to the very top. He could now release all the pent-up anger from years of teasing and bullying in one public burst of aggression. In his mind, it refuted the claims that he was weak or gay and provided definitive evidence that he could be every bit the man to the kids who had thrown him into lockers. As Michael put it, "I thought maybe they would be scared and then no one would mess with Michael."

The seemingly random choice of targets also speaks to the boys' need to send a message rather than simply to exact revenge. Random firing has been the most distinctive aspect of rampage school shootings, and the most frightening. As former principal Bill Bond pointed out, if Michael had wanted to shoot the preps, he would have gone upstairs to where the preps hang out. But when Michael shot randomly into the prayer circle, and when Mitchell and Andrew fired at their fellow students from across a field, they were demonstrating their anger with an entire social system that had rejected them rather than trying to take out particular tormentors. For this purpose, any target would do just as well as any other, so long as the shootings occurred on a public stage for all to see.

Finally, it is no coincidence that the boys used the school as the outlet for their anger. Schools are both the location of their adolescent social failures and the center of community life, not just for students but for everyone in these small towns.

For Michael, seeking to reverse years of negative perceptions that had accumulated in his family, church, and community, what better place to do it than in the school, the one institution that links all these spheres? It is the only public stage with strong connections to the entire community, and by opening fire randomly at school, shooters issue a public expression about how they have been treated in their communities and about the way they want to be remembered.

CULTURAL SCRIPTS RECONSIDERED

Journalists and social critics have suggested that exposure to violent films, television, and videos is at the heart of rampage shootings in school. We believe that the media plays a role, but not quite the one that has been assigned to it. Why don't girls who are exposed to the same songs, movies, and videos commit these horrendous crimes? What is being glorified is not simply violence, but rather the role that violence plays in enhancing the status of men. As Jackson Katz, an expert on masculinity and gender violence, writes about school violence: "The issue is not just violence in the media but the construction of violent masculinity as a cultural norm."[40]

We can see how this played out in Michael's case. Michael had watched violent movies and played point-and-shoot video games since he was a child, and they clearly had made some impression on him. But Michael's fantasies were not just about senseless brutality—they were about carnage perpetrated by a powerless or oppressed male who boosts his status by blowing people up. And on this front, he drew his cues not only from movies but also from his local environment. Michael perceived that violent behavior was often condoned by adults—as when he was hit in the head by a bully and a teacher did not intervene—and that the bad-boy image was glorified by other students. When asked how he would be seen for going to jail, he said that "people who go to jail in our school have lots of friends, and all the kids say 'Wow!'"[41]

Cultural scripts also affected the design of the Westside shooting. Andrew was a hunter, and the way that the two boys set up the shooting was similar to the way one might organize a hunt. They dressed in camouflage clothing, exactly as Andrew did when he went hunting. Andrew's pulling the fire alarm can be likened to setting a trap and luring the prey into an open area. From across the field, their classmates and teachers seemed less like the human beings they went to school with than like quarry to be killed. The set-up was familiar and psychologically distant: killing as sport.

This script has spread. Michael, Mitchell, and Andrew came up with their own solutions to their problems of social marginality and psychological distress.

To do so, they selected from available but general cultural scripts and applied them to their particular situations in order to solve their problems. Since then, however, some school shooters—the copycats—adopted their script, rather than writing their own. Hence, we now have a new and deadly cultural script on our hands. It is a powerful explanation for the recent spike in these highly publicized shootings.

———

Adults often think back to adolescence as the worst period of their lives. Few of us would turn the clock back to those teen years. Unsure of their own social standing, adolescents relentlessly attack one another verbally and physically as part of a strategy to gain a foothold in the status hierarchy. The pressure is worst for those at the bottom who, like Michael, are socially awkward and least able to defend themselves. But it can also be debilitating for "wannabes" like Mitchell, who hover just outside the popular group and are repeatedly called out for their attempts to make a status jump beyond their bona fides. This adolescent social hierarchy is itself supported by both a broader set of cultural ideals that valorize money, athleticism, beauty, and gender conformity and by the tacit and explicit support of adults in their midst who reinforce the very same values.

Although we have focused here primarily on the social and cultural side of the story, the way those factors intersect with individual psychological vulnerability can help explain why rampage school shootings are so rare. Michael's mental illness and Mitchell's history of sexual abuse magnified the social failures that provided much of the motivation. As we will see in chapter 10, when we look across the broader universe of rampage school shootings, serious individual-level predisposing factors are almost always present.

When social marginalization and psychological vulnerability are added to a mix that includes weapons and scripts of violent masculinity, the result can be horrific. Kids who in the past might have just coped with their problems, attempted or committed suicide, or lashed out with their fists now have the rampage shooting pathway before them and the means to pursue it. No longer willing or able to try to accommodate themselves to their social betters, they act spectacularly. They claim the power and status their peers have denied them, a very appealing script for those who would love nothing more than to bring the adolescent world crashing down around their feet.

7

WHY KIDS DON'T TELL

ON THE MORNING OF WEDNESDAY, FEBRUARY 1, 1997, TWO DOZEN STUDENTS in the Bethel Regional School in Alaska gathered on the library landing overlooking the lobby. Apprehensive, but abuzz with anticipation, they awaited the appearance of sixteen-year-old Evan Ramsey. Evan had spent a busy Tuesday night on the phone, calling a number of them to announce "something big is gonna happen" and that he was planning "an evil day."[1] While his friends weren't completely sure what Evan had in mind, they had heard him say that he was going to bring a gun to school to shoot the principal.

Evan arrived at Bethel with a shotgun hidden in his baggy black jeans just before the opening bell of the day. Searching everywhere for Josh Palacios, another sixteen-year-old student and popular star of the basketball team, Evan finally found the young man and blasted him. Evan screamed at the terrified students in the lobby to get out of his way, as he began roaming the halls, firing randomly at the ceiling and rows of steel lockers. Pushing and shoving, students stumbled over one another in the rush to get out of the lobby and away from the gunfire. Meanwhile, Evan swaggered down the halls, firing now and then, injuring several students along the way.

He finally reached his destination: the office of the strict but well-liked principal of Bethel, Ron Edwards. Evan shot him at point blank range as Edwards emerged from his office, in full view of the students on the library balcony. Evan barricaded himself behind a door for a shoot-out with the police, who by this time had arrived on the scene. Twenty minutes after the rampage began, Evan held the shotgun to his own head and then put it down: he surrendered. Evan Ramsey was eventually convicted of two counts of first-degree murder and sentenced to 210 years in prison; he will be sixty-eight years old before he is eligible for parole.

Why was it that no one on that balcony came forward in advance? Adults working at Heath and Westside were similarly dumbfounded when they discovered that some of their students knew of threats from Mitchell, Andrew, and Michael in the weeks and months before the shootings. One Westside teacher held her shock in check for fear of disturbing her students even more than they already were:

> When I got into the gym [after the shooting], there were some boys [who] said they knew what happened. I said "What do you mean you knew what happened?" and I thought, "OK, how I react to this is going to determine whether these kids feel guilty the rest of their lives or not." 'Cause I wanted to just grab them and say, "Why didn't you tell somebody?" but I thought, "They can't help it."

Michael issued at least a dozen threats (see Table 7.1)—comments such as "something big is going to happen on Monday" or that Monday was the "day of reckoning." He went as far as to tell some of the kids he liked to stay away from the prayer circle on Monday. No fewer than twelve students gave the police first-hand accounts of threats made by Mitchell Johnson (see Table 7.2); dozens of others heard the warnings secondhand. Mitchell told several students that "someone is going to die" or that "he was going on a shooting spree." Other students had heard that he had made a hit list that included all of his ex-girlfriends. Nine weeks before the shooting, Andrew informed one girl that he was planning to pull the fire alarm, go out in a field and shoot at his classmates, although he later told her he was not going to go through with it.

Westside and Heath were not unusual in the frequency or character of these broadcasts. A Secret Service report examining thirty-seven school shootings between 1974 and 2000 found that at least one friend was told before the fact in 81 percent of the cases. More than one friend was warned in 59 percent of the cases.[2] Other researchers have corroborated the Secret Service findings. A media analysis of nine school shootings between February 1996 and May 1999 found that in every case, the perpetrator had let people know what he was planning beforehand.[3]

Why didn't kids tell adults what they heard?[4] In this chapter we let the kids in Westside and Heath answer that question, drawing on our own interviews as well as police interrogations and civil suit depositions.[5] Our goal is not to appor-

Table 7.1: What Michael Carneal Told Other Students Before the December 1, 1997, Shooting

Where?	When?	Who Heard It?	What? (as told by the friend who heard it)
Cafeteria	November 26*	Group of three or four around the lunch table	"Something big is going to happen on Monday." Some heard it would be at the prayer group.
Cafeteria	November 26	Twelfth grade boy	"Something big is going to happen on Monday." When pushed, Michael said it would involve "blood and guts," prompting both boys to start laughing.
Cafeteria	November 26	Twelfth grade boy	"Something big is going to happen on Monday." Warned not to be at the prayer group.
English class	November 26	Two ninth grade boys and a ninth grade girl	Monday was going to be the "day of reckoning"; he was going to bring a gun and go off. Were also warned not to be at the prayer group. One of the boys, Hollan Holm, was shot but survived.
Unknown	November 26	Tenth grade boy	"Michael said, 'We should go into the principal's office and shoot them while they are in their offices,' and I said, 'Yeah' but I didn't think anything of it."
Friend's birthday party	November 22	Tenth grade boy	Michael said it would be "cool to walk down the hall and kill people." Also had seen Michael with a gun at school on several occasions.
Unknown	Months before the shooting	Ninth grade girl	Heard Michael fantasize about taking over the school. Had seen Michael bring a gun to school around Halloween.

* The shooting happened on the Monday after the Thanksgiving break. Wednesday, November 26, was the last school day before the shooting.

Source: Police reports and our interviews.

Notes: Each item represents a different student (or students) who heard a threat. This list is limited to students who heard about it firsthand from Michael. Numerous other students claimed to have heard about it secondhand before the shooting. Other students had also seen Michael bring a gun to school, but had not heard a threat, as best as anyone was able to determine.

Table 7.2: What Mitchell Johnson and Andrew Golden Told Other Students Before the March 24, 1998, Shooting

Who Said It?	Where?	When?	Who Heard It?	What? (as told by the friend who heard it)
Mitchell	Cafeteria	March 23	Seventh grade boy	"Some people are gonna die" and then we both started laughing."
Mitchell	Bus	March 23	Seventh grade boy	"He said he was gonna kill a lot of people."
Mitchell	Bus	March 23	Middle school girl	Mitchell "was going to kill some people tomorrow."
Mitchell	Hallway	March 23	Seventh grade boy	"He was telling a lot of people that he's gonna kill someone. "All my girlfriends who ever broke up with me, I am gonna kill them." "He was tired of the school, pretty much."
Mitchell	Seventh grade wing	March 23	Seventh grade girl	"I was out in the seventh grade wing, and I heard Mitchell saying that he was going to 'cut school tomorrow, and bring a gun to school, and we'd find out if we'd live or die.' We didn't believe him because he'd said things like that before."
Mitchell	Unknown	March 23	Seventh grade girl	"If she ever told anyone that him and his girlfriend had broken up that he would kill her." Said when she heard about the shooting she "knew it was him before it was announced."
Mitchell	Unknown	March 23	Middle school girl	Mitchell asked her if she was going to live or die. Girl asked him what he was talking about, and he said that if she went outside the next day during fifth period, she would die.
Andrew and Mitchell	Hallway, just before school let out	March 23	Two seventh grade girls	Approached by both Mitchell and Andrew. Mitchell said he wanted to give one a note today because he wouldn't be here tomorrow. She asked why not, he said, "because something big is going to happen," and "you'll find out tomorrow." He liked her, but she didn't see him as a boyfriend—too into that "gangs stuff".

(continues on next page)

Table 7.2 *(continued from previous page)*

Who Said It?	Where?	When?	Who Heard It?	What? (as told by the friend who heard it)
Mitchell	Bus	March 23	Middle school girl	Mitchell said this was his last day of school
Mitchell	At Mitchell's house	Sunday, March 22	Monte (Mitchell's fifth grade brother) and Monte's friend	Friend of Mitchell's brother overheard him say to his brother (from the next room) that "he was going on a killing spree." Also heard him discussing plans on the phone.
Mitchell	Cafeteria	Twice in two weeks before shooting	Middle school boy	"People were going to die."
Andrew	Cafeteria	Unknown	Middle school boy (reported by father)	Stood on table and said, "You're all going to die."
Andrew	Unknown	9 weeks before the shooting	Sixth grade girl	Andrew said that he and Mitchell were going to pull the fire alarm, go to the field and shoot people. Two days later, Andrew said that he was not going to do it because he did not want to ruin the friendship between himself and the person he was telling.
Mitchell	Unknown	Earlier in the year	Seventh grade boy	Was going to "get back at some people from last year" and "kill them and stuff." I didn't believe him. "If we get caught, someone else will finish the job."
Mitchell	Hallway	Sometime before Christmas break	Seventh grade boy	He and Andrew were going on a killing spree. Also threatened, "If I am caught, someone else will come back and finish the job."

Source: Police reports and our interviews.

Notes: Each item represents a different student who heard a threat. This list is limited to students who heard about it firsthand from Mitchell or Andrew. Numerous other students claimed to have heard about it secondhand before the shooting.

tion blame or intensify the guilt they already feel; indeed, each individual youth appears less blameworthy as it becomes clear that telling is the exception and not the rule. Rather, we seek to answer questions that are critical for averting future attacks: What "rules" do kids employ when deciding whether to report a threat? What role do peer norms against "ratting" out one another play in this process? What makes some threats seem more serious than others? How do adults unintentionally contribute to kids' reluctance to come forward? And finally, are kids any more likely to come forward now that they have seen what can happen when they don't?

KID STUFF, VIOLENT LANGUAGE, AND THE PRESUMPTION OF INNOCENCE

Most of the kids who "knew" did not take the warnings from Mitchell Johnson and Andrew Golden seriously. Much of what they'd heard had come from the rumor mill, was vague, or appeared to be so "over the top" as swagger and bravado that they dismissed the prospect that Mitchell—the more talkative of the two— was actually planning to gun down his classmates. Stacey Hunt didn't give Mitchell's comments much credence:

> [Mitchell] said something about it, like joking around, but . . . nobody takes him serious, like that's going to happen.

Had you heard anything about it beforehand?

> About the shooting? Yeah. He'd like talked about that he had this list or something planned out that everybody was going to pay. But he didn't say that he was going to go and pull the fire alarm, get everybody outside and shoot them, you know? . . . He was going around bragging like any other kid would when they were mad.

Samantha Deacon, who had sung with Mitchell in the school choir, remembered a vaguely troubling conversation along similar lines, which she, too, had dismissed:

> Mitch stopped me at choir practice . . . and he told me, "You won't be seeing me for awhile because I'm going to be running from the cops." And I'm thinking, "What do you mean by that?" I said, "Well, what are you talking about? You're not going to be running from the cops." He said, "Yeah." . . .

[Mitch] said something once [before that about how] he was going to run away. I don't remember it word for word, but you know, I believed that was what he was [talking about so]. . . . I just kind of blew it off.

The very commonality of these threats is a big part of the problem. School shootings remain extremely rare events, surrounded by a great deal of threatening chatter. A 1999 *Washington Post* poll showed that about a third (32 percent) of students had heard someone threaten to kill someone in their school—the majority of those said they heard the threat more than once.[6] A 2001 *USA Today* poll showed that 52 percent of high school students had heard a weapons-related threat.[7]

Making outrageous claims to get attention is such a common habit among adolescents that the warnings issued by the shooters did not stand above the daily din. Luke Fallon, a senior headed to seminary school and a friend of Michael's, ignored the boy's warnings for exactly this reason. "Any . . . reason why you didn't contact authorities?" the civil attorneys for the victim families asked Luke. "To be honest with you, sir," he replied, "when somebody said they were going to do anything, for the most part, they were probably lying, or just trying to get attention."

Michael had long been known as a jokester who would do anything for attention. The "frame" students had in place for Michael made it hard to separate a serious threat from an inane stunt. Michael told Luke specifically to stay away from the prayer group because "something big was going to happen on Monday." It is a measure of how little credence Luke gave these statements that he stood in the lobby leading the prayer group on the morning of the rampage.

Luke was not alone in dismissing Michael's warnings. Hollan Holm had heard Michael say the same kinds of things, ignored him, and with his head bowed in prayer, suffered a gunshot wound (though not fatal). After David Maxwell, a member of the Goth group, heard Michael warn his friends in the cafeteria, he pressed Michael for details so that he could be in on the joke. During his police deposition, Maxwell explained how he tried to find out more:

I kept asking him, . . . "Well, what does it involve?" And he was, like, "Don't worry about it. . . . You'll see Monday." I was, like, "Does it involve violence? Does it involve, you know, killing people? Does it involve blood and guts?" you know, laugh, jokingly. And he said, "Yeah." Shrug your shoulders, kind of laugh, you know, jokingly about it. And I was, like, okay, whatever.

These threats won Michael a measure of respect from David, an older boy, but in the "whatever" world of adolescence, "blood and guts" are the subject of jokes, not cause for alarm.

Everyday language, especially among teens, is laced with violent talk which makes it even harder to sort out a threat from a casual line. "'I'm gonna kill you' doesn't always have the same meaning in our language," noted Bill Bond, the principal at Heath at the time of the shooting. "In sports, 'we killed them' . . . 'we beat them.' We didn't really *beat* them. We just won the game."

Violent imagery is hardly limited to sports. Everyday conversation among teenagers would be barely recognizable without it.[8] Mrs. Holden, who had been teaching in Westside for almost twenty years at the time of the shooting, described the constant references to violence she hears in the hallways every day:

> I'm teaching eleventh-graders . . . right now, and one of the girls, she did terrible on one of the practice [tests] that we did, and she said, "Oh, Mrs. Holden, just shoot me!" and I thought, "Oh, don't say that!" And she said, "Oh, I'm sorry!" and she felt horrible about it. . . . It's just part of our vocabulary that we don't think about. After you've been shot, . . . then you hear things that you didn't hear before.

Given the frequency with which language of this kind is bandied about, it is hardly surprising that hearing it one more time does not cause anyone to sit up and take notice. When a Westside seventh grader and his buddy heard Mitchell say, a day before the shooting, that "some people are gonna die" by their own accounts, the boys "both started laughing." Cory Giles explained to the police why he was unfazed by a similar remark coming from Michael:

> GILES: Michael told me [about ten days before the shooting] that he thought it would be cool to walk down the hall shooting people. Just to walk down and just like shoot people like that. . . .
> POLICE: Did you ask him anything about it? If he was serious? Or did he act like he was serious?
> GILES: No. I don't believe he was serious, because, like, you know, when you say you want to kill people, like when you're really mad at your sister or something—like, "I want to kill her"—but you never really do. So I didn't take him seriously.

Adults and students in both communities reported that even after the shooting, "I'll kill you" was still common parlance, although it gave them a bit more pause than it had before.

Students who heard more specific threats did not dismiss them as easily, but dismiss them they did, and for similar reasons. These students were usually closer friends of the shooter and thus had access to more specific information, but they were also likely to conclude, on the basis of past experience, that it was bluster. Courtney Walsh, a ninth grader and a family friend of Michael's, had heard Michael threaten to do something at the prayer group that Monday. He had said that Monday was the "day of reckoning" and that she should avoid the prayer group.

POLICE: What did Michael tell you?

WALSH: . . . He didn't say it to me directly, but we were in our second hour English class [the Wednesday before the shooting]. Michael was just talking. . . . He was saying how . . . Monday, he was just going to bring a gun and go off. But, of course, we thought he was all joke. . . . I'm like, "Yeah, shut up, Michael." 'Cause he couldn't have been seriously . . . talking about it [where] anyone can hear him. He has a loud voice. . . . After a while, he just stopped talking about it and we didn't really think anything about it at the time.

Yet when Courtney called Michael the night before the shooting to ask him to bring her favorite scrunchie to school the next day, his comments in English class stuck in her mind. When she arrived at school, a little late that fateful morning, students were running out in a panic as she was trying to make her way in. Courtney heard an acquaintance say a student had been shot, and she immediately realized that her worst fears had come to pass.

Courtney wrote a letter to Nicole Hadley the day after Nicole died. The letter makes it clear that Courtney was given just enough information before the fact that she was overwhelmed with guilt afterward. At the same time, she was not told enough to convince her that this boast was any more real than those Michael had made in the past. As she put it in a handwritten statement the morning of the shooting: "I didn't take him seriously, because he has been known to say things like that, but has never followed through."

Chris Jackson, a seventh grader at Westside and one of Mitchell's best friends, also heard a specific threat, but convinced himself that Mitchell was not serious, although he suspected enough to have serious misgivings after the fact:

Michael had this death list he wrote out of who he wanted to kill. That's where like messing around with me and stuff, made me mad. Some of the teachers were on it, some of the students, all the [principals] were listed, all this stuff. . . . I knew he was insane, but I didn't think he'd do it.

Chris saw the "death list" and heard Mitchell make threats against teachers, students, and administrators but surmised that Mitchell was "on stage" as he so often was, performing the character of the tough guy, flashing signs, or talking of past gang exploits. Chris concluded that Mitchell was bluffing, but when he heard shortly after the shooting that Mitchell was one of the shooters, he blamed himself for not going forward with what he "knew."

Most of the students on that balcony in Bethel were in a similar position, and they seem to have dismissed Evan Ramsey's warnings for the same reason. "People knew about it, but they didn't think [Evan] was going to go through with it," said one Bethel student.[9] "He was always saying things like, 'I'm going to bring a gun to school. You'll see who's better then,'" said another classmate.[10] When students heard Evan say he was going to "do something big," they showed up on the balcony to watch the show. Yet, given past experience with Evan's false boasts, they weren't at all convinced that anything serious would happen.

Students were also inclined not to believe the threats because nothing like that had ever happened before. Since the whole idea of a school shooting was not part of their reality, there was insufficient "evidence" to consider reporting a fellow student.

> If I ever seen a guy bring a gun to school . . . I would look at him and be like, "You are a dumb butt." . . . And I probably wouldn't do nothing. . . . If you go to school and [a shooting has] never happened there before, no, you're not going to think something like that's going to happen. . . . When it happens, it's a shock.
>
> —Brenda Dilworth, Heath student

When the frame shifts, what was previously unthinkable becomes reality, and students' behavior shifts accordingly.

THE ADOLESCENT CODE

The strictures of the adolescent code further ensured that no one would come forward to report what they heard from the shooters. Being overly compliant with adults' wishes is hardly cool. Living up to these expectations requires shaping one's values in contradistinction to those demanded by adults, and at least to appear to be defiant in the face of their authority. In a study by Joyce Canaan of cliques in suburban middle-class schools very much like Heath and Westside, a student explained what the "rules to live by" require of a teenager:

> Don't say you like school. Don't . . . get good grades. Don't brag about your good grades. Don't punch people out. You gotta ridicule people that are supposed to be "fags." Don't be quiet and be crazy.[11]

Elliot Anthony, a Heath senior, echoed the same sentiment, reflecting on his eighth grade view of adults:

> At that age, the adults were enemies. . . . The adults didn't know anything. They were the Gestapo waiting to bust you. They weren't friends, and they certainly didn't know more than you did. All they were going to do is get onto your case and not be able to help you.

Students who are too much in league with adults, including those who overperform academically, are in a similar position to scabs in a firm or plant—they have mistakenly cast their lot with management as opposed to with workers—and as such are subject to severe sanctions.[12] Peer pressure drives achievers underground. They do well quietly, or they clown around on occasion, so as not to violate the social expectations their friends impose to resist adult authority. Even when both teachers and parents have basically good relationships with kids, as was true in both Westside and Heath, maintaining good standing within a peer group requires obeisance—at least on the surface—to the adolescent code.

In a climate where students are supposed to dislike school, threats that involve taking power over adults are, at least according to some students, commonplace. Here the police ask Vicky Whitman, Michael's former girlfriend, about her reactions to his threats:

CIVIL ATTORNEY: Did you ever hear Michael talk about taking over the school?

WHITMAN: Yeah. Not as in seriously. A lot of kids talk about taking over the school.

CIVIL ATTORNEY: Do they?

WHITMAN: No one likes school, so.

CIVIL ATTORNEY: Okay. Nobody liked it at Heath, so a lot of kids were talking about taking over the school?

WHITMAN: Every school I've been to, someone would mention we should burn down the school. It's not strange for someone to not like school.

Bill Janson, a sophomore and friend of Michael's, came under considerable heat from police because he admitted to taking part in some similar fantasizing with Michael.

JANSON: Wednesday morning, . . . Mike was talking about . . . how he disliked Mr. Bond or hated him and . . . I was like, yeah, uh, I hope he gets in a car wreck or something. . . . And then he was like, we should . . . shoot 'em while they're in their offices, and . . . I was like, yeah, yeah, but I mean I didn't think anything of it.

POLICE: Why was he gonna do this to Mr. Bond? . . . Was there a problem between them or something or just . . . ?

JANSON: Not really, I mean just, you know, he's the principal—you don't really like your principal.

Michael had had a run-in with Bond when he was caught picking at the wall with a screwdriver, but his animus was directed more toward authority in general than toward any particular individual. Bill Janson was open to this logic—he too said it would be cool if the principal died a painful death. At the same time, the very familiarity of this fantasy made it obvious that Michael couldn't be serious.

Neither Heath High School nor Westside Middle School is riddled with students who harbor murderous thoughts and abiding hatred for their teachers or principals. The natural course of adolescent rebellion is likely to lead to some degree of antagonism toward authority figures, although it is generally mild. But the drama of youth culture encourages more extreme talk. We do not believe that Bill Janson really wanted to see Principal Bond die. Rather, we believe that Bill, Michael, and dozens of others wanted to appear cool to one another and thought that violent imagery would help them strike the pose.[13]

For students who are deeply immersed in the adolescent code, even the idea of coming forth is inconceivable. Michael's friend Cory Giles identifies himself (and Michael) with the most juvenile part of this code: "[Michael] was just this goofy kid that just did really silly stuff. And I liked that, because I'm a silly guy myself. And it's like, you know, you see somebody, and you're like, wow, he's cool. So you talk to him and you get to know him." For students like Cory who have so completely adopted the adolescent outlook, there is no ambivalence about telling—it's out of the question.

POLICE: Did you ever tell anybody in charge that you had seen him at school with a gun on several occasions?

GILES: No.

POLICE: Why not?

GILES: The thought never crossed my mind.

POLICE: Why?

GILES: I just don't know. I mean, it just never occurred to me that I should tell on him.

POLICE: Because why?

GILES: I don't have a reason why, because I didn't think of a reason to tell on him, so I didn't think of a reason not to tell on him.

Students who are not as invested in defiance still want to avoid being tagged as tattletales. Even Luke Fallon, the prayer group leader who was widely respected by both students and adults, failed to come forward in part because he didn't want to be stigmatized.

CIVIL ATTORNEY: Any other reason why you didn't call authorities?

FALLON: No, sir. . . . If you did tell something on somebody, usually you'd cause more trouble than what it's worth. Because, usually, they didn't do it. And then you ended up just looking kind of weird, or whatever.

CIVIL ATTORNEY: Like a rat?

FALLON: Yeah, for the most part.

The price kids pay for coming forward can be high.[14] Much as union members ostracize scabs, kids have a variety of social and even physical sanctions that they apply to those who break rank. We interviewed one Heath student who was quite familiar with the price the code-breakers pay for ratting on their peers. "There's a kid in my class," he told us, "and he always tattles on everybody. . . . If you do the slightest thing wrong, he's going to tell on you. He just does it to annoy people." How do people treat this kid? we asked.

Oh, he's been beaten up like twice this year already. . . . Not really beaten up like really bad. One time, outside the bus, [the tattletale] said something to [an acquaintance who] turned around and just popped him. And it was really funny because everybody [was] standing around saying, "Yeah," because nobody likes him. He had a black eye but he didn't really get any broken bones or, I mean, he's never bled, I don't think.

The desire to avoid betraying a friend also contributes to teenage reticence. Whether the issue is about reporting friends for making threats or cheating on a test, students are hesitant to break the code when it would almost surely cost them a friend. Brendan Hayes is a thirteen-year-old who lives in Bono. We visited with him at his mother's office, where he could sit in her oversized swivel chair. The conversation made Brendan nervous, and he swung back and forth in the chair, now putting his feet up on the desk, now crossing his legs. It seems nobody likes talking about the rules for telling on a friend.

What if you saw another student cheating on a test, would you go tell?
BRENDAN: Oh, yeah.
Yeah? How do you decide what's appropriate to tell an adult and when it's not appropriate to tell?
BRENDAN: By the way everybody reacts to it. . . . If somebody's cheating on a test, and they say, "Don't tell. Don't tell."
What does that tell you?
BRENDAN: That tells me that if I don't tell on them, they're going to be happy. And if I do tell the teacher, that they're going to be mad at me.
So what would you do?
BRENDAN: Well, if it was my friend, I wouldn't tell. If it wasn't my friend, I would.
What would happen to you if you told? Let's say it's your friend, what if you tell on your friend, what would happen, do you think?
BRENDAN: He'd ask me why I told on him and probably wouldn't talk to me.

The adolescent code is to beat the system, not to rat out one's compatriots. Being known as a tattletale might be an undesirable but acceptable social consequence, but losing a friendship is clearly not worth it. And when the information in question is riddled with ambiguity, hard to interpret, and quite fantastic, the basis for this difficult calculation becomes even weaker. Why risk something of value—a friendship—with such uncertainty in the air?

Cheating on a test is not on par with threats of murder, but the calculations students employ in thinking about telling are very similar. Indeed, kids seem to apply the logic from moral quandaries like cheating—which they witness fairly often—to the more infrequent question of whether or not to report a threat. Christine Olson, an eighteen-year-old senior and choir member at Westside High, said that the desire not to betray a friend would be a paramount consideration in deciding whether or not she would report a threat:

Is there anything that you feel like you couldn't talk to an adult . . . or did you feel comfortable talking to them about everything?

CHRISTINE: If I heard someone had a gun or a weapon . . . at school, if it was someone that was really close to me and I would have this fear of losing them as a friend. But if I felt that it was serious enough, well, I'm sure I would say something, especially now.

At Heath, students followed Christine's logic almost exactly, with tragic results. For example, Craig Holt had done some target shooting with Michael Carneal outside of school, and he had seen Michael bring a gun to school on a previous occasion. Even with this background knowledge, Holt did not come forward.

CIVIL ATTORNEY: What is that rule [about bringing guns to school]?

HOLT: That if you bring in weapons, I think you can be suspended or expelled.

CIVIL ATTORNEY: Okay. And you knew that at the time that Carneal had the pistol there, didn't you?

HOLT: Yes.

CIVIL ATTORNEY: Then why didn't you do anything about reporting it?

HOLT: Well, he was a friend of mine. I didn't really want to get him in trouble.

If reporting to adults means getting a friend in trouble or being labeled a rat, many adolescents simply will not take the risk, especially when they can't imagine that their peers will follow through with an outlandish threat.

The flypaper effect, where reputations stick, is responsible for student reluctance to confide in adults when they do observe worrying behavior in their peers. Being pegged a tattletale is serious baggage at an age when loyalty can be paramount. Hence, young people are reluctant to tell adults compromising information unless they are very sure of its meaning. The warnings shooters make public are typically ambiguous enough to leave others unsure of their intentions. No one wants to risk their own good name if they cannot be certain that the threat is serious.

NEW FRAMES OR OLD?

Since the shootings, students have reconsidered the wisdom of their reticence about reporting threats. Those who failed to come forward the first time live with tremendous guilt. Some of their best friends died and they see themselves as to blame. At the same time, students at these schools still think that "I'm gonna kill you" is more likely to be a joke than a threat, and the prohibitions of ratting out one's peers are unchanged. Students try to navigate these competing imperatives by assessing the seriousness of a threat. The adolescent code, it seems, makes an exception for serious threats, but not for jokes. Here Mellody Wilkins, a Westside ninth grader who was a fifth grade student in the middle school when the shooting happened, explains how her peers would see the revelation of a serious threat:

Do you think most kids would tell if [someone made a threat]?
MELLODY: If the person was really, really serious, if "I'm really going to hurt you." But usually some people just kid around and say, "If you say that again I'm going to smack you," but they just barely touch you. . . . If [I ever heard a serious threat], I'd probably tell a teacher. He would get detention because it's a threat and everything.

Would that be considered ratting if it was a serious threat?
MELLODY: Everyone would respect you for it because you could have got hurt.

The difficulty, of course, is how to tell a serious threat from a joke. Even *after* the shootings, in the very same communities where memorials serve as reminders of the consequences of not telling, well-intentioned students still say they would try to distinguish between threats that were serious and those that were not. And despite the life-and-death consequences attached to making the right judgment, the criteria they lean on is maddeningly vague. We asked Mellody how she could tell the difference:

MELLODY: I don't really know. If I know that they know how to use a gun or something, and they say that they are going to hurt somebody, and they look really, really serious, then I probably would tell.
Has that ever happened, where you had to tell someone?
MELLODY: No.
Have there been people who have said threats but you thought they weren't serious?
MELLODY: Yes. They say, "I'm going to hurt you," but they never do.

Mellody wants to do the right thing. She doesn't want anyone to get hurt, and she is not averse to telling an adult if needed, even if that means ratting out a close friend. But she will only go forward if the threat is a serious one, which she judges on the basis of clues that lack a great deal of specificity. Or at least that's how she thinks she would decide. On the occasions when she has confronted such a situation, she has refrained from coming forward because she has never heard a threat she thought was serious. Each empty threat reinforces the sense that the next one should be ignored.[15] The vicious circle breaks down only after a great deal of damage has been done, and sometimes not even then.

Students' efforts to distinguish between serious and nonserious threats also flounder because they are based on inaccurate assumptions about who is likely to carry through a threat. Consider the responses of Christine Olson and Gillian Moyer, both Westside seniors:

How can you tell when something's, when a threat is serious or not?
CHRISTINE: You know, those boys have never caused any trouble before, and . . . they come from okay homes, and it's not like you would classify [them] as . . . a problem child. So I don't know how you would tell if [a threat] was serious or not. It would just kind of depend on who it was. You know the ones that joke or just talk. But . . . if something was said . . . about a few certain people that they had a gun and they were going to bring it to school . . . Wouldn't you know that they have guns because they're the big hunters and everything? That would probably be hard to tell on something like that.

How do you determine whether the threat is serious or it's not so serious?
GILLIAN: Well, I think it depends on the situation and also how they say it. If they're just aggravated at someone and they just say it without even thinking, I wouldn't think anything about that. But if it had been like that loner and like the day he got so mad and that had been building around that, I might do something about that.

Christine assumes that "fake threats" come from kids who are known to joke or talk big, but both Michael and Mitchell were known for their talk. She would be inclined to disregard talk coming from boys who have no disciplinary history, but none of our shooters had been in serious disciplinary trouble. Gillian says she might "do something" if the student was a loner, but Michael, Mitchell, and Andrew had friends and wouldn't be described as loners by anyone. In short, like the adults in their community—and across the nation—students work from stereotypes about what school shooters must be like. They are wide of the mark.

This is exactly what happened in Michael's case. Students said they did not take his threats seriously because he was known as a jokester and had never shown any signs of violence. "[Michael] told us that he was going to do something that day," one female friend recalled, "but he [was] one of those people that was just kind of little and you just want to give him a hug because he's so funny and nice. Didn't seem like somebody that could possibly do something like that."

If students have misperceptions about *who* is likely to be issuing serious threats, their conception of what a "serious" threat looks like also differs in *type* from the kind that actually circulate. Because school shooters are seeking the admiration of others, they tend to make broad or even indiscriminate pronouncements intended to win them attention, fear, and respect. The shootings rarely target those with whom they have had specific disagreements, and targets often are random, signaling a generalized anger at the institution or the pecking order. Yet when students think about serious threats, they have in mind comments directed at specific opponents who are on the wrong side of a grudge. Bill Janson, the boy who fantasized about the principal dying in a car wreck, tries to describe the difference to an unfriendly lawyer during his deposition:

CIVIL ATTORNEY: You considered a statement that Michael Carneal wanted to go in and shoot school personnel an idle statement?

JANSON: Sure. People, all over the place, say random things like that not meaning anything by them . . . like, "I really hate this" . . . and they don't mean anything by it. And people don't take them seriously.

CIVIL ATTORNEY: And so, people, according to you, don't take threats to murder like this seriously?

JANSON: It wasn't a threat to murder, though.

CIVIL ATTORNEY: All right. What would you call it?

JANSON: I don't know what I'd call it. I think if you go up to someone and say I'm going to kill you, that's a threat to murder. Talking about something like this is not a threat to murder, I don't think.

Tragically, dismissing the shooters' threats is often interpreted by the shooter as a challenge or a form of disrespect, either of which can propel an insecure student beyond the fantasy stage. It is possible that Michael Carneal would not have gone through with the rampage in the Heath lobby had his display of guns had the desired impact: the immediate adulation of the Goths. It was, at least in part, their dismissive attitude that persuaded Michael that he had to be bolder to get what he wanted. He interpreted their lack of interest as an insult or a dare, and it could not go unanswered.

Students privy to threats represent the most promising prospect for heading off school shootings. Yet the decision-making rules they employ may vitiate the potential. Even *after* the shootings in Westside and Heath, students in both communities filter what they hear through criteria that would probably classify the kinds of threats issued by Michael, Mitchell, and Andrew as "just talk." We visited with Mrs. Holden, a Westside teacher, in her home in Jonesboro. The aroma of homemade blueberry muffins wafted out of the kitchen as she sat down to talk about how the kids she teaches think about threats. Mrs. Holden despaired of being able to change this filtering practice.

> Everybody thought that Mitchell was not-so-serious. . . . If some person's talking about it over and over, I believe now that they're asking for help. I believe he was. And I hope we can pick up on it because the kids thought he was just joking. . . .

For a variety of reasons, students have trouble screening what they hear and figuring out what kinds of threats warrant telling. Adults might do better. Mrs. Holden:

> Maybe that's what we need to be trying to find out, how to determine if a threat is serious. Kids, sixth graders, they don't have the capability . . . that adults have of knowing what's a serious threat and what's not. . . . I don't think they have the capability of understanding.

Of course, whether adults would really be any better at making these distinctions is far from certain. The vast majority of "threats" *are* just kids' talk, and it would take an adult of some sensitivity to be able to pick up when a threat might not be a hollow one. We will discuss in chapter 11 how some experts have suggested this can be done. But our research made it clear that teachers and school personnel *want* to be the ones trying to make these distinctions; they want the matter out of students' hands.

HOW ADULTS DISCOURAGE KIDS FROM TELLING

Some school staff and members of the community suggested that adults may have unwittingly discouraged students from coming to them with threats. One church leader we met in Westside illustrated the point. A teenager named Sam reported that another boy, Greg, had threatened to kill himself and his family.

Sam went to a counselor to report this information, but instead of keeping it confidential, the counselor confronted Greg and then revealed his source. The church leader was appalled:

> All that did was show Sam that . . . if you tell, you're going to have to deal with the consequences of Greg knowing who told. And there are some upset parents and—do you blame them? So sometimes we're not making good choices. . . . If you're a teenager, are you going to give out information if it's going to come back to hurt you? I wouldn't.

We know that at least one kid brushed these sorts of reservations off and stuck his neck out by coming forward with the news that Andrew was threatening to shoot his classmates. He sat for a deposition in which he explained exactly how he came forward and how quickly Andrew found out about his breach:

> In October 1997, Andrew Golden told me that he was going to bring a gun to school and shoot some people. The statement upset me because I believed it was serious. I told my father . . . about Golden's statements and we contacted . . . the school counselor. I told [the counselor] about the threat that Andrew had made against the other students.
>
> The next morning at school . . . the principal asked me the boy's name again. I told her it was Andrew Golden. Later that same day, Andrew Golden told me that [the counselor] had spoken to him. He said that he knew that I had told on him, but he did not threaten me. He said that he was going to have to go through one day of counseling. All of this took place before Christmas of 1997. Andrew never made any further statements about shooting people at school to me.[16]

The school denies that the reported threat was against other students, claiming instead that Andrew was threatening suicide. We take no position on the facts of this issue. Our point here is simply that the school also did not move effectively to protect the identity of the student who had the courage to risk his social reputation by coming forward. It is not likely that others will follow his lead.

In practice, it can be difficult to maintain confidentiality and simultaneously act on private information. Sometimes the "informant" is the only person who could possibly be privy to the threats. Merely taking action to stem an incident could "finger" the speaker. But in Westside and Heath the threats were widely known and heard by so many people that no one individual could have been identified as a source.[17] Reluctance to come forward under these circumstances has more to do with the wariness of kids over the reliability of the adults they deal with.

This dour conclusion may suggest that something was terribly wrong in these schools. Not so. All bureaucratic environments are mixtures of good intentions and caring people who abide by the rules of the cultures in which they are immersed. There is a gap in all institutions between the formal rules—all relevant information should be reported—and the actual behavior—only favorable risk assessments reach NASA officials. This is not on account of corruption but rather reflects the imperatives of running an organization that has goals to achieve and a tendency to act on information that furthers achieving them.

At the same time, elements of the surrounding culture help to shape the way those bureaucratic practices unfold. The greater community provides no less respect to sports heroes than does the school. And high schools are but a gateway to college and professional sports, which have seen their share of stars engage in behavior that makes the school athlete behavior we have described here pale by comparison. If basketball star Latrell Sprewell can choke his coach and then be cheered on his return to the court, can we really get on a high horse if high school teachers let sports stars out of class to watch a movie but expect the calculus students to hit the books? We want students to come forward with sensitive information, but in the neighborhoods where they live, neither they nor their parents are comfortable telling on a child who is killing cats or talking about using weapons in a church youth group. Schools do not exist in a vacuum.

———

In every recent case of rampage school shootings, the perpetrators have sounded off to other kids before they have acted. Kids don't snap—they build toward these devastating moments. They talk about their plans, because one impetus for shooting in the first place is to secure a position in the status system that is an improvement over the marginal position they occupy beforehand. Winning attention, winning respect—this is often what the shooters are after. They try to achieve these goals by making their classmates curious about their intentions or afraid of what they might do next. Hence, they talk, and usually a lot.

In the Heath and Westside cases, the threats increased markedly the last school day before the shooting, with Mitchell and Michael indiscriminately spilling their plans—perhaps, as Mrs. Holden suggested, asking to be stopped. But these threats often go unheeded by other students, dismissed as simply kids' talk, only one more in the string of ridiculous things that they have said.

Even adolescents who had heard more specific threats—those who had seen a hit list, or were warned to stay away from the prayer group—were not convinced that their friends would follow through. They concluded that they were hearing an extended adolescent fantasy. The fact that Michael and Mitchell were both known to be full of bluster and bravado, with little to back it up, was taken as a sign that they were probably not serious this time either. Armed with only vague suspicions, students face loyalty norms and social sanctions that reinforce them, which combine to discourage them from coming forward.

For those who buy into the adolescent code completely, telling is not even an option; even for more mature and reflective students, the social imperative to adhere to the code works against conveying loosely held suspicions to adults. When students see that adults cannot be completely trusted with their secrets, or fail to take serious action in the face of a reported threat, they file this information away and act with it in mind. They remain silent.

For the students who were closest to the shooters, like Courtney (Michael's friend) and Chris (Mitchell's confidante), the fact that others did not report it is likely to be of scant consolation. They have both been wracked with guilt about not coming forward with their premonitions. Chris has been in therapy for years since the shooting. Courtney left town for almost a year to try to shake the sense of guilt she carried. Both students blame themselves in retrospect, but given the vagueness of the threats, their friends' general tendencies to make empty boasts, and the fact that school shootings were not yet a part of the public consciousness, it is hard to see how they could have known better.

But what is more surprising—and alarming—is that students we talked to *today* would likely repeat the mistakes of their classmates. Even after seeing all the damage that can be caused when those with information don't come forward, the kids we talked to say that they would try to distinguish between serious and joking threats. The ways that they make these distinctions are strikingly similar to the ways that students at the time went wrong—ruling out students who are all "talk" or those who don't seem threatening enough to follow through. Despite all of the painful self-criticism and legal cross-examination that students who were there at the time have endured, the difficulty of distinguishing serious threats remains, as does the tendency to hold back.

PART THREE

8

BLAME AND
FORGIVENESS

We wanted. . . someone to accept the blame, the guilt, for my
daughter's murder, and even today I haven't gotten that. Because [Michael] never accepted the guilt. The parents say it
wasn't their fault, the school says it wasn't their fault, the
shooter says, "Well, I'm not accepting fault," so my daughter
just went to school one day, got a hole in her head, never came
home, and it's nobody's fault? That's hard to live with.

—Wayne Steger, father of Kayce Steger

THE MORNING AFTER THE SHOOTING, A SMALL GROUP OF STUDENTS AT HEATH
High gathered at the front of the school and stretched a homemade banner across
the entrance: "We forgive you Mike." "As God has forgiven us," some were heard
to respond. Surely there had never been another time when the messages of faith
were more resonant, or more difficult to live by. The attack had cost the Heath
student body three friends, left a fourth in a wheelchair, disabled a star athlete,
and shattered their sense of security. Yet the carnage was committed by one of
their own, someone many had known since elementary school, whose family had
deep roots in the community. To shun the Carneals for the actions of their son, or
to turn a collective back on Michael, would have been very hard in such a tight-
knit community. Better to call on the tenets of their faith—be it Baptist or
Methodist, Lutheran or fundamentalist—and proclaim forgiveness in a hurry.

Too fast, as it turned out, for some. For every person who tried to turn the
other cheek, there was another who thought the time was not yet right—both in

Heath and Westside. "[Westside residents] were enraged," remembered Thomas Gardner, a professor of social work at Arkansas State University. "They wanted vengeance. I heard anger. I heard: 'Can you try these guys for murder?' 'Can you put them away?' 'Can you give them the death sentence?' Rage!" The shooters had a long road to travel before they were eligible for their communities' forgiveness.

For those whose daughters died, that day may never come. Their losses were so devastating that they cannot accept the notion that these young men deserve any understanding at all. They want the shooters, their parents, their teachers, and their conspiratorial friends to confront the enormity of their crimes and be held accountable for the damage they have done. Hiding behind youth, mental illness, or confusion over the shooters' intentions will not do. This insistence set the parents who lost children apart from their neighbors, who were ready to move on after a year of mourning. Disgusted by the criminal process, the victim families pushed on, turning to civil suits to force the real story out into the open, to find justice for their daughters and a measure of peace for themselves.

Christian teachings provide a powerful sense of morality, define the rules by which transgressors should be dealt with, and govern the public reputations of the main characters in our story. Yet it is a tradition replete with contradictory messages about the proper stance to take under these sad circumstances. Those who tried understanding and those eager for vengeance could both find justification in Scripture.[1]

Criminal law also assigns blame and metes out punishment, although with a different playbook. American legal culture, especially criminal law, emphasizes process over outcome, and our tradition urges the law to protect the welfare of defendants. This is especially true where juvenile justice is concerned, for the theory has long been that children can be rehabilitated and that the mission of the system is less to punish than to rescue them.

The shootings in Westside and Heath brought these two realms—religion and law—into direct conflict on almost every issue. The process, the evidence, the outcomes, the sense of closure—in all of these domains, the two systems clashed. Whereas religious conventions emphasized the need for full disclosure of faults and mistakes from everyone concerned, legal custom drove the same people toward silence and self-protection. Juvenile law placed the rights of the accused and the desire for positive change in their lives foremost, but religious teachings called for public confession and shaming, and then alternated between punishment and forgiveness. Among the faithful, there was little consensus about what a good Christian should do when confronted with the cold-blooded killing of innocent children.

Questions of blame and forgiveness were pondered in the glare of the national spotlight. Dennis Prager, a Los Angeles radio talk show host, took note of the banner at Heath High and responded with a harsh editorial in the *Wall Street Journal*. "I am appalled and frightened," Prager wrote, "by this feel-good doctrine of automatic forgiveness."

> This doctrine undermines the moral foundations of American civilization because it advances the amoral notion that no matter how much you hurt other people, millions of your fellow citizens will immediately forgive you. This doctrine destroys Christianity's central moral tenets about forgiveness—that forgiveness, even by God, is contingent on the sinner repenting, and that it can only be given to the sinner by the one against whom he sinned. . . . no one has the moral right to forgive evil done to others.[2]

The *Paducah Sun* was quick to respond to Prager's critique. Local columnist, Pat Brockenborough was particularly incensed by Prager's claim that her community lacked religious backbone. Rising to the defense of the students who posted the banner, she argued that forgiveness is the essence of Christian faith.

> Here in the Bible Belt, our faith is demonstrated by love, compassion, forgiveness—something that Prager finds abhorrent. To believe good comes from evil, and that God's will be done may be platitudinous, but it helps good people work through their troubles. . . . Simple faith eases pain.[3]

This turned out to be a much harder prescription than Brockenborough might have imagined. Figuring out who was to blame for the crimes committed by juvenile shooters proved an exceedingly difficult task, driven by the differences between faith and law. In this chapter, we explore the moral quandaries facing the townspeople as the enormity of the crimes registered. The impact of rampage school shootings reaches beyond the personal losses. Divisions buried in normal times surfaced with a vengeance. When legal outcomes seemed inexplicable, they became evidence for the conspiratorial view that hidden hands of power, class, and influence were moving behind the scenes.

At first sight, preoccupations with punishment and forgiveness may appear peculiar to Bible Belt communities. Yet we see in their reactions a mirror of national concerns about accountability for crime, the legitimacy of shame and retribution, and the controversial status of mental illness or a troubled life as mitigating factors in the judicial system.

THE TROUBLE IN COURT

Michael Carneal was charged with three counts of murder, five counts of attempted murder, and one count of burglary. Unlike the Westside shooters, who were clearly underage, Michael was tried as an adult. In the end, he pleaded "guilty but mentally ill" to all charges and received a sentence of life without possibility of parole for twenty-five years, the maximum permissible under law given his age (fourteen at the time of the crime).[4]

Because Mitchell and Andrew were younger than the legal threshold for adult charges, they were tried for murder but convicted only of "delinquency," the most serious finding available for juvenile offenders. The maximum penalty for delinquency is indefinite detention in a Department of Youth Services juvenile center until the age of eighteen—four years for Mitchell and six for Andrew. The law provides for their continued incarceration until the age of twenty-one only if the state of Arkansas builds or locates a special facility for 18-to-21-year-olds, which would segregate them from both younger offenders and adults. When they are released, neither boy will carry a felony record.

Objections to the process and the outcome deluged the airwaves, editorial pages, and backroom conversations in both communities. In Michael's case, the protests focused on two issues. First, the victim families argued, he wasn't mentally ill, or at least was not incapacitated to the point where he had no idea what he was doing. Michael had maneuvered to conceal the weapons he used in the shooting, moved the guns from place to place to avoid detection, and covered the cache with blankets so that no one would see them. Second, he plotted days, even weeks, ahead of time to acquire the weapons and discussed his evil plan with a dozen other kids. There was nothing spontaneous about his crime, and from the layperson's perspective, serious mental illness is simply incompatible with the extensive evidence of his capacity to plan.

Experts agreed with the families, at least insofar as a classic insanity defense was concerned. None of them thought Michael was unable to tell the difference between right and wrong—the legal definition of insanity. Defense experts claimed that Michael suffered from schizotypal personality disorder, often a precursor to schizophrenia. This disorder manifests itself as an extreme inability to manage social interaction, a tendency to magnify negative encounters, and to feel—despite evidence to the contrary—unloved and unwanted. Prosecutors objected to the diagnosis, arguing that Michael's concern with his "lack of popularity and acceptance by peers . . . did not appear to have been very different from many teenagers." In other words, Michael wasn't crazy, he was just upset that no one liked him.

Even more distressing to the parents whose children died was the failure to even charge the Goths, with whom, some believed, Michael had plotted the rampage. As the criminal investigation gathered force, the sheriff himself made it clear that other students bore some responsibility. He made public pronouncements to the effect that other people would find themselves in court, charged with conspiracy, in short order. Much to his dismay, not to mention the fury of the victim families, this never happened. Despite a special grand jury with the power to force people to testify, the prosecutor never charged anyone else.

The Commonwealth Attorney felt from the beginning that the investigation was stymied by a lack of cooperation on the part of the Goths. Questions about their involvement in the plot were never clearly answered, although not for lack of trying by his office. "Did we find out answers to everything?" he asked rhetorically. "I think the answer is no."

> Do I think that everybody was candid with the police? Do I think everybody was completely candid with the grand jury? The answer is no. Do I think that there was anywhere near sufficient evidence to bring charges? The answer is again no.

Detective Baker, the lead investigator for the McCracken County Sheriff's Department, voiced the same sentiments in a confidential memo he wrote to the prosecutors: "Based on the evidence . . . I have, I believe we have gone as far as we can at this time. I also believe that if Michael Carneal would tell the whole truth, we might get a conviction on one or maybe two other people."[5]

Under the circumstances, the alleged coconspirators were left untouched, and the real story of their involvement remained a mystery. Families of the dead were outraged.

The legal disposition of the Westside case provoked an equally furious response. At least Michael would be locked up for twenty-five years or more. But Andrew and Mitchell will be out in no time, not because their crimes were less appalling but, as many in community saw the matter, because of our misguided precepts of juvenile justice. U.S. law inherited from English common law the view that the capacity to form intent is critical in assessing culpability for murder. In most states, children, particularly those under age fourteen, are deemed inherently unable to form the requisite intent to murder. We have embraced this principle since colonial times, although we continue to lower the age at which we believe mental capacity matures enough for adult charges to be filed.[6]

The case of Nathaniel Brazill in Lake Worth, Florida, a thirteen-year-old boy who shot and killed a teacher after being sent home from school for throwing water balloons, fueled a serious discussion nationwide about letting the nature of the crime, rather than the characteristics of the accused, determine whether a defendant should be tried as a juvenile or an adult. Proposals have been advanced to drop the age of adulthood for the purposes of criminal prosecution to eleven, spurred by the outrage over the Brazill case.[7]

More than a few Westside parents could see the wisdom in that. Had Mitchell and Andrew exploded without warning or acted on sheer impulse, the line that stands between children and adults on the capacity to form intent would have remained sharp. However, Andrew and Mitchell engaged in extensive, careful planning, carried on over a number of weeks, and made threats well in advance. This taught the Westside community that it was entirely possible for children as young as eleven to act intentionally.

Does intent include a full understanding of the consequences of one's actions, though? Here lies the rub in the case of Mitchell and Andrew. First, the evidence is mixed as to whether they actually intended to *kill* anyone. Mitchell claimed, although few believed him, that the boys meant to aim above the heads of the students and teachers. There were bullet holes at the school roofline that might constitute corroboration of his statement. The boys packed the van with sleeping bags and explained that they thought they'd go camping for a few weeks and return when things had calmed down to enjoy a celebrity reception among their peers. It's not clear that anyone—even a naïve child—would concoct such a plan if they expected to commit murder. Yet Andrew was an expert marksman, and Mitchell was equipped with a rifle whose scope was designed for hunting at a distance. Someone who had won awards for target practice, as Andrew had, would not have hit people if he intended to fire over their heads. For parents of the victims, these subtleties were beside the point. The boys planned and executed a mass murder, and that was that.

The utter failure of the criminal justice system to come to terms with this simple truth seemed a symptom of a larger meltdown in American society. The view from pew and pulpit in this small Bible Belt town was of a culture gone crazy, a retreat from responsibility, authority, and discipline. The county coroner, whose family has lived in Jonesboro for generations, complained, "No one is being held accountable any more."

I was beaten as a child, so that makes it all right for me to go out and kill someone? There's so much of that [kind of excuse] out there now. You're going to have to make them responsible and you're going to make them have to pay a penalty. I'm down here in the South and I believe in the death penalty. There's a lot of people who don't, but I've seen . . . the blood, I've seen the victims, I've put them in body bags.

CIVIL ACTION

On December 2, 1998, a year and day after the shooting, the James, the Stegers, and the Hadleys filed civil suits in Paducah against those they held responsible for their daughters' deaths.[8] Among their targets were: Michael Carneal, his parents, the neighbor from whom Michael had stolen the guns, students who had seen Michael with a gun at school before the shooting, students who had heard that something was going to happen on Monday, students who might have been involved as coconspirators, teachers and principals at Heath High and Middle schools, the producers of the film *Basketball Diaries,* the makers of the "point-and-shoot" video games that Michael played, and the Internet pornography sites he had visited.[9]

In Westside, families of the victims sued the shooters for wrongful death, the Goldens and the Woodards for not controlling their children or being aware that something like this could happen, Doug Golden—Andrew's grandfather—for failing to adequately secure his guns from the known risk of burglary, and against the gun manufacturers for failing to ensure gun safety by installing trigger locks.[10]

The legal machinations are not particularly important here. What matters more for our purposes is the motivation behind the civil suits, which were clearest in the Heath case. The victim families believe that the full truth of the Heath massacre has never been told. They cannot find peace until they determine whether there were others whose malice, carelessness, or self-interest contributed to the deaths. Above all, they want all of the responsible parties to own up to their roles in this tragedy, something they believe did not happen in the course of the criminal trial.

Why didn't the Carneals ask what had become of the knives missing from their kitchen? (They were found after the shootings under Michael's mattress.) Why didn't they know their son was downloading violent media from Web sites in the middle of the night (as the contents of his hard drive made plain)? Why didn't they punish Michael when he behaved outrageously, pushing screwdrivers into the school walls, throwing bikes into bonfires?

To the parents of the slain girls, Michael was known to be a boy with problems, a kid who never behaved appropriately anywhere.[11] He was broadcasting weird, worrying signals that there was something wrong with him. How come nobody was looking deeper into his behavior? Either Michael was truly sick, in which case John and Ann Carneal were at fault for not having sought treatment, or he was perfectly healthy and therefore deserving of condemnation. Either way, responsibility lay with the shooter and his family.

Yet adversarial practice prevented such a clear assignation of responsibility. Had the complainants in the civil suit prevailed, the Carneals would have lost all of their assets. Legal maneuvers designed to thwart such an outcome make perfect sense to defense lawyers. They instruct their clients to avoid answering questions when possible, to defer to experts, to say they "can't recall" events that most people believe they do indeed remember. When John Carneal was asked in a civil suit deposition whether he thought Michael had been behaving strangely in the weeks before the rampage, he responded that he was not a psychiatrist and that only a qualified expert could answer the question. To wounded parties, who were sitting in the background listening, his response was nothing more than an attempt to shirk his responsibility. Having been almost willfully blind to Michael's instability, he was now pretending that only a medical expert could have seen the truth. The civil suits were supposed to force the Carneals to come out from behind the psychiatric defense in the criminal trial and admit their own culpability. They succeeded only in making plain how far from the Christian mandate of self-examination the Carneals had strayed.

Unwittingly, having insisted on accountability through the civil law, the victim families created conditions that blocked their access to people with whom they desperately needed to communicate. Having filed lawsuits that named teachers and administrators as defendants, a wall of silence descended at the behest of lawyers who were engaged to protect their clients. Teachers who had done everything they could for the dying children—staunched their wounds, administered CPR—found themselves on the other end of a subpoena and under instruction not to talk to anyone about the shooting. This put an end to any prospect of a conversation between the victims families and the people who had tended their children as they lay dying. Judy James, the mother of one of the victims recounted:

> [Jessica] was alive for . . . fifteen, twenty minutes [after the shooting] that she lay there. They say she didn't pass out until they started moving her, getting her in the ambulance and she screamed because something hurt all of a sudden. And that was about it. But there was fifteen minutes we don't know what actually happened.

One's last minutes on Earth are of great moment for devout Christians. Last minutes tell Christian families something poignant and precious about the dying as they approach the afterlife. It has been an unbearable sorrow to be cut off from these witnesses, and it is a dereliction of duty within the faith to hold back.

Of course, as families saw it, teachers were not merely innocent bystanders in this drama. Some of them were privy to Michael's mental disintegration in the form of bizarre stories like the "Halloween Surprise" described in chapter 4. Why didn't they take notice of his fixations? To people of the "old school," remembering the days when teachers paddled students at will, when kids who talked back or failed to remove their hats were punished in short order, the notion that teachers had lost interest in the content of their students' writing was simply stunning. Do we really look the other way when kids start writing about murder? Do we not look to teachers as moral guardians *in loco parentis* as well as technicians who teach grammar?

If they didn't know Michael was on a path to violence, despite the many warning signs they observed, the teachers were guilty of something: malfeasance or incompetence, perhaps, as opposed to murder, but implicated just the same. If the students knew what Michael had in mind that Monday morning but failed to come forward, they too were in some way responsible. And if they planned and encouraged the assault, they were almost as guilty as the boy who pulled the trigger. But since none of these parties owned up to their failures—indeed, they refused to admit any responsibility at all—it was left to the families whose daughters were in the grave to force the truth out—in court. Painful as the consequences might be, the civil process was the only means of holding people accountable.

Very few of their neighbors, particularly in Heath, agreed. Indeed, sympathy for the Carneals and the educators named in the suit led most of the townspeople to the conclusion that the plaintiffs were creating a new class of victims, perhaps out of grief, but possibly out of self-interest. Some critics thought they were looking for financial compensation for a loss that cannot be translated into dollars. Others viewed the civil suits as a vendetta pursued by parents who simply could not accept the awful truth that nothing was going to bring their daughters back. Whatever the motive, the outcome seemed clear enough to the critics: The town was going to be held hostage to this tragedy for years as the lawsuits dragged on.

THE PATH TO FORGIVENESS

Secular institutions such as the law offer one route to resolution, but it is not the path that Bible Belt communities find most compelling. Hiding behind procedure, privileging experts over common sense, and permitting people to evade scrutiny—these are not palatable means of getting at the truth, determining who is at fault, or deciding how the guilty should be punished. Faith provides a better method.

The New Testament recognizes the need for society to respond when it is wounded by one of its own. A believer who has committed a heinous crime can come back into the fold, but only after deep reflection, admission of guilt and responsibility, acceptance of punishment, and the public shame that comes with it. The pathway is intentionally hard and cannot be short-circuited. Forgiveness should cost the transgressor, force him to lay bare his most grievous faults and unambiguously accept blame for his actions. Moving too fast risks the legitimacy of contrition and casts doubt on whether the community itself has walked the hard road of confronting the sinner. This arduous path cannot be traveled in the short time it took to paint a sign and stretch it across the school entryway.

Cultural rules drawn from the ordinary Sunday sermon come into play here. On a June Sunday in 2001, we attended morning services at the Heartland Worship Center, the interfaith church where the funeral was held for the three students who died at Heath. Walking into the church complex from a parking lot that held nearly 1,000 cars, we were welcomed by the pastor and his assistants into a huge, white foyer. The main church hall holds 2,000 visitors, who face forward to a stage flanked by projection screens that scroll through Biblical texts and hymns.

Our visit opened a window into this congregation's views about human flaws, the responsibilities of sinners, and the power of God's love to forgive. That Sunday morning, the pastor stepped forward and began his homily by talking about his own faults. He explained that he had made many mistakes since he had last seen his flock. He had harbored bad thoughts, uncharitable feelings. Faces turned toward him with a nod of recognition as everyone in the room mulled over their own mistakes, petty actions, and malevolent thoughts.

The pastor humbled himself before his own congregation, drawing a parallel between his own weaknesses and theirs. Through this rhetorical device, he pointed toward two tenets of the faith that are of central importance. First, we are all equals in God's eyes. Only God has the right to judge, and He is merciful. Second, all people are flawed and should feel a powerful sense of humility in the face of this truth. They must recognize that even the best among them will make mistakes and deserve disapproval. The pathway to forgiveness lies in giving oneself over to God, trusting in Jesus to accept His errant children for what they are: imperfect.[12] Acknowledging personal failures publicly is an essential and ongoing part of being a devout Christian.[13]

Dr. Bruce Tippit, pastor of the First Baptist Church in Jonesboro, offered a similar message in a sermon he delivered in October of 2000, entitled "Coming Clean." Pastor Tippit engaged the congregation in a discussion of the mistakes we make in handling our faults, the ways we permit frustration to build up inside when guilt rules. He urged his flock to walk down the "Road to Recovery," which begins when each of us recognizes that

> I'm not God, that I'm powerless to control my tendency to do the wrong thing and my life is unmanageable. . . . I have problems I can't seem to control. . . . None of us are faultless. We all have sins, we've all made mistakes. So we all have remorse.

Yet before God can make much headway, the sinner must "openly examine and confess my faults to God, to myself, and to someone I trust." A thorough, unflinching, embarrassing moral inventory is required.

As the congregation is reminded that everyone is capable of sinning, they shed their own corrosive anger.[14] This is how many in Westside understood the proper pathway to forgiveness in the aftermath of the shooting. The question before them, though, was whether the sinners had really examined their faults and exposed themselves to shame.[15] Christian forgiveness is contingent on taking responsibility for one's faults and "ownership" of the unimaginable costs they have imposed on the innocent.[16] To expect to be forgiven just because one comes from a good Christian family merely demonstrates a self-interested misinterpretation of what the Bible calls for. To offer forgiveness before the requisite hard work of self-examination, public confession, and shame is equally wrong.

Yet that is precisely what appeared to be under way. Michael had not properly "asked," nor had his family "worked through the feelings," before the whole town was urging that the community "put it behind them," accept whatever passed for Michael's self-examination, and make the forgiveness final. "I don't know who put up the banner at school," Chuck Hadley remarked. "It rubbed us the wrong way."

> He has to ask for forgiveness. We can forgive his actions, but only God can forgive him for what he did. . . . I think a lot of people on the outside [of the tragedy thought,] "Oh, yeah, we forgive him." That's a knee-jerk reaction because of what you're taught as a Christian.[17]

This rush to absolution created a great deal of pressure on the victim families, who seemed to cling stubbornly to the role of persecutors. Judgment was passed on them rather than on Michael and his family, because they were not prepared to join the crowd. Their own religious faith was under attack by those who claimed that a real Christian would show compassion. Nicole Hadley's parents were outraged by what they saw as an effort to skip over the hard part and pressure them to move too quickly to accept the apologies offered by the Carneals.

GWEN HADLEY: I was very much aware of [whether] I was coming across as a Christian. I didn't want to come across as angry as I was. . . . And for me, trying to keep up the image of a good strong Christian when I didn't feel like it. You know, there was times . . . I've had yelling conversations with God. I questioned my faith. I questioned God.

CHUCK: Everybody, the whole town was in this forgiving mode. And you know, the three parents of the girls that died, what's wrong with them?

THE VOICE OF SHAME

Ironically, one of the few opportunities to subject the shooters to public shame occurred not in church but in criminal court. Over a year after Michael's rampage, the Heath community came together in the McCracken County Courthouse for his sentencing hearing. Although the criminal case was over, there was still a great deal of unfinished emotional business. The anger in Heath was so great, and the opportunities for direct confrontation between victims and defendant so few, that Judge Hines invited the families of the dead and the wounded themselves to speak their piece.

In Jonesboro, the first opportunity for the Westside community to publicly confront the shooters also came at a sentencing hearing. Here too, the introduction of victim impact statements was unprecedented. Mitchell and Andrew were facing sentences that were fixed, so the testimony of the victim families had no bearing on the outcome. What the judge was after was a chance to let the suffering people of Westside drill the enormity of this crime into Mitchell and Andrew, cleansing the community of its grief.

In both courtrooms, the victims began by trying to impress upon the shooters how their crimes had robbed the families of everything they cherish. In Paducah, Sebrina Steger, mother of the slain Kayce Steger, took the stand, faced the judge and in a determined, but strained voice, explained that "Kayce's murder . . . has affected every aspect of our lives, from our daily routines to our belief systems."

Not only have we lost our daughter, we have also lost being a normal family. We have lost the ability to be the parents we want to be to our surviving children. . . . Answering the simple question, "How many children do you have?" has become very complicated. . . . We have a life sentence of grief. We have no hope of parole.

First to the stand in Jonesboro was Mitchell Wright. "I not only lost a wife," he told the boys, "I lost a best friend because of you two."

Zane looks for his mother to come back and I have to explain to him that his mother is in Heaven and she can't come back. . . . You know, most three-year-old boys are more worried about playing games and watching "Barney." But do you know what my three-year-old boy come up to me and told me last week? He . . . said, "Dad, don't worry about those two bad boys, because if they ever break out of jail, I'll take care of you."

. . . I want you two to know one thing: If you, Andrew and Mitchell, if you had been the ones out there on that playground . . . that day, she would have got in front of you and covered you.

Regina Kaut, aunt of the slain Britthney Varner, spoke on behalf of her sister Suzanne:

If I had to describe our life after the 24th of March, I would say it's like living in a world with no color. We continue to go about the same routine as before, only now we're missing a vital and important element. That was . . . Britthney . . .

Roy Brooks, whose niece Natalie was killed and whose daughter Jenna was wounded, took a harder tone. He wanted the boys to know that they destroyed the childhoods of the kids in the whole Westside community, taking away their innocence and replacing it with fear. Why should the system treat them with understanding and leniency?

I'd like to say that this whole bloody crime has changed my family in several ways. The questions from my daughter Jenna, such as what [her cousin Natalie] did to deserve to be shot. And . . . could we move now . . . from the home . . . move away? And what if . . . these two boys returned to finish the killings, the job they started. . . . [These] are questions that a father thinks a child should never have to ask. . . .

The pain I see in my brother's eyes and the other family members leaves us wondering why. . . . I know that [Mitchell and Andrew] will leave our community for now, but my hope is that they'll never return.

A small measure of satisfaction came from simply airing publicly the private toll the rampages had taken on the families of Heath and Westside. But it was not enough; what the victim families really wanted was to deprive the shooters of any refuge from the pain the victim families have to live with day in and day out. Missy Jenkins, former president of Heath High School's chapter of the Future Homemakers of America, a blond beauty known for her strong faith, slowly turned her wheelchair to the podium, pushing herself past Ann, Kelly, and John Carneal. She stared hard at Michael and practically willed him to confront what he had done to her body:

> I want Michael to look at me. I want to tell you that I'm paralyzed from my chest down. . . . I really feel helpless. I can't go to the bathroom like regular people. It is hard to get dressed. . . . I have to live with this every day. . . . I don't know why you did this to me and to everybody else, but I know I'm not going to forget it, because I see it everyday in my mind. . . . I don't have any hard feelings toward you. . . . I can live this way. It's going to be hard, but I can do it.

When Stephen Keene, the older brother of the wounded Craig Keene, addressed the court, he demanded that Michael acknowledge the proceedings before him:

> Michael, I watched you gun down three girls . . . I watched you shoot my brother and try to kill him and four other people. . . . You look at me right now! [Michael looks up]. Thank you. . . . I don't know what was going on in your head. What would drive somebody to do this? Respond! . . . I wish I could just hide [like you]. . . Today you will get sentenced. Today you will spend the rest of your life in jail.

If the essence of Christian process is that forgiveness must be preceded by acknowledgment of one's faults, it seemed clear to the victim families that this was far from complete. "Today some will say that Jesus would plead that Michael doesn't need to be jailed and that we should forgive his actions," Joe James acknowledged. "Jesus never excused an unrepentant sinner."

> Repentant sinners were expected to pay their penalty to this world. And I must state that Michael has never shown any remorse for his actions. There has only been a statement of repentance . . . that John and Ann Carneal have suffered more than any other people in this county did. C'mon, give us a break. John

and Ann Carneal still have a son and will be able to shower him with gifts and affection for years to come, and I get to clean and polish a marker in a cemetery.

So please Judge Hines, tell the community and the world that there is a reaction that is just and swift for the type of action that Mr. Carneal committed, that you believe the actions of Mr. Carneal are so reprehensible that to give him a lesser sentence would be not only a crime against man, but a slap in the face of God.

REPENTANCE

Did the shooters understand what their actions had done to families of their victims? Had they any idea of the magnitude of the grief they had caused? Andrew sat silent as a stone in court, never looking at the victims, never acknowledging the words streaming from the stand. Indeed, while the lawyer for the Golden family issued a statement to the press, Pat and Dennis never spoke on their own behalf to the town that their family had lived in for three generations. Never content to let a tragedy go unexplained, their neighbors began to put the pieces together without them. "Oh, my heart goes out to them so bad," said Sandra Banks, a Westside mother, shaking her head. "But I don't know, they never would talk to the public."

> I don't know if it was embarrassing or just not knowing what to do, but they never really showed remorse of any kind. And I think this sort of community sort of shuns that family out. It was just like a wall was built after that. . . . [Mitchell's family], the mother . . . was on TV crying and telling everybody she was sorry, you know, I mean, what can you do? But the Goldens would never come forward with anything ever, so I don't know why. . . . They always said it wasn't Andrew's fault . . . And they probably believed that.

The Goldens' failure to comment publicly on the part their son played in the massacre seemed to fit with other perceptions of their parenting. Andrew was deemed an overindulged child, whose cussing and acting out was just laughed away by his family. And why didn't the Goldens bring Andrew to church? This was a child with a dark side that his family did not recognize because they loved him so much.

Those who knew the Goldens personally thought otherwise. Remember, they admonished, this is a hardworking family, honest and upright. Dennis and Pat put in long hours as postal service employees. The boy's grandparents helped take care of him because they loved him so dearly and because they wanted to help their adult children maintain good jobs. How many families these days can claim such solidarity across the generations?

Mitchell Johnson did speak his piece in court. He was unable to explain why he shot and killed his classmates; it is not clear that he really knew himself. He merely tried to apologize as best he could in a statement delivered on the eve of his fourteenth birthday:

> As I have sat in jail the past four months, I have had an opportunity to think about what happened on March 24th, 1998. First, I want to tell the judge and all these people who have been hurt by my actions, that I am sorry. I understand that . . . it may be impossible for some of you to forgive me.
>
> If I could go back and change what happened on March 24th, 1998, I would do so in a minute. I really thought that no one would actually be hurt. I thought we would just shoot over everyone's head. When the shooting started, we were not shooting at anybody or any group of people in particular.
>
> I have caused pain not only to my victims . . . and their families who are in this courtroom today and to my family and friends. I hope that anyone who will listen to these words will know how sorry that I truly am for what I have done.
>
> I have also asked God for forgiveness and I pray that He will heal the lives of the people who have been hurt by my actions. And that's all, Your Honor.[18]

Michael Carneal provided his victims no satisfaction. He did not make a statement explaining his actions, nor did he apologize or ask for forgiveness. He did not speak at all. Except for the times when his victims insisted that he look at them, he did not lift his eyes from the table. Michael's lawyer made a brief statement on his behalf instead, noting that the boy was remorseful and fully expected to receive the maximum punishment the law allowed: life in prison without parole for twenty-five years. Soon afterward, Judge Hines pronounced just that sentence, and the case was closed.

APOLOGIES UNHEARD

Ted Koppel and the ABC news program *Nightline* landed in Jonesboro a few days after the Columbine High School rampage. Koppel called a "town meeting" in a large Jonesboro church. New England austere, with high white walls and deep red pews, it was large enough to hold the hundreds of affected residents who appeared on national television in an electronic conversation with the shattered families of Littleton, Colorado. This little town in the middle of nowhere was caught once again in the klieg lights.

Koppel was particularly keen to have Gretchen Woodard, Mitchell Johnson's mother, appear on the show. Gretchen was skittish about the idea and initially refused to participate. In the end, though, she was coaxed into it, persuaded by Koppel's producers that Columbine families might learn something. No one else in Jonesboro was asked whether it would be fitting for Gretchen to appear. Some were furious that she did, to the point of tearing into her for the entire world to see. Others quietly admired her courage.

Gretchen's presence riveted the attention of the community and the television audience on the question of forgiveness. She began by trying to explain how grateful she was for the gracious behavior of her neighbors and acquaintances who had every reason to turn their backs on her and her family.

> What this community has done as far as being kind and the love that has shown everyone, including us, [is wonderful]. . . .
>
> I want Littleton to know [that] the kindest thing anyone has ever done for us was say that they've kept us in their thoughts and prayers. It helps me go on every day. . . . The pain don't go away. For me, I will carry this the rest of my life. My kids, Mitchell's siblings, will carry this the rest of their lives. . . .

In the face of death threats streaming in her direction and maps to her house posted on the Internet for all to see, Gretchen still felt safe in the embrace of her neighbors. The essence of Christian humility, Gretchen was well aware that she had no right to this comfort. "We've been blessed, truly blessed," she said, "I've never had to change my phone number."

A few minutes later, during a commercial break, Mitchell Wright spoke up to complicate Gretchen's moral profile. On the air, live before the entire nation, Koppel turned to Gretchen and asked her to respond to Wright's broadside:

> TED KOPPEL: A very difficult moment occurred just a few minutes ago when [Gretchen Woodard] . . . expressed a sense of how warmly she felt toward everyone in the community. . . . Sitting right here in the front row is a man who will introduce himself and who [was] having a very hard time with that. . . .
>
> MITCHELL WRIGHT: I'm Mitchell Wright. I'm Zane Wright's father, just three and a half years old now, and I was Shannon Wright's husband. . . . [She] was a teacher at the school that was murdered by Mitchell Johnson. The young man shot my wife twice and then he had the audacity to go to jail and brag to others how he watched her go down on her hands and knees and hold herself across her chest and was rocking back and forth like she was rocking a baby and she was saying no, no, no . . . [19]

. . . One bit of advice I'd like to give the two families in Colorado [whose] boys did [the shootings] is this. . . . If you are remorseful, if you are truly sorry for what your boys did, the victims' families, they need to hear that. They need you to contact them and just say hey, I'm sorry. I don't know what I could have done but I'm sorry.

Mitchell Wright was not satisfied with any of Gretchen's public statements. He was of the view that she had never adequately apologized, nor had the Goldens.

MITCHELL WRIGHT: See, it's been thirteen months and we've been told through bits of TV and newspaper that families are sorry, but no one's ever contacted my mother-in-law or my father-in-law or myself or my baby. . . . Don't . . . make the victims feel like they have to ask for that [apology]. . . .

No justice was served or will be served. [Johnson and Golden] will walk out [of youth corrections] in four years, and they committed five murders and possibly could have been ten others or more. They have emotionally scarred teachers [and] children. . . .

Mitchell Wright was not an uncomplicated character in this drama, which is why it is hard to know how his comments struck Westside residents. Just as there are proper paths to forgiveness, there are proper ways to grieve, and some in the Westside community felt Mitchell Wright had chosen poorly in seeking the limelight after the shootings, talking too much to the press, and pushing too hard to have the school and awards named after Shannon. Others, however, were more hesitant to judge. People have different ways of grieving. Some sink into privacy; others feel that to honor the dead, something good must come of the tragedy.

TRASHING THE FAMILY

From the very beginning, townspeople asked themselves, "Is it possible for a shooter to grow up inside a good Christian family?"[20] If the family is truly admirable, some thought, this could not come to pass. The community must have been mistaken, fooled, or just blind to the defects on the inside of families such as the Goldens and the Carneals. Mitchell's family was most eligible for revisionism. Terry Woodard, a former felon, and Gretchen, thrice married, did not make a picture-perfect pair, as the Carneals did. The bizarre, attention-seeking behavior of Scott Johnson, Mitchell's father—who tried to sell his story for money, who hired a lawyer-promoter, whose own angry, belligerent behavior had done so much to terrify Mitchell in the first place—did not endear the family to the world either. It was an impossible situation for Gretchen:

> Lord, any mud, any dirt. "You're a divorcee and that's what you put your kids through," [they'd say]. People judged me through the press and they still do. Oh, yeah, . . . I've tried hard to apologize. I won't apologize for who I am. And I've never agreed with what happened and what my son was a part of. I can't stop loving him. I will stand beside him and help him. I don't know any other way.

Mitchell Wright was having none of this. Ted Koppel asked him directly whether he blamed the parents for the son's crime.

> TED KOPPEL: You have every right to feel whatever anger you feel. . . . But you don't hold the mother responsible, do you? Or the little brother? Or the sisters? In a sense, can you accept that they have been victimized? Not as much as you have. No one has been victimized as much as those who've lost family members. But they are also victims. Can you accept that?
>
> MITCHELL WRIGHT: . . . I'm trying so hard to forgive and to go on. But it's very tough. . . . I'm not blaming the families all in all but, something was missed somewhere. . . . Their sons committed murder. Kids being brought up . . . in a Christian environment with parents that are actually paying attention to them, I don't think do this. You know, Mitchell Johnson was kicked off the basketball team a few weeks before this happened for engraving, doing self-mutilation into his skin, OK? If I'm a parent, which I am, and my son's doing that, I'm going to be looking into it and finding out what's going on.

Wright turned the spotlight back onto Gretchen, blaming her indirectly for her son's crime by casting her as an inadequate parent.

Never one to waste a dramatic moment, Koppel seized the opportunity to affect a catharsis on television. He asked Gretchen if she wanted to explain just how sorry she was for Shannon Wright's death. This time, perhaps sensing that she was on trial for her own conduct as a mother, she backed away:

> GRETCHEN WOODARD: I . . . would not [want] words from me to ever hurt anyone any more than anyone has already suffered. . . . I

come here with good intentions and to let the people know that we all do have to work through this. . .

TED KOPPEL: But I can't begin to know what Mr. Wright is going through. I don't pretend to know what you're going through. . . . But I've just heard an anguished cry from one man saying it's been thirteen months and I haven't heard an apology yet and I . . . don't want to be the one to lead you to it. That wouldn't be appropriate either. If you don't feel it, you shouldn't say it.

GRETCHEN WOODARD: . . . I don't begin to know what Mr. Wright has gone through either. I do know what I live with every day of my life and . . . the rest of my family does [too] . . . I don't feel it is my right to be here and cause any more hard feelings. . . . Standing here and pointing fingers at someone and saying you're a bad person . . . There isn't a quick fix answer. . . .

I do feel that with my heart, and I have said many times that I'm sorry. I don't know what I could say or do to help. Is there words? And I am very sorry. My family's very sorry and my son lives with this every day, struggles with this, Mitchell does.

During the next commercial break, Gretchen left the show, regretting her decision to come.

Gretchen apologized, but never actually asked for forgiveness for herself or her son. One person who did, at great cost to herself, was Stacey Worthington, whose job it is to oversee the treatment of juvenile offenders in the detention system. Stacey attended the *Nightline* taping because she was convinced of Mitchell's sincerity. On national television, Stacey made the case to her friends and neighbors that they needed to remember that in addition to the children who died, two others were "lost."

STACEY WORTHINGTON: I'm kind of coming at this situation from the other side. I deal with juvenile offenders and I dealt with Mitchell Johnson and Andrew Golden. I wasn't much involved in the victim side of this situation.

I know that everybody that I work with and everybody I've come in contact with will never be the same [but] I . . . have a bond with [the Woodard] family . . . and with Andrew Golden. I went to see [them] two weeks ago at [Alexander] DYS where they are being housed.

Mitchell shares things with me. . . . Mitchell prays on a daily basis; he prays for forgiveness. He prays for the victims. He prays for his family. He prays for me. He prays for everyone who's been involved in this. There's nothing more heartbreaking—and I am a parent also, I have an eight-year-old son—to sit there . . . with this fourteen-year-old young man who is changing, who's growing up, who's incarcerated and will be till he's twenty-one and to hear him talk about the free world. It's heartbreaking.

I've always felt on that particular day when this tragedy happened at Westside that not only did we lose five valuable, precious lives, we lost two others, also.

Three years later we asked Stacey to explain what she was trying to accomplish that day. "Well," she said, "People were saying that [Mitchell and Drew should have been [dragged] behind a horse in Times Square and strung up [so that we can] gawk at them. . . . [They] said we should . . . let them watch the autopsies of their victims." Stacy was shocked by the belligerence and violence of the recommendations coming at her for the treatment of eleven- and thirteen-year-old offenders. Surely, she thought, she could make them understand that Mitchell, at least, was genuinely remorseful. For her pains on the *Nightline* show, Stacey was rewarded with icy stares, angry outbursts, and some scary encounters with relatives of the dead. "It was nearly midnight [before the taping was over] and I was in the midst of this church pew," she remembered.

I felt somebody push, not tap, push on me. I turned around and I looked up and there's this huge, silver-haired man. I don't know who he is to this day. I figured he was an extended family member of one of the deceased. And he said, "How dare you!" Then he spit in my face. I said, "Sir, I didn't mean to hurt you or your family, but that's the way I feel. We have to learn to forgive. We have to be able to find [peace or it will] eat you from the inside out."

Stacey managed to get away from her antagonist and collapsed into the arms of a close friend who happened to be in the church. She was sobbing from the tension all the way home. Her husband met her at the door, with a phone in his hand:

It was the deputy prosecuting assistant. He said, "Stacey, I'm sorry. I know what you meant. And I'm sorry for the way they treated you. I know you've been dealing with those kids."

She cried all night, hardly sleeping at all. When she got to work the next day, Stacey was afraid to answer the phone for fear of bomb threats. But when she finally did, she heard a woman's voice on the other end:

> She started crying on the phone. She said, "Somebody needed to say it on behalf of those two boys. Because if you're a God-fearing person you have to learn how to forgive. . . ." She told me, "You touched my heart, and I'm so sorry for the way those people treated you."

Outside of the criminal court hearings, the Carneals escaped the kind of public critique that the Woodards and the Goldens were treated to. In Heath, the community examined its collective memory for evidence to support their view of John and Ann as exemplary parents. We heard many times over how Ann Carneal rushed to the school with blankets in hand the instant she heard about the shooting, before she knew that Michael was the perpetrator, and how John Carneal helped the ambulance crews by lifting up the crime scene tape to let stretchers pass underneath. The Carneals were as close as it comes to model parents. Middle-class pillars of the community, the Carneals were more attractive candidates for community empathy than their unfortunate counterparts in Westside.

The Schaberg family, whose daughter was badly injured in the Heath shooting, were particularly sympathetic toward John and Ann. Their daughter, Shelley, a senior and star athlete with a college sports scholarship waiting for her, was struck in the spine by a bullet that has caused her endless pain requiring extensive physical therapy and ended her promising basketball career.

Such a trauma might have inclined the Schabergs to dismiss the Carneals' apology. Instead they followed the advice of their Episcopalian priest, who urged them to set aside their own pain, to see the horror that had visited Ann and John. On the day of the funeral for the three girls who died, the Carneals' Lutheran minister asked the Schabergs' permission for John and Ann to visit Shelley in the hospital. The scene that followed has never left Julie Schaberg:

> John came in the room and he just melted in the floor. . . . He kept saying, "I am so sorry.". . . Ann [was] at the bed just rubbing Shelley. . . . Every nerve ending was terrible pain. . . . So here's Ann just rubbing her arm, and Shelley's in terrible pain, but she just let Ann do it.

Though never discounting the far worse price that parents of dead children paid, the Carneals' suffering was all too real. Julie Schaberg thought to herself, "You know what? This could be so much worse for us."

This could be our child that did this [shooting]. . . . I think that's worse, to be this person with the shooting than to be the person that died or that is injured. How are they going to live with themselves?

From the most public occasions—especially the *Nightline* "town hall"—to the most private conversations, the people of Westside debated the fundamental moral questions posed by the shooting. How much responsibility do parents bear for the conduct of their children? Should children who have committed terrible crimes *ever* be forgiven? What does a truly meaningful, Christian apology consist of? Under what conditions should we turn the other cheek? In the end, no real resolution was possible. Every person on the stage came to the drama from a different vantage point. Though their own religious culture emphasizes moral absolutes, they came away with competing principles and, as a consequence, endless arguments about who was in the right. There was no closure.

READING CLASS CONFLICT

Small town life encourages residents to paper over material differences in their standard of living and ignore the divergent pathways their kids are likely to take, submerging these distinctions in a common devotion to the football team, the band, or talent shows. Everyone turns out for these occasions, whether they come in fancy cars or jalopies. But when conflict is in the air, as it was in the course of the legal wrangling surrounding the civil suits, those who feel most aggrieved call on a subtext of class division to explain what happened. Elites, they believe, have a vested interest in hiding the truth. "Little people" like themselves have no clout and are at the mercy of those with power.

We visited a small Baptist church in Jonesboro in June 2001. It was a Wednesday night, the evening when many devoted members of the faith come to hear a midweek service. As the pastor dug into his sermon, the urgency grew in his voice as he delivered a message familiar to audiences at protest rallies in the 1960s. "Life is unfair," he remarked, "but it is also unfinished." Oppressors gain power and crush the little people, he explained. You work hard and go unrecognized, while lazy people above you are praised. The rich and powerful take your jobs, he intoned, robbing you of your livelihood and your security. They are ruthless, hiding behind facades of power, and that is why good people come up short while bad people prosper.

Having drawn his flock into the drama of class conflict and included himself among the souls trampled by hidden hands, the pastor then introduced the key dramatic element: judgment day is coming. "If you fear God," he told them solemnly, "a different truth will emerge. God knows who is the righteous one. With God you will never be alone." When the judgment day comes, all of that worldly power will evaporate and the real and true Power will assert itself. Ordinary people will rise up and claim their rightful place in the Kingdom of Heaven. Their oppressors will be cast down.

Northerners are schooled to think of southern small towns as places where the divisions between black and white are sharp, enduring, and key to understanding the social structure. Yet in Jonesboro, as in Paducah, the African-American population tends to live within the city limits. Both Heath and Westside are far enough outside those boundaries that they don't see many black residents. They are geographically separated to the point where interaction between racial groups is rare.

In Heath and Westside, it is class rather than race that defines the social pecking order. It is a fault line running between the prosperous farmers of Cash and Bono and the day laborers living in the public housing projects and trailer parks near Westside. It separates the engineers and programmers who work for the uranium processing plant outside of Paducah and the parents of the Future Farmers of America, whose way of life is all but disappearing now. Below the surface of conviviality and abundant social capital, some people are living in mansions, and others are barely eking it out in trailer parks.

Victim families in Heath interpreted the lack of enthusiasm for investigation, the release of the Goths from any further scrutiny, and the soft landing implied in Michael's "guilty but mentally ill" plea as examples of social inequality at work. John Carneal's work as a lawyer ensured that his son would have special privileges. John had so many ties to the prosecutor's office, they complained, that Michael was bound to get off lightly. The James family noted with suspicion that most of the people involved in the criminal investigation were friends of the Carneals:

> JUDY: Supposedly the wife of the sheriff went and interviewed John and Ann [for the criminal proceedings].
> JOE: They were good buddies. She had the least training . . . of any deputy they had down there, but she was paid more than anybody else. She was the only one to interview John and Ann and that was because [the Carneals] approved that she would come because they knew her from years back.

The Carneal family was also close to other elites in Paducah who were thought to have helped Michael's case. The *Paducah Sun,* the main newspaper in town, was highly critical of the families who filed civil actions against the Carneals, suggesting that the suits were preventing the community from getting beyond the tragedy. Given that the newspaper publisher lived only "three houses away" from the Carneals, the families felt they knew why the paper would take such a strident stand. Personal ties, they thought, had tainted the paper, influenced the composition of the legal teams, and snared all of the powerful people in a web of influence that the plaintiffs could not match.

They saw a pattern: the prosecutors did not consult with them about plea bargaining,[21] the investigations of Michael's hard drive[22] and phone records[23] were delayed, and the criminal investigation was closed after a month.[24] They reasoned that things would not have proceeded this way if the prosecution had been truly independent. It could only mean one thing: Ties among a professional clique had corrupted the whole case.

Most Heath families rejected this view of the Carneals as players in the Paducah power structure. John Carneal's law practice focuses on workmen's compensation claims, a far cry from corporate law, which might have fit the elite image the victim families had in mind. But class is in the mind of the beholder. The families who lost their children were looking at someone who had connections. The rest of the town was looking at a man they considered an upstanding citizen, as the Carneals' Lutheran minister explained:

> John's a defense attorney, he's always for the underdog. How many things he's done for me on behalf of members of the church and so forth, when we're having legal problems and couldn't afford [his services, but] John never charged us. . . . In John's law office. . . , the secretary-receptionist doesn't dress fancy. The common man feels very comfortable there. . . . He's just that kind of guy, and Ann too. Ann is not stylish or anything like that. She's not out in the community as much as John is, but very respected in her own way too.

The class argument for the conduct of the prosecutor's case failed to convince Heath residents who knew the Carneals personally. For those who were several steps removed, though, it not only had resonance; it helped to account for how a murderer could grow up inside a comfortable family. One working-class father and son thought they knew exactly what the connection was: professionals make bad parents because they are too caught up in their work to spend time with their kids. "It seems they're just so wrapped up," the father told us. "I think that's why Michael did it," the son continued. "He wasn't getting enough attention from his parents."

His dad was busy. And he was trying to make as much money as he could. And it's not bad, it's just he got wrapped up in his work. And instead of going to somebody and talking about his problems, he did the thing that we never thought he would do.

Did the same class division surface in Jonesboro? We found little evidence of it in Westside, although the national media certainly played on the theme in its own treatment of the case. Since the Woodards live on the wrong side of the tracks, in a trailer park, and possessed all the wrong biographical background (abuse, divorce, criminality, and poverty), the makings of a class divide were all there. And yet, Gretchen Woodard's public conduct cut across this potential gulf and rendered it less salient in the Westside community. Gretchen never hid from public view; she appeared on national television, accepted publicly her son's culpability, and never tried to rebut the criticism that was flung in her direction. She stood by her son but also apologized on his behalf. Gretchen was the essence of Christian "process," having scrutinized herself and her child, opened herself to shame, and asked for forgiveness, expecting none. It might be argued that by behaving in an open and responsible fashion, Gretchen reconfirmed a tenet of Christian faith that the most honorable people on this Earth are not the powerful, but the meek.

CULTURE WARS

Tragedies have a way of throwing into high relief the fractures that lie below the surface of a community. In the Bible Belt South, those tensions have grown steadily as the distance between conservative views of family life, discipline, and the role of religion have diverged from a more liberal or laissez-faire impulse elsewhere in the country. Defenders of the "old ways" point to the loosening of moral standards as an explanation for almost any kind of damage. From this perspective, we should not be surprised if Mitchell and Andrew ended up committing a mass murder, because boys raised by divorcees or in latchkey households are destined for bad ends. Michael's rampage reflects the absence of standards in schools, the intrusions of violent media, the cultural cancer spreading through the Internet, and the ill-advised tolerance shown to irreligious counterculture groups like the Goths. That all this should come to no good is even less surprising to cultural conservatives who are convinced that a lack of accountability is running rampant through our society and that we no longer insist on punishment for wrongdoers. Because Bible Belt tradition is suffused with an underlying, populist suspicion of elites, the notion that rampage shootings come about because of a failure to discipline—or that judicial processes are tainted by class privilege—made sense to people who had come to expect "business as usual," in which ordinary people suffer at the hands of the powerful.[25]

The sharp strain between Christian ideals, which call for public confession and shame, and the legal process, which requires strategic maneuvering, increased the anger of the victim families.[26] The notion that the truth was concealed from them, that people who bore responsibility for their daughters' deaths were protected from prosecution or coddled in "country club" detention centers rather than harsh prisons, was consistent with their view that power trumps justice. These things happen when the true foundation of religion and a more authentic egalitarian social system is overthrown by secular institutions and class-based hierarchies.

Religious beliefs and local readings of class conflict played a critical role in the search for closure in Heath and Westside. For those who lost their children and were desperate for a full accounting of why, that closure may never come. They see forces arrayed against them that have prevented the truth from surfacing. Those who lost less find inspiration in Biblical teachings of forgiveness, look past the class differences to see good parents who loved their children but inexplicably raised kids who turned out to have serious problems. They can accept those parents back into the fold, or let them go (as the Goldens would prefer), but without rancor.

These sentiments are hardly confined to the Bible Belt South. Families elsewhere in the country who have lost loved ones to murder do not forgive easily, religiosity notwithstanding. They often feel, as these victim families felt, that the judicial system turns a blind eye to their interests by being overly protective of the rights of the accused. American culture, inspired by its early Protestant origins, has always put a great deal of store in the idea of personal responsibility. Tensions between individual accountability and the mitigating factors in criminal cases—from abusive childhoods to mental illness—have always been pronounced and remain so in Bethel, Alaska, or Littleton, Colorado, as in Westside or Heath. Many Americans feel that criminal justice system is too lenient in focusing attention on the bad hand that criminals have been dealt, to the neglect of the punitive side of the equation. After all, lots of people have bad experiences growing up, but most of them overcome them to lead good lives. On this theory, we should continue to hold maximally accountable those people who do otherwise. A "victim's rights" movement has gathered force to accelerate the change.

Pressure is being felt all over the United States—although perhaps with greater fervor in conservative regions—to abandon the line that separates juvenile cases from the adult ones. The ferocity of high-profile crimes committed by teenagers has provoked a harsh response among the public. The desire for vengeance through punishment has been gathering steam for some time, while confidence in rehabilitation has declined.

The religious tone we heard in Heath and Westside does not render the experience of these two communities unique. They have their own way of expressing the conditions under which miscreants should be punished, shamed, forgiven, or forgotten. But they are not alone.

9

PICKING UP
THE PIECES

Natural disasters can produce a powerful euphoria. Neighbors on the outs, religious factions, and political antagonists set their differences aside and come together in a burst of unity. Initially, that is exactly what happened in the wake of these shootings.[1] But it didn't last. If the first fissures broke open over questions of blame and forgiveness, chasms later developed as both communities grappled with the problem of healing. Jonesboro Family Life minister Ron Deal compared the aftermath of the shootings to an earthquake, with many concentric circles around the epicenter representing the different rates at which people would heal. After the initial period of common shock and grief, neighbors recovered differently, creating yet one more fault line for conflict. How much support and attention did the peripherally affected owe to those who were at the epicenter? How fast should victim families be expected to recover? Agreement proved hard to achieve and feelings hardened. In these small towns, where one cannot avoid the neighbors for long, people who expected sympathy discovered that friends were ducking their company, avoiding the subject.

Not recognizing the differential rates of healing, each side thought the other was wrong—or worse, that they were "damaged goods." The emotional needs of some placed them in direct opposition to the well-being of others. How close people were to the epicenter of the shooting created tension when others further removed tried to claim that they, too, had been damaged. Who had the right to claim true victim status? Rampage school shootings produced divisions reminiscent of the gaps that opened up among residents of Oklahoma City in the wake of the 1995 bombing of the federal building.[2] Survivors of terrorism who failed to "get over it" were thought to have a mental illness, victims of posttraumatic stress disorder.

Yet in this divisive environment, decisions had to be made that would affect the whole community. How should counseling be handled? How should donations be distributed? How should the victims' memories be honored? Public officials and charity directors were inevitably caught in the middle, unable to please everyone and fearful of causing harm to someone at every turn.

CLOSING RANKS

Raw emotion flowed through both towns for many weeks after the shootings. Numbness, disbelief, anguish, anger, and loving affection jumbled together on the sidewalks, in classrooms, across store counters, behind the polished desks of law firms, and inside the homes of countless families. Grim survivors of a terrible ordeal, residents turned to one another for solace. Ironically, some felt that they had never experienced such a closeness before in their lives. A Paducah pastor compared the sentiment in town to the solidarity he remembered during the Second World War.

In the days after the shooting at Westside, the entire Jonesboro area stood together as well. People worked together toward recovery, as they had in the wake of tornadoes that leveled the town about thirty years earlier, one of which killed more than forty people. Before the shooting, ministerial groups in Jonesboro were at loggerheads with one another over whether the county should remain "dry" or allow the sale of alcohol. It was a tense period, with open conflicts between denominations. In the wake of the shooting, the major antagonists put their differences aside and formed a Ministerial Alliance that was responsible for organizing a memorial at the Arkansas State University's Convocation Center. A moment of true unity, the service symbolized their ability to grow stronger and closer in the wake of tragedy.

Community members also had a new enemy in common: the media. Seventy U.S. and foreign news organizations sent more than 200 reporters, photographers, and support personnel to cover the shooting in Westside. Out-of-town reporters began arriving at the school within ninety minutes of the first report of the shooting, and by the following morning, fifty satellite trucks and camera crews, including international representatives from the United Kingdom, Germany, and Japan occupied the school grounds.[3] In Paducah, national media outlets, in fierce competition with one another, staked out the school, the local barbecue, and the courthouse.

The media besieged both towns, disrupting daily life, straining the nerves of residents already fraught by shock and grief. Sam Cartright, who manages a small bank in Jonesboro, said, "It was overwhelming. To become the center of

TIME

Mitchell Johnson, 13, and Andrew Golden, 11. Right, Golden as a toddler

Armed & Dangerous

An up-close look at the lives of two gun-happy kids and the murderous ambush of their Arkansas classmates

Andrew Golden was given his first rifle for his sixth birthday and had trained as an expert marksman by age 11. TIME-LIFE PICTURES/GETTY IMAGES

Mitchell Johnson's yearbook photo in the 8th grade, age 13. Known to most teachers as polite and respectful, Johnson had a boastful, angry side familiar to his classmates.
BISHOP'S PHOTOGRAPHY / CORBIS SYGMA

Jackie and Doug Golden, Andrew's stricken grandparents. Mitchell Johnson and Andrew Golden stole most of their arsenal from the gun rack visible in the rear. JIM LO SCALZO-U.S. NEWS & WORLD REPORT

Westside teacher Shannon Wright's gravesite. Neighbors and friends climbed out of their cars and stood with their heads bowed as her funeral procession passed. AP/WIDE WORLD PHOTOS

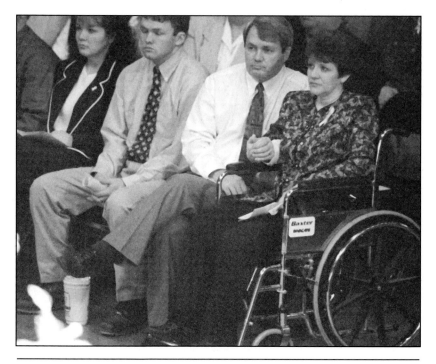

Lynette Thetford, a teacher wounded in the shooting, attended the memorial service for the victims. She later transferred out of Westside Middle School because of the trauma. AP/WIDE WORLD PHOTOS

Gretchen Woodard, Mitchell Johnson's mother, reads a prison letter from her 14-year-old son. To this day, she has no idea why he killed his classmates. KEN HEARD-ARKANSAS DEMOCRAT-GAZETTE (MARCH 21, 1999)

Westside victims—Shannon Wright (middle), and (left to right), Paige Ann Herring, Natalie Brooks, Britthney Varner, and Stephanie Johnson. This portrait was given to Westside Middle School, but they took it down because it was too painful. Today it hangs in the back of the District Attorney's office in Jonesboro. AUTHORS' PHOTO

Students and parents react in horror, moments after Michael Carneal shot into the Heath High prayer group. AP/WIDE WORLD PHOTOS/THE PADUCAH (KY.) SUN

A depressed and delusional Michael Carneal, age 14, at his arraignment for murder, with his lawyer, Chuck Granner. Carneal could not bring himself to look up from the table. THE PADUCAH (KY.) SUN

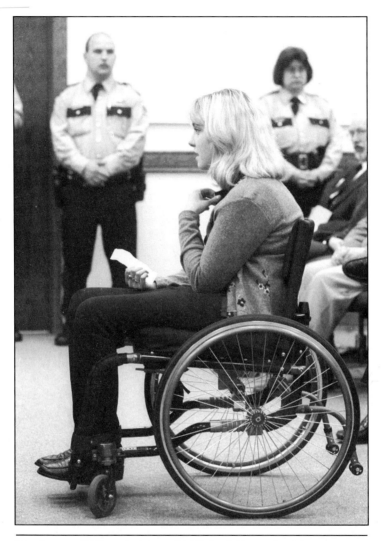

"Look at me," Missy Jenkins told Michael Carneal at his sentencing hearing. "I'm paralyzed from my chest down. . . . I don't know why you did this to me and to everybody else." THE COURIER-JOURNAL

Mass funeral service at the Heartland Worship Center for the three victims of the Heath High shooting. Thousands watched the televised ceremony. THE PADUCAH (KY.) SUN

The Steger family, who lost their daughter Kayce (in photo), explain why they were filing civil law suits against the Carneals, the unindicted co-conspirators, gun and video game manufacturers, and Heath teachers and administrators. ROSHANFOTO.COM

Michael Carneal at age 19 in the Kentucky State Reformatory. Carneal explained that he never looked at who he shot and described himself as a "compassionate person." KEITH WILLIAMS-AP PHOTO/COURIER-JOURNAL

Kayce Steger, age 15, Jessica James, age 17, and Nicole Hadley, age 14: the three members of the Heath prayer group who died in the shooting. THE PADUCAH (KY.) SUN

the world in Jonesboro, Arkansas, overnight was really difficult for us. . . . It caused a little bit of a feeding frenzy."

Even worse than the sheer size of the press corps was their aggressive behavior. Just when families most needed privacy, cameras followed them home, reporters pretended to be close relatives in order to get into victims' hospital rooms, and children were waylaid by journalists scrambling for emotional, on-camera interviews without parental consent. One Heath student described how a reporter chased him all over the school grounds:

> Me and my friends were sitting outside, at the back of the gym, . . . and a news reporter showed up in one of the big vans with the camera and jumped out, trying to get us interviewed on tape. We were like, "No, we don't want to talk, leave us alone," and we started walking away. He called [after] us about some questions, until finally we ended up . . . running around the front of the gym, trying to get into the school [to find] the security guard, [who] stopped them. . . . Obviously they were doing what they had to do, but . . . they were harassing people because they want to have their story. They just want some thirteen- or twelve-year-old kid who just saw some-one shot . . . Have some respect!

Banding together against these invaders, both communities drew distinctions between insiders and outsiders. Members of the community were seen as sharing a common experience. Even the local media personnel, unlike the national and international reporters, were accepted as allies rather than foes in this battle. Communal solidarity strengthened in the face of this external force.

Aspects of teen culture changed for the better. Football players and band members, geeks and Goths, all had something in common, perhaps for the first time since they hit adolescence. Barriers between them broke down as students offered sympathy and support to one another. "From a student's perspective," Chris Jackson recalled, "[life] has changed for the better."

> People talk to each other more. They're more in synch. . . . Before this, . . . people weren't supportive. But now . . . we're like people grown up. . . . Like if something bad happens, then [kids] talk to each other and they support each other. Before [the shooting], we never really cared about nobody else. So we have changed for the better.

A Heath student, Albert Fisher, saw the same solidarity break down the walls that had separated cliques.

When I was in sixth [grade] there used to be like a lot of little groups together. . . . After the shooting, . . . everybody just kind of sat down and everybody gets along now. . . . I wouldn't say there was much problem with groups nowadays like there used to be. . . . Like it's a totally different school.

Initial media accounts placed the blame on bullying, which increased students' feelings of guilt about their role in pushing the shooters toward mounting a rampage. The potential truth in that observation led students to work overtime to cut back on the harassment. Heath students, such as Rick Bowman, a senior, told us that fighting declined considerably. In the few months before the shooting, there was a fistfight about once a month; in the four years after the shooting, though, he estimated that a little more than one fight per year occurred. "People learned that if you've got a problem you can talk about it," Rick explained. "You don't have to keep everything in. Everyone has the same problems. . . . It's better to go through it together than to just trying to go it alone."

CRACKS IN THE FOUNDATION

It didn't last. As time passed, the atmosphere returned to normal and the good graces in which jocks and geeks held each other faded away. "People still make fun of other people," Elaine Johnson, a Heath sophomore commented. "Kids put them down to make themselves feel better."

It might have changed for a little, while but it's back. . . . If somebody is a little clumsy and, like, drops their books on the floor, people aren't . . . as mean as they were in middle school. . . . But they'll still talk about each other behind their backs and make fun of people. Not in front of them.

Adolescent life may have been affected for the specific students who lived through the shooting, but enduring change is another story.

Community cohesion seems to have been short-lived as well. Even the Ministerial Alliance, a beacon of unity, tarnished as neighbors realized that the previous conflicts had been put aside but not forgotten. "It was, like, come on, can't we just get along?" said one Jonesboro youth minister. "And all of a sudden, we're together. We're not together. No values changed, no convictions changed. Those things did not disappear when a bullet flies through the air." A similar fate awaited Columbine. Tom Galland, a senior pastor in Jonesboro, described an interaction he had with a minister in Littleton, Colorado, who called him for advice after their shooting. Galland told the Littleton minister that for a period after the shooting, it would feel like everyone was coming together and people were very caring, but it would be false. Everything would fall apart and it would turn ugly. Six months later, the minister from Littleton called him back and told him, "Have you heard? It's just like you said. We had a false sense of cohesion and togetherness, and now everyone is suing each other."

Why did the togetherness fade? Old sources of friction, which predated the shooting, became sharper under the stress. Class conflicts that were already present in these communities were given new, dark meanings, driving wedges into cracks that already showed on the surface. The rampage created entirely new sources of division in the community as well. How people dealt with the shooting drove them into different emotional camps. Differing views of who was most affected spurred territorial battles over ownership of the tragedy.

THE EARTHQUAKE: HEALING AT DIFFERENT SPEEDS

Family Life Minister Ron Deal caught the dimensions of the aftermath with tremendous accuracy in his earthquake analogy.

> Those closest to the epicenter . . . are going to be the ones who have the greatest psychological, emotional, social impact on their life. . . . Everything has been destroyed; all they have is rubble and ashes. . . . The trauma, the shock, once you get past that, then you still have to figure out how to go back in your house every day knowing "my daughter's not going to be there." And just living with that reality is just terrible. . . . The further you get away from the epicenter, the less impact there is. "Severe damage": most everything destroyed, some things are salvageable, so the house is gone but the garage is still there. They've got something. "Partial damage": the foundation's been shook, there's a few cracked walls, so they've definitely felt it and boy was that weird and, okay I think we're going to be all right. . . . "Shaken, not stirred," felt the ground move, but they're back to life.

For those at the epicenter, moving on is exceedingly difficult. Their lives have been completely torn apart, and they seem unable to pick up the pieces. Denise Simpson, a Westside administrator, has been burdened by a heavy sense of responsibility, an inability to reach out to others, and exhaustion with the traumas that others lay at her feet, fairly or not. It was hard for her to talk about the shooting at all, but when she did, a dam of emotion broke open. "It's been a life-changing event," she said with a heavy sadness in her voice, "I feel like I've aged ten years."

> The "ongoingness" of it is unbelievable. It was such a tragedy. A car accident, you have a wreck and someone will get killed and that was a very tough thing to go through, but eventually, over the years, time seems to come to heal those things. This one was not healing. This is just continuous. . . . There doesn't seem to be an end in sight.

Those closest to the shootings continue to suffer from nightmares or panic attacks. Children startle at loud noises. "We went to a Christian music concert," a Paducah pastor mentioned, "and of course they bounce balloons back and forth."

> And somebody popped a balloon. And all of our kids started ducking, because that's what it sounded like to them. And that was months after the shooting.

Westside children know exactly what he means. One of their teachers recalled a softball trip that students from Westside and a neighboring school, Middleton, took to Little Rock, Arkansas:

> All the girls had been in seventh grade that year [of the shooting] . . . And a car had backfired and all the Westside girls got down. And the Middleton girls are sitting there looking at us, kind of crazy, but that was just our reaction . . . and we all started crying.

Many children are still in counseling several years after the shooting.

Teachers at the epicenter have been severely traumatized; even the simplest acts force them to relive painful memories. Watching movies with guns, violence, or death reminds them of what they went through. Jane Holden, a Westside Middle School teacher, was unable to continue her duties as a history teacher because she got too upset when the subject of the world wars came up; she is now a reading teacher instead. Some teachers find themselves becoming hysterical during routine fire drills. When they visit churches, walk down hallways, or enter auditoriums, they check for the exits and think about what they will do if someone starts shooting. On occasion, teacher Mary Curtis looks down the hallway of the middle school and still sees the blood on the floor.

Emotional problems led to illness as well. The Westside staff has seen some of its youngest members become quite sick or pass away. One person had an aneurysm; another—only forty years old—was diagnosed with cancer. Although these unfortunate cases might have come about anyway, teachers are of the opinion that the stress of the shooting was responsible. Burdens of this kind took their toll on the personal lives of teachers. Some marriages broke up, and other people rushed to marry for the emotional support, only to divorce shortly afterward.

———

The shooters and their families were caught in the middle of this earthquake, too. As much as anyone, their lives have been turned upside down. The experience was particularly hard on Monte Johnson, Mitchell's younger brother. Gretchen had always known that the two boys were close and that Mitchell was protective of Monte, and suddenly that rock, that shield, disappeared. "The first month was a living hell," Gretchen recalled, sitting at her kitchen table, staring out the sliding door to the backyard. "The police wouldn't let us touch anything in [Mitchell's] room."

> Things had been scattered, but it was just that part of Mitch that was still there. . . . We couldn't let loose of it yet. . . . After three weeks I looked at Terry and I said, "You know, I really think in my heart [we have to get back to] normal for the rest of the family. . . .
>
> So I said to Terry [that Monte] doesn't make his bed. I [told Monte] "Look, the least you can do is make the bed." [Monte] give me this kind of funny look and didn't say much of anything. Well, three days had gone by and his bed hadn't been made, and so I had to call him on it. . . .
>
> He got this sheepish god-awful look on his face, and he looked down on the floor, and he looked at me all apologetic, and he [whispers]: "I don't know how to make my bed" . . . I said, "Monte, you've been making your bed since you were five years old. What do you mean you don't know how to?" And [he said], "Mitch has been doing it for me like that."

Monte was scared to return to school after the shooting. Although many people went out of their way to welcome him back, his life at Westside would never be the same. Jane Holden had him in her class, and the resemblance between the two brothers made her squirm inside.

They said he was loud and wasn't quite as polite as what Mitchell was, but just looking at his hands and knowing that the same hands exactly like that were the ones that shot Shannon and killed her, and then seeing him walk down the hall because he's very similar in build and the way he walks to Mitchell. We got along fine, but I was always nervous about him. What if? What if?

Monte has since moved away to Minnesota to live with his father.[4]

Andrew's parents, Dennis and Pat Golden, have also moved out of town, to another community in Arkansas, where they still work for the postal service. They lost many of their lifelong friends as a result of their son's rampage shooting. Some describe the atmosphere after the shooting as so tense that some people were nervous about what kind of message being friendly to the Goldens would send to others. Ironically, those who were wounded or lost a relative were immune to criticism if they extended a hand to the Goldens. For everyone else, the rules were unclear. Was being civil to the Goldens betraying the victims?

GETTING STUCK, MOVING ON

For those nearest the epicenter, life will never be the same. But for others who were further out on the fringes of the event, life goes on, and getting beyond the tragedy is a natural evolution.[5] If healing were a purely private matter, this would not be problematic—but because there is a public element to the process, it is. Those who were badly damaged need the support of everyone around them, while those on the periphery cannot fathom why these neighbors are burnishing this awful memory. "At first [the community] lifted us up and held onto us," Jane Holden, a Westside teacher, confided. "Now they got tired of hearing about it before we got tired of talking about it."

> The kids and the teachers needed to keep talking, because we were so hurt. But the people on the outside . . . didn't want to talk about it, and so we ended up having to talk to each other [instead].

As the wider community retreats from the healing process, suspicion grows that there is something profoundly "wrong" with the people who are stuck, like broken records, rehearsing the shooting, month after month. To be thought of as a little unbalanced is hardly what the victims of the shooting need. Yet teacher Julia Sampson found, to her dismay, that she was being asked to smother her emotions in order to get along with her neighbors:

I don't want to talk about it in gory details, but . . . I have flashbacks of the ambulances. When I heard the sirens . . . north of town last year and I fell apart, I want people to understand. . . . I'm not ready for [my friends] to forget . . . [because] I need to talk about it. . . .[6]

The same disjuncture undid some of the victim families as well. Suzann Wilson lost her daughter, Britthney Varner, in the Westside shooting, and found herself divorced not long afterward. Speaking with newspaper reporters in Jonesboro on the five-year anniversary of the shooting, she explained that she and her husband simply couldn't adjust to one another's approach to grief. "He didn't want to talk about it. That was his way of handling it. We stopped talking about everything. The house changed. It became empty. I stopped cooking and we didn't eat together, and the house became a prison." People in town "wanted to get on with their life," she noted. "I wanted to dwell on my loss."

Jonesboro residents find they have to tiptoe around trying to anticipate how the person on the other side of the table will react to a show of emotion. "You don't want to bring it out unless you're sure the person you are talking with wants to hear it," Betsey Woods, a Jonesboro counselor, said. She needs to be sure that her conversation partners won't think poorly of her.

The social norm is you don't [talk about the shooting]. Or if you [do, you] get an attitude from people like, "What's the matter with you? Why are you still talking about it?"

Those who lost their children, who desperately needed to be embraced by the community, found themselves losing again as the initial period of sympathy and support came to a close. "The people I work with avoid me because they don't want to talk to me about it," said the mother of one of the victims. "It's almost like I have a contagious disease."[7]

Support networks atrophy under these conditions. Beverly Ashford developed a friendship with a fellow teacher at Columbine High School by mail after the Littleton disaster. She is the only person Beverly can talk to, since no one else in her community can bear to hear it again.

We talked last night for about three hours. . . . But she's about the only person—other than my therapist and my husband, she's the only person I talk at all about the shooting because [people] around here want to pretend like it [didn't] happen.

The fault lines splintered the ranks of teachers and students. With their prescribed exit routes for a fire drill, about half of the Westside teachers walked into the line of fire, while others were safe from harm's way. Were they all victims? Mary Curtis, a teacher who was caught on the front lines, felt a deep division—and powerful resentment—between those who had and those who had not actually "touched a child" that day. Mary felt that some of her colleagues judged her unfavorably, even though they had not been forced to contend with the horror. She had had to make instant decisions over the life of a bleeding thirteen-year-old, while others huddled behind the protection of the building. How dare they criticize her now that she was having trouble coming back to work?

> I heard secretaries [say,] "What's wrong with her? She needs to get her shit together.". . . Those remarks being made by people who never touched a child, who never had to make any decisions, can I really not feel a pulse or I just don't know what I'm doing? Is this dangerous? Do I need to leave and go on? Some people didn't have to deal with the little bleeding, the little breathing. . . . By the time I ran back down that same hall, there was so much blood on it that I was trying to hold on to the lockers. There are people that judge me that don't know.

Some teachers who did go out the west exit managed to get back into the building to take cover. The shooters were still at large and no one knew whether the rampage was over or still in progress. Everyone had to decide whether they were going to stay at the scene with the wounded children or go inside and protect themselves. Staying outside meant risking one's own life.

No response coming from teachers who had not "touched a child" came out right because—Mary Curtis felt—they simply *couldn't* understand the emotional state of the teachers who had stayed with the wounded. A teacher who ran back inside the building would sometimes try to offer Mary her support, but usually pretended the shooting never happened. Mary resented both reactions.

Divisions like this did not erupt at Heath, partly because of the differences in the shootings. At Heath, the shooting was over in seconds. Michael Carneal was in full view the entire time, and there were no questions about the shooter's identity or location. After firing eight shots, Michael put his gun down and was taken to the principal's office. At Westside, by contrast, eighty-nine students and nine teachers were in the line of fire. They could not see the shooters and were not even sure where the bullets were coming from at first. A full ten minutes passed between the end of the firing and the capture of Johnson and Golden, and more time passed before word got back to the school that the shooters were in custody. During those intense moments, teachers faced crucial decisions about where to go and what to do. That was the center of the lasting trauma, and it fueled subsequent moral critiques and mental health problems.

A parallel divide erupted among the students at Westside. The summer after the shooting, sixty-eight Westside students attended Ferncliff, a residential camp for children affected by violence and war. Another camp was held the spring before we arrived in Westside, but only twenty students attended. The kids who continued to attend were sometimes mocked by classmates. Who was and who was not "over" the shooting became a public label.

Minister Ron Deal's account of the way these fissures developed over time recounts how solidarity collapsed as conflicts gathered force and moral judgments hardened. Differential rates of healing were causing the community to come unglued:

> The first three months after the shooting, unbelievable support, unbelievable outpouring of love, compassion, money, time, volunteerism. . . . Phase Two: We set it aside. School got out . . . and everybody went on an emotional vacation. . . . There was also a growing saturation. . . . It was just ongoing, and you get to a place where you just hate to hear another word about this. Phase Three: . . . With the onset of school came back all the emotion, and a lot of the fear, security, safety issues. But also . . . we began to have a little bit of the splitting. . . .
>
> You start hearing talk about "moving beyond this. When are we not going to hear about it anymore?" . . . The further we went in time—six months, nine months, twelve months—the more that polarization just began to show itself. . . .
>
> Phase Four: "Don't forget our losses" . . . nothing has changed, when will they ever get over this? Those were kind of the polarizing messages that I'd hear.

Mental health counselors believe that denial and survivor's guilt are at the base of the division. Perhaps. Yet from our perspective, the hostility derives at least as much from a concern over what the shooting represents. Its very mention reminds residents of their vulnerability. "We certainly don't want to have it happen again," noted a Westside administrator, "but at the same time there is no assurance that we can keep it from happening again." Putting the shooting behind them helped assuage that anxiety and guilt, and those who insist on remembering for the sake of their own mental health force those emotions onto those who want the subject to disappear.

The civil suits in Paducah dredged up similar emotional aftershocks. Long after peripheral bystanders were ready to move on, the suits kept the shooting on the front pages of the local newspapers. While the victim families thought of their legal actions as a means of getting at the truth, holding people accountable, and achieving closure, their neighbors rejected this motivation altogether. Helen Banning, a Heath High school teacher, broke down in tears as she told us about how the lawsuits attacked the very people who had come forward to help the wounded. "That [plaintiff's] attorney has no idea what it's like, . . . how he's making me feel . . . being sued. 'Cause he didn't know what it was like for me." But it was not simply the civil suit defendants who were upset by the cases. The legal maneuvers touched raw nerves far and wide. Books that had been closed and shelved were opened to scrutiny again, leaving the community feeling unsettled and insecure once more.

WHO OWNS THIS PROBLEM?

Much as they hated the shooting, groups that had been affected fought over who had the right to authentic victim status. As some parts of the community tried to use the shooting to their advantage, others drew lines in the sand. It took a more distant set of eyes to see how this unraveling developed. Betsey Woods works at Arkansas State University as a professor of social work and is not from the area originally. Her outsider eyes picked up on the tensions emerging from the wreckage of the shooting as the months wore on and the divisions became sharper:

> Who owns this problem? Who owns the solution? Who did it happen to? . . . Who is "us"? . . . A lot of people wanted to say they helped but not all the people [would agree that] they helped. But it seemed important to people to be able to say they did something. And so there was a debate over who is allowed to say that and who isn't allowed to say that.

Initially, Jonesboro and Westside came together as one. City residents rushed out to the Westside area to help with counseling. They volunteered their time, gave generous donations to the victims' families, and genuinely felt as affected by the shooting as their Westside counterparts. Over time, though, the connections dwindled and residents began to distinguish more sharply between the two places as a way of clarifying where the shooting *really* happened.

The national media had dubbed the rampage the "Jonesboro shooting." Residents were quick to correct us on this point: the rampage had not happened in

Jonesboro.[8] Underlying this distinction were more serious sources of division about whom the shooting belonged to: who had to deal with it, and who got to claim whatever positive came of it. Jonesboro residents tired of the negative associations the rampage attached to their city, especially because it had not really happened there. Westsiders thought Jonesboro courted the attention on purpose.

After the shooting, a number of schools in the Jonesboro school district won a Federal Safe Schools/Healthy Students Grant, which provides some important services, including security measures, educational reforms, teacher training, and mental health services. New case managers were hired on the strength of these resources for several schools to work with kids who needed counseling or therapy. Westside was written into the grant and receives important benefits as a consequence. Yet as Denise Simpson, an administrator at Westside, noted with grim irony, the Jonesboro school district rode in on the popular misconception that they had been victims of the shooting.

> We're a school *outside* of Jonesboro, it's not a Jonesboro tragedy. It's a Westside School tragedy. . . . Everybody wants to lay claim now after the fact that this happened to them. It didn't happen to them.

Tussles over who could legitimately claim "credit" as victims continued for months. Denise was infuriated by the efforts of uninvolved parties to benefit from the grief of real survivors:

> A lot of people trying to get on the bandwagon. And the people that were actually . . . in the middle of it, they don't want the glorification. . . . We resent the fact that someone else is taking any type of credit for anything they had done. . . . You'll find most resistant to talking about it will be the people that were involved directly. . . .
>
> Some people . . . wanted to take ownership of what's happened and they had nothing to do with it. They showed up two days later as a counselor and learned what they learned from somebody who told them their experience. And so a lot of people were interviewed on television. . . . They were never even here. . . .
>
> One man that knows nothing about what happened at the school . . . came in as a person who was supposed to reassure the staff, and he had no feelings for us. And he walked away from here and he wrote a book. . . . He writes this book like he's Mr. Somebody. . . . He wasn't on this campus thirty minutes and he writes a book as if he knew what all happened.

CHARITY: WHO ARE
THE "REAL" VICTIMS HERE?

The first day after the shooting, all Westside students received a flower. The second day they were given little golden angels, or gold rings. The next day they received teddy bears. After that, they received little poems. Bills for medical services, coffins, ambulances, funeral expenses—all of it was covered by loving friends and neighbors, as well as complete strangers. One Westside student who was shot lived in a house trailer that lacked sufficient furniture; a local business came in and furnished their home for free.[9] Heath High School received $72,000 in the immediate aftermath from people as far away as New Jersey. Gifts, good wishes, and money poured into both communities—over a half million dollars to Westside—from around the world, and it still does.

But every silver lining seems to have its cloud. In both communities, victims' funds were established. The issue that loomed over them was one now familiar to those who have had to administer disaster relief funds to victims of the World Trade Center attack: who was and was not a victim, an issue that played directly into the conflicts of who "owned" this tragedy. In Westside, the funds were given to the families of those who were shot. This strict definition did not sit well with everyone. Jane Holden was worried about students whose problems surfaced years down the road. How would their needs be supported if all the funds were doled out immediately to the wounded and the families of the dead?[10]

> They only counted . . . the ten who were injured and five that were killed. . . . But . . . that day there were 89 kids on that playground and nine teachers, and they were all victims too. . . . They've overlooked them. I think it's sad. . . . They're going to have some problems later. . . . They should've used [the fund] for counseling. These are babies. These are sixth-graders. They're little. And they watched their friends die. You don't get over something like that.

In Heath, too, there was conflict over how narrowly to define the category of victim. The kids who were shot? The ones who witnessed bloodshed, but emerged physically unscathed? Holly Gates, now in her senior year at Heath, was part of the prayer group in the line of fire at Heath. A thin, fidgety young woman, Holly looks deeply sad, perpetually on the edge of tears. She escaped unscathed physically, but her mental state is another matter. A wider definition of "victim" would be needed to take Holly into account:

I was diagnosed back in October with [Raynaud's] syndrome,[11] posttraumatic stress syndrome and panic disorder. I ended up having to quit [sports] because of these things, because it brought my immune system down so low, I was so weak all of the time, I lost a lot of weight. . . . In class . . . I got to a point where I couldn't concentrate, because there were so many other things in my mind. . . . I actually failed Algebra III last semester because after I was diagnosed with some of this stuff, I couldn't do anything.

My doctor . . . and my mom [wrote] . . . and called the school board several times. We haven't had any cooperation with them. . . . My mom had to fight in order to get help with psychiatrists and medications and stuff, which is what that [charity] money was for. . . .

This conflict also grew over the issue of who would be invited to the Ferncliff camp. The organizers of the camp invited the 89 Westside students who had exited the West door on March 24 and walked into the hail of bullets. The camp's own resources were limited, and funds to run the camp had to be raised from national church organizations and foundations.[12] This turned out to be but one example of a larger tendency to single out only those directly in the line of fire and to ignore everyone else. Either explicitly or implicitly, every service and every program defined who were the victims, and however those lines were drawn, some people who saw themselves as victims were left out.

Community leaders had to tread lightly around questions of "ownership" to make sensitive decisions about who should receive charitable donations. Similarly, in the midst of emotional turmoil, school administrators, ministers, and town officials had the job of getting their communities back on track, which could not be set aside. It fell to them to figure out how to get the schools running again, what to do about memorializing the dead—problems that had an effect on everyone. Each decision directed how community-level healing was "supposed" to take place. With people recovering at different rates, this process pitted the needs of some against the desires of others, making community-level healing more and more elusive.

The first judgment call involved the school day itself. Should students be asked to come back right away, or hold off and recover at home? A consensus emerged that students should return to normal routines quickly.[13] Teachers and administrators responded to that call, with little thought of their own traumas. This plan took a toll on some of the teachers, though. Later on, resentment built up over this decision. "After being shot at, after having our friends and students killed, not getting sleep, . . . " complained one teacher, "we had to go back to school the next morning and act like everything was okay." Another teacher said, "You know, I don't think I've ever gotten over the fact that I needed a day to just roll in the fetal position and cry."

Of course, not everyone wanted to stay home. Some were distraught when they were alone and wanted more than anything to be with fellow victims at school. "I had to go back," Julia Sampson recalled. "While I was at home, I was miserable. When I was at school, I was better. . . . The place I wanted to be was with the people I experienced [the shooting] with." People grieve in different ways, which complicates the task of those making decisions that affect everyone.

CIRCLING THE WAGONS

In the aftermath of the shootings, the Westside and Heath communities were clearly in need of counseling services, but rather than face an insufficient supply, they had to contend with the opposite problem: an inundation of support. Handling the massive influx of offers and volunteers—from as far away as Lockerbie, Scotland—was a full-time job that school staff could not manage. These offers were made out of kindness, but the schools eventually closed the gates, excluding "outsiders" and turning inward.

Principals and their assistants did not know how to separate the well-meaning professionals from the attention-seeking busybodies, and their insecurity grew because they had lost control of the grounds and property. Was it a good idea to have so many strangers on-site when students and teachers already felt anxious and vulnerable? Westside administrators were forced to weed out some bad eggs, grandstanders who were looking for a little notoriety for themselves.

NOVA—the National Organization of Victims Assistance—which was invited by both schools to help students, ended up attracting some criticism in Westside. A documentary about the organization was being filmed for the television news magazine. They decided to film some of the group's activities in Westside for the program, without properly informing the students' families and teachers of the purpose. The Jonesboro prosecutor had to call the show's network to try to get the footage removed, an effort that succeeded at the last minute. Even those who arrived with noble purposes, it seemed, could not be fully trusted. Outsiders got a bad name as a consequence, a sentiment we encountered in our initial forays into the Westside community as well.

After experiencing an invasion of helpers and the extra burden of having to pare down nuisance volunteers and grandstanders, the communities quickly reached a saturation point.

[Schools] feel very protective of their students. You have to understand there's a book this thick of offers . . . everybody wants to come and help. . . . I think the longer it went, the closer the circle became of who they would trust then to intervene. It became, I think, an atmosphere of circling the wagon and saying, "We're opened up during this time of crisis, now we've got to close back down and get control of our situation."

—Thomas Gardner, professor of
social work, Arkansas State University

Self-reliance is a virtue, but not an uncomplicated prescription in a community with such high levels of social capital. Even though therapy was formally encouraged, some who needed help were reticent when it became clear that their main options were closely tied to the social networks "on the inside." Counseling or therapy is a stigmatized enterprise in these culturally conservative communities.[14] A Westside staff member told us, "I think . . . people here wouldn't suggest that they get counseling. A lot of times they're not open to it, because they see it as a sign of weakness." The worry that neighbors could find out that a child was in therapy was enough to discourage parents from it. "I don't know that I would have [my child] go to the school counselor," one parent told us.

Because they are going to be seen, . . . and that's probably going to make it a little bit worse. Not that the school counselor couldn't help. . . . I just mean that being visibly seen going in would probably hurt the situation a bit more.

Circling the wagons helped some people gain control over the situation; the unfortunate result for others was to cut them off from help they really needed.

REVISITING A TRAGEDY . . . OR RELIVING IT

Among those who rejected psychological treatment, the view was that the only way to get over a tragedy of these dimensions was *not* to talk about what had happened, since revisiting trauma just makes it worse: Best to just get on with life.[15] Teachers were aghast at this attitude. "We still have kids that freak out on a fire drill," Beverly Ashford pointed out.

We still have kids that don't sleep at night. . . . The least little thing like the slamming of a locker door or the dropping of a book just [sets them off].. . . You're dealing with parents that want to shove things under the rug. You're dealing with the school that [doesn't know what to do about that] since it is really the parents' choice.

Emotions that are swept under the rug at home bubble up in the classroom, where children turn to the faculty, and teachers who cannot find a sympathetic ear for their own fears lean on one another. Some students complained to their teachers that their parents would not listen to them, saying instead, "It's time to get over it." Teachers understood their dilemmas, because some of their husbands were losing patience with the subject as well. Westside teachers had one another. Their students had no one.

> [One student] was talking to me . . . she was crying, upset. We . . . were sitting outside talking. The first time she'd been out [in the courtyard] since the shooting had happened. She was hit and it had glanced off of a rib. . . . It was just a flesh wound. But . . . people had told her that the bullet that went into her probably had [killed another child] first. . . .

> Well, she's looking at me and she said, "You think maybe that bullet should've gone into me first, that maybe [the other child] would have lived . . . ? She was just hurt so bad. She needed somebody to talk to about that, somebody besides me. . . . I didn't know what to say to her. I did the best I could do without having any counseling [training] at all. But they just, all the parents felt like these kids will be okay, they're young, they'll bounce back. And I don't think they will.
>
> —Jane Holden, Westside teacher

Some parents may not recognize how much their kids need mental health services[16] or may be understandably wary of local stigma. Their own desire to return to normal may cause them to push their children's problems away. Yet parents are also reacting to the legitimate fear that therapy will do their children more harm than good. Rehearsing a traumatic incident can be harmful,[17] and parents who are concerned about this possibility are simply trying to shield their children from repeated injury. Thomas Gardner, an Arkansas State University professor of social work who lives in Jonesboro, knows that the fear of retraumatizing is real, but he tried to persuade Westside parents that professionals knows how to avoid "volatile kinds of questions" and instead let natural reactions to tragedy seep out. It was an uphill battle. "There is such a desire . . . to get back to normal," he sighed. "This is not us, this is not real." Talking about the shooting, even in therapy, would keep those unhappy memories alive.

REMEMBRANCE

If mental health is not an exact science, ritual observance is even less so. Questions that arose about the wisdom of counseling surfaced all over again in discussions of memorials. Should an annual observance of the deaths be held? For how long? Is this a healthy remembrance or a morbid reminder?

The initial memorial service at Arkansas State University's convocation center a week after the Westside shooting embraced the entire Jonesboro area. After that, public memorials contracted in scope, and soon faded away. The school itself was particularly silent: memorials were confined to the one-year anniversary, which was a small service, mainly for the staff. Fear of a media circus impelled Westside leaders to close ranks and make sure it was tightly controlled. The result was a memorial that seemed to many too minimalist, and when that anniversary passed, no further services were held at Westside.[18] On the two-year anniversary, a group of teachers and students who had been at the shooting scene and knew of each other's desire to keep talking, gathered informally. They met for dinner at a restaurant and then all went out to the cemeteries together.

A memorial garden created to honor those who had been killed was planted by a group of volunteers, but six months after their labors were finished, it still had not been dedicated. As one minister pointed out, the garden has "never been recognized by the Westside School. . . ."[19]

> That is a telling illustration of where we are as a community. We have tried to forget. We have tried to pretend. . . . I don't even think the community at large knows it's there. . . . It certainly has not been able to provide the kind of healing that it was meant to provide, a ritual if you will, to help people pass from one phase to another. And they don't even know it's there. . . . I just think that's so sad.

Why would the garden be ignored? Westside wanted to distance itself from tragedy—a mistake in the minister's view, because "the whole idea of anniversaries . . . these ritual rites of passage, is to help people heal." Reminders of tragedy, through memorials, tributes, and anniversary ceremonies, bring back unwanted memories.[20] The concrete path where the students and teachers were mowed down was relaid to remove bloodstains; the fire drills were replaced, at least for a time, with bells that had a different tone. After the shooting, a portrait was drawn for the school of the five victims who were killed. Three years later, when we arrived in the area, the drawing was hanging in one of the conference rooms of the Jonesboro District Attorney's office. The school didn't want it.

What some saw as denial, administrators saw as a necessary attempt to carry on with the school's purpose. Community attempts to memorialize conflicted with the administration's judgment of how to get the school back on track. "Just when is it going to end?" asked Susan Miller, a Westside administrator.

> The first-year, the third-year, and it will be the fifth-year anniversary. . . . People donating things to you that you don't even want, huge cemetery-looking stuff. They want you to put it in your playground. With names on it. In memory of . . . whatever. It's not that we want to forget those kids. We can't have a cemetery-looking playground.

Wallowing in painful memories, Miller believed, was self-destructive for staff and students. "We have a school to run," she reminded us.

Taking the position that the school has to, almost willfully, push beyond the shooting has hurt many Westside teachers we interviewed. The school did not do enough to provide counseling or compensation for those who needed to take time off. One middle school teacher who ministered to children at the scene of the shooting told us that her pay was docked for days when she simply did not have the emotional wherewithal to fulfill her duties. At the same time, she was told to "forget it," when she wanted to file a workers' compensation claim, because it would not cover PTSD-related problems.[21]

Morale sank to an all-time low. A new superintendent arrived, a former military man who made no allowances for teachers' emotional frailties. His rigid, severe management style was difficult for the emotionally scarred teachers to handle, as it reinforced the view that emotional weakness should not be tolerated. Teacher turnover rose sharply in the wake of his arrival. Some estimated that half of the teachers who had been there on March 24, 1998, had left Westside by the summer of 2001.

Administrators burned out on the stress as well. The leadership was trying to do the impossible: keep the school afloat under the hardest of circumstances, and deal with the anger and criticism of teachers and parents who felt they hadn't done enough. It was a no-win situation. Westside administrators had their own memories to live with but found themselves on the receiving end of constant and bitter criticism. "One of the teachers that . . . was in the shooting . . .

said, 'I want you to know that I'm having a real hard time,'" one administrator told us.

> "I might not be back next year," [she told me]. I said, "That's a shame. Why?" She said, "I've been in therapy for two years . . . because of you." I'm like, "What in the world did I do?" She said, "I just keep going through my mind that the day that this happened, you didn't come check on me . . ." I'm like, "Oh, I'm sorry, I only had 250 kids and 30 teachers and 5,000 parents and the media and policemen and . . . "
>
> Good grief, who came to see about *me*? . . . I'm telling you, that was a blow. As an administrator, I've been hit from every angle and every side, and I've seen angry parents who lost their kids, who thought the world of me before, because I didn't protect their kid they're mad at me.[22]

Some of these same issues arose in Heath, yet the conflict was minor by comparison, and the urge to memorialize was respected. Quilts, one for each girl who died, were hung in the local quilt museum, each square denoting a special passion or event in the lives of Kayce Steger, Nicole Hadley, and Jessica James. A memorial fountain was placed behind the school. A large rock in the fountain cites a Biblical passage, and smaller rocks are engraved with the names of each of the shooting victims. There is also a memorial in front of the school in the form of an engraved stone; some claimed this looked too much like a tombstone.

The observations of sociologist Kai Erikson on catastrophes give us some purchase on the different responses of these two schools.[23] He contrasts "individual trauma" that arises out of exposure to death and devastation, with "collective trauma," which is "a blow to the basic tissues of social life that damages the bonds attaching people together." A traumatic event can send individuals at the epicenter into a lifetime of fear and anxiety but leave most of the community untouched and therefore able to reach out to their damaged members. A collective trauma, which emerges when the damage affects everyone, shatters the very structure of the community, leaving no one able to help. The flood at Buffalo Creek, which Erikson studied at close range, left no one unscathed, no one stable enough to help other survivors. Everyone was a victim. Although the circumstances and the scale are not comparable, the scope of those affected in Westside was nevertheless fairly broad, as eighty-nine people had been in the shooters' target area and fifteen had been struck by bullets, with five killed. The Heath shooting, terrible though it was, had a more delimited impact, and the community's social structure was in better shape.

In both Heath and Westside, however, communities where people share a history, the conflicts that developed from public tragedies had particularly destructive consequences. In small, densely interconnected communities, it is harder for groups with warring emotional needs to coexist peacefully. There are fewer escapes for people who need to heal in their own way or whose own needs do not coincide with those of a surrounding culture.

10

TESTING THE THEORY

M ORE THAN A DOZEN HYPOTHESES HAVE BEEN ADVANCED TO ACCOUNT FOR rampage school shootings, including media violence, bullying, gun culture, family problems, mental illness, peer relations, demographic change, a culture of violence, and copycatting. Most contain an element of truth, but none of them taken alone suffices. Rampage school shootings are so rare that any particular episode arises from multiple causes interacting with one another. What we would like to understand, then, is which *combination of factors* is necessary to produce these violent rampages.

Based on our research at Heath and Westside, we propose five *necessary but not sufficient conditions* for rampage school shootings.[1] The individual parts of our theory are not novel; variants of them have been proffered before. Nevertheless, this approach is useful because although it is parsimonious, it combines elements at the individual, community, and national levels, providing a more realistic understanding of how each one contributes to these explosions of rage. Take away any one of these elements, and the shootings at Heath and Westside would not have happened.

The first necessary factor is the shooter's perception of himself as extremely marginal in the social worlds that matter to him. Among adolescents, whose identities are closely tied to peer relations and position in the pecking order, bullying and other forms of social exclusion are recipes for marginalization and isolation, which in turn breed extreme levels of desperation and frustration. Particularly in tightly knit rural and suburban communities, where ties are multiplex, anonymity scarce, and homogeneity the rule, those who are different are all the more easily pushed to the fringe.

Second, school shooters must suffer from psychosocial problems that magnify the impact of marginality. When mental illness, severe depression, abuse, and related vulnerabilities dog a young man, his emotional and psychological reserves for coping with social exclusion erode. Under these circumstances, even students who enjoy a fair degree of acceptance may see themselves as alone, disliked, rejected.

"Cultural scripts"—prescriptions for behavior—must be available to lead the way toward an armed attack. Cultural scripts provide models for problem solving: The shooter must believe that unleashing an attack on teachers and classmates will resolve his dilemmas. When we see films featuring macho heroes or villains who shoot their way to greater notoriety, we are looking at the traces of a cultural script that links manhood and public respect with violence. The script provides an image of what the shooters want to become and a template for action that links the method to the goal. Of course, this is not the only available image of masculinity in our culture, but it is one that attracts the attention of boys who have suffered ridicule from their peers for being insufficiently strong or socially capable. These blueprints for the masculine self may help explain why rampage school shooters direct their anger and hopelessness outward, rather than inward.

The fourth necessary factor is a failure of surveillance systems that are intended to identify troubled teens before their problems become extreme. School shooters fall under radar range because they tend not to exhibit the types of behavioral problems schools associate with potentially violent or troubled kids. Peers fail to report threats that are issued in advance.

Finally, we come to gun availability. Clearly a school shooting cannot occur unless a youth can attain unsupervised access to a weapon. Here we emphasize the ease with which young men can put their hands on guns.

Acknowledging that school shootings are the product of a combination of factors moves us away from futile discussions about the explanatory power of any single cause. Boys who are the target of the worst bullying or who routinely watch the most violent movies are not necessarily the ones who commit rampage school shootings. Rather, *it's the boys for whom a range of unfortunate circumstances come together*—those who are socially marginal, are psychologically vulnerable, are fixated on cultural scripts that fuse violence with masculinity, live in areas where firearms are readily available, and attend schools that cannot identify this constellation—who constitute the likely universe of school shooters.[2]

A theory made up of five necessary but not sufficient conditions limits the population of children, communities, or eras in which rampage school shootings will tend to occur. But it is not a profile. It cannot predict which communities will be next or which students will explode. To achieve that kind of predictive power would require knowing the *sufficient* conditions—conditions that, where present, will *always* lead to a school shooting. It is unlikely that such a theory will ever be developed. Rampage shootings are (thankfully) too rare and the factors too omnipresent. Almost every kid in America has seen a violent movie, and a substantial number are socially marginal or psychologically troubled. A smaller but still sizable number of students would "qualify" as potential school shooters under our theory by virtue of having all five factors.

Although this "constellation" theory cannot predict who will become a school shooter, it does not have to in order to suggest avenues for prevention. If all five factors are necessary for a rampage to occur, eliminating any one of the factors will reduce the chances of another rampage. Policies that help identify troubled children before they explode, or that decrease the prevalence of bullying or social marginalization, or that make guns less accessible will decrease the prevalence of rampage school shootings.

TESTING THE THEORY

A theory of this kind is not very useful unless it can help explain other instances of school shootings. So how does it fare? Does it explain Columbine or Santee or Pearl? The evidence confirms the theory for a specific kind of attack: *rampage school shootings*. This does not cover all shootings on school grounds. For example, it does not address the reasons Jacob Davis shot and killed another senior in his high school parking lot in Fayetteville, Tennessee, in a dispute over a girl on May 19, 1998, three days before graduation. Our thesis does a better job explaining cases that are more similar in form to the shootings at Westside and Heath. These attacks differ from other forms of violence because they constitute deadly assaults on an *institution*—the school. An institutional attack takes place on a public stage before an audience, is committed by a member or a former member of the institution, and involves multiple victims, some chosen for their symbolic significance or at random. This final condition signifies that it is the organization, not the individuals, who are important.[3]

Three principal sources of data make it possible to test the adequacy of this approach. First, the Centers for Disease Control and Prevention (CDC) generously gave us access to their national database of school-associated violent deaths.[4] The Safe School Initiative report by the U.S. Secret Service and the U.S. Department of Education contains an additional source of data.[5] Finally, we created our own data set, based on media accounts and case studies of other rampage school shootings.[6] Table 10.1 gives an overview of the three data sets used in this chapter, including each study's definition of a school shooting, the years and regions covered, and the methodologies used in defining the samples.[7]

Table 10.1: Overview of Three Data Sets

	CDC	Secret Service	Our Dataset
Definition	School-Associated Violent Deaths[†]	Targeted School Shootings	Rampage School Shootings
Location of Incident	At school, at school-sponsored event, or on way to or from school	On school property or at school related event	On school property or at school-related event
Significance of Location	None	School was deliberately selected as location of attack—not just a site of opportunity	School as a public stage
Status of Offender	Student of school targeted[†]	Student or recent former student of school targeted	Student or recent former student of school targeted
Weapon Used	Firearm[†]	Lethal weapon	Firearm
Lethality	Violent death required for inclusion in study	Attack "with lethal means," no deaths required	Attack with a firearm, no deaths required
Number of Victims	Multiple fatalities or one fatality plus at least one injury that results in hospitalization[†]	Single or multiple-victim event	Multiple-victim/target event
Symbolism or Randomness of Victims	None	None	Although there may be specific targets, some victims are shot for their symbolic significance or at random
Years Considered	1994–1999	1974–2000	1974–2002
Countries Considered	United States	United States	United States plus two cases from other countries for comparison

(continues on next page)

Table 10.1 (continued from previous page)

	CDC	Secret Service	Our Dataset
Sources Considered	One school official and one law enforcement official familiar with the case	Investigative, school, court and mental health records. Conducted supplemental interviews with ten of the perpetrators	Media reports, the Columbine Commission Report, and studies of rampage school shootings from the National Academy of Sciences report
Significant Limitations	Only two sources consulted, and estimates on many aspects of the case, including evidence of bullying or marginality, likely to be conservative. Data limited to recent period	Because of concerns about confidentiality, we are limited to data in published report.	Media reports often inaccurate or contradictory. Estimates of presence of mental illness and bullying likely to be liberal
Primary Benefits	Uniform survey instrument. Can compare with suicides on school property	Access to perpetrators gives rare insider perspective	Considers only rampage school shootings. Breadth of sources considered by the media reports and case studies
Total number of Cases	12	37	25
Total number of Offenders	19 (Includes all charged)	41 (Includes main offenders)	27 (Includes main offenders)
Percentage Male Offenders	100%	100%	100%

(continues on next page)

233

Table 10.1 *(continued from previous page)*

	CDC	Secret Service	Our Dataset
Offender Race/Ethnicity			
White	57.9% (n=11/19)	76% (n=31/41)	85% (n=23/27)
Black	15.8% (n=3/19)	12% (n=5/41)	7% (n=2/27)
Hispanic	0.0% (n=0/19)	5% (n=2/41)	0% (n=0/27)
Asian or Pacific Islander	10.5% (n=2/19)	2% (n=1/41)	4% (n=1/27)
Native American, Alaska or Hawaiian Native	15.8% (n=3/19)	5% (n=2/41)	4%[††] (n=1/27)
Location of Shooting			
Urban	25% (n=3/12)	N/A	8% (n=2/25)
Suburban	25% (n=3/12)	N/A	32% (n=8/25)
Rural	50% (n=6/12)	N/A	60% (n=15/25)

[†] The analysis of the CDC data is limited to cases that best fit our definition of a rampage shooting.
[††] This offender was bi-racial: Alaska Native and white.

Media reports are somewhat unreliable sources of information. News accounts often provide incomplete and inaccurate information. That is why we took great pains to compare the evidence of the media reports with studies that rely on other sources of information, including investigative, school, court, and mental health records, as well as interviews with school and law enforcement officials and the perpetrators themselves. Still, our data set based on media accounts and case studies is useful because it is the only one that narrows the lens down to rampage school shootings as we have defined them.[8]

Table 10.1 also presents the basic characteristics of the incidents and the offenders for the three data sets.[9] The majority of school shooters are white, although by no means exclusively so: two were black, one Asian, and one mixed Alaska Native and white. There are no cases in which girls were implicated in rampage school shootings; it is a genre of violence that attracts boys exclusively.[10]

Table 10.2 identifies the twenty-five cases of rampage school shootings in our own database and provides basic information on the incidents and the twenty-seven offenders.[11]

No region of the United States is immune to rampage school shootings, as the map in Figure 10.1 indicates. However, population density matters: 60 percent of the rampage school shootings have occurred in rural communities and 32 percent in suburbs. Only 8 percent happened in urban areas.[12] This is no accident. As we argued in chapter 5, big cities offer a larger variety of social niches—escape hatches—than small, tight-knit communities where boys who fail to live up to masculine ideals may be ostracized.

To gauge our theory's explanatory power, we now turn to the five factors and subject each one to as many empirical tests as we can muster. Statistical findings are illustrated with accounts drawn from newspaper coverage of rampage school shootings far beyond Heath and Westside.

FACTOR 1: MARGINALITY

Peer Groups and Extracurricular Activities

In the wake of the shootings at Heath, Westside, Littleton, and many others, journalists were quick to suggest that school shooters were "a host of alienated loners downloading nihilistic rock music from the Internet."[13] Yet, as Figure 10.2 (and Table A.2 in the appendix) makes clear, few school shooters were actually loners. According to the CDC and Secret Service, about one in ten were known to have no close friends.[14] Yet neither were school shooters socially successful.

Table 10.2: Rampage School Shootings, 1974–2002

1974 **Anthony Barbaro** **Olean, New York**	On December 30, 1974, 18-year-old Anthony Barbaro entered his high school, which was closed for Christmas, and set several fires. When a custodian investigated, Barbaro, who was a member of the school's rifle team, shot him dead, then fired from a third-floor window at firefighters and passers-by, killing two more people and wounding nine.
1982 **Patrick Lizotte** **Las Vegas, Nevada**	On March 19, 1982, thinking that his teacher wanted to have him committed to an institution, 17-year-old Patrick Lizotte killed his teacher and shot two students.
1983 **David Lawler** **Manchester, Missouri**	On January 20, 1983, 14-year-old David Lawler opened fire in a junior high school study hall, killing one student and injuring another before he shot himself to death.
1985 **James Alan Kearbey** **Goddard, Kansas**	On January 21, 1985, 14-year-old James Allen Kearby walked into his school brandishing weapons. When confronted by the principal, he opened fire, killing the principal and injuring a teacher nearby. He headed toward the classroom area where he shot another teacher and a student.
1986 **Kristopher Hans** **Lewiston, Montana**	On December 4, 1986, 14-year-old Kristopher Hans went to his French classroom in hopes of killing a teacher who had flunked him. Hans knocked on the classroom door and asked the teacher to come out. His teacher was coaching basketball in the gym that morning, and a popular substitute teacher answered the door instead. Hans shot her in the face and then fired several additional shots as he fled the building. He killed the substitute teacher and injured the vice principal and two female students.
1988 **Nicholas Elliot** **Virginia Beach, Virginia**	On December 16, 1988, 16-year-old Nicholas Elliot went to two classrooms in search of a student who had been tormenting him. He killed an algebra and French teacher and shot the window of a locked classroom to reach a student he wanted to kill. He also opened fire on a crowded classroom.
1992 **Eric Houston** **Olivehurst, California**	On May 1, 1992, 20-year-old Eric Houston returned to his former high school and killed a teacher who had previously flunked him and prevented him from graduating three years earlier. He then went on a shooting spree through the hallways and held 85 students hostage for over 8 hours before finally surrendering to the police. In addition to the teacher, he killed three students and injured nine others.

(continues on next page)

Table 10.2 *(continued from previous page)*

1992 **Wayne Lo** **Great Barrington,** **Massachusetts**	On December 14, 1992, 18-year-old Wayne Lo, a student at Simon's Rock College of Bard, an experimental school designed for gifted high school students, walked up to the school security shack and shot the female security guard, then fired at a professor driving through the parking lot and killed a student who heard the car crash and came running to help. He then fired at several students studying in the library and then went to a dorm and opened fire in the hallways. In all he killed a teacher and a student and wounded four others.
1993 **Scott Pennington** **Grayson, Kentucky**	On January 18, 1993, 17-year-old Scott Pennington walked into his seventh period English class and shot his teacher in the head. He killed a custodian who came to investigate the noise. He held the class hostage for 40 minutes before he gave himself up to policemen.
1995 **Toby Sincino** **Blackville, South Carolina**	On October 12, 1995, 16-year-old Toby Sincino walked into his math teacher's classroom and shot him in the face in front of a room full of students. He moved down the hall and killed another math teacher before fatally shooting himself.
1995 **Jamie Rouse** **Lynnville, Tennessee**	On November 15, 1995, 17-year-old Jamie Rouse walked down the hallway of his school and shot the first two teachers he saw. He continued into the crowded cafeteria, where he fired again. The rampage ended when he was tackled by a teacher and several students. He killed one teacher, seriously injured another, and killed an eighth grader.
1996 **Barry Loukaitis** **Moses Lake, Washington**	On February 2, 1996, 14-year-old Barry Loukaitis walked into his ninth grade algebra class and shot a student sitting at a desk. He then fired at two students behind the first victim and at a teacher who walked toward him. He attempted to hold the class hostage but was overpowered by the gym teacher. Two male students and a teacher were killed in the attack.
1997 **Evan Ramsey** **Bethel, Alaska**	On February 19, 1997, 16-year-old Evan Ramsey entered the school lobby and sought out and shot a fellow student and then went on a 20-minute shooting spree. He held the gun to his own head before he surrendered to authorities. He killed the principal and a student and injured two others.
1997 **Luke Woodham** **Pearl, Mississippi**	On October 1, 1997, 16-year-old Luke Woodham walked into the crowded courtyard just as school buses were arriving and started shooting. He shot his former girlfriend and then randomly shot at others. He killed two students (including his former girlfriend) and wounded seven others. Earlier, he had smothered his mother with a pillow, beaten her with a baseball bat, and stabbed her to death with a kitchen knife.

(continues on next page)

Table 10.2 *(continued from previous page)*

1997 **Michael Carneal** **West Paducah, Kentucky**	On December 1, 1997, 14-year-old Michael Carneal opened fire on a prayer circle that had gathered in the school lobby just before classes started. He killed three students and injured five others.
1997 **Joseph "Colt" Todd** **Stamps, Arkansas**	On December 6, 1997, 14-year-old Joseph "Colt" Todd stood in the pines on the edge of school grounds and fired at students walking to class. He hit two students, neither of whom died.
1998 **Andrew Golden and** **Mitchell Johnson** **Jonesboro, Arkansas**	On March 24, 1998, 11-year-old Andrew Golden and 13-year-old Mitchell Johnson lured their classmates out of the school building and onto the playground by pulling the fire alarm. From a shielded position in the woods, they fired approximately 30 rounds at their peers and teachers, killing four students and a teacher and injuring another ten.
1998 **Andrew Jerome Wurst** **Edinboro, Pennsylvania**	On April 24, 1998, 14-year-old Andrew Jerome Wurst brought a gun to a school dance. He shot and killed a teacher who came out to the patio to tell students to come back inside, then walked through the doorway and called for another student. He fired three additional shots, wounding two classmates.
1998 **Kip Kinkel** **Springfield, Oregon**	On May 21, 1998, 15-year-old Kip Kinkel walked into his high school cafeteria at 8 a.m. and opened fire on 400 students congregating before the start of classes. He killed two boys and injured 22 others. He had also shot his parents either the morning of or the night before the attack.
1999 **Shawn Cooper** **Notus, Idaho**	On April 16, 1999, 16-year-old Shawn Cooper brought a gun (bundled up) on the school bus, telling the bus driver it was a science project. At school, he took the gun out and pointed it at a secretary and a student in the foyer outside the principal's office and then fired two shots in the direction of female students. No one was injured.
1999 **Eric Harris and** **Dylan Klebold** **Littleton, Colorado**	On April 20, 1999, 18-year-old Eric Harris and 17-year-old Dylan Klebold entered the school cafeteria and began a four-hour shooting spree that ended with their own suicides. They killed twelve students and one teacher and injured 23 others before booby trapping the bodies with bombs and killing themselves.
1999 **T. J. Solomon** **Conyers, Georgia**	On May 20, 1999, 15-year-old T. J. Solomon opened fire at his high school. He fired twelve shots from his rifle, then fled from the building. He then pulled out a handgun and fired three additional shots before kneeling on the ground and placing the gun in his own mouth. He didn't fire. Instead, he surrendered to school officials and was taken into custody. He wounded six students, one seriously. No one was killed.

(continues on next page)

Table 10.2 *(continued from previous page)*

1999 **Seth Trickney** **Fort Gibson, Oklahoma**	On December 6, 1999, 13-year-old Seth Trickney randomly opened fire on his classmates before the start of the school day. He fired 15 shots and wounded four students.
2001 **Charles Andrew Williams** **Santee, California**	On March 5, 2001, 15-year-old Charles Andrew Williams walked into a packed boys bathroom and began firing. Williams reloaded at least four times during his six-minute spree, which took him out of the bathroom and to the school's nearby courtyard. Two students were killed and another 13 were injured, including a campus monitor and a student teacher.
2001 **Jason Hoffman** **El Cajon, California**	On March 22, 2001, 18-year-old Jason Hoffman walked into the school with a single-barrel shotgun slung over his shoulder. He found his target, the dean of students, right outside the school, and fired as the administrator dove out of the way. Hoffman fired two more shots, aiming indiscriminately at people in the school's attendance quad area. He wounded two teachers and three students.
Cases in other countries	
1999 **Unidentified** **14 year-old boy** **Taber, Canada**	On April 28, 1999—just eight days after the Columbine shootings—a 14-year-old boy walked into a high school during the lunch hour and opened fire. He killed a fellow student and wounded another. The shooting ended when the school's liaison officer quickly rushed to the scene, took the gun from the boy, and placed him under arrest. The boy did not resist. (Neither the boy nor his family can be identified under Canada's Young Offenders Act.)
2002 **Robert Steinhaeuser** **Erfurt, Germany**	On April 26, 2002, 19-year-old Robert Steinhaeuser left home with two guns and more than 500 bullets. The previous fall, he had been expelled from school, and now returned to get his revenge. He walked through the schools' hallways, entering classrooms along the way and shooting teachers in front of students. In all, Steinhaeuser fired about 40 rounds, killing 12 teachers, two students, a school secretary, and a police officer before taking his own life.

Most rampage shooters had only a few friends, and those they had tended to come from outcast cliques like the Trench Coat Mafia (at Columbine) or the Goths (at Heath).[15] Taken together, nearly four out of five shooters were marginal kids at school.[16]

Many popular students undoubtedly have serious problems at times, but they tend not to take their anger or hopelessness out on the school or the adolescent

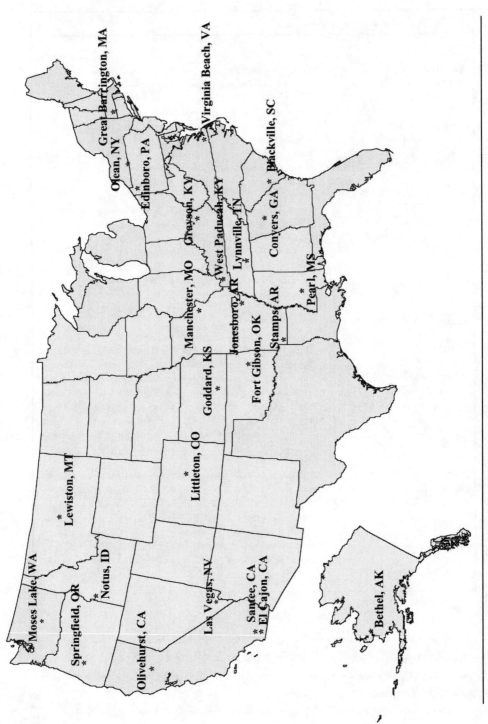

Figure 10.1 Locations of Rampage School Shootings, 1974–2002

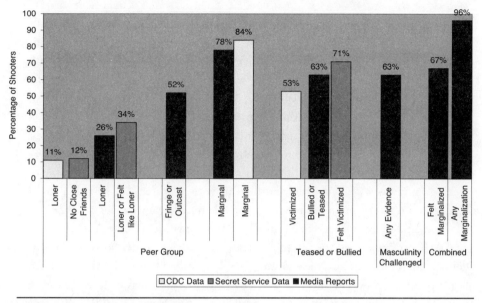

Figure 10.2 Social Marginality

social hierarchy, because that pecking order has served them well. The CDC data make it possible to compare characteristics of students who committed rampage-style school shootings with those who committed suicide at school but harmed no one else. A quarter of students who committed suicide on school campus were described as popular, preppies, jocks, or athletes, compared with only 5 percent of shooters in multiple-victim incidents. The numbers on which these statistics depend are very small, so we should be cautious about giving them too much weight. Nonetheless, they suggest that although popular kids may also become angry or desperate, they are less likely to strike out at their peers than students who are socially marginal.

Bullying and Teasing

Over half of the offenders in the CDC data were victimized in at least one way: called names or bullied, physically threatened, assaulted, or witnessed their personal property damaged or stolen by their peers.[17]

This measure underestimates harassment, because the CDC data were gathered solely from school and law enforcement officials. Our fieldwork suggests that peer and offender reports of bullying often contradict adults' perceptions.[18] According to the Secret Service report, almost three-quarters of the offenders "felt persecuted, bullied, threatened, attacked or injured by others prior to the attack."[19]

Sometimes the bullying was particularly severe, as in the case of Charles Andrew (Andy) Williams, a fifteen-year-old boy who killed two students and injured another thirteen in Santee, California. Classmates saw the small kid with jug-handle ears as a social misfit. "He was picked on because he was one of the scrawniest guys," said one acquaintance. "People called him freak, dork, nerd, stuff like that."[20] They also called him gay.[21]

Williams wasn't just called names; he was also bullied, and some of the incidents bordered on torture. Among the eighteen assaults outlined by his attorney at trial, Williams was "burned with a cigarette lighter on his neck every couple of weeks," "sprayed with hair spray and then lit with a lighter," "beat with a towel that caused welts by bullies at the pool" and "slammed against a tree twice."[22]

Williams's peers didn't make much of the harassment. Like Michael Carneal, Williams appeared to take the bullying in stride.[23] Inside, however, he was devastated. Shortly before the shooting, Williams called friends in Maryland and told them how miserable he was. He frequently broke down in tears and even mentioned that he was contemplating suicide.[24] On March 5, 2001, Williams walked into a packed boys' bathroom and began firing.

The media tends to describe school shooters like Andy Williams as small, skinny or overweight, with glasses and sometimes acne, and usually nerdy, awkward and withdrawn. Very few of these boys seem to meet the physical and social ideals of masculinity—tall, handsome, muscular, athletic, and confident.[25] Furthermore, in three out of five cases,[26] the shooters had suffered an attack on their masculinity, either by being called gay or "faggot,"[27] by being physically bullied, mercilessly teased or humiliated, sexually or physically abused, or having been recently rejected by a girl.[28] Unable to protect themselves from attacks on their manliness, they found a bloody way to "set the record straight."

School shooters are not all loners and they are not all bullied, but nearly all experience ostracism and social marginality. For some of these boys, like Andy Williams, exclusion takes the form of bullying bordering on torture. Others, like Andrew Golden are invisible. For still others, like Mitchell Johnson, it's the *perception* of marginalization, despite evidence to the contrary, that matters most.[29] Overall, there is evidence of social marginality in all but one case.[30]

FACTOR 2: INDIVIDUAL VULNERABILITIES

Shooters are plagued by individual problems—especially psychological conditions—that magnify the impact of their marginalization. When mental illness, severe depression, abuse, or other forms of vulnerability are in the picture, emotional resources for dealing with marginality diminish. Small slights loom large in the shooter's imagination. Bullying and exclusion, tolerable to adolescents who learn to live with it, become impossible volcanic pressures.

Mental Illness

In this section, we report on the evidence for the mental illness of the shooters in our database. We have not had the opportunity to do an independent analysis of their mental state using a clinical standard. Instead, we are relying on the views expressed in news coverage, which in turn report on court testimony from psychiatrists, a plea of insanity entered by a defense attorney, statements in court offered by defense attorneys, and commentary from judges summarizing the court's views of the defendant's mental state. How prevalent is mental illness among rampage school shooters? The short answer is that we do not know for sure. The Secret Service study determined that only one-third of offenders had ever received a mental health evaluation and less than one-fifth had been diagnosed with a mental health or behavior disorder *prior to* the shooting.[31]

The data drawn from media accounts show that at least 52 percent of offenders (14 of 27) suffered from a serious mental illness such as schizophrenia or bipolar disorder *at the time of the shooting* (see Figure 10.3 and Table A.3 in the appendix).[32] However, this figure must be treated with caution. Most of the evidence

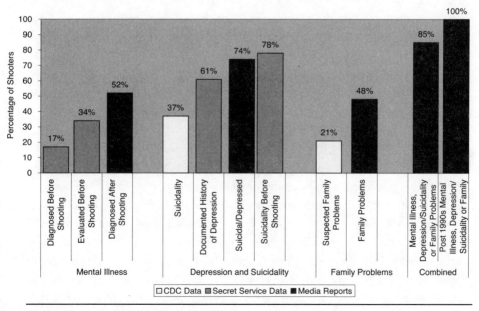

Figure 10.3   Individual Vulnerabilities

was revealed during court proceedings by the offender's defense attorney. These findings were nearly always challenged by prosecutors. It's impossible to adjudicate between the competing claims of the prosecution and the defense, and we make no attempt to do so here. For the purposes of our theory, however, it does not matter whether the shooters were criminally insane. It is critical merely to determine how the shooter's mental state interacted with his social exclusion to foster hopelessness, despair, and rage. Still, the figure derived from the media reports is an upper bound estimate of the prevalence of mental illness: somewhere between 20 percent and 52 percent of school shooters suffered from a mental illness or a behavior disorder at the time of a shooting.[33]

Depression and Suicidal Ideation

Severe depression and suicidal ideation[34] may come as a result of severe marginalization, but they may also impair a boy's ability to accurately perceive his social position and may prevent him from coping with the problem or exacerbate the underlying sense of insecurity. Suicidal teens may feel they have little to lose, which lowers an important social barrier to violence.

As we noted in chapter 4, approximately 20 percent of adolescents seriously consider suicide each year, and 8 percent attempt it. According to the CDC, evidence of suicidality is present in more than a third of school shooters.[35] The findings in the Secret Service study are even more startling. The vast majority of school shooters studied had a history of severe depression, desperation, and suicidal impulses. Although most attackers had never been evaluated or diagnosed, nearly *four out of five* school shooters had a history of suicide attempts or suicidal thoughts before they opened fire.[36] A similar pattern is evident in the media reports.[37] [38]

Family Problems

What about family life? Did school shooters tend to have serious family problems? The Secret Service researchers found scant evidence of family problems, in part because they limited their analysis to living arrangements, in which few patterns emerge. Nearly two-thirds of the shooters lived in two-parent families.[39] This is not what many criminologists have come to expect when they write about family disorder as a source of criminal behavior; they have in mind single-parent families. Clearly, however, family structure is not the key variable in school shootings.[40] The *quality* of family life—the extent to which parents get along with one another, the degree to which they express excessive or harsh disapproval of their sons, and the like—may be much more important than whether there are two of them in the house.

The CDC asked school and law enforcement officials whether offenders came from homes with suspected family problems. One in five (4 of 19) fit this bill. In our media accounts database, almost half of the offenders lived with discord at home.[41]

Jamie Rouse, the 17-year-old Tennessee boy who killed one teacher, seriously injured another, and killed an eighth grade student in 1995, is a textbook example of family dysfunction and abuse.[42] His father, Elison Rouse, was a truck driver who spent most of his time on the road. When he was home, Elison was often drunk or on drugs, and he would often fly into rages and beat his children with belts and paddles. After the shooting, Jamie recalled an incident in which his father grew so angry at the family cats for eating the chicken he'd brought home for dinner that he took out a twelve-gauge shotgun and killed them all.

At school Jamie was smart but also lonely, withdrawn, and intensely shy, and he rarely showed emotion. In high school he began to wear black and listen to "death metal" music,[43] and he etched an upside-down cross into his forehead. Other students shunned him, and he had few friends. He grew depressed and felt he couldn't relate to anyone. In an interview with the *Los Angeles Times,* Jaime described what it felt like to be so disconnected from his peers.

> I really didn't fit in. I didn't see myself reaching out to any adult. I just didn't see anybody I could trust. . . . I thought it would always be like that. I couldn't see no future whatsoever. I just had a hopeless feeling. It was a tired feeling. It was kind of an empty feeling. Although I'm locked up, probably for life, I'm still happier now than when I was free."[44]

Eighty-five percent of the shooters in our database were said to come from dysfunctional homes, were suicidal or depressed, or suffered from a major mental illness.[45] If we limit the analysis to the more recent cases (beginning in 1990), for which information is more plentiful, 100 percent of the shooters suffered from at least one of those individual predisposing factors.

FACTOR 3: CULTURAL SCRIPTS

If marginalization and individual vulnerability motivate the shooters, cultural scripts delimit the options for reaction. Boys who commit murders of this kind are deeply troubled, angry, and desperate. How do school shootings enter their heads as the best solution to their problems? If extreme options were "required," why not target the agents of their oppression? Mitchell Johnson could have gone after the neighborhood boy who molested him and his brother. Michael Carneal could have decided that the best way to deal with the demons that haunted him was to end his own life instead of shooting into the prayer group. Jamie Rouse could have killed his father. These might well have been the solutions these boys would have chosen only a decade ago. Had they done so, both the courts and the people around them might have been less outraged. After all, most of us could understand why someone in Jamie's shoes would choose to strike back at a father as abusive as Elison Rouse. But after 1990, a new script emerged that directed their plans toward rampage shootings.

It is a mistake to think of shooters as impulsive or erratic, for they are virtually the opposite. They ruminate on their difficulties, consider a variety of options, try a few—although generally to no effect—and then decide on shooting as a last resort. That decision is not random, though. It is a consequence of cultural scripts that are visible in popular culture.

How powerful is the notion of cultural scripts in accounting for school shootings? It is the hardest element to "test," because a shooter's thought processes and motivation are difficult to recover. Shooters either land in jail, where they are often inaccessible, or kill themselves. Given the uneven nature of the available data, variables as measurable as mental illness or marginality are hard to construct for cultural scripts. Nonetheless, qualitative accounts in the news coverage point toward a set of blueprints that lead boys in the direction of escalating violence.

Trying Alternatives

When they feel ignored or mistreated by their peers, teens try to change their social position. Kip Kinkel, who killed two students and injured twenty-two others in Springfield, Oregon, first tried to act the class clown, but his antics fell flat. Kinkel was too outrageous, and as a result his peers described him "most likely to start World War III." Toby Sincino, who shot two math teachers before killing himself, took on the clown role as well but found it hard to maintain while fellow students were stuffing him into garbage cans or slamming him against lockers. While there was perhaps nothing Columbine killers Harris and Klebold could do to get in with the jocks, they developed an alternative identity group—the Trench Coat Mafia—to insulate themselves from the taunts and public humiliation. But many school shooters were clearly not able or willing to pursue these strategies for long. Often their social skills were simply too weak.

They could have gone to an adult for help, but this is hardly what "real men" do. The young man who asks for help risks being viewed as a "wimp." Worse yet, adults are reluctant to intervene in adolescent hazing. A few shooters claimed that they did turn to adults, and in some instances adults witnessed the abuse. Yet these adults proved largely ineffective in addressing the problem. Like Mitchell Johnson, Nicholas Elliot—who killed two teachers and sprayed a classroom with bullets—asked teachers for help when fellow students were teasing and bullying him. The commission set up to investigate the rampage at Columbine High School reported that Harris and Klebold had allegedly been "surrounded in the cafeteria by other students who squirted ketchup, laughed at them, and called them "faggots," and that teachers were present at the time but did nothing to intervene."[46] Evan Ramsey said that teachers told him to just ignore the teasing he endured at school. "The response I always got from all these people was to ignore it, it will go away. I got tired of people telling me it will get better."[47]

Some school shooters do try simply to live with it. Fourteen-year-old Andrew Wurst had been trying to deal with his depression on his own for over four years. Through a veil of tears, Wurst told the police, "I died four years ago. I've already been dead and I've come back. It doesn't matter anymore. None of this is real." He started having suicidal ideas when he was only ten years old. By the time he was in eighth grade, he was drinking alcohol and using marijuana, which he said "made his body go numb." Wurst was ambivalent about whether he was going to kill himself or take others out with him. He left a suicide note on his pillow and then shot four people at his school dance. When Wurst brought a gun to school at the end of his eighth grade year, it wasn't his first effort to deal with his powerful emotions. It was his last.

The Masculine Exit

In the months and weeks leading up to rampages, most shooters felt trapped and in need of a "manly" exit. Their options seemed to be running out; they could not see past the crises facing them. Mitchell Johnson thought he was about to be moved back to Minnesota live with his father. Michael Carneal's mental health was rapidly deteriorating and his ability to concentrate diminished markedly. Kip Kinkel was facing expulsion and possibly a "boot camp for wayward youngsters." Jamie Rouse was feeling hopeless and couldn't imagine that things would ever change.[48]

Defense attorneys argued that fourteen-year-old Barry Loukaitis was facing just such a no-exit situation when he opened fire on his classmates. According to his mother, Barry began to slide into a depression at the age of twelve when his parents began to have marital difficulties. His home life was plagued by tense silence punctuated by loud arguments and fistfights. JoAnn Loukaitis was certain her husband was having an affair, and she filed for divorce in January 1996.

Shortly thereafter, JoAnn told Barry that she intended to confront her husband and his mistress, tie them up, and force them to listen to how much pain they had caused her. "They destroyed my life," JoAnn Loukaitis testified in court, "I was going to shoot myself and make them watch. I told Barry all that."[49] She planned to carry out her plan on Valentine's Day, when she "knew for sure" that her husband would be with his girlfriend.

Just twelve days before his mother's planned suicide, Loukaitis arrived at Frontier Junior High School, walked into his ninth-grade algebra class and opened fire. Barry Loukaitis didn't just wake up one morning and snap. He was depressed, possibly also mentally ill, had suffered at the hands of bullies in school for years,[50] and now faced an excruciating situation: his mother's plan to kill herself. Barry felt trapped.

Shooters do not typically face this brutal an emotional landscape, but the feeling of being trapped and needing a "manly" exit from an unbearable situation is common to many of them. They want to die to end their torment. As we saw earlier, the vast majority had considered or had attempted suicide before the shooting; many follow through or try to kill themselves. Eric Harris, Dylan Klebold, Toby Sincino, and David Lawler all killed themselves during the shootings.[51] When Michael Carneal gave up his gun, he told fellow student Luke Fallon, "Kill me now." Before surrendering to authorities, Evan Ramsey held his gun to his own head. Letters later found in his bedroom showed that he expected to die in the shooting. When police found Andy Williams in a school bathroom after his shooting spree, they found him kneeling on the floor, with a revolver cocked above his head. After T. J. Solomon opened fire on his classmates, he dropped to his knees and put the handgun in his mouth.[52] Andrew Wurst left a suicide note and a will.[53] Luke Woodham did the same. Eric Houston told his hostages that "he didn't expect to make it out alive—either that he'd kill himself or that police would shoot him."[54] Virtually no one ever gets away with a rampage shooting, and almost everyone who commits this type of crime is aware of that. (Mitchell and Andrew, because of their age, may have been exceptions.)

Yet these boys do not go quietly into the night. What the shooters want is to end their torment in a way that reclaims their social standing. There is immense power in deciding who lives and who dies, a fact not lost on many school shooters. Eric Harris drew a gunman in Dylan Klebold's yearbook standing in a sea of dead bodies. His caption read, "The only reason your still alive is because someone has decided to let you live."[55] When Scott Pennington held his class hostage, he taunted students, threatening that "there's one [a bullet] for each of you." He then asked the terrified students, "Does anyone want to leave?" When none responded, he chose two students that he would release. "I love you, Scott," said one. "Thank you, Scott," said the other.[56] Powerless in their normal day-to-day existence, school shooters gain a few moments of invincibility when they wield a shotgun and are not afraid to use it.

Sending a Message

School shooters want their exit to send a final, powerful message, not only to their tormentors but to everyone who hurt or excluded them. Minutes before opening fire, Luke Woodham handed his manifesto and a will to a friend. He wanted no ambiguity over the meaning of his final performance. With this one act of extreme violence, Luke was going to invert the adolescent social hierarchy. "I am not insane," he argued, "I am angry."[57]

> I killed because people like me are mistreated every day. I did this to show society push us and we will push back. *Murder is not weak and slow-witted, murder is gutsy and daring.*[58] . . . I suffered all my life. No one ever truly loved me. No one ever truly cared about me. . . . All throughout my life, I was ridiculed, always beaten, always hated. Can you, society, truly blame me for what I do? Yes, you will. The ratings wouldn't be high enough if you didn't, and it would not make good gossip for all the old ladies.[59] . . . It was not a cry for attention, it was not a cry for help. It was a scream in sheer agony saying that if I can't pry your eyes open, if I can't do it through pacifism, if I can't show you through displaying of intelligence, then I will do it with a bullet."[60]

A friend (later charged as an accessory) said that Woodham "was tired of society dealing the thinkers, the learners, a bad hand. He felt that why should Johnny football player get the glory when in fact he does nothing."[61] School shooters often target those at the top of the social hierarchy, the jocks and the preps, at least in their initial hit lists, a pattern that supports the notion that it is the entire institution that is under attack.[62] School shooters are seeking to overturn—possibly destroy—the status system that has relegated them to the miserable bottom.

There is also a righteous element in Woodham's "manifesto." Shooters often feel that their wrath is justified: "I have a right to be angry, society treated me like dirt." Therefore, just about everyone at school—often a shooter's entire social world—is fair game.

Fame

"If it bleeds, it leads": Few things are more terrifying than random violence, and the media is drawn to gory stories like moths to a flame. If fame and glory are the goal, school shooters know that celebrity status will be granted only if they can outdo the last rampage. This cultural obsession with violence was satirized in *Natural Born Killers,* a 1994 film directed by Oliver Stone. The movie's protagonists, Mickey and Mallory, go on a three-week murderous rampage, killing more than fifty people before they are caught by the police. Because Mickey and Mallory always leave someone alive to tell the story of their crimes, they gain worldwide attention—even adulation—from teens and adults who admire their murderous deeds and their stunning ability to evade capture. Antiheroes become celebrities, known the world over: Mickey and Mallory live happily ever after. Although the movie is intended to be a parody of this cultural and media obsession, many reviewers complained that it only served to glorify violence further.[63]

Eric Harris and Dylan Klebold were big fans of *Natural Born Killers.* Their notebooks are filled with references to this favored film.[64] Although Harris and Klebold claimed to have come up with the idea to do a school shooting well before Westside—bristling at the thought of being labeled mere copycats—they openly compared their plans with the Westside shooting, boasting that they could do it better. Their attack would eclipse all others: they would shoot more students, plant bombs throughout the school, and booby-trap the bodies in hopes of causing even more casualties after they had taken their own lives. Unknown and powerless within Columbine High School, they were determined to leave this Earth victorious and notorious. Committing suicide in a blaze after their rampage, they sought to secure a final image of themselves the world would never forget.

T. J. Solomon had a few ideas of his own about how to up the ante. He critiqued the Columbine boys for taking the time to aim. Their rampage could have been bloodier, T. J. thought, had they been less discriminating. Solomon told friends that "the kids at Columbine were aiming at certain people and that slowed them down, and that if he [T.J.] ever shot at Heritage [High School], that he wouldn't take any time to aim, that he would shoot at everybody." Solomon told a prosecution psychiatrist that on the morning of his rampage shooting, he was thinking about Columbine, about how much media coverage the incident received, and about how much attention he might win if he followed suit.[65]

Evan Ramsey's rampage came before all of these, but he, too, wanted to go out in a blaze of glory. His original plan was to commit suicide, and he wanted to do it at school so that everybody would watch. He told friends one day after being picked on that he wanted to "go out with a bang" and bring a gun to school "to scare the hell out of everybody and kill myself." But a friend of his convinced him that he could accomplish much more if he killed others as well: "[My friend] said that my face and name would go across the world. He said I'll become famous. He said lots of people will know about me. He said I should live out the fame."[66]

Threats and Escalating Commitments

School shooters rarely seek anonymity. Like Michael, Mitchell, and Andrew, they advertise their crimes in advance. According to the Secret Service study, "in over three-quarters of the incidents, at least one person had information that the attacker was thinking about or planning the school attack."[67] Our media database reveals evidence of threats in 78 percent (21 of 27) of the cases.[68]

They advertise their impending crimes for a variety of reasons. Some no doubt hope that the threat alone will serve to alter their social status. Threats can serve to redefine the self in a way that playing the class clown simply cannot. A manly image can be burnished if fellow students see the shooter as someone to be feared and not ignored.

Shooters are initially deeply ambivalent; they know they are about to do something terrible. What pushes them past the point of anxious indecision? They are convinced that failure to act will publicly confirm their weak character. They *have* to shoot. When other kids learned that Andy Williams was planning to bring a gun to school to kill his classmates, one of them dared him to make good on his boast.[69] In Pearl, Mississippi, an older kid told Luke Woodham that he would be "spineless and gutless" if he failed to follow through on his threats. If Williams or Woodham had kept their plans to themselves, failing to shoot wouldn't have been an issue. But they didn't: They broadcast threats in order to attract attention and change their public image. Boasting boxed them in.

T. J. Solomon knew he couldn't turn back when others saw that he had brought the guns to school.

> When I got to school I was walking up there. I didn't even know what I was going to do yet. . . . I was walking . . . and the bullets started dropping out [of the gun]. . . . After that . . . I pretty much felt I had to do it, because, you know, there was somebody that had already seen me with it at this point."[70]

Secret Service data confirm that escalating commitments are important factors in many school shootings. "Nearly half of the attackers were influenced by other individuals in deciding to mount an attack, dared or encouraged by others to attack, or both."[71]

Designing a Rampage

Cultural scripts do more than provide the range of possible solutions to a potential shooter's problems; they shape the *design* of the rampage. Barry Loukaitis spent the morning of his attack carefully preparing his clothes—a black cowboy hat and boots, an oversized black trench coat—and his weapons. Sporting a cartridge belt with seventy rounds of ammunition, two pistols in holsters slung across his hips, and a hunting rifle concealed in his trench coat, Loukaitis arrived at school around 2:00 p.m., walked into his ninth grade algebra class, and shot three people, including a popular student who had bullied him and a teacher. He then ordered the other students to line up against the wall, and he talked about taking a hostage before he was overpowered by a gym teacher. Students later said that his demeanor was calm throughout and that his actions seemed organized and rehearsed.

In fact, his actions *were* organized and rehearsed, according to police detectives, because Loukaitis was acting out the plot from one of his favorite novels: Stephen King's 1977 book, *Rage,* which police detectives found on Loukaitis's bedside table. In the novel, a teen holds his algebra class hostage with a revolver, kills a teacher, and talks about killing a popular student. During Loukaitis's shooting spree, classmates reported that he turned to one of them and said, "This sure beats algebra, doesn't it?"—a direct quote from the book.[72]

After Westside and Columbine, few students had not heard of rampage school shootings.[73] Rather than find inspiration in a *Terminator* movie, *Natural Born Killers,* or Stephen King's *Rage,*[74] adolescents could simply use the pathways taken by previous school shooters. With each new shooting, the script becomes ever more widely available. Copycat shootings provide a powerful explanation for the recent rise in school shootings, although the trend cannot be quantified with any precision.[75]

Are violent video games, lyrics, and movies to blame for the recent spate of rampage school shootings? Or, as the movie *Scream* suggested, is it that movies just make killers more creative?[76] Watching and listening to violent media doesn't brainwash otherwise happy and healthy teenagers so that they murder teachers and peers. That is why millions of youths ingest countless hours of bloody films and come out none worse for wear. But for school shooters—whose social status is marginal *and* who are beset by vulnerabilities such as mental illness, depression, or difficult home lives—scripts that connect manhood to guns, domination, and the power that comes from terrifying the innocent, offer a template for action. Books, TV, movies, and song lyrics influence decisions that direct their anger outward instead of inward; they provide the justification for random attacks. They are a set of stage directions.

FACTOR 4: UNDER THE RADAR

Mitchell, Andrew, and Michael were all well below the radar at their schools. They did not give off the sorts of warning signals that school authorities would notice. Signs that did surface were dismissed because the signals were weak and contradictory evidence, such as good behavior and rapid apologies, introduced even more "noise" in the signal. The surveillance systems in place were not up to the complex task of decoding their broadcasts.

Evan Ramsey did not generate much concern among school officials. But they should have been worried about him.[77] Ramsey's father is an infamous ex-convict who was released from prison after serving ten years for assault with deadly weapons. After the father's arrest, Evan's mother became an alcoholic, moved the family around, and took in a series of violent boyfriends. The state intervened in the family's chaotic life: Evan was placed in a foster home at age seven and was shuttled around among ten different foster families in the succeeding years. Abused by older children in several of these placements, Evan developed a serious case of depression. None of this was known by the school system, even though eventually Evan and his younger brother were placed with Sue Hare, an experienced foster parent who was superintendent of schools in Bethel.

Evan had trouble during junior high school because classmates "knew how to push his buttons." He exploded frequently, throwing trash cans, books, and other debris before storming out of school. Instead of continuing to lash out, though, Evan turned to teachers and administrators for help in junior high. Sue Hare took this as a good sign: her son was maturing.

[I thought,] "You know, he's had a hard time and he's really using good judgment [now]." This was just a month or so before [the shootings], and I thought, "It's going to be all right, it's going to come together for him. He's going to be OK."

Evan was not OK. But the downward spiral was not easy for Bethel High School to catch because, if anything, Evan seemed to be on an upswing. After twelve disciplinary infractions the year before, including two suspensions for smoking, he had received just five minor detentions the year of the shooting. The signals were mixed. The school thought that Evan's situation was improving, that he had weathered the storm.

Disciplinary and Academic History

Evan Ramsey's lengthy disciplinary history at school does not represent the norm. Most rampage shooters give far fewer warning signs of what is to come. According to the Secret Service study, "nearly two-thirds of the attackers had never been in trouble or rarely were in trouble at school." Only one-quarter had ever been suspended from school and only a few attackers had ever been expelled from school.[78]

Likewise, only a small fraction had ever been reported for disobeying authority, and only a minority were reported to school authorities for fighting, name-calling, or teasing peers.[79] Our media data analysis shows that only four offenders (15 percent) had serious disciplinary histories (see Figures 10.4a, 10.4b, 10.4c and Table A.4 in the appendix).[80]

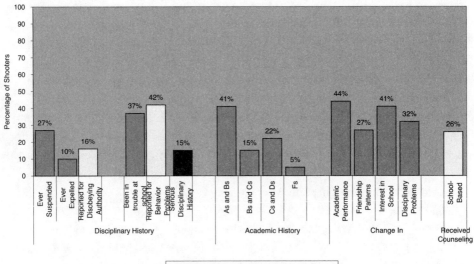

Figure 10.4a   Under the Radar

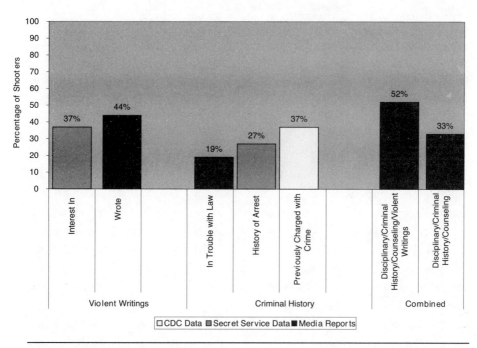

Figure 10.4b   Under the Radar

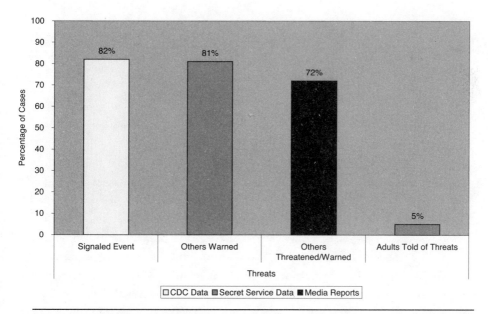

Figure 10.4c   Under the Radar

Most of us might imagine that someone disturbed enough to shoot people at school would leave a trail of bad grades. Not so. The Secret Service study found that most shooters were doing well in school at the time of the attack, and some had been on the honor roll regularly. Only 5 percent (2 of 41) were known to be failing.[81]

Downward Spiral

Signs of a downward spiral may serve as a warning for school authorities that a child's mental status is deteriorating and that he needs special attention. Michael Carneal's grades plummeted the year before the shooting. Yet his experience was atypical. The Secret Service analysis indicates that most attackers showed no marked change in academic performance, friendship patterns, interest in school, or school disciplinary problems before their attack.[82] Some offenders, such as Ramsey, even displayed improvements in academic performance or declining disciplinary problems at school before the shooting.[83]

Moreover, school counselors were often unaware of the serious problems these youths were experiencing. According to our analysis of CDC data, only one-quarter (5 of 19) of offenders had received school-sponsored psychological counseling.[84]

Violent Writings

Violent writings by shooters were not uncommon, but they are absent in the majority of cases. About two out of five shooters had written violent essays, and most of these writings were turned in to school authorities.[85] We know little about how teachers interpret these essays. The limited evidence we have suggests that they find it hard to read what shooters are trying to communicate, as was the case for Michael's English teacher and "The Halloween Surprise."

Scott Pennington's English teacher, Deanna McDavid, had a better fix on what she was seeing in his essays.[86] Scott was perhaps the smartest boy in her class and had never been suspended at school, but the violent writings he turned in worried her. His stories were "laden with violence, death, and dying," and McDavid was concerned that he might try to take his own life. For an assignment to write about the worst day of his life, Scott wrote about the day he was born.

McDavid grew increasingly worried about Scott, talked to other teachers about him, and considered calling his parents, but she worried that she might make things worse for Scott if she got them involved. In early January 1993, McDavid voiced her concerns to the director of a new state youth services program and asked about getting him help, but she remained reluctant to do more. Less than three weeks later, Scott Pennington walked into his English class and shot McDavid in the head because he was angry at her for giving him a C.

Even when school authorities are aware that a teenager is troubled and are rightfully concerned, the solution is not always obvious. Because school shooters are usually suicidal (in addition to being homicidal), it's not always clear that the violence will be turned outward. McDavid thought Scott was going to kill himself, not her.

Involvement with the Law

Most school shooters had no history of violent or criminal behavior.[87] Even students who have a criminal history, though, can fall below the radar. Mitchell had been in juvenile court for molesting a two-year-old, but no one at the school knew anything about that offense, because juvenile records are sealed and the offense occurred in a different state.

Eric Harris and Dylan Klebold had also been in trouble with the law and at school, but information about them was never put together because it was spread across multiple actors.[88] For example, the school had suspended Harris and Klebold for hacking into the school's computer. The school appears to have been unaware, however, that in January 1998, Klebold and Harris were arrested after breaking into a van and stealing tools and other equipment. Both boys were required to attend a juvenile diversion program for a year, which required them to pay fines, attend anger management classes, undergo counseling, and perform community service. Once they successfully completed the diversion program, all charges were dropped and their records were wiped clean.[89]

In March 1998, the local Sheriff's Office took a "suspicious incident" report from Harris's neighbor, Randy Brown, who said that his son, Brooks Brown, had been threatened with death on Harris's Web page.[90] The Sheriff's Office was apparently unable to trace the Web page, and because the Brown family insisted on anonymity for fear of retribution, particularly against their son, the case was left open. No search warrant was ever issued.[91]

Although the school resource officer at Columbine High was aware of the Web page, he was unable to tell other officials at the school about the investigation because of a law that prevented the sharing of such information unless formal charges are filed.[92] Furthermore, when Harris and Klebold appeared in front of the county magistrate on theft charges days after the Browns made their complaint about the Web page, the magistrate was not informed about the threats. Information wasn't moving smoothly among school officials, among law enforcement officials, or between the two organizations. No individual, it appears, had all of the information in one place, and this, the Columbine Review Commission argues, was a central component in Harris and Klebold's falling under the radar.

Threats

In roughly four out of five cases, offenders gave some sort of signal of what was to come.[93] In most of the incidents, more that one person was privy to the warnings.[94] Unfortunately, such information tends to go no farther than their peers. Students generally dismiss them as false bravado and as a consequence refrain from warning even trusted adults.

Andy Williams was explicit about his plans. He told his friends three times in the week leading up to his rampage that he was going to shoot people at school. None of the fifteen to twenty students who knew about the threats told officials. "He jokes around a lot," said a friend of Williams. "We didn't believe him."[95] "He said he had three shotguns and a .22 that he was going to take to school to shoot up the school. We were like, 'Yeah, right.'" Williams even invited some of his friends to help him.[96] Clearly, some of his friends were worried: They patted Williams down before school on the day of the shooting, but found nothing. The pistol was inside his backpack.[97]

One adult found out about the boasts and confronted Williams, threatening to call the Sheriff's Department and have him arrested if he was even "thinking about" hurting anyone. Williams told him that it was all a joke and that he didn't even know where his father kept the keys to the gun cabinet.[98]

Despite the fact that, in general, peers were concerned about the shooter's threats to kill himself or others—some stayed home from school or stayed away from what would become the site of the shootings—the Secret Service study found that adults were privy to these threats in only two cases. That's not to say that adults were all completely in the dark. In nine out of ten cases, at least one adult was worried about the shooter's behavior in advance.[99]

What Parents Know

Although most parents were completely shocked to learn of their sons' murderous deeds, there are a few tragic exceptions, instances when parents were all too aware of their sons' violent potential. On hearing news of the Columbine massacre, Dylan Klebold's parents called authorities before any suspects had been identified to suggest that their son might be responsible.[100] Kip Kinkel's parents also knew very well that their son might turn violent. Unlike most school shooters—who give off few clear warning signs—many of Kinkel's troubles became clear in early adolescence.

In middle school Kinkel had several encounters with the police. He was caught shoplifting CDs as well as throwing rocks from a highway overpass onto cars. He was suspended twice from school. Thinking that his aggressive behavior was due to peer influence, his parents removed him from school and home-schooled him for a time.

Bill and Faith Kinkel were considered concerned, attentive parents who knew their son was troubled and did everything in their power to help him. Alarmed about the boy's fascination with weapons, his mother took him to a psychologist in 1997. The therapist diagnosed Kinkel with severe depression and anger management problems, and prescribed Prozac.[101]

The day before the shootings, school officials caught Kinkel with a stolen gun. Kinkel was arrested, suspended, and released into the custody of his parents, pending an expulsion hearing. Desperate, his father called the Oregon National Guard Youth program, described as a "boot camp for wayward youngsters",[102] and begged them to take his son. By the next morning, both his parents were dead and Kinkel was on his way to school with a rifle under his trench coat. When he arrived, he opened fire. In addition to his parents, he killed two boys and injured twenty-two others.

Kip Kinkel is an exception to the rule. Few school shooters leave the kinds of clues he did. Most remain under the radar until the shooting, leaving teachers and parents alike shocked that such seemingly normal boys could commit such crimes. Unnoticed, their problems fester until they explode into the sacred sanctuary of the school.

FACTOR 5: ACCESS TO GUNS

Clearly a school shooting cannot occur unless a potential shooter can get hold of a weapon. The critical question is not whether the shooter was able to access a gun, but the *ease* with which youths in the community can do so.

How hard was it for school shooters to find guns? Most shooters got their weapons from home or from a relative.[103] Sometimes the shooters purchased the weapons themselves or got help from a friend (see Figure 10.5 and Table A.5 in the appendix).[104] In only two cases did the shooter resort to stealing the gun from someone other than a relative.[105] In only one case for which evidence is

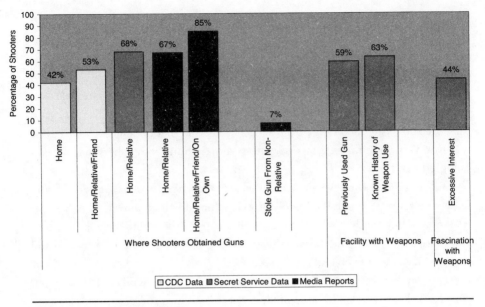

Figure 10.5   Gun Availability

available did the shooter have to look beyond his own, relatives', or friends' households for guns: Toby Sincino stole the gun he used from a car. Furthermore, most of the shooters had used weapons before the attack.[106]

Are guns more readily available in places where shootings occur than elsewhere? There is no way to get detailed data on levels of gun ownership and availability. Many states do not require individuals to register their guns, so there is no national database that would enable us to determine the prevalence of guns in the localities where the shootings occurred. We do know that approximately two-thirds of the shootings occurred in rural areas, and national surveys of gun ownership have shown that rural communities tend to have higher gun ownership rates than urban or suburban communities.[107]

The presence of guns is clearly causally related to school shootings. Without guns they would not happen. However, as we argued in chapter 3, it is not clear that the increasing availability of guns accounts for the spike in rampage shootings in schools. Although the number of guns in the United States has doubled since 1970, most of that increase is due to existing gun owners' adding to their stock.

Nonetheless, without relatively easy access to guns, it is likely that many of these shootings would never have occurred. Youths could use other weapons, such as knives or homemade bombs, a few have done so. It is notable that Germany, a country with very strict gun control laws, has had only one rampage school shooting, and the attacker in that case had legally purchased his weapons. Canadian households are half as likely as American households to contain a firearm, and the school shooting in Taber, Alberta, which occurred just eight days after the Columbine rampage, was notable in part because it was the first fatal school shooting in Canada in twenty years.[108]

ATTACKING THE INSTITUTION

Our research suggests two overlapping types of rampage school shootings. Some rampages are directed against the teachers and others against the students, and most fall somewhere in between. In the first, the attacks are directed at the adult power structure for what it may represent—authority, discipline, and a failure to protect or teach—and in the second, the attacks are directed at the adolescent social hierarchy. Still, each type targets aspects of the institution or the institution as a whole (see Figure 10.6).

Our five-factor theory works best to explain cases in which shooters are targeting the adolescent social hierarchy, which accounts for four-fifths of our cases (20 of 25). It also helps us understand at least one non-U.S. case, the rampage school shooting in Taber, Canada.[109]

Thus far we have focused on peer mistreatment and peer exclusion. There is another form of marginalization: being pushed out of the institution altogether, which appears to better explain cases such as the shootings in Olivehurst, California, and in Erfurt, Germany, in which the attackers more explicitly targeted teachers and administrators.[110]

Robert Steinhaeuser was a senior at Erfurt's elite Johann Gutenberg Gymnasium. Steinhaeuser did poorly in school and had a record of skipping classes. When school officials learned that Steinhaeuser had forged a doctor's note in order to cut class, he was expelled and asked to switch to another school. He failed to enroll there, and school officials did not pursue the matter because Steinhaeuser, over age eighteen, was legally an adult. He never told his parents that he had been expelled, and, until the shooting, the Steinhaeusers believed that their son was on track to successfully pass the Abitur, the national entrance exam for universities.[111] Unlike in the United States, where students are afforded many second chances with schools and with admission to college, Germany has a more rigid educational track. The expulsion prevented him from taking the entrance exams. Five months after the expulsion, Steinhaeuser showed up at school to take his revenge.

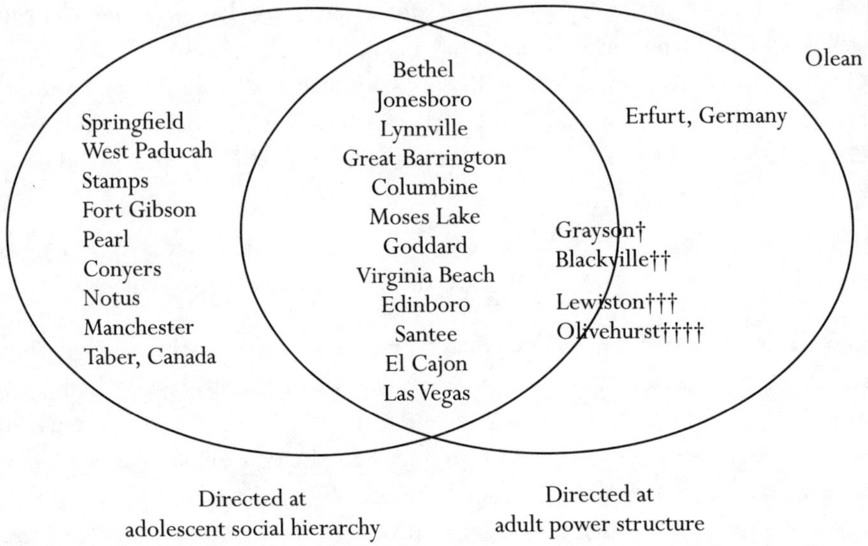
Springfield
West Paducah
Stamps
Fort Gibson
Pearl
Conyers
Notus
Manchester
Taber, Canada
Bethel
Jonesboro
Lynnville
Great Barrington
Columbine
Moses Lake
Goddard
Virginia Beach
Edinboro
Santee
El Cajon
Las Vegas
Olean
Erfurt, Germany
Grayson†
Blackville††
Lewiston†††
Olivehurst††††
Directed at adolescent social hierarchy
Directed at adult power structure

† This case falls on the margins because only teachers were targeted and hit. However, Pennington was a loner who had been bullied, and he held the class hostage for 40 minutes before he gave himself up to policemen.

†† Toby Scincino killed two teachers, then himself. There is no evidence that he shot at any students. However, he was bullied: he was often thrown into lockers and stuffed into garbage cans. Scincino had a tough time with the teachers at school and had a serious disciplinary history. His mother suggested that "racism at her son's school might have played a role in his death," and black community leaders charged that black students tended to be "disciplined more harshly than white students."

††† There is little media evidence on this case, but what exists suggests that Hans was targeting teachers and only hit students as he was fleeing the building. There is also only slim evidence that he was marginalized at school.

†††† On May 1, 1992, twenty-year-old Eric Houston returned to his former high school, killed a teacher who had previously flunked him and prevented him from graduating three years earlier, went on a shooting spree through the hallways, and held 85 students hostage for over 8 hours before finally surrendering to police. In addition to shooting the teacher, he killed three students and injured nine.

Figure 10.6 Attack on an Institution

Carrying a pump-action shotgun and nine-millimeter pistol, Steinhaeuser moved from classroom to classroom, shooting teachers in front of their students. The rampage lasted twenty minutes; by the end, Steinhaeuser had fired about forty rounds, killing twelve teachers, two students, a school secretary, and a police officer. Another six people were seriously wounded. It was the bloodiest massacre in Germany since World War II.

A similar incident took place in the United States in the early 1990s. After being laid off from his job on the assembly line at a Hewlett-Packard plant because it emerged that he didn't have a high school diploma, twenty-year-old Eric Houston returned to his former high school in Olivehurst, California, and killed a teacher who had previously flunked him and prevented him from graduating three years before. He then went on a shooting spree through the hallways and held 85 students hostage for over eight hours before finally surrendering to police. In addition to shooting the teacher, he killed two male students and one female student and injured nine others. According to a friend, Houston felt, "If I ain't going to graduate, these kids ain't going to graduate." The negotiator who reached him by phone reported that "he wants to air his grievances about how [badly] he was treated by the school system."[112] Although Houston intended to harm students, the students were targeted as members of an organization that had failed him—not for what the adolescent status hierarchy represents.

There is only one shooting that does not fit our theory at all. Unfortunately, there is little information about this incident, which happened almost thirty years ago and is the first known instance of a rampage school shooting. Eighteen-year-old Anthony Barbaro was an honor student who was generally described as a kind and considerate altar boy. Friends said that he kept to himself and that he didn't have a girlfriend, but there was no other mention of his social status at school.

On December 30, 1974, Barbaro entered his high school, which was closed for Christmas, and set several fires. When a custodian investigated, Barbaro, who was a member of the school's rifle team, shot him dead, then fired from a third-floor window at firefighters and passersby, killing two more people and wounding nine. An investigation of his home turned up homemade bombs and a diary detailing five months of planning for the attack. The only information that Barbaro offered to explain the shooting before he hanged himself in his cell was that "the pressure just got the best of me."[113] Given the scant evidence that Barbaro was marginalized and that he broke into the school when classes were not even in session, his attack seems to have been directed neither at the adolescent social hierarchy nor at the school's teachers and administrators. Rather, it was an attack against the school as an institution.

NEAR-MISS CASES[114]

The focus in this chapter has been on testing a five-part theory that pinpoints the necessary conditions of rampage school shootings. A key part of the model involves the broadcasting of threats, the circulation of information about the shooter's intentions, which is intended to increase the attention of the audience the killer is hoping to impress—fellow students. When shootings have occurred, those messages have failed to reach the right ears, because the adolescent code excludes the adults in their institutional world.

There are, however, near-miss cases that did not turn into shootings because critical information *was* intercepted and dealt with effectively. Indeed, in the aftermath of the string of shootings that occurred in the late 1990s, the number of plots uncovered and defused began to rise. Reporting behavior changed; kids were more willing to break the adolescent code, because the potential costs of failing to do so became more salient in their eyes, thanks in part to the publicity attending rampage shootings.

Understanding near-miss cases is critical, precisely because we are unable to predict who will become a school shooter. One thing we might be able to do better, though, is to intercept the information circulating about the shooters' intentions and make more effective use of it. We take up that subject—and other prevention measures—in chapter 11. Here, though, we consider whether the near-miss cases support our theory and we look at how the tip-offs emerged that prevented these plots from becoming school shootings.

We should note at the outset that available information on near-miss plots is sparse and uneven in quality, particularly compared with the detailed investigative journalism that follows rampage shootings. When people are shot, the media jumps to attention. When the plot unravels before anyone is hurt, journalists tend to dig less. Hence they often do not examine issues that are essential to evaluating our theory: Were these would-be shooters socially marginal? Was there evidence of mental illness? Often the news articles do not comment on these issues. Since journalists are the "remote sensors" for our database, we can only hazard some tentative observations from our data.

As Table 10.3 shows, twelve plots were stopped in their tracks in the years between 1999 and 2001. What can be gleaned from them? First, like the other cases we examined, the perpetrators were all boys, with one exception (in New Bedford, Massachusetts), where a girl was at least initially involved. The cases might well have become real shootings had someone not heard a threat and then repeated it. Hence, almost by definition they involve the spread of information.

We do have information about the targets in the near-miss plots, and they largely confirm our suspicion that school shootings are attacks on institutions rather than on individuals. In particular, they are attempts to destroy the very status system that plagues the marginal boy in adolescence. Where targets are identified at all—and in some cases they are not—high on the list we find preps, jocks, principals, and teachers as categories of victims. For the near-miss cases,

Table 10.3: Near Misses, 1999–2001

Location	Sex	Race/ Ethnicity	Age	Single/ Group	Freak/ Goth	Targets	Tip Source
New Bedford, MA	M	White	15–17	Group	Y	Thugs, faculty, preps	One girl included in plot
Ft. Collins, CO	M	White	14–15	Group	N	Preps, jocks	Four girls
Cupertino, CA	M	Latino	19	Single	N	Random	One girl working in photo shop
Millbrae, CA	M	Asian-American	17	Single	N	Random	Boy who was subjected to threat
Port Huron, MI	M	White	13–14	Group	?	Students, teachers	Fellow students
Palm Harbor, FL	M	White	14	Single	?	Teachers' office	One girl on instant messenger
Twenty-Nine Palms, CA	M	White	17	Group	?	Neighboring school	One girl
Fullerton, CA	M	White	14	Single	?	Classmates	No data
Anaheim, CA	M	??	13–14	Group	?	??	Fellow student
Cleveland, OH	M	White	14–15	Group	?	Random, cafeteria, principal's office	Anonymous tip
Elmira, NY	M	White	18	Single	N	Random	One girl
Hoyt, KS	M	White and Latino	16–18	Group	N	Random	One girlfriend

would-be shooters appear to be aiming at a structure or system of prestige rather than particular people.

Most important to us, though, is the information Table 10.3 provides about how plots were stopped. Whereas all of the would-be shooters were boys, in seven of the nine cases, those who spoke out were girls. In two cases the tipsters are identified only as "classmates" or "fellow students." The data indicate only one boy—a young man who had been threatened by a lone attacker at Mills High School in Millbrae, California—coming forward. Every other case where we have information on the gender of the tipster, it is a girl. We believe this is an important finding—although with such a thin database, it can hardly be considered conclusive.

Why do girls break the code of silence? To answer this question, we turn to the New Bedford, Massachusetts, plot that was exposed in November 2001, for it is the one about which we have the most detailed information. Five members of the New Bedford High School "Trench Coat Mafia"—Eric McKeehan (age seventeen), Eric's brother Michael McKeehan (fifteen), Steve Jones (fifteen), Neil Mello (sixteen), and Amylee Bowman (seventeen)[115]—hatched a plot to kill "thugs, preps, and faculty" in a spectacular explosion of bombs and guns. They wished to create a spectacle that would make Columbine pale in comparison, ending in a glorious suicide.

Although the news broke on November 24, the investigation started on October 17, 2001, when two school resource officers confronted Neil Mello and Michael McKeehan about rumors that they had issued threats. Michael denied it, saying that people were suspicious of his friends (who called themselves "the Freaks") for their trench coats, body-piercing, and musical tastes. According to Mello, at this point Michael called the plot off.

On November 4, Amylee Bowman—by now a student in a Plymouth, Massachusetts, school—approached one of her former New Bedford teachers, Rachel Jupin, to warn her about the plot. Bowman thought of Jupin as a "mother figure," who had been good to her throughout her years at New Bedford. Amylee was worried that her favorite teacher might be hurt in the rampage and wanted to make sure she was safe from harm, so she told Jupin there was a plan afoot to shoot the staff, thugs, and preps. Jupin quietly informed the police, who immediately brought Amylee in for questioning. Bowman finally opened up to the investigating officer on November 7, when she described a rather messy plot for a massive shoot-out including rooftop snipers and careful videotaping of the event, culminating in a rooftop party and mass suicide on the part of the shooters. According to Bowman, the plot was scheduled for sometime the following year, and she herself had already been assigned a target. Confirmation of her information came to police attention on November 20, when a janitor found a note stating that something would happen on a Monday. The note mentioned "getting back at everyone for calling us names" but provided no names or dates.

Four days later, the McKeehan brothers and Steve Jones were arrested. Police found bomb-making instructions, Nazi literature, Satanic paraphernalia, a knife collection, and a varied assortment of ammunition and spent cartridges in the McKeehan household. The final indictment charged all five with conspiracy to commit murder. Michael pleaded guilty to a reduced charge in May 2002.[116]

During the investigation, a number of students claimed that Eric McKeehan tried to recruit them to the plot; others said that they had heard rumors of a kid who had stolen a gun and was planning to shoot the school up. But it was Amy Bowman who came forward. Why? We speculate that the cultural script involved in most school shootings is a particularly male enterprise, and not just because boys are the ones who have turned up as shooters. The evidence leading to cultural patterns that sanction male violence, that throw up for our collective admiration the gutsy shooter, appeals to boys who are socially excluded. Boys are more susceptible than girls to the combination of social exclusion and out-group formation. Girls are both more likely to retain social ties to others—fraught as they may be—that tug on their heart strings. They are more likely to have affection for teachers, empathy for potential victims, and functioning ties to adults in whom they can confide. Girls do not become socially isolated in quite the same way that boys do.

Girls do not always experience a smooth path through adolescence. Many books have been written about the social torments girls experience, usually at the hands of other girls, who make them feel inadequate, unattractive, and unloved. It is possible that Amy Bowman felt exactly this way, which is what caused her to gravitate toward an unholy bunch of boys with murder on their minds. But Amy kept ties to at least one teacher whom she really cared about. There is no evidence that any of her coconspirators had a relationship of this kind. Had this been the case, they might have felt a similar degree of anticipatory concern. But apparently they did not, and we submit that this is more likely to be the case with boys than with girls.

How well does this speculation hold up in other near-miss cases? The only relevant information we have about them is the identification of tipsters as girls. The other eleven cases simply did not become the subject of extensive journalistic inquiry. The case of Jeremy Getman (age eighteen), is at least somewhat similar. Getman was arrested in February 2001 carrying a gym bag with fourteen pipe bombs, three CO_2 bombs, a propane bomb, and a sawed-off shotgun, and he was armed with a loaded .22-caliber pistol. The school resource officer knew Getman from a Drug Abuse Resistance Education (DARE) program, and he credited their acquaintance for Getman's peaceful surrender.[117] The only reason the officer knew that Getman was getting ready to blow up the school was that Getman gave a note to a girl who then came forward.

In several of the near-miss cases, the girls who revealed the plots were the current or former girlfriends of the would-be shooters. They knew about the plots because the boys they were linked to wanted to impress them and bragged about their plans. Unlike the boys who were coconspirators, sworn to silence and loyal to the end, the girls broke ranks, informed on their boyfriends and sided with safety, often despite threats against them.

Girls are not alone in their capacity to cross the boundaries that separate adolescents from adults. It is quite possible to cultivate social links between adults and teenagers of both genders, and we address this issue in chapter 11. It does bear notice, however, that without special efforts boys seem to be more susceptible to the sort of marginalization that leads to violence. Among adolescents, it takes someone with meaningful relationships that span these out-groups and the adult world to break free of the adolescent code and come forward.

SUMMARIZING THE EVIDENCE

The U.S. Secret Service determined that it is impossible to profile school shooters, and we agree. Even when the cases are limited to rampage school shootings, there is still too much diversity among them to predict which students could become rampage shooters. But there are other means of working toward prevention besides attempting to create profiles. By looking for patterns and opportunities to challenge popular stereotypes, we take important steps toward answering the questions we all have: Why the rage? Why in these communities? Why boys and not girls? Why these particular boys? Why a rampage? Why did no one notice? How did they get the means to live out their violent fantasies?

School shooters weren't all loners; most actually had a least some friends. And they weren't all bullied or teased either. But virtually none of them were high up in the adolescent status hierarchy. Most of them lacked the physical and social qualities that would have given them a leg up in the social pyramid—looks, height, an athletic build, or self-confidence. And nearly all of them were bullied or teased or were outcasts—or at least felt as though they were. Their marginal-ization was compounded by the fact that they tend to live in small, tightly knit, homogeneous rural and suburban communities where being different can often be all the more painful.

These findings make sense. Why would students attack a status hierarchy that had served them well? Why would popular students attack an institution that placed them at the top? Should parents and teachers assume, then, that they can just ignore popular students because they tend not to become rampage shooters? Surely not. For one thing, some students whose objective social status is fairly high—like Mitchell Johnson—still *feel* like nobodies. Moreover, popu-lar students, too, can have problems that warrant intervention.

Contrary to some popular perceptions, rampage school shooters did not all come from broken families or dysfunctional households. In fact, the majority lived in two-parent families. But if shooters had generally stable homes, other problems were afoot. Quite a few had a serious mental illness such as schizo-phrenia or bipolar disorder, which often went undiagnosed, and most were so desperate or depressed that they had considered suicide prior to the shooting. Such vulnerabilities tended to make these boys less able to handle their social marginalization. Downright vicious taunts and bullying (but also small slights and general ostracism) that other students would be able to brush off were un-bearable to this group of seriously troubled youths.

The shooters appear to be working from widely available cultural scripts that glorify violent masculinity. Most of the shooters were suicidal, a fact that must be kept in mind when we think about prevention. School shooters generally know that they will not escape with their crimes. Most expect to die at their own hands or at the hands of others. The shooting solves two problems at once: it provides them the "exit" they are seeking and it overturns the social hierarchy, establishing once and for all that they are, in Luke Woodham's words, "gutsy and daring," not "weak and slow-witted." The problem is they didn't just fail at popu-larity—they failed at the very specific task of "manhood," or at least they felt that way. The solutions to this failure are popularized in the media in violent song lyrics, movies, and video games. But the overall script of violent masculinity is omnipresent. "Men" handle their own problems. They don't talk; they act. They fight back. And above all, "men" must never let others push them around. Once a potential shooter has shared his violent fantasies with peers, this script virtually assures that there's no turning back.

The shooters' rage and hopelessness evaded detection because school shoot-ers typically failed to give off the kinds of warning signs that parents and schools are used to watching for. Few had serious disciplinary histories or criminal records. Most gave off signs that concerned at least one adult—writing violent essays, threatening suicide, or less obvious behaviors, such as starting to pull back or turning in sloppy homework at school—but the signs were often weak signals, either because there are so many false positives or because the boys were able to stave off inquisitive and concerned adults.

They also evaded detection because although they tended to broadcast their threats among their peers, those students typically didn't come forward. They dismissed the often general threats as jokes or gross overstatements: Maybe "something big" would happen, but murder? Inconceivable.

Finally, the shooters were able to commit rampages because they had access to guns. Guns are widely available: only two shooters had to look beyond their own, relatives', or friends' households for the guns they used to commit their crimes. Guns strike fear into observers; when the goal is letting others know who is powerful, other methods aren't as effective.

Identifying the patterns behind rampage school shootings hardly excuses the shooters. "They were bullied or ostracized; disturbed; bombarded with images of violent masculinity; ignored by adults; and practically handed the guns with which to commit their evil deeds—we, society, practically told them to do it." Not at all.

But the sad truth is that *we are all implicated.* We *do* play into the petty status hierarchies at school and teach our kids that it's not good to snitch. We defend them when they get in trouble and pay less attention than we should to what those behaviors are telling us. We often fail to recognize the pain and hopelessness they feel. Every day, we help to recreate a culture that embraces a narrow, often destructive definition of masculinity. We don't pay close enough attention unless they make our jobs as teachers or administrators too difficult—not because we are uncaring but because we don't have the training or bureaucratic organization to accomplish this task well. We keep guns in our homes and expect that our kids will never use them in crimes.

But there is an upside to taking a broader sociological view of the problem. If school shooters were simply bad seeds or pathological deviants, there would be little we could do. If blame lay only with dysfunctional families, policy prescriptions would be virtually useless. Looking at the social roots of school shootings helps us understand how to prevent such catastrophes in the future.

11

PREVENTION, INTERVENTION, AND COPING WITH SCHOOL SHOOTINGS

No one wants to see another rampage shooting headline, cradle another dying child, suffer through another funeral, or send any more troubled adolescents to jail. Everyone hopes the epidemic of school shootings has petered out, so that the nation's children can go back to the more innocent lives they led before it began. Yet because the problems recounted in this book—particularly the status tournament of adolescence—show no signs of disappearing, it is worthwhile to consider what this examination of school shootings yields that might make a difference.

We approach these issues with a hefty dose of humility. Ideally, we would like to have conducted the kind of rigorous evaluation that social science is known for: experimental evidence, with treatment and control schools, or before and after studies. This was not possible: We arrived on the scene too late, and the opportunity to conduct evaluations of this kind had long since passed. More sobering still, the focus adopted here on the causes of school shootings does not lead to straightforward solutions or policies whose effectiveness is guaranteed. Indeed, in almost all cases, interventions that might make a positive difference have negative consequences that may be intolerable.

It is up to our society—students, parents, teachers, administrators, politicians, and citizens at large—to weigh the pluses and minuses. Are security measures that lower the risk of a rare event like a rampage shooting worth the loss of freedom they impose? Are the costs of additional mental health services, school-based counselors, and the like affordable? Is this the best way to spend precious resources at a time when so many parents and teachers are concerned about academic achievement or test scores? If urban violence is more common, shouldn't we concentrate our attention there instead? There are important trade-offs in such decisions, and the choices communities must make are all the more difficult because school shootings are simultaneously rare and devastating. Ask the community that has suffered from one of these tragedies, and the answer is likely to be, "Spare no expense to keep our children safe." Ask the typical town that has never seen a rampage shooting, and the response will be more cautious.

While the suggestions we offer in this chapter would make a difference in addressing school shootings, they also address problems that are far more common. For example, improved mental health services may make it easier to identify a depressed boy before he progresses to the stage that Michael Carneal or Mitchell Johnson reached. But for every one of these rare cases, there are thousands more children who suffer from depression who would benefit from such an investment.

At the outset, we must state the obvious (which is often overlooked): There are no policy solutions that can reduce the risk of a school shooting to zero. As we saw in the case of Mitchell and Andrew, who used a blowtorch to try to break open a safe loaded with guns, a determined killer is hard to stop. Nonetheless, as the adage goes, we do not want perfection (zero risk) to be the enemy of improvement. If we can intercept more plots before they become rampage shootings, we will be better off even if some get through.

One final caveat: We focus attention on what schools can do, because policy change is often most effective when funneled through an institution. Yet in concentrating on the responsibilities of schools, we are not advocating letting the rest of us off the hook. Parents have responsibilities in regard to their children. Community institutions, ranging from civic organizations to the Boy Scouts and churches, can play a role. Industries—particularly media firms—can do more to help. For example, disclosure of the content of films, video games, and the like is helpful to parents who are trying to take responsibility for monitoring what their kids consume. To the extent that boys are taking their cues from the scripts they see on the screen, it will make a difference if parents can make intelligent choices about which images of masculinity they want their children exposed to. Parents can teach their sons that a "real man" is not measured by his muscles; a real man is a responsible and caring person, an individual who works hard to achieve goals, an individual striving for more education or a contributor to the civic betterment of his community. The short message here is that there are things that all of us can do to shift the cultural baggage that burdens young men in our society. We cannot leave it all to the schools.

POLICY OPTIONS IN THE
AFTERMATH OF A SCHOOL SHOOTING

Westside and Heath were among the first in the series of school shootings that shook the nation in the late 1990s. Administrators at these schools had no contingency plans in place to guide their responses—and neither did any of the other schools that suffered these tragedies in those early days. The sheer number of problems they had to contend with was overwhelming, and the fact that so many of them touched powerful emotions made them that much harder to resolve. The cascade of decisions they had to make posed a daunting challenge even for seasoned administrators.

Sadly, there are now more principals in U.S. schools have had experience with school shootings, and they have found ways to communicate with one another. An informal network of administrators, media affairs specialists who work for school districts, and sheriffs' departments has taken root, dedicated to helping each new addition to this unhappy list deal with the public and the press. The FBI lent a hand by organizing conferences of community leaders from Heath and Westside, Pearl, Mississippi, Eugene, Oregon, and Bethel, Alaska, among others, to discuss school responses and community reactions.[1] Harvesting from the experience of Westside and Heath as well as from these other communities, it is possible now to draw some conclusions about better and worse ways to deal with rampage school shootings.

The Media: Lessons Learned

Media attention created the single largest headache for school authorities in the immediate aftermath of the shootings. Schools, sheriff's departments, investigators, the courts, and the juvenile justice systems were all flooded with requests for information and interviews. Heath and Westside leaders responded to these requests in ways that should be emulated elsewhere: they assigned one person to organize media access and keep reporters at bay so that everyone else could focus on the students, the teachers, and the families. The bottom line for almost everyone in the schools was to restrain the media when their presence could interfere with the ability of the police and emergency personnel to do their jobs. It was not a policy the media took to with alacrity.

The Freedom Forum, a media watch foundation, was sufficiently disturbed to publish a report entitled "Jonesboro: Were the Media Fair?" Westside residents agree that the answer is "No." The Freedom Forum itself concluded that the media failed to police itself and breached ethical lines in the rush to compete.[2]

Schools should insist that news organizations pool their resources and send one representative, rather than multiple reporters to cover rampage school shootings. Bill Sadler, a media specialist with the Arkansas State Police, first suggested this idea and we endorse it. The news industry is likely to reject it because competition is its lifeblood. Nonetheless, we believe the media needs should take a back seat to respect for privacy, which would have been much easier to maintain had there not been a mob of reporters angling to beat each other out for the most dramatic angle on a stunned community's grief.

Dealing with Trauma

After the immediate shock of the shootings wore off, the question remained of how to treat the long-term impact of the trauma. The schools offered services to the entire community, at least in the immediate aftermath of the shootings. Long-term psychological needs were left to individuals and families to manage, although the schools did what they could to provide referrals and to be sympathetic to children's needs. Nevertheless, a number of people reported symptoms of posttraumatic stress disorder even three years after the shooting. The severity of their symptoms may have deepened with time as worries and anxieties festered without appropriate release.

In light of this observation, it would be wise for all communities to develop postshooting crisis plans that provide for mental health services on a widespread basis. Providing support services is costly. Figuring out how to deploy needed resources is a challenge, and not one easily met under the extraordinary pressure of a shooting aftermath. Thus, it is important to include screening procedures in crisis plans, to examine both children and school personnel for physical symptoms and psychological distress in order to determine the best way to target services.

School administrators are respected in their communities, especially in small towns. Where they lead, others will follow. For this reason, *educators need to be both well informed about the symptoms of trauma and open with parents about the importance of counseling.* Without being dogmatic, they need to remind parents that children often do not heal on their own and that counseling may be necessary even if it does cause some pain as troubling memories surface. Flyers and checklists that inform parents of symptoms they should look out for—problems sleeping or eating, inability to concentrate, jumpiness, and fear—are helpful. Principals and teachers are the first line of defense against the stigma that mental health services often attracts.

Putting children in contact with people they know—teachers, ministers, school counselors, and perhaps police officers—is critical. Hotlines that permit people to seek help easily and with minimal public exposure can be very helpful.

It is a mistake to permit the intrusive presence of outsiders, however well-meaning, especially in the early days after a school shooting. Westside and Heath were burdened by having to ask strangers who came to help to get out of their way when they experienced an overload of attention and needed to turn inward for a time. In the longer term, access to counselors from outside the community is important, particularly if victims are uncomfortable about confiding in people who are embedded in local social networks.

Open meetings proved to be reassuring to parents, children, and other members of the community who were not directly affected by the shootings. Everyone wants to be apprised of the plans schools put in place for moving back to a regular schedule, the rights of victims to protect their privacy, the progress of criminal investigations, what to do about funerals and memorial services, and long-term treatment. There is a great hunger for information and for fellowship among survivors after a school shooting, and meetings that are inclusive but barred to the media are an essential response to those needs.

Special attention should be paid to the needs of teachers and staff in the wake of school shootings. We found it distressing to learn that Westside teachers, in particular, felt so neglected, undertreated, and drained by the needs of others. Teachers do naturally respond to their students and they are "on call" in the classroom, often because kids are more comfortable with them than with unfamiliar professional therapists. However, teachers are not mental health specialists. Moreover, they often have psychological needs themselves as a result of the traumatic experience or of a sense of guilt because they might have done more. In this respect, teachers are very much like survivors of wars who return home to discover that no one wants to listen to their stories. But since the school is their workplace, they have little choice but to return—often quite quickly—to the scene of their distress. Administrators and others should be sensitive to the stress they endure and offer as much support, counseling, and time off with pay as can be mustered.

Counseling needs are not short term. Even three years after the attacks, we spoke with dozens of people in both communities—children and adults—who were still in need of therapy. No one should be made to feel inadequate because they are still in shaky condition several years after a school shooting. It is a miracle that so many could cope with their daily responsibilities after the deaths, injuries, and grief. Communities need to be sure that the medical resources are available to those who need them and accept the fact that recovery can be a lengthy process.

In Jonesboro, funds were available to teachers to receive counseling even three years after the shooting, but the hoops they had to jump through to gain access to them were off-putting. The Arkansas Crime Victims' Reparations Board provided for counseling services for six months but would extend their provisions only if written requests were approved. This may seem a simple requirement, but for teachers burdened by PTSD, bureaucratic hurdles can be insurmountable.

The duration of benefits is particularly important because of the latent emergence of psychological distress. Some people—especially children—show symptoms immediately. Others may take years to call for help.[3]

Finding someone to listen to them is often a matter of money. Therapy is expensive, and in many communities it is not covered by existing health insurance plans. *At a minimum, we recommend that mental health benefits be included in teachers' insurance coverage for emergencies.* Even better would be routine coverage of mental health so that beyond the emergency stage, teachers can be assured that their needs will be met.

Dealing with Damaged Children

A generation of Westside and Heath students will find it impossible to forget the tragedy they lived through. One reason it will remain fresh in their minds is that the rest of the world responded to their distress with an avalanche of presents, trips, and attention. Charitable impulses are motivated by the best of intentions, but the largesse has its downside. The attention can become a crutch for kids who need to get themselves back on track. Students who were at Westside Middle School have now progressed to high school, where some are known for having become close to unmanageable. Teachers and administrators are genuinely worried about what the future holds for these students, because they seem to expect special treatment indefinitely.

It is difficult for everyone to resume a normal life after an event that is so traumatic. For those who lost a loved one or who were seriously injured, it may never happen. However, schools and communities owe it to the rest of the children to set some limits on the length of time those special privileges and protection from expectations should be extended. This is not a matter for legislation. Parents and teachers need to use their judgment, bearing in mind that people heal at different rates. And again, counseling may be needed for years. But in the public sphere of school and community, children must be held accountable for their behavior when the community feels that it is time.

Restoring Security

"Is this place safe?" That was the first question on everyone's mind in Heath and Westside. Residents demanded that schools take steps to tighten up on everything from access by strangers to misbehavior among students. How else, parents asked, could they continue to trust schools to care for their children in their absence?

From the day of the shooting onward, Heath posted teachers at the school entrances in the morning to search students' bags for weapons. The practice continues to this day. Teachers were ambivalent about adopting this role. One Heath instructor apologized to each and every student for the invasion of privacy and lack of trust that the searches implied. Students are also required to store their backpacks in their lockers once in the building; they cannot carry them around, as they were accustomed to doing in the past.

Both Heath and Westside closed their campuses to outsiders. Officials were posted at the doors so that they could see who entered and ask for identification from anyone they were unfamiliar with. These measures were needed more in response to the media, milling around in large numbers, than because of fears of violence. Yet students and faculty needed reassurance that only those who belonged in the school building were there.[4]

New fences were built around both schools. At Heath, every student was required to wear an identification tag. The combination of security measures led a number of students to complain that Heath was starting to feel a bit more like a jail than a school. "Heathcatraz" emerged as a nickname for the school. The fences were a source of puzzlement. Built to keep intruders out and to funnel all visitors and students through two manned entrances, fences could do little to stop a shooting by a student who actually belonged in the facility and would do a lot to prevent people from fleeing if they needed to. Moreover, they were not much of an impediment to intruders, as students were fond of demonstrating, by climbing over or under them.

The chain-link fence that had surrounded Westside was replaced with a wooden slat fence that was intended to make the school feel more protected by blocking it from the view of outsiders. Teachers and students worried that the fence actually blocked those inside the school from seeing who might be lurking out there. The sheriff's deputies also noted that the wooden slats of the fence would still allow someone to push the barrel of a rifle through, while remaining hidden from view, providing better cover than Johnson and Golden had. The limitations of these measures led skeptics to believe they were put in place "for show," a knee-jerk response to demands that the schools "do something." There was some resentment that the school board imposed the changes without sufficient consultation with the local leadership of the school, which would have made a different set of decisions.

Schools do have a legitimate need to reassure the public and to create an aura of greater security so that students and teachers feel safer, even if the measures at issue would not stop a determined criminal or an "inside job." As long as the process of developing new security measures respects the consensus of school staff, the changes will be embraced by teachers, if not by students. School boards also have legitimate responsibilities for school safety, but it is important for those in charge locally to feel that they have a voice.

Keeping intruders at bay was especially important at Westside, since the school's notoriety attracted unwanted attention. A bomb warning three days after the shooting forced the evacuation of the gymnasium, and there have been additional threats against the school since then. News of the shooting brought oddball characters to the school—for example, a clown the school had denied permission to perform for the students showed up anyway and was found performing magic tricks in the cafeteria. A man with a car full of newspaper clippings about different school shootings around the country turned up at Westside as well. The presence of such strangers wandering onto campus caused additional security concerns for the administration. Even several years after the shooting, some parents and students continue to feel that the school is a target of violence because of the limelight. Some therefore welcomed security procedures and tighter entry restrictions, even if measures of this kind could not have prevented a rampage.

A great deal of thought went into figuring out the best options for coping with both short-term and long-term problems in both schools. They have a lot to teach other communities facing school shootings. We offer their experience here as an extension of their own mission to spread the word about what worked for them and what did not.

PREVENTION

Our diagnosis of the causes of school shootings is a resource for thinking about prevention. What does the sociological approach we used—focusing on schools as organizations, on the dark side of social capital, and on the social organization of adolescence—yield in the way of new ideas that may prove useful to schools, parents, communities, and law enforcement agencies in efforts stem the tide of lethal violence?

Adjusting the Radar

Although trying to predict which kids will turn into shooters is futile, we should nevertheless focus attention on children who manifest signs of disturbance or broadcast an intention to do harm. How might we reorganize schools so that it is easier to "see" what is right before our eyes? How can we consolidate the information that currently resides in separate nooks and crannies about troubled kids who are not major disciplinary problems?

First, *academic, counseling, and disciplinary records should be maintained across the bureaucratic boundaries that separate different grades and different schools in the same district.* The commitment to second chances, and the desire to avoid labeling kids in ways that prejudice future teachers is socially worthy, but it exacts too high a cost. Had Heath High School personnel been aware of Michael Carneal's rocky eighth grade experience and put it together with his disciplinary problems early on in his freshman year, they might have looked into his life more closely. Nevertheless, there are incidents that never make it into any record at all, and short of creating a paperwork nightmare, there are few palatable options for change. Nor can we be sure that the preservation of records would have stopped Michael from committing murder. Yet without a paper trail, the patterns of behavior he exhibited went unnoticed. School districts simply cannot afford to burn materials that, at a minimum, help guidance counselors and administrators spot kids who need more attention.

Hiding inside this recommendation is a complicated question: who ought to possess this information? It may create more problems than it solves if disciplinary histories become self-fulfilling prophecies. Teachers' expectations can easily be shaped by what they learn about a student's errant past. For this reason, *student records should remain the province of guidance counselors and administrators, to be revealed to teachers only when a current spate of misbehavior causes concern and raises the need for additional vigilance.* Erecting a firewall of this kind is not easy, especially in a small school system, but both the transfer of information and maximum protection against poisoning a child's chance to start over again are vital.

The "radar" problem would also be diminished if schools provided more opportunities for teachers to exchange information amongst themselves. At Westside and Heath, teachers were privy to observations about the shooters that they had very few opportunities to share with one another. Again, there is no *guarantee* that greater communication would have created a more comprehensive picture of the boys whose cases we examined. It would certainly have made it easier.

Many middle schools are experimenting with the use of grade-level teacher teams, often pairing math/science teachers with humanities/social science counterparts in planning joint curricula and overseeing the progress of individual students. In schools that make use of this model, students who are exceptionally isolated, appear depressed, let their schoolwork go, or act up are more likely to be noticed and dealt with because teachers recognize that their individual perceptions are shared. They place a child onto their collective radar screens when they have the opportunity to compare notes. *Schools should adopt a team model. Both the child's behavioral adjustment and his or her academic achievement should be front and center when teams meet together or with parents.* Happily, there are solid pedagogical reasons for supporting such a program. A positive by-product would be a more sensitive radar that is more likely to pick up on the marginal child. Had this kind of practice been the norm, teachers across several classes might have noticed that Michael Carneal's handwriting in fact had deteriorated, that he was turning in homework that bore no relationship to the assignments in more than one class, and that his creative writing was on the violent end of the spectrum.

This is not to advocate a culture of gossip, with a lot of private information about a student's family problems circulating among teachers. Moreover, teachers are not mental health experts. Indeed, they have enough to do just making sure their students master academic skills. Yet teachers are the adults in closest daily contact with students, and when they observe troubling behavior, they need to be able to confide in someone with the training to intervene. A teacher who has an Evan Ramsey in her class needs to be able to convey her concerns to a counselor who can address the problem.

At the elementary school in Westside, guidance counselors and social workers meet with the principal every week to discuss students who seem to be troubled. This is a valuable practice that should be adopted as a companion to the kind of discussions teachers can have with one another when they meet to discuss academic progress.

School Resource Officers

School resource officers (SROs) are an important answer to the problem of an ineffective radar: They are an additional set of adult eyes and ears that have the advantage of being independent of the school system. SROs, who are trained law enforcement officials, spend most, if not all, of their time at the schools. Both Heath and Westside have added SROs and see them as an unqualified success. Like traditional police officers, SROs carry a radio, a gun, handcuffs, and a club, but they try to blend in at the school by wearing a "soft" uniform. By acting as a presence on the school campus and reaching out to students, they combine the functions of security and communication.

Students seem to feel more comfortable confiding in an adult who does not have the same authoritative relationship over them as their teachers. SROs are supposed to get to know students and establish a bond of trust with them. Teenagers need to feel that they can turn to the SRO if they hear threats or learn of students who are in trouble. This is precisely what happened in Heath and Westside after the shootings. In both schools, the SROs successfully integrated themselves into school life, befriending a number of students, often joining groups to chat socially during the lunch periods. Tips they have received from students have led to several arrests for drugs, knives, and other contraband violations. SROs also assist with drug education, contribute their understanding of the law to the school administration, and sit in on difficult disciplinary meetings with parents. Teachers support their presence because it relieves them of some of the disciplinary duties they do not relish.

SROs make the daily process of maintaining order easier on the educational staff, and their presence is helpful in preventing school violence. As one Heath teacher put it, "An ID badge and a fence won't stop a potential shooter, but a security officer might." In truth very few school shootings have been ended by the police or by security guards because they are generally over very quickly.

The "value added" of an SRO lies much more in the officer's capacity to intercept threats by being a friendly and trusted face. Standard law enforcement strategy is weak in the face of determined shooters. However, the fact that school shooters tend to broadcast their intentions opens opportunities for stopping plots before they become realities—as long as the information about their intentions gets into the right hands. In May 2003, a Kings County sheriff's deputy working as an SRO at Evergreen High School, south of Seattle, was tipped off that a seventeen-year-old student was carrying a loaded "Mac 10" machine gun in his backpack.[5] He seized the student and the gun. Had there been no SRO to warn, who knows what might have happened?

SROs can work in consort with counseling staff to identify kids who need additional attention and supervision. Long before the plot stage, SROs may realize that particular kids are troubled and assist the school by making it clear that steps need to be taken to address the problem before it festers. Yet we should recognize that for both tasks—detective and confidante—a trained, skilled person is required. In some school districts, the SRO job is poorly paid and of low status. Under those circumstances, the only people who have both the necessary training and the interest may be retired police officers looking to supplement their pensions. People like this can do a great job, but there may not be enough of them to fill the bill. If we want quality, we will have to pay for it.

The main worry for Heath and Westside now is how to ensure the continued presence of SROs. Short-term grants given to the schools in the wake of the shootings cover the cost for now, but it is not clear that the state legislature or the local authorities are willing to pick up the tab over the long run. In the current climate of state budget deficits, we worry that this kind of program will wind up on the chopping block, which would be unfortunate. *SROs represent a worthy investment in the safety of all schools and the peace of mind of the nation's children and teachers.*

Moreover, there is an advantage to be gained in freeing educators from some of the disciplinary duties that currently take up so much of their time. A division of labor that places some of the most disagreeable tasks of monitoring drugs, weapons, and fighting in the hands of quasi–law enforcement personnel and leaves teachers to teach is beneficial for many reasons, not least of which is that the arrangement actually preempts violence rather than treating it after the fact.

There are unintended consequences to having law enforcement personnel on campus. The presence of an SRO clearly leads to more student interaction with the criminal justice system. Where school authorities might have invoked their own "law" in the past, these days all violations that can be construed as "criminal," including fighting in the hallway, have become the province of the Sheriff's Office. The Westside SRO told us, "Fighting is illegal. Fighting is battery." Local juvenile court officials process more students from schools with an SRO than without one. Kids who might once have had a discipline record at school now have an arrest record in the courts. This can create problems for them later, because employers are often troubled by delinquency. However, as with all interventions, the consequences of the change are mixed, and on balance we think the pros outweigh the cons.

Leavening Social Capital, Tweaking Adolescent Culture

Despite the benefits of living in tight-knit, highly stable communities, towns that are high in social capital and low in geographic mobility are hard on adolescents who do not fit in. Marginal boys come to feel that there is "no exit," that the problems they face as teens will follow them forever. Going to a distant college, the escape hatch for many unhappy high school students, may not be an option. Graduates of Westside and Heath tend not to head for distant colleges. Most opt for local colleges, live at home, and stay in the community to work, marry, and raise the next generation. This is all well and good for those who fit in; it magnifies the social insecurity of those who do not.

How might the grip be loosened without eroding the beneficial aspects of social capital? Oddballs and eggheads who emerge from adolescence in good shape often remember with gratitude a special teacher or two who showcased an alternative set of values, an accepting culture, or a set of activities that honored a divergent self. Teachers create the social space students need to be different. They give kids who don't care for football or cheerleading a safe space to stretch their wings in like-minded company.

Bill Bond, the former principal of Heath High, recognized the importance of this special breed and argued that they should be considered an important resource:

> Every kid in the building should have an adult that he or she can relate to, to go to with problems or issues that they can identify with. And so your faculty doesn't need to all be of one set mind. It doesn't need to look like the school board. I don't want my faculty with a bunch of people who are all valedictorians of their school. . . .
>
> You've got to have some diverse academics in your school, but you've got to have some diverse kind of personalities too. . . . So if you've got weird kids, you need to hire some weird teachers also. Sometimes we forget that. . . .

Younger teachers are particularly valuable in this role. Recall that all of the shooters we have identified in the United States have been adolescent boys. Girls seem to find ways to stay connected to one another and to adults, although they have their own share of psychosocial problems. It is the boys who seem to find it harder to locate themselves in the social landscape. How, then, are we to reach them? *Recruiting young or "hip" teachers is one way to give these boys another model of adulthood, another kind of grown-up to bond with.* In small towns, in particular, such teachers may be in short supply. Hence, when one or two make an appearance, it would be a blessing for schools to recognize their good fortune and provide them with the support they need to run activities that will include the round pegs who do not fit in the existing square holes.

Schools could also explicitly challenge reductionist notions of masculinity that prevail in adolescence. Masculinity in adulthood can mean a range of things, but for adolescents it often signifies physical strength, athletic accomplishment, and sexual conquest. Exposing adolescents to a more expansive range and challenging them to confront their own parochialism is an important strategy in diversifying the range of viable options for manly behavior.[6]

Sports culture is responsible for a great deal of the damage done to the egos of boys who cannot compete. Teams bring a great deal of positive spirit to their schools and communities, serving as a magnet for loyalty and an opportunity for intergenerational engagement in an institution most would agree is central to the health of any community. But there is no reason these positive contributions have to be buttressed by the kind of "star culture" that attends them. No matter how valued, no matter how talented, athletes should not be exempted from the requirement of treating their fellow students with respect. We teach them all the wrong lessons when coaches look the other way as they slam smaller boys into lockers. *Adults who fail to discipline flagrant rule violators should be removed from positions of authority.* Evading their responsibility to keep order is placing the safety of other children in jeopardy.

Good, old-fashioned ideals of sportsmanship are important to emphasize. But as we noted earlier, this is easier said than done. Schools do not exist independently of the society in which they are situated. Dozens of examples of violent, illegal, and disreputable behavior crop up every year among professional athletes. Because they bring in big money, they are tolerated, even embraced by team owners. Can we expect high school coaches to do any better? Yes. Public schools are not private, professional organizations. They belong to their communities and everyone in them has a right to expect a higher standard of behavior. Playing on a sports team is a privilege, not a right.

This matters a great deal in small towns where the football and basketball teams, pep rallies, cheerleaders, and the homecoming game seem make the world go around. When everyone rivets their attention on these central social events and then permits their stars to behave badly, they send a message to the marginal boy: you are not respected, you are not welcome. This tacit policy needs to be reversed. Persistent bullying should be grounds for forfeit of the privilege of representing one's school in athletic competition.

The community has a role to play as well. *It would be helpful if local businesses, civic leaders, and parent groups extended some of the positive support they currently give to sports teams to other kinds of achievements.* Why not ask the Chamber of Commerce to throw a celebration for the debate team or get the local supermarket to sponsor awards for students with high achievement in the creative arts or engineering? Some schools give varsity letters for chess teams or science teams. Kids pay attention to what the surrounding community values and rewards. They know that an outsized fuss is made over only one kind of achievement in most towns: the sports teams. Why not diversify the winners of public recognition?

It makes a big difference when kids can find a diversity of nonschool activities to participate in. When this is not possible in a small town, providing transportation to other communities for chess tournaments, art festivals, science fairs, rock concerts, or ultimate Frisbee may provide the oddball kid with opportunities to meet like-minded friends, see a bit of the country, and recognize that the closed social universe of his own high school is just one corner of a bigger world.

To the extent that this happens in American schools now, it is the high school that is likely to be at the forefront. *Middle schools should try to develop more activities that will engage the interest of kids who are not involved in sports.* The troubles we have recounted in this book begin in middle school, where the resources are often least abundant for creating extracurricular activities. Younger kids have less need for alternatives, and high schoolers tend to have at least some options. Middle school is getting lost in the shuffle.

Zero Tolerance Policy

Controversy surrounds the tightening of school disciplinary procedures in favor of zero tolerance. In general, these policies require schools to follow formalized disciplinary procedures after any threat of violence and leave administrators with little discretion to separate serious offenders from casual jokers. The strictest of such policies have mandatory suspension penalties for all threats, regardless of the circumstances or the credibility of the threats. Schools no longer have the flexibility to determine that the student who says, "I'm gonna get you," is merely using a common phrase uttered daily by millions of adolescents (and adults for that matter), none of whom have any intention of hurting anyone. In Jonesboro, a five-year-old child pointed a chicken finger at another child and said, "Bang, bang, you're dead." He was suspended and his parents were summoned to a meeting at the school. The press had a field day with the incident, ridiculing school authorities for overreacting.

A punitive approach is counterproductive, because it does little to change the underlying dynamics of peer relations and the flow of information in schools—factors that lie closer to the root of the problem. Moreover, rigid disciplinary policies often backfire, because they create greater distance between students and the staff who need to enforce these measures. A 1994–95 study of seventh to twelfth graders found that students felt less connected to their school when it temporarily adopted a policy of expelling students for infractions such as possession of alcohol and for their first major rule infraction.[7] Given what we have learned about the importance of breaking down communication barriers between adolescents and adults, the last thing we need is policies that widen the social gaps between them.

Electronic surveillance, security staff, and adult supervision are among the more common school security procedures. In 2000, 82 percent of high schools reported having staff or volunteers monitor hallways, and 45 percent reported routinely checking bags, desks, and lockers. Thirty percent of high schools reported having uniformed police officers, 24 percent used surveillance cameras, and 10 percent used metal detectors.[8] The effectiveness of these strategies is debatable.[9] Two national studies found that schools using these strategies had higher levels of violence and lower levels of safety, but this is probably because unsafe schools are the first to make use of these security measures.[10] We do know that students and teachers sometimes develop negative perceptions of regulation security guards as ineffective and harassing. However, in schools that have experienced the shock of gunfire in the hallways, the presence of uniformed police or guards may have a reassuring effect in the first few weeks after the rampage. Those negative perceptions may soften in the face of the increased vulnerability that students and teachers feel after a shooting.

Zero tolerance policies have the advantage of assuring families that their children are in an environment where the risk of violence is taken seriously. It is possible, although far from proven, that less violent behavior crops up in schools like this. However, the cost may be too high. Suspending kindergarten students for playing Wild West games makes no sense. For better or worse, much of our casual, daily conversation is laced with metaphors that, taken wrongly, could get a lot of perfectly innocent people in trouble. *The "Big Brother" aspects of zero tolerance policies are too extreme; discretion is an important tool for keeping order.* If students believe that their teachers and administrators are unable to exercise any judgment, they are not likely to consider them people they can confide in or trust.

A military climate may not be conducive to education, but neither is an atmosphere of fear. Students and parents need assurances that the institution is in good order, that any hint of real violence is taken seriously, and that troublemakers will be punished. We know this is not the case where the behavior of sports stars is concerned. At Columbine High School, harassment by athletes was particularly problematic. Football players were given wide latitude to abuse their fellow students, and this atmosphere was an important factor in the rampage shooting. Columbine paid dearly for looking the other way. *No one who intimidates, pushes, punches, slams kids into lockers, or threatens them with worse should be permitted to continue their reign of terror.* They should be disciplined and excluded if they cannot learn to respect the human rights of their peers.

Some might argue that such a policy would not have deterred a Michael, a Mitchell, or an Andrew because they were not regarded as serious disciplinary problem cases. That is true. But the policy would have been helpful, at least in

Michael's case, not because it would have snared him, but because it might have discouraged the people who made him so miserable that he wanted to shoot people to "get them off [his] back." There certainly are cases in our database where there is no evidence of torment or where the shooter was in such a bad mental state that the torment was really in his head rather than in the hallways. But in many cases, shooters were victims of bullying. Had the bullying not occurred, their lives and perceptions might have been very different.

Heath and Westside did react to the shootings and the associated trauma by tightening discipline, and their experience is instructive. Westside had always had a zero tolerance policy on weapons in school or other gross violations. The federal government embraced the same approach when Congress passed the Gun-Free Schools Act in 1994. This law mandates a one-year expulsion for possession of firearms and requires that such students be referred to the criminal justice or juvenile justice system.[11] In effect, then, all schools have zero tolerance policies for weapons and this we heartily applaud.

The terrain becomes more slippery when we shift from weapons—which are unambiguously inappropriate at school—to speech. After the shooting, Westside began to include threats that would previously have been ignored under the heading of offenses warranting automatic discipline, including comments made in the heat of an argument. Some teachers described the policy as "commonsense zero tolerance" that still allowed some flexibility for administrators to judge the severity of incidents. Students and staff alike agreed that the climate of Westside is very different now and that transgressions are dealt with more harshly.

Westside teachers fear that zero tolerance policies for speech will disrupt the lines of communication between students and teachers, fragile as they are. Donna Randall, a classmate of Mitchell's, told us that she was much *less* likely to talk to teachers about her concerns or problems now because of the way teachers have to respond. Before the shooting, detention and paddling were much more common forms of punishment for disciplinary problems. After the shooting, the school made mountains out of molehills. Expulsion, in particular, is much more common now, and more students are turned over to the SRO or the Sheriff's Office if they get in trouble, something that rarely happened in the past. Even though students are told to report threats of any kind to their teachers, they worry that they could get fellow students into trouble, forcing the school to respond with a suspension or expulsion. It is hard for them to know when a threat is really serious, they claim, and with harsher punishments becoming the norm, they're much more likely to hold their peace.

Students are not above manipulating a zero tolerance policy for their own aims. Students know that threats—which often cannot be substantiated—must be punished. Adolescent power games can reach whole new levels under these circumstances.

The harsher punishments meted out for such infractions can produced another kind of unintended consequence: driving violence off of school grounds, where it can become more severe. Knowing that they will be dealt with harshly for fighting on school grounds, students have arranged meeting places for fights off campus, where school officials lack jurisdiction. For Westside students, a nearby gas station and a local field host these old-style showdowns. This is cause for concern, because however distasteful and disruptive fighting on school grounds may be, it could be more severe and dangerous if it occurs where no adults are in range. Of course, because fighting has never been acceptable on school grounds, this is not an entirely new development, but increasing surveillance has pushed more conflict off campus.

On the whole, zero tolerance policies are too inflexible and should be avoided. School authorities need to take disciplinary problems seriously, and threats should provoke intensive investigation and, when warranted, punishment. Yet preserving the capacity for school authorities to make nuanced judgments is important not only for ensuring students' trust and encouraging communication (especially of threats) but for preserving the exercise of adult authority. Rigid policies restrict principals from exercising the judgment we pay them to cultivate in the first place.

ENCOURAGING KIDS TO REPORT THREATS

Despite the best efforts of communities to squelch violence, we are not likely to see the end of it any time soon. While the nation looks for ways to attack the root causes of adolescent rage, it must apply equal effort to increasing the likelihood that kids who hear threats come forward and tell someone who can make a difference. Intercepting threats is the most promising avenue for prevention of school shootings, but for that to happen, kids must feel comfortable coming forward with information that they typically conceal. Teenagers face a minefield when they cross the barrier that separates them from adults: They risk their reputations and their friendships, two of their most valuable possessions. They will not do so lightly.

Having reviewed the many reasons why teenagers are reluctant to confide in adults, it is worth considering how their hesitation might be reversed. First, *kids must come to trust that the information they report will be kept confidential.* Heath High School instituted an anonymous tip line, which allows students to report potential threats without the possibility that the information can be traced. A nationwide hotline for students to report weapon-related threats (866-SPEAK-UP) opened in October 2002. It is sponsored by PAX, a nonprofit organization dedicated to ending gun violence, with partners including Atlantic Records, Channel One Network, MTV, and several national organizations that represent school boards, law enforcement personnel, and secondary school principals.[12]

Second, *SROs represent an important resource for intercepting threats of violence and should be supported in every community.* Because SROs do not report to the school authority system, teens in Heath do seem to believe that the officers will keep their confidences private and will act on the information teens give them. Of course, there is potential for abuse here too. SROs must be on their guard for false complaints made to get an innocent in trouble. Background investigations must be discrete. Nonetheless, the SROs make it easier for teenagers to come forward and repeat threats they have heard—which is critical to safety in our schools. Hotlines can achieve a similar purpose, but we recommend that they not be instituted alone. Students need adults to confide in when they hear frightening warnings.

Third, *efforts should be made to increase direct contact between parents and teachers, especially in middle school.* Children are particularly vulnerable during early adolescence. They don't yet feel secure in their identities; they are constantly jockeying for approval; and they can become depressed when their status falls. Yet middle school is precisely the period when we seem to push parents out of the picture. The hallways of a typical elementary school are often swarming with parents visiting classrooms, chaperoning field trips, and chatting with teachers. But in most communities parents get the message that they must withdraw when their children hit middle school in favor of greater adolescent autonomy.

This is a delicate dance. Kids *do* need to learn how to navigate the social world on their own. But there is no reason why the need for independence must necessarily break the bond between parent and teacher.

Why does this matter where school shootings are concerned? To the extent that kids confide in adults at all, their own parents are more likely to become sounding boards for their fears than teachers or church leaders. If parents have a direct relationship with teachers, they may be able to complete the loop, transferring information about credible threats without exposing their children to the opprobrium they fear the most from their friends. This will not always work. Indeed, we know that at least one parent whose son had heard Andrew Golden's threats went to the school with the information, and the school authorities' intervention did not go far enough. The point here is that the parent knew what to do with the threat and had enough of a relationship with the child's school to act.

This is not the norm. Most parents of middle school children are virtual strangers to the classroom and the principal's office. This may be less so in small towns where parents are also neighbors of teachers. But in many American communities parents are simply not in the picture and would not know what to do with delicate information if it came their way. We recognize that such a process must be handled with discretion, lest kids conclude that they cannot trust their parents to keep their confidences. However, after looking at the pattern of discussions kids engaged in with their parents, we believe they are frightened when they hear threats and want their parents to "do something," even if they balk at the thought of being identified as the source. If parents have meaningful relations with their children's middle school and high school teachers, they can find ways to come forward that will not publicly implicate their kids.

What else tips the balance toward reporting threats to authorities? We can take some comfort from the change in the willingness of teens to come forward in the wake of highly publicized shootings. For instance, in the week after the shooting in Santee, California, in March 2001, a variety of threats—some serious and others less so—were reported at schools throughout Southern California. At one school in South Corona (about 95 miles from Santee), several students came forward, after a speech by a teacher on the importance of reporting threats, to say that a thirteen-year-old boy had been threatening to kill classmates for months. Police investigated and found a handwritten list of people the boy wanted to kill and an online list of teachers and students he disliked. That same week, a girl in Twenty-nine Palms, California (175 miles from Santee) told her father about a hit list that she had overheard two students bragging about at school. During a search of the boys' homes, police found the hit list, containing the names of sixteen students at a nearby school, and a .22 caliber rifle.[13] In these near-miss cases, we cannot say for sure that the students making threats and writing hit lists would have become shooters. Nevertheless, the fellow students who came forward may have saved lives.

Mass school shootings did not seem a realistic prospect before they actually happened. There was no pattern to rely on in making such an assessment. Now that there is, perhaps the reporting pattern will look more like these near-miss cases than like Heath or Bethel, Alaska. But it takes an awareness of present danger to motivate young people to push past their normal reluctance to breach the confines of the adolescent code.

How long does such an awareness last after a widely publicized school shooting? A year? Two years? If we are fortunate and there is a long lull with no rampage shootings, will kids remember that it could still happen in their high school and continue to be courageous in reporting threats? Two years is a long time in the adolescent world. The sense of urgency is not likely to remain unless it is nourished by the concerted efforts of teachers and principals to remind students forcefully of how important it is to tell them if they hear threats of violence. Students need to be reminded periodically of the horrors of school shootings and the precipitating pressures they may be generating when they tease and exclude the peers they don't care for. Antibullying curricula tend to focus on the latter domain. Programs developed for schools to try to sensitize kids to the damage they do to one another are probably useful, although doubt that they will affect reporting behavior. Instead, we recommend that schools include in their curriculum periodic discussions of a very straightforward sort about school shootings in general.

Several fine videos have been produced—such as a PBS *Frontline* special on the Moses Lake shooting and a *Dateline NBC* program on the Jeremy Getman case—that recount the terrible cost that these rampages have exacted. The programs are blunt and graphic, but in that respect they are doing no more than reporting the events themselves. *Films of this kind need to be shown periodically in schools across the country, followed by classroom discussions in which teachers ask students to analyze what they have just viewed.* This would help to bring home the unhappy message that the possibility of school shootings is real and that even the safest of surroundings holds the potential for explosive violence. The further actual rampage shootings recede in time, the less necessary such programs will seem. But administrators must recognize that declining to implement and maintain them leaves us with the kind of response to threats that prevailed at Heath and Westside: Threats were not reported because the prospect of a shooting seemed so fantastic and remote. Only when they are aware that shootings can and do happen will teens learn to ignore the adolescent code that holds them back.

When students do take that courageous step, it must be met with decisive action. Unfortunately, this is not the outcome they have come to expect. Bureaucracies are often inclined to avoid trouble or to push it out of the way, particularly if the normal operation of the institution is not concretely threatened. But when students make the effort to confide in teachers, parents, or counselors about a rumor of impending violence, they must see that their concerns are taken seriously. Otherwise, they will lose confidence in the capacity of adults to act.

The key here is to act in a way that students perceive as both efficacious and fair. In this respect, zero tolerance policies are of little use. In a culture where violent language is common and kids often say things they don't mean, punishments must be proportionate to the severity of the offense. In practice this means that principals have to do the laborious work of assessing the context in which words were spoken and the state of mind of the student issuing the threat.

At the same time, when such an investigation determines that a threat is serious, the school must behave in a decisive fashion to protect its student body if students are to be expected to come forward in the future.

Under pressure from the broader community, schools may be tempted to try to divide the world into two simple categories: innocent students and moral monsters who seek to target them. This view provides the rationale for zero tolerance policies, which essentially try to exclude by means of expulsion those who are dangerous in order to protect the rest. This approach is wholly inconsistent with the morally messy views and perceptions of students themselves: They feel that they have obligations both to protect the welfare of fellow students and to look out for friends and peers who often say things they don't really mean. If schools want to make use of their most valuable resource in heading off potential attacks—the knowledge of students—schools will have to adapt to this reality.

If adults want kids to speak up in the future, they will have to instruct students on exactly what kind of threats they are expected to report; disabuse them of their stereotypes and convince them that anyone could potentially be a school shooter; protect the confidentiality of those who come forward with information; accurately assess the danger of each threat; and respond in a way that balances the twin goals of student safety and fairness to the accused.

To do so effectively, schools can benefit from the research the FBI has conducted on threat assessment.[14] The essence of the bureau's advice is that the more specific the threat, the more serious it is. The report also provides rules of interpretation to help us separate out casual comments ("Oh man, I'm gonna kill that guy!") from something more threatening ("You'll see who lives or dies on Monday"). Obviously our interpretive equipment is not foolproof. In a context where the unthinkable had not yet happened, kids dismissed fairly specific threats as boastful fantasies designed to attract attention. Threats containing specific information as to dates, times, and weapons, however, must be reported even if the context is ambiguous.

Bullying

Readers may get the impression that bullying and shaming are merely sideshows to the athletic star culture. They are not. Most athletes are not bullies, and not all bullies are athletes. Harassment is not perpetrated by a single group, and it is a serious problem in U.S. schools. It is a source of depression for teenagers, especially boys, and it requires attention in its own right. Educators are aware of this and have taken steps to address it. Nonetheless, nearly 70 percent of the nation's students believe that their schools respond poorly to bullying.[15]

Westside has added adult monitors, as well as some student monitors, to its school buses since the shooting in an effort to reduce the chaos and harassment that attended the school commute before the shooting. Students told us that the monitors have helped, although teasing has not disappeared. Nonetheless, this has improved the climate during those early morning and afternoon hours, and it illustrates the general principle that reducing unsupervised time increases social order. *Children should not have to run a gauntlet of intimidation at the hands of their peers. Wherever it is possible, we should reduce harassment and demonstrate to students that their sense of security matters to us.* This is particularly important for young children, who are not well treated by the older students left to their own devices.

Existing prevention programs tend to emphasize the importance of making bullies aware of their victim's feelings, forcing harassers to make amends to victims, increasing the social skills of bullies so that they will not lapse into victimizing behavior, and enrolling bullies in anger management classes.[16] Very few of these programs have been subjected to rigorous evaluation, and hence we cannot offer an informed view of their efficacy.[17]

However, they have their limitations. Efforts to focus on changing either the bullies or the victims are unlikely to be effective, because they leave the underlying power dynamics largely unchanged. Shaming is held in check only by the desire to behave better, which is a weak motivator compared with the status gains that came from teasing and harassment. Bystanders stay out of it, because they do not want to endanger their own social status. The victims have no real way out of these situations, because their low status makes most of the recommended strategies—ignore the teasing, exit conflict situations, tell the teacher—ineffective at stopping the problem at its source.[18]

Rather than focus attention on the subset of students who are causing trouble, treat entire schools for the bullying problem. One particularly effective model was developed by Dan Olweus in Norway.[19] His program begins with a series of steps, including a schoolwide questionnaire to assess the baseline incidence of bullying and to build momentum for solving the problem.[20] Olweus recommends following up with a schoolwide conference to discuss the results and share best practices among teachers and administrators. Thereafter, a three-part process unfolds. First, at the school level, supervision is increased in the locations where bullying seems to crop up—such as bathrooms, corridors, buses, lunchrooms, and locker rooms. Teachers have to be trained to understand that prevention of harassment is part of their jobs.

At the classroom level, Olweus recommends posting rules about bullying and insisting that teachers intervene aggressively when they see evidence of harassment. Students must see teachers taking the message seriously and acting on their behalf, as much to improve the disciplinary climate as to remove from children's shoulders the full responsibility for defending themselves. Finally, at the individual level, rules must be enforced—although with room for adult judgment—in a no-nonsense fashion. Any hint that adults are winking at offenders will undermine the whole edifice.

These recommendations are not particularly novel, but they have been effective. The Olweus program reduced bullying in forty-two Norwegian schools by 50 percent, according to before-and-after evaluations. The key to success is to change the school climate regarding bullying so that it is *universally* understood to be unacceptable. The role of teachers is critical. They must not assume that bullying is inevitable. They can do something about it. When the change is thoroughgoing, it increases the motivation of bystanders to intervene on the side of victims, it strengthens the resolve of victims to come forward and seek help from adults. No child should have to tolerate the fear, stigma, and sense of weakness that persistent victimization creates.

Mental Health Services in Schools

Whatever good comes of tightening security—and there is good to be had—it is clear that security policies have only a modest impact on the underlying forces that led shooters to feel they had no other way out of their dilemmas. Such policies may deter the more aggressive bullies, and that is all to the good. But kids like Mitchell or Michael are disturbed by behavior that is less severe, because their interpretations of the intentions of others are warped by their own psychological problems. For kids like this, *we need to move away from a law enforcement model and toward devoting greater resources to counseling, mental health services, social workers, and development of communication skills.* Recall that 80 percent of the school shooters in our database were suicidal, and 20 percent of the U.S. high school population has considered suicide.[21] School shooters may be a tiny minority, but there are clearly thousands of other teens for whom these services would be helpful.

The Safe Schools/Healthy Students Grant, which was awarded to Westside and other schools in the area, provided funds for additional social workers and full-time counselors for the school. Counselors are available to meet with students who are referred to them by teachers or administrators for behavioral problems or therapy, and they meet with some students on an ongoing basis. Social workers make home visits to parents, refer them to more specialized services or information if they are unable to come to the school, and teach students character education, such as building social skills, anger management, and coping with bullying.

These are significant resource commitments that have proved to be popular at these schools. Counselors are fully booked, week in and week out. The more staff with this kind of training in our schools, the better. Among other benefits, the additional staff permits a beneficial specialization, or what sociologists call "role segregation." Counselors who specialize in guidance functions—scheduling, college counseling, record keeping—can be distinguished from those with training in psychological assessment or emotional development. With this division of labor, it might be possible to be more proactive in offering support to students like Mitchell Johnson or Michael Carneal, the kids with minor but more than occasional disciplinary problems or marginal social lives. Kids at the frictional edges of social cliques might be offered greater attention before they act out in ways that damage themselves or others.

Teachers need to be especially attuned to identifying boys with depression or suicidal tendencies, because traditional signs of despair—crying, expressing hopelessness, or commiserating with others—are more socially acceptable for girls than for boys. Boys may mask their unhappiness by internalizing, as Michael did, making it very hard to pick up when they are having serious problems. Given the potential costs of failing to identify depressed students, teachers should be more attentive to "male" signs, such as withdrawal from friendships, increased aggressiveness, greater risk-taking behavior, or more frequent angry outbursts, as well as less gender-specific criteria, such as academic difficulties or trouble eating, sleeping, or concentrating.[22]

Curriculum-based programs have also been introduced that force problems that might have been kept under wraps in the past out into open discussion. Bill Bond explained that the "life skills" program at Heath is comprehensive, tailored to different age groups, and intended to instruct students on how to cope with conflict. As the children grow up, they are accorded greater responsibility not only for their own conduct, but also in assisting troubled peers through mediation.

Human Resources

Many of the policy changes undertaken at Heath and Westside as well as those suggested here can be implemented by redirecting existing efforts on the part of parents, teachers, administrators, and students. However, there is only so much that can be done without some additional investment in the safety and well-being of students. The nation's educational workforce is not equipped to handle the additional task of monitoring the mental health of millions of students. Educators need to focus on the demanding work they must do in the classroom. Although it will make a positive difference if teachers learn how to spot troubled children, they need skilled professionals to turn to when they recognize that a student needs help.

Where are those professionals in the schools? Guidance counselors are those most likely to meet this task, but the workload they typically carry is too high to permit the kind of individualized care that is needed. As Table 11.1 shows, the ratio of counselors to students has been decreasing, but at a pace way too slow to make a difference for the kinds of problems we have identified in this book.

When counselors are responsible for nearly 500 students each, it is no wonder that their jobs are confined to scheduling. The American School Counselor Association recommends that schools set a standard of no more than 250 students per counselor at an annual cost that, according to some estimates, would be comparable to what we are spending on security cameras and metal detectors.[23] Few public schools come close to this level of staffing.

We believe that increasing investment in counseling staff would make a positive difference in stemming lethal violence in schools while simultaneously improving services for students who would never dream of hurting anyone. Each year, 5,000 Americans aged fifteen to twenty-four commit suicide. Suicide rates for those aged fifteen to nineteen doubled between 1970 and 1990. The problem is especially acute in less densely populated areas (such as Western states and rural areas). The vast majority (90–95 percent) of people who commit suicide had a potentially diagnosable mental disorder (this includes substance abuse), but only about half had received any treatment.[24] These data suggest that the population of students who need treatment is growing.

Table 11.1: Ratio of Counselors to Students in U.S. Public Elementary and Secondary Schools, 1959–1999

School Year	Number of counselors	Pupils per counselor
1959–60	14,643	2,402.7
1969–70	48,763	934.1
1980–81	63,973	639.0
1990–91	79,950	515.5
1999–00	95,697	489.6

Source: Adapted from the National Center for Education Statistics, Digest of Educational Statistics 2001, Table 82. Available at http://nces.ed.gov/pubs2002/digest2001/tables/dt082.asp.

Guidance counselors may not be able to provide counseling themselves, but their ability to identify kids who need referrals will be hampered as long as they are responsible for nearly 500 students at a time. We need to do better by the nation's youth so that fewer seriously disturbed individuals go without treatment. At least since the late 1980s, a growing chorus of voices has been calling for increasing the mental health services provided schools, both within the school itself and through referrals to services in the community. Proponents argue that mental health problems are among the greatest barriers to learning in American schools.

By attending to the emotional, social, and developmental needs of students, we can boost achievement, prevent problem behaviors, and reduce violence. Researchers and practitioners at UCLA, University of Maryland, and Yale have been developing support materials, providing assistance to schools, and spreading information about the role of mental health resources in schools. Schools and communities need to take advantage of these resources to learn how to identify students who have mental health problems and get them the help they need.[25]

For better or worse, schools are the only universal institution that has access to teenagers: It is the place where we are likely to do the best job of screening and referral—but not if we fail to provide the human resources necessary to identify those in need before they harm themselves or others. Michael Carneal exhibited at least six of the warning signs of suicide.[26] He never received any treatment at all until he was incarcerated.

Guns

Finally, society as a whole can reconsider what we can do about access to guns. Many people we met in Heath and Westside are gun owners who respect the need for safety in handling them. Some believe in the virtues of gun control, but many are skeptical. "People kill people," they told us, "guns don't kill people." This may be so, but it bears repeating that most of the school shooters in our database did not have to go far or put much effort into obtaining the guns they used in their rampages—and that these rampages most likely would not have happened in the absence of guns. It would be wise to consider ways of making it harder for potential killers to gain access to guns.

One useful approach worked its way into New Jersey law in December 2002, when that state became the first to require that new handguns be equipped with devices that prevent anyone but the licensed user from firing them.[27] The bill will take effect as soon as the technology for user identification is commercially available. Although dedicated criminals will find ways to defeat the technology, ambivalent teens are less likely to do so. Clearly, however, with some 200 million guns already in Americans' hands, other measures are needed too.

———

The rage that fueled the outbursts of Michael Carneal, Mitchell Johnson, and Andrew Golden is harbored by many young people—particularly boys—who are on the losing end of the fierce competition among adolescents for respect and masculine identity. We hope this book will help parents, students, teachers, administrators, law enforcement personnel, and policy makers in understanding the cross-pressures that led these boys down the path to becoming rampage shooters. There are choices to be made by all parties that can make a difference. Teenagers can come to understand the damage they inflict if they treat one another with such disdain that they cause depression and violent impulses. Parents can do more to connect with their children's teachers, and neighbors may recognize their responsibilities to approach one another when they see evidence of bad behavior, animal abuse, or weapons in the wrong hands. Teachers must take responsibility for ensuring that students respect the rules of conduct and not hesitate to discipline those who step out of line. Schools must think critically about the importance of preserving student records and see to it that they remain in the hands of professionals who can make positive use of them while protecting students from the self-fulfilling prophecies that may attend negative expectations from teachers who learn of their difficult pasts.

School shootings are rare events. Yet the fear of explosive attacks in the middle of communities that consider themselves safe places to raise a family is real enough. It is a fair question whether we should devote the kinds of resources we have discussed in this chapter to preventing eruptions that occur so infrequently. This is a matter for taxpayers, parents, students, school officials, law enforcement officials, and mental health specialists to debate. We hope that when they engage with this question, they will keep in mind that adopting the recommendations we make here would improve the school climate in general and help many thousands of kids who are not potential shooters—as well as the few who are and the thousands who might have to face them.

EPILOGUE:
WHAT BECAME OF
THE SHOOTERS

MITCHELL JOHNSON AND ANDREW GOLDEN WERE CAPTURED BY LOCAL LAW
ENFORCEMENT officers within ten minutes of opening fire on Westside Middle
School. They were taken to the Craighead County Detention Center, where they
remained for several months, throughout their juvenile adjudication. Their
lawyers and Department of Youth Services officials spent this period searching
high and low for facilities that would house them, which were few and far between in the state of Arkansas.

One night, under cover of darkness and with no warning, National Guard
troops maneuvered a large, black helicopter to a landing site in a remote corner
of Jonesboro. The blades whirred overhead, slowly winding down as the grass
and trees whipsawed in their wake. The headlights of the helicopter cast a ghastly
white glow over the field behind the Craighead County Detention Center.
Armed guards piled out of the doors with guns drawn and scanned the area for
snipers. Convinced the grounds were secure, they entered the jailhouse, found
Jean Rittman, the night supervisor, and instructed her to get Mitchell Johnson
and Andrew Golden ready to travel.

The two young boys emerged in prison issue clothing, blinking at the bright
lights. Mitchell looked apprehensive but excited. Andrew was sobbing. The helicopter lifted into the night sky and was joined by airplanes flying alongside,
guardians against sniper attacks. Mitchell and Andrew disappeared from Jonesboro, with neither their families nor their lawyers the wiser. Only the National
Guard knew where they were headed. When the chopper finally came down, the

boys found themselves in the exercise yard of the maximum-security unit of the Department of Youth Services in Alexander, Arkansas.

Alexander lies in a heavily wooded area twenty miles south of Little Rock, a two-hour drive from Jonesboro. It is not easy to find, on purpose. Down a long, winding, country road, surrounded by forest, the facility is secluded from the surrounding countryside. Nonetheless, angry people bent on doing harm to the boys seemed to know precisely where it was. Ever since the announcement of their sentences, death threats had been arriving via mail and phone, spurred both by the heinous nature of the crime and the widespread conviction that justice had not been served. The Ku Klux Klan announced that it would exact its own death penalty; freelance militia, angry individuals, and assorted nut cases joined in the cacophony. Given this threatening climate, authorities were taking no chances at the jail, en route, or at Alexander itself. Tarps were placed around the exercise yard of the maximum-security unit where Mitchell and Andrew would be held, and part of the nearby woods was cleared to prevent snipers from gaining a vantage point.

The facility, a sprawling, green campus dotted with pine trees, sits amid gently rolling hills. A chain-link fence with spiral barbed wire across the top encloses Alexander. The swimming pool lies empty, filled with dead leaves. Most of the prisoner units—single-level, wood buildings that look like outdoor camp dormitories—are for lower-level security "residents." Mitchell and Andrew, however, never leave the concrete maximum-security unit, except to take exercise in the adjoining yard.

To enter the concrete slab where the boys live, we had to ring a buzzer and be identified by a husky guard who peeks through a peephole from the other side of a bulletproof steel door. Just inside the door, we passed through a metal detector and walked past another guard. Inmates walk around freely, dressed in identical green polo shirts and khaki pants. Their unit is a cross between a soulless, concrete-block institution and an elementary school. Colorful construction paper signs note the name of each inmate on his cell door, yet all movements are monitored by video cameras or in the bathrooms, motion sensors.

When Mitchell and Andrew first arrived at Alexander, they were held in solitary confinement in cell-like rooms. Alexander workers observed that they were fairly well behaved, and over the course of the succeeding years they compiled good disciplinary records. With the exception of one incident early on, when Mitchell was placed in solitary confinement for losing his temper, the pair has adapted without much difficulty. They have since reached the highest level of Alexander's system of privileges. Mitchell in particular is regarded as one of the best-behaved boys in the facility and often helps out the staff in teaching the other boys. Mitchell's mother, Gretchen Woodard, told us how Mitchell is often called on to help with the other inmates, and takes pride in doing so:

> Mr. Abrams said that there's a class that's taught and it's Life Skills. He said that it's tough, and it's structured for a bunch of teenage boys. This is a serious offender program, and . . . most of them don't do the work involved. . . . Mr. Abrams said . . . Mitch can explain to them where [he's] failing [to get an] idea . . . across. . . . He helps with this class. Mitch will get so they understand, and they know him. . . .
>
> And there's two boys that had come in, and they were totally illiterate, they could not even spell their names. One was seventeen and the other one was fifteen, I believe. And Mitch worked and worked and worked, he's like a mama hen, he's so proud because they can write their name now. And every week we get an update on how good they're doing. And the one boy is fixing to leave soon, and [Mitch] says he's really proud of him. It's good for all of them. I think it gives him a feeling of hope. . . .

The Golden family and the Woodards are among the few parents who have remained a presence in the lives of the inmates at Alexander. They visit nearly every weekend, and their involvement is noted with gratitude by the staff. Few families make the effort to stay in touch with their incarcerated sons. One year, a Christmas party was held for the inmates and their parents. Pizzas and sodas were ordered for the 300 parents who could potentially have come to celebrate Christmas with the 150 young men. Only ten parents showed up, the Goldens and the Woodards among them.

During his months in the Craighead County jail, Mitchell's contact with his father pushed him into fits of rage, leading the jail staff to crack down on the boy. He would slam his cell door on days when his father came to visit, and he once broke the phone receiver after a call from Scott Johnson. According to reports, the last Mitchell heard from his father was an angry phone call in which Scott Johnson yelled into the phone, "You're the reason I stopped believing in God!" and hung up. Since then, Gretchen noted, Mitchell has not received so much as a Christmas card from his father.

Johnson and Golden have matured in the years since the shooting; Mitchell has grown taller, has put on weight, wears glasses, and now seems like a young man rather than a child. Golden, while still small and boyish, carries himself with confidence. The families have complained about the quality of the education their sons received at Alexander, however. Most of their lessons involve worksheets rather than classes, and Johnson has already completed the highest education level available, at the seventh or eighth grade level. "I feel bad for his education, because Mitchell is very smart," Gretchen said.

> He was an A/B student. Of course, they were giving him worksheets. Mitch did most of his last year's work, and that's discouraging for me. And for him. You need to keep his mind [alive]. He's been writing a lot of poetry lately, which is good. He's trying to keep his mind occupied.

In the spring of 2001, Mitchell and Andrew both pleaded guilty to federal gun-related charges that were brought against them. Little is known about the nature of these charges, because a gag order ensures their secrecy. Arkansas does not have an appropriate state facility to hold them beyond their eighteenth birthdays. They are now inmates somewhere in the federal prison system, where they can be held until they reach age twenty-one. According to the U.S. Attorney's Office, their exact locations are known only to their parents and their attorneys.[1] When their placement was still uncertain, Gretchen worried about where Mitchell might be sent and whether it would still be possible for her to see him:

> There's only five facilities in the United States—California, North Dakota . . . I'm not sure, they're all far away. . . . And I don't know what that's going to be for me. 'Cause I'd be lucky to see him once a year. Terry and I live a pretty hand-to-mouth existence.

No one knows when the boys will be released or whether they will be rehabilitated. Gretchen Woodard has fought to get her son into a facility where the chances of a turnaround would be higher, but she worries still that the Mitchell who comes out may bear little resemblance to the son who went in. She speaks from experience here, having worked for years as a prison guard herself. "Please don't misunderstand me," she said over her kitchen table, "I don't believe he should go through a whole resort-type place . . ."

> On the other hand, . . . you take an animal, . . . and you take him for eight to ten years and you don't . . . give him the proper education . . . what comes out of that cage is going to be a hell of a lot worse than whatever went in. . . . These boys will come out, and what kind of life [will] they have then? I don't know. . . .
>
> Mitchell has forgotten—he's now sixteen [the interview was conducted in 2001]—he's forgotten what it is to hold a piece of silverware, or a glass for that matter. He's told when he can go to the bathroom. He's told when he

goes to bed. He's so institutionalized that at the age of sixteen I can't imagine what it's going to be when he's twenty-one and someone truly—I feel with all my heart—needs to be looking at preparing him to come back into this world.

Already I hear [from him], "Maybe I don't belong in the real world.". . . You know, "This is where I belong. I need to stay.". . . That's kind of disheartening for me to see the institutionalization [pause] and it's a big part of why we go [visit] as often as we possibly can and to keep him . . . upbeat.

———

Michael Carneal began his sentence in the Northern Kentucky Youth Correctional Facility, a maximum-security facility for juvenile offenders set amid rolling hills near Lexington. The youth prison is far away from any residential community, down a long, narrow road that winds through forests. The facility, built in 1972, is known as the "Alcatraz" of the Kentucky juvenile correction system—the last stop for violent offenders thirteen to eighteen years old who have perpetrated serious crimes or been ejected from the other parts of the youth prison system. It has had a rocky history and has operated under a consent decree for some time now in response to documented instances of brutality, lack of psychological care, and inadequate educational provisions for a high school age population.

Low, squat buildings cover the extensive grounds of the facility, which are surrounded by a high chain-link fence topped with razor wire. There are baseball diamonds, basketball courts, and big grass fields. The facility houses a school, a medical unit, isolation facilities, and dormitory rooms, which accommodate about ten boys to a room.

Clad in different colored T-shirts—mainly neon orange and green—signifying the level of privileges they have earned, the young men walk down the hallways with their hands perpetually clasped behind their backs. When they are not locked into their rooms, they are escorted everywhere they go. Newcomers start at the bottom of the pile and have to work their way up, slowly gaining access to television time (strictly educational programs) or recreation. The facility houses mainly white kids, almost all of them from the poorest families in Kentucky. No one on the staff could remember ever having had a boy from a professional middle-class family like the Carneals before Michael arrived.

When he arrived, Michael was in terrible condition. Delusions ruled his mind, and they got progressively louder and louder. He suffered from severe depression and his paranoia increased markedly. Michael was sure that evil demons were trying to get at him through every window and floorboard. He heard ants crawling at night. Dr. O'Connor, who began treating him not long after his arrival, described Michael as "psychologically very, very fragile," in far worse shape than the other inmates she has known. At times he would shut down so tight that he would curl up in a fetal position in a chair, refusing to communicate with anyone. Michael would not speak to any members of the staff at all.

Michael's first attempts to climb out of his shell-shocked state involved not words, but Bible verses. He would slip notes with Biblical references to members of the staff. As Dr. O'Connor recounts:

> He would come to Peter [a staff member] and give him Bible verses, like John 3:16 through 19 or whatever, and Peter and I would look these Bible verses up, and those verses would be something to do with damnation, killing, redemption, those kinds of things. So his first real communication with us was not really communication. It was like a puzzle. We'd have to look in the Bible and come up with these verses to figure out what he was trying to tell us.

Somehow Michael managed to make the Bible speak for him, a means of expressing the shame and remorse he felt over his crime.

Michael was overwhelmed by guilt, and he told Dr. O'Connor that his sentence had been too lenient. He felt the death penalty was the only just outcome. Michael was put on suicide watch. Not long after he learned of the massacre at Columbine High School, Michael slit his wrists with a razor. A month later, he drank from a bottle of cleaning fluid. Dr. O'Connor explained that Michael felt that Klebold and Harris had followed his example. "I personally told him about the Columbine shooting," she recalled, "and he was a mess, an absolute mess. Felt a lot of responsibility for that. . . . He takes a little responsibility for every school shooting that happened after his own."

Over time, with intensive therapy and antipsychotic medication, Michael's condition began to improve. "It was a long struggle," O'Connor recalled. "I mean it was months and months before we saw him starting to come back from the psychosis. . . ." Being in a secure facility actually helped. In a way, she added, Michael found a niche that he had been unable to secure before, in a place where he was no longer ridiculed or teased.

John and Ann Carneal remain extremely supportive of their son and are actively involved in his life. They participated in every aspect of his treatment program at the facility, a rarity among the parents of inmates. Dr. O'Connor knew that she could count on this middle-class couple in ways that have often proved unrealistic for poor parents:

I would call and [say] Michael's struggling, I need you to come up, they were here. . . . They never ever missed a weekend of visiting. And they have a six-hour one-way drive. Our phases of treatment are differentiated by the color shirt [each inmate has].. . . When Ann would come for visitation, she would wear whatever [color] Michael was wearing.

Today, Michael Carneal is almost unrecognizable from the slight, awkward adolescent he was at fourteen. Once one of the shortest boys in the Heath freshman class, he is now over six feet tall and has long since passed the 200 pound mark. He towers over his parents, his sister Kelly, and his diminutive psychologist. One can only wonder how different his life at Heath High School would have been had this growth spurt come earlier.

Once the medication quieted the voices in his head, Michael set about finding worthy goals for himself. Not long before his eighteenth birthday, he earned his general equivalency diploma—GED. Dr. O'Connor showed us the photos she took on his graduation day. A sheet cake emblazoned with "Congratulations Mike" on the top, sits on a table. A round-faced Michael stands beaming behind it, his arms around his mother's shoulders, the rest of his family smiling alongside him.

Dr. O'Connor noted, "He . . . was very confident with himself when he left here."

And he had never been confident in his entire life. Made good eye contact, laughed a lot, relaxed around a lot of the staff. I mean he knew me particularly well and . . . would relax. Just really a very different Michael. And what he learned here, in one of the last conversations we've had, he said, "You know, I guess I've come to realize that thinking people didn't like me and thinking that I was this weird, awful person was just all in my mind."

When Andy Williams opened fire on his classmates in Santee, California, in the spring of 2001, Michael was able to distance himself enough not to feel the full weight of the crime on his own shoulders. His current goal is to find some sense of purpose in his life, so that some good may be salvaged from it. To this end, he gave Dr. O'Connor permission to speak about him, including the time she spent with us, in the hopes of educating others about the causes and consequences of school shootings[2]:

[Michael] would agree that he didn't think the Lord put him on this Earth to perpetrate that shooting. But since he did perpetrate it, . . . [there] had to be some reason for him to go on and if he had to, bring whatever good he could out of that. . . . I don't think he's clearly defined [his sense of purpose yet]. But I think in giving me permission to speak about him publicly, part of his sense of purpose is to prevent other kids from going down the same path that he chose to go down.

Michael turned eighteen in June 2001 and was transferred to an adult medium-security facility for mentally ill criminals in La Grange, Kentucky. He made the transition without becoming depressed or psychotic. Looking back on his improvement since entering the Northern Kentucky Youth Correctional Facility, Dr. O'Connor noted with some pride that, "the Michael who left here on . . . bore no resemblance to the Michael who came here."

Appendix A

DATA TABLES
FOR CHAPTER 10

Table A.1: Offender and Case Descriptions

	Name	Sex	Age	Grade	Race/Ethnicity	Date	Location	Population	Urbanicity
1	Anthony Barbaro	Male	18	12th	White	December 30, 1974	Olean, NY	15,347	Rural
2	Patrick Lizotte	Male	17	12th	White	March 19, 1982	Las Vegas, NV	478,434	Urban
3	David Lawler	Male	14	8th	White	January 10, 1983	Manchester, MO	19,161	Suburb
4	James Alan Kearbey	Male	14	N/A	White	January 21, 1985	Goddard, KS	2,037	Suburb
5	Kristofer Hans	Male	14	9th	White	December 4, 1986	Lewiston, MT	5,813	Rural
6	Nicholas Elliot	Male	16	10th	Black	December 16, 1988	Virginia Beach, VA	425,257	Urban
7	Eric Houston	Male	20	Dropout	White	May 1, 1992	Olivehurst, CA	11,061	Rural
8	Wayne Lo	Male	18	10th	Asian	December 14, 1992	Great Barrington, MA	2,459	Rural
9	Scott Pennington	Male	17	12th	White	January 18, 1993	Grayson, KY	3,877	Rural
10	Toby Sincino	Male	16	9th	Black	October 12, 1995	Blackville, SC	2,973	Rural
11	Jamie Rouse	Male	17	12th	White	November 15, 1995	Lynnville, TN	345	Rural
12	Barry Loukaitis	Male	14	9th	White	February 2, 1996	Moses Lake, WA	14,953	Rural
13	Evan Ramsey	Male	16	10th	White/Alaska Native	February 19, 1997	Bethel, AK	5,471	Rural
14	Luke Woodham	Male	16	10th	White	October 1, 1997	Pearl, MS	21,961	Suburb

(continued on next page)

Table A.1: Offender and Case Descriptions *(continued from previous page)*

#	Name	Sex	Age	Grade	Race/Ethnicity	Date	Location	Population	Urbanicity
15	Michael Carneal	Male	14	9th	White	December 1, 1997	Paducah, KY	26,307	Rural
16	Joseph "Colt" Todd	Male	14	8th	White	December 15, 1997	Stamps, AR	2,131	Rural
17	Mitchell Johnson	Male	13	8th	White	March 24, 1998	Westside,† AR	1,907	Rural
18	Andrew Golden	Male	11	6th	White				Rural
19	Andrew Jerome Wurst	Male	14	8th	White	April 24, 1998	Edinboro, PA	6,950	Rural
20	Kip Kinkel	Male	15	9th	White	May 21, 1998	Springfield, OR	52,864	Suburb
21	Shawn Cooper	Male	16	10th	White	April 16, 1999	Notus, ID	458	Rural
22	Eric Harris	Male	18	12th	White	April 20, 1999	Littleton, CO	40,340	Suburb
23	Dylan Klebold	Male	17	12th	White				Suburb
24	T. J. Solomon	Male	15	10th	White	May 20, 1999	Conyers, GA	10,689	Suburb
25	Seth Trickney	Male	13	7th	White	December 6, 1999	Fort Gibson, OK	4,054	Rural
26	Charles Andrew Williams	Male	15	9th	White	March 5, 2001	Santee, CA	52,975	Suburb
27	Jason Hoffman	Male	18	12th	White	March 22, 2001	El Cajon, CA	94,869	Suburb

Sources: Media reports and case studies; population data from 2000 census. †Includes the towns of Bono, Cash, and Egypt, which make up the Westside School District.

Table A.2: Social Marginalization

	Peer Group	Teased	Physically Bullied	Physical or Social Description	Masculinity Challenged	Felt Marginalized	Any Evidence
Anthony Barbaro (Olean, NY)	Not popular, few friends	No evidence	No evidence	Balding, Altar boy, conscientious student, played chess, kept to himself.	No evidence	No evidence	Little evidence
Pat Lizotte (Las Vegas, NV)	Loner	No evidence	No evidence	Quiet but stiff	No evidence	No evidence, but feared being institutionalized	Yes
David Lawler (Manchester, MO)	No evidence	Yes	No evidence	No evidence, but outgoing	No evidence, but peers told him his brother was a "pussy"	No evidence	Yes
James Alan Kearbey (Goddard, KS)	Loner	Yes	Yes	Slight build	Bullied	No evidence	Yes
Kristofer Hans (Lewiston, MT)	No evidence	No evidence	No evidence	No evidence	When pulled gun, kids laughed and said they didn't think he'd do it	No evidence	Little evidence
Nicholas Elliot (Virginia Beach, VA)	Loner	Yes	Yes	He was black in an almost exclusively white school	Bullied	Yes	Yes
Eric Houston (Olivehurst, CA)	No evidence	No evidence	No evidence	No evidence	Fired from job and recently rejected by girl	No evidence[1]	No evidence
Wayne Lo (Great Barrington, MA)	Some alternative friends, loner	No evidence	No evidence	Small	No evidence	Yes	Yes
Scott Pennington (Grayson, KY)	Loner	Yes	Yes	Lanky, thick glasses, stuttering problem	Bullied	Yes	Yes

(continued on next page)

Table A.2: Social Marginalization *(continued from previous page)*

	Peer Group	Teased	Physically Bullied	Physical or Social Description	Masculinity Challenged	Felt Marginalized	Any Evidence
Toby Sincino (Blackville, SC)	Some friends	Yes	Yes	Small, baby-faced	Bullied	Yes	Yes
Jamie Rouse (Lynnville, TN)	Loner	No	No	5'7", 122 lbs. Wore black	No evidence, but father obsessed with boy's masculinity	No evidence	Yes
Barry Loukaitis (Moses Lake, WA)	Few friends	Yes	Yes	Tall and slender, slight build	Called "faggot" "gaylord" & bullied	Yes	Yes
Evan Ramsey (Bethel, AK)	Some friends	Yes	No evidence	Goofy, acne-prone. Called "Screech"	Abused in foster care	Yes	Yes
Luke Woodham (Pearl, MS)	Outcast/The Kroth—cult	Yes	Yes	Overweight, nerdy, wore glasses, not athletic	Rejected by girl and bullied	Yes	Yes
Michael Carneal (West Paducah, KY)	Some friends	Yes	Yes	Small and wore glasses	Called "faggot," bullied	Yes	Yes
Joseph "Colt" Todd (Stamps, AR)	No evidence	Yes	Yes	No evidence	Bullied	Yes	Yes
Mitchell Johnson (Westside, AR)	Some friends	Yes	No evidence	Chubby, "wannabe"	Sexually abused, recently rejected by girl	Yes	Yes
Andrew Golden (Westside, AR)	Some friends	Yes	No evidence	Small, slight build	No evidence	Yes	Yes
Andrew Jerome Wurst (Edinboro, PA)	Some friends, but characterized as outsider	Teased by brother for bedwetting	No record	Average size, not athletic, wore glasses. Wanted to get contacts and to bulk up	Turned down by former girlfriend, laughed at by another, teased for bedwetting	Yes	Yes

(continued on next page)

Table A.2: Social Marginalization *(continued from previous page)*

	Peer Group	Teased	Physically Bullied	Physical or Social Description	Masculinity Challenged	Felt Marginalized	Any Evidence
Kip Kinkel (Springfield, OR)	Some alternative friends, loner	Yes	No evidence	Skinny. Class clown	No evidence	Yes	Yes
Shawn Cooper (Notus, ID)	No evidence	Some evidence	No evidence	No evidence	No evidence	No evidence	Little evidence
Eric Harris (Littleton, CO)	Trenchcoat mafia	Yes	Yes	Lean, baby-faced, not athletic	Called "faggot," bullied	Yes	Yes
Dylan Klebold (Littleton, CO)	Trenchcoat mafia	Yes	Yes	Tall, blond, and well off, not athletic	Called "faggot," bullied	Yes	Yes
T. J. Solomon (Conyers, GA)	Loner	Yes	No	Physically average, altar boy, Boy Scout	No evidence	Yes	Yes
Seth Trickney (Fort Gibson, OK)	Popular or loner[2]	No evidence	No evidence	Small, slender	No evidence	Yes	Yes
Charles Andrew Williams (Santee, CA)	Some friends	Yes	Yes	Scrawny kid with big ears	Bullied	Yes	Yes
Jason Hoffman (El Cajon, CA)	Loner	No evidence	No evidence	Burly and intimidating but had a very serious skin condition	Abused by father	No evidence	Yes

Sources: Media reports and case studies

[1] No evidence that he was marginalized at school but clearly felt marginalized by others. "My hatred toward humanity forced me to do what I did." Fired from job, being kicked out of parents' house, and had just lost girlfriend.

[2] Peers generally said he was popular, but psychologist said he felt like a loner.

Table A.3: Individual Predisposing Factors

Name	Mental Illness	Suicidality	Depressions/ Desperation	Family Problems	Number of Issues
Anthony Barbaro (Olean, NY)	No evidence	Yes**	No evidence	No evidence	0
Patrick Lizotte (Las Vegas, NV)	Possibly. Feared institutionalization	No evidence	No evidence	No evidence	0.5
David Lawler (Manchester, MO)	No evidence	Yes*	Yes	No evidence	2
James Alan Kearbey (Goddard, KS)	No evidence	No evidence	No evidence	No evidence	0
Kristofer Hans (Lewiston, MT)	Yes	No evidence	No evidence	Stressful home life	2
Nicholas Elliot (Virginia Beach, VA)	No evidence	No evidence	No evidence	No evidence	0
Eric Houston (Olivehurst, CA)	Yes	Yes	Yes	No evidence	3
Wayne Lo (Great Barrington, MA)	Paranoid schizophrenia	No evidence	No evidence	High expectations	1.5
Scott Pennington (Grayson, KY)	Schizoid personality disorder	No evidence	Yes	Abusive home life	3
Toby Sincino (Blackville, SC)	No evidence	Yes*	Yes	No evidence	2
Jamie Rouse (Lynnville, TN)	Paranoid schizophrenia	Yes**	Yes	Abusive home life	3
Barry Loukaitis (Moses Lake, WA)	Bipolar disorder	No evidence	Yes	Neglect, verbal abuse	3
Evan Ramsey (Bethel, AK)	No evidence	Yes	Yes	Abusive home life	3
Luke Woodham (Pearl, MS)	General psychological problems	Yes*	No evidence	Neglect, verbal abuse	3

(continued on next page)

Table A.3: Individual Predisposing Factors *(continued from previous page)*

Name	Mental Illness	Suicidality	Depressions/Desperation	Family Problems[1]	Number of Issues
Michael Carneal (West Paducah, KY)	Schitzotypal personality disorder	Yes	Yes	No evidence	3
Joseph "Colt" Todd (Stamps, AR)	No evidence	No evidence	Yes	Abusive home life	2
Mitchell Johnson (Westside, AR)	No evidence	Some Evidence	Yes	Abusive home life	3
Andrew Golden (Westside, AR)	Possibly	Yes	Yes	No evidence	2
Andrew Wurst (Edinboro, PA)	Psychotic thinking with delusions of persecution and grandeur	Yes	Yes	Stressful home life	4
Kip Kinkel (Springfield, OR)	Paranoid schizophrenia	Yes*	Yes	No evidence	3
Shawn Cooper (Notus, ID)	Bipolar disorder	No evidence	No evidence	Neglect	2
Eric Harris (Littleton, CO)	Obsessive-compulsive disorder	Yes	Yes	Frequent moves	3.5
Dylan Klebold (Littleton, CO)	No evidence	Yes	Yes	No evidence	2
T. J. Solomon (Conyers, GA)	Psychotic	Yes	Yes	Tense home life, upset about parents' divorce	4
Seth Trickney (Fort Gibson, OK)	Schizoid personality disorder	Yes	Yes	No evidence	3
Charles Andrew Williams (Santee, CA)	No evidence	Yes	Yes	Difficult home life	3
Jason Hoffman (El Cajon, CA)	No evidence	No evidence	Yes	Abuse	2

Source: Media reports and case studies

*Evidence of suicidality present during or immediately after shooting only. **Evidence of suicidality present while in jail after shooting only.

[1]The coding for this variable is necessarily subjective. We have reviewed all of the newspaper coverage regarding each case. Where the coverage indicates that there was any evidence of exceptionally pronounced internal conflict, physical violence, or extreme verbal harassment, we have assigned a code of "abusive home life."

Table A.4: Under the Radar

Name	Disciplinary History	Received Counseling	Violent Writings	Trouble with the Law	Jekyll/Hyde Personality	Issued Threats/ Peers had knowledge
Anthony Barbaro (Olean, NY)	No evidence	No evidence	No evidence	No evidence	Some evidence	No evidence
Patrick Lizotte (Las Vegas, NV)	No evidence	No evidence	No evidence	No evidence	Yes	No evidence
David Lawler (Manchester, MO)	No	No evidence	No evidence	No evidence	No evidence	No evidence
James Alan Kearbey (Goddard, KS)	No evidence	No evidence	No evidence	No evidence	No evidence	No evidence, but seen with gun in school right before shooting
Kristofer Hans (Lewiston, MT)	No evidence	No evidence	No evidence	No evidence	No evidence	Yes
Nicholas Elliot (Virginia Beach, VA)	No evidence	No evidence	No evidence	No	No evidence	No evidence
Eric Houston (Olivehurst, CA)	No	No evidence	No evidence	No	No evidence	Yes, but not at school
Wayne Lo (Great Barrington, MA)	Minor	No evidence	Yes	No	Yes	Yes
Scott Pennington (Grayson, KY)	No evidence	No evidence	Yes	No evidence	No evidence	Yes
Toby Sincino (Blackville, SC)	Yes	No evidence	No evidence	No evidence	Some evidence	Threatened suicide
Jamie Rouse (Lynnville, TN)	No evidence	No evidence	Yes	No evidence	No evidence	Yes
Barry Loukaitis (Moses Lake, WA)	No	No evidence	Yes	No evidence	No evidence	Yes
Evan Ramsey (Bethel, AK)	Yes	No	No evidence	No evidence	Yes	Yes
Luke Woodham (Pearl, MS)	No	No evidence	No evidence	No	Yes	Yes

(continued on next page)

Table A.4: Under the Radar *(continued from previous page)*

Name	Disciplinary History	Received Counseling	Violent Writings	Trouble with the Law	Jekyll/Hyde Personality	Issued Threats/ Peers had knowledge
Michael Carneal (West Paducah, KY)	Minor	No	Yes	No	Yes	Yes
Joseph "Colt" Todd (Stamps, AR)	No evidence	Yes, not at school	No evidence	No	No evidence	No evidence
Mitchell Johnson (Westside, AR)	Minor	Yes, not at school	Yes	Yes	Yes	Yes
Andrew Golden (Westside, AR)	No	Yes	No	No	Yes	Yes
Andrew Wurst (Edinboro, PA)	No	No	Teacher found a will	No	No evidence	Yes
Kip Kinkel (Springfield, OR)	Yes	Yes, not at school	Yes	Yes	Yes	Yes
Shawn Cooper (Notus, ID)	No	No evidence	No evidence	No evidence	No evidence	Yes
Eric Harris (Littleton, CO)	Minor	Yes, not at school	Yes	Yes	Yes	Yes
Dylan Klebold (Littleton, CO)	Minor	Yes, not at school	Yes	Yes	Yes	Yes
T. J. Solomon (Conyers, GA)	Minor	Yes, suicidal ideation reported	Yes, not at school	No	No evidence	Yes
Seth Trickney (Fort Gibson, OK)	No	Yes, not at school	No evidence	No	No evidence	Yes
Charles Andrew Williams (Santee, CA)	Minor	No evidence	No evidence	No	No evidence	Yes
Jason Hoffman (El Cajon, CA)	Yes	Yes, not at school	No evidence	Yes	Yes	Yes

Source: Media reports and case studies

Table A.5: Guns

Name	Guns from Home of Relative?	Source of Guns	Displayed Interest in Weapons?
Anthony Barbaro (Olean, NY)	No evidence	No evidence	Member of school's rifle team, fascinated by guns
Patrick Lizotte (Las Vegas, NV)	Yes	Father	Interested in military books, habitually wore army fatigues
David Lawler (Manchester, MO)	Yes	Family	Often went hunting, sometimes practiced target shooting
James Alan Kearbey (Goddard, KS)	Yes	Father	Fascination with military weapons, talked frequently of war
Kristofer Hans (Lewiston, MT)	No evidence	No evidence	No evidence
Nicholas Elliot (Virginia Beach, VA)	Yes	Second cousin	Read gun magazines frequently
Eric Houston (Olivehurst, CA)	No*	Owned by shooter	Intense fascination with guns
Wayne Lo (Great Barrington, MA)	No*	Owned by shooter	No evidence but father was in Taiwanese army
Scott Pennington (Grayson, KY)	Yes	Mother	Hunted with father, but not that interested in shooting animals
Toby Sincino (Blackville, SC)	No	Stolen from a car	No evidence
Jamie Rouse (Lynnville, TN)	Yes	Family	Liked to hunt. Once threatened brother with a rifle during an argument
Barry Loukaitis (Moses Lake, WA)	Yes	Family	Read gun magazines and played with guns at home
Evan Ramsey (Bethel, AK)	Yes	Foster mother's adult sons	Had not handled gun previously
Luke Woodham (Pearl, MS)	Yes	Owned by shooter	Hunted with friends

(continued on next page)

Table A.5: Guns *(continued from previous page)*

Name	Guns from Home of Relative?	Source of Guns	Displayed Interest in Weapons?
Michael Carneal (West Paducah, KY)	Yes	Father's and stolen from friend	Brought gun to school on 2 occasions
Joseph "Colt" Todd (Stamps, AR)	Yes	Family/belonged to shooter	No evidence
Mitchell Johnson (Westside, AR)	No	Golden's grandfather	Hunted, played with BB gun
Andrew Golden (Westside, AR)	Yes	Parents and grandparents	Intense Fascination with guns
Andrew Wurst (Edinboro, PA)	Yes	Father	Played with Father's gun
Kip Kinkel (Springfield, OR)	Yes	Family, belonged to shooter	Intense fascination with guns
Shawn Cooper (Notus, ID)	Yes	Grandfather	No evidence
Eric Harris (Littleton, CO)	No	Friend	Interested in bombs
Dylan Klebold (Littleton, CO)	No	Friend	Interested in bombs
T. J. Solomon (Conyers, GA)	Yes	Stepfather's	Intense fascination. Guns described as "love of his life."
Seth Trickney (Fort Gibson, OK)	Yes	Father	Obsessed with military tactics, identified with WWII General George Patton
Charles Andrew Williams (Santee, CA)	Yes	Father	Not that interested, but father would occasionally take him skeet shooting and he had played with a BB gun
Jason Hoffman (El Cajon, CA)	No*	Owned by shooter	Loved guns, read gun magazines

Source: Media reports and case studies

* In these cases, the gun was bought by the shooter and the family appears not to have been involved in the purchase of the weapon.

Appendix B

QUALITATIVE
RESEARCH DESIGN

QUALITATIVE CASE STUDIES OF EVENTS AS HORRIFIC AND AS PUBLIC AS THE RAM-page school shootings at Heath and Westside present special challenges to social science researchers in data collection, analysis, and presentation. As Herbert Gans noted in the appendix to his classic *The Urban Villagers,* conclusions are only as strong as the research on which they are based. Many readers will want to know on what bases we have drawn our conclusions. In this appendix, we describe our fieldwork in Heath and Westside and how we dealt with some of the challenges it presented us. In Appendix C, we describe the data and methods we used in our analysis of other school shootings in chapter 10.

THE FIELDWORK

The fieldwork was initially conducted as part of a National Academy of Sciences study of lethal school violence. We conducted two of the six in-depth qualitative case studies of school shootings that formed the backbone of the National Academy report.[1]

We spent approximately one month in each of these communities, with two researchers primarily responsible for each community (Fox and Roth in Westside, Harding and Mehta in Heath, and Newman coordinating and conducting interviews in both sites). Our methods were a combination of participant observation and in-depth unstructured interviews. We identified some individuals to interview through media accounts, including all the officials who were involved in the investigations and criminal adjudications. We then relied on snowball sampling, asking each interviewee, as well as most other people we met, whom we should speak with about the shooting and the events that followed. Often this information was volunteered as soon as we described the nature of our project. Interviews were conducted in homes, offices, classrooms, and public places such as restaurants and cafés—wherever was most comfortable or convenient for the subject.

We also immersed ourselves in the social life of these communities, attending church services, softball games, public festivals, potlucks, and picnics and accepting invitations to meals in people's homes. These activities all provided opportunities for generating contacts for interviews, talking with people informally about how the shooting affected their community, and for participant observation. In doing our analyses, we also relied on documents gathered during the fieldwork.

In Westside, we conducted eighty-seven interviews in June 2001 with a total of ninety-eight students, teachers, school administrators, criminal and civil suit lawyers, judges, police and court personnel, parents of the victims and of one of the shooters, church and business leaders, political officials, counselors and therapists involved in the response to the shooting, and community residents. We also used national and local media reports, police investigative materials, and court documents. We were able to tour the juvenile facility where Mitchell Johnson and Andrew Golden were held, although we did not have access to the shooters themselves. We also did not have access to the psychological evaluations of either Johnson or Golden, because they were sealed by the juvenile court. Gretchen Woodard, Mitchell Johnson's mother, was particularly helpful.

Some key individuals were unwilling to be interviewed, particularly members of Andrew Golden's family. We were also unable to contact Scott Johnson, Mitchell's father. Hence, as we have tried to make clear, we were only able to capture how others in the community saw the boys. The Westside school system also declined to formally participate in our study, although it gave its employees permission to speak with us, and many did.

The Heath research is based on seventy-six interviews conducted in late May and early June 2001 with more than 100 individuals and participant observation in the school and community. Information from this fieldwork is supplemented by local and national media coverage, police investigative materials, Carneal's own writings, depositions from civil lawsuits, psychiatric evaluations of Carneal and an interview with his most recent treating psychologist, and materials from Heath High School and the McCracken County School District. We interviewed legal professionals from both the criminal and civil proceedings that followed the shooting, police officials, victims' families, teachers, high school and middle school administrators, business, political and religious leaders in the community, journalists, parents, and students, both those present at the time of the shooting and those who were in the ninth grade at Heath at the time of our fieldwork.

While we interviewed Kelly Carneal, Michael Carneal's older sister, we were not able to interview Carneal himself or his parents. However, we did review three lengthy interrogations of Carneal by the police, reports and interview transcripts written by Carneal's numerous psychiatrists, and an exhaustive 500-page deposition of Carneal taken in preparation for the civil suits.

We were also unable to interview the Heath students who were suspected by some in the community to be coconspirators in the crime, although we did read the police interviews and the civil depositions they provided.

In addition, Katherine Newman spent a day at the Northern Kentucky Youth Corrections facility near Lexington to interview Dr. Kathleen O'Connor, who was Michael Carneal's psychologist for the four years he was incarcerated there.

The events described and analyzed throughout this book have been variously described and interpreted by the people involved. Although we have done our best to present what we believe to be the facts, school shootings, like other emotionally charged events, produce contradictory accounts that elude complete resolution. Especially in Heath, civil litigation naming many of the people we interviewed was still pending on appeal at the time of our fieldwork, which discouraged the participation of a number of key figures who may someday be able to contribute their perspectives.

GAINING ACCESS

In both Westside and Heath, the school shootings were seemingly senseless murders that were not explicable by notions of simple "revenge." They were instead (depending on one's vantage point), attacks on a whole community or institution, adolescent cries for attention gone murderously awry, or the desperate acts of adolescents whose extreme mental illness had gone undetected until it exploded into acts of mass murder. Both communities were torn apart by the loss of young people, accusations that warning signs were overlooked, implicit (and explicit) criticism of the shooters' parents and their parenting, and, on occasion, the postshooting responses of the victims' families. In each case, the shooting occurred more than three years before the research began. Despite the time that had passed, wounds were still raw, and community recovery—if such a thing is possible—was only partial.

These circumstances imposed major obstacles for the project. First and foremost, these traumatized communities had become extremely wary of the intentions and behavior of outsiders, particularly the national media. The Westside and Heath communities are small and close-knit and were largely unknown to the outside world prior to the shootings. Residents were distressed that their communities had been put on the map through these terrible events, leaving them to explain how such a thing could have happened in places that residents had defined as wonderful places to raise kids. They were not eager to open old wounds or to put themselves at the mercy of a new round of external scrutiny. Many had closed the doors to further research, which challenged us to find ways to enlist their trust.

Second, even though the criminal cases that followed the shootings had long since ended, some residents were dissatisfied with the outcomes. Some community members rejected the very premises of juvenile justice, which limit culpability even for heinous crimes, on the principle that children cannot form the requisite intent. The sense of injustice fueled the demand for civil lawsuits, which could and did reopen old wounds. Even three years after the shootings, the appeals process for the civil cases was still ongoing. Lawyers advised their clients not to cooperate with our research for fear of the impact of new disclosures. As a result, some of the most important actors in these events were unwilling to cooperate.

Third, it was impossible to interview the juvenile offenders themselves. Understandably, many protections are in place that limit their communication with outsiders. Because most school shooters suffer from serious depression, even suicidal impulses, and are incarcerated in institutions that are officially rehabilitative rather than punitive, the facilities that hold them make sure that they cannot be contacted. Hence, our only access to the central actors was through the documentary evidence of psychiatric reports, trial records, and writings they left behind.

Heeding the early warnings we received from local officials about the sensitivity of this topic to people in the community, we proceeded with caution. To preserve their privacy, we did not contact the families of the victims or the shooters directly. The victims' advocates in Jonesboro and Paducah both agreed to forward letters to the victims' families indicating our interest in talking with them; they were free to contact us, either through the victims' advocate or directly. We followed the same course with the shooters' families, sending through their lawyers word of our interest in speaking with them.

Those closest to the shooters varied in their attitudes toward the research effort. Mitchell Johnson's mother took the view that she could help to make amends to the community and the country by trying to help us understand her son's rage. Others, such as Andrew Golden's parents, have moved away from the community and regularly refuse all requests for interviews. Some of the shooters' relatives considered our requests for interviews but in the end expressed concern that anything they told us might be used against them in future legal actions.

Despite these obstacles, many people were willing to speak with us, despite having nothing to gain personally from participation. Four important factors made it possible for the project to proceed. First, the project began as a report for the National Academy of Sciences, mandated by Congress. The imprimatur of Congress and the sense of civic obligation to contribute to prevention efforts helped distinguish our research effort from what were regarded as the more mercenary or profit-driven motives of the media. Second, respected individuals in the community—judges, former school principals, and lawyers—responded to our requests for their help and vouched for us among community members who were more skeptical. These requests, which began months before the fieldwork, proved essential to clearing the way for interviews with individuals who had been seriously affected by the rampage shootings. Third, the reputation of Harvard University conveyed legitimacy to the effort. Fourth, once we arrived in the field and began conducting interviews, people in the communities heard by word of mouth about the experience of being interviewed, demystifying our research project. In Jonesboro, local newspapers and television stations asked to run stories about our research. The spread of information about us through locally trusted sources led some people to come forward or agree to speak with us. We also owe a debt of gratitude to the hospitality of the community residents, which greatly facilitated our efforts.

PROTECTING HUMAN SUBJECTS

Social science research, like medical research, has the potential to harm its subjects. We took great pains to minimize the risks to our respondents, but only they can judge whether we succeeded.

As is customary, our research was reviewed and approved by human subjects review boards, both at Harvard and at the National Research Council, before we went into the field. Before each interview, we informed those we interviewed of the terms of the interview, including their right to stop the interview at any time, to refuse to answer any question, or to refuse tape recording of the interview. Minors were interviewed only with a parent's permission, and some were interviewed in the presence of parents (parents always had the option to be present). Traditionally, interviewees are promised anonymity when findings are reported, but the public nature of school shootings and the small size of the communities we studied made it impossible to guarantee anonymity, especially to those in particularly public positions or with notable roles in the events surrounding the shootings. We informed our subjects that even with pseudonyms and altered identifying details, neighbors might be able to figure out who was who.

Many of the people we interviewed appeared on national television, and some were featured in national newsmagazines, state and local newspapers, and local television broadcasts. Under these circumstances, it was impossible to guarantee anonymity for certain key actors in our story, and as we explain in the preface, we did not attempt to do so. We felt this was ethically justified since our consent forms, which every interviewee signed, made it clear that we would not be able to guarantee anonymity to everyone who participated.

Because our interviews were originally conducted under the auspices of the National Research Council, they are covered by a certificate of confidentiality from the U.S. Department of Health and Human Services, which prohibits other researchers, the courts, government officials, or anyone else from gaining access to them.

We had two concerns when debating whether to use individuals' real names in this book. The first was protecting people from fallout from those in their own communities who might object to a particular version of events, a particular opinion about others, or even participation in our study at all. Some subjects did not want it known that they had even spoken with us. The shootings and their aftermath had already created enough fracture and pain in Heath and Westside, and we did not want to create any more. The second was the possibility that people from outside the community would try to locate individuals on the basis of information provided in this book. After each of the shootings, various strangers seemed to come out of the woodwork, arriving at the schools and seeking to talk with parents, students, teachers, or community leaders, such that some were concerned about safety issues.

In the end, we decided to err on the side of caution, using the real names of only those who were public officials or already identified repeatedly in national media, primarily the victims and their families, the shooters and their families, and a few school officials. We struggled with what to do with individuals we did not interview (and therefore had made no commitments to) but who still played an important role in the events surrounding the shooting, such as the suspected coconspirators at Heath. Would we diminish the power of our account if it could not be easily checked by other researchers or by journalists? Again we erred on the side of caution, lest our use of their real names to describe events in their youth hound these individuals into their adult lives.

Although we tried to avoid asking participants to recount or relive the horrible events that led us to their communities, our very presence was a reminder of the trauma they had experienced. To prepare for potentially emotional interviews, we consulted a psychiatrist trained in grief counseling on what to expect and came prepared with a list of counseling services available in their communities. Neither proved relevant for the vast majority of our respondents, however.

ANALYZING CONTESTED EVENTS

In the preceding chapters we attempted to convey that the interpretations and understandings of the events leading up to and following the shootings in Heath and Westside were highly contested. The shootings sent profound shock waves through these communities, both because of the horrific nature of the acts and because of the locations in which they occurred. It was partly the senseless and unexpected nature of the shootings that led to disagreement and contestation as community members struggled to make sense of what had happened and what it meant. In each community, there were multiple vantage points, multiple interests, and multiple emotions. The preceding chapters have shown that there was much at stake in the story that was told.

As researchers, we found this contestation to be both an important source of data and a source of confusion when trying to piece together various bits of information. In some instances we have tried to convey the multiplicity of perspectives because the divergence of perspectives is itself interesting and important in understanding these events and their consequences. In other instances, however, we have privileged one version of the events because claims about causes and effects require, as a basis for analysis, a single coherent account. This tension reflects a basic tension within the social sciences, particularly sociology and anthropology, between positivist and interpretivist modes of analysis. Such a tension is in many ways a false one; we have relied on both positivist and interpretivist analysis in writing this book.

Positivist Analysis of Contested Events

The positivist approach is modeled on the methods of the natural sciences. It seeks knowledge based on systematic observation and experiment, with the goal of discovering social laws analogous to the natural laws uncovered by the methods of natural science.[2] Positivist analysis seeks to hypothesize and then evaluate causal inferences about social phenomena that will be generalizable beyond the specific data analyzed.[3] Qualitative and quantitative approaches to research differ in their methods but share a unified logic of causal inference.[4] Analyses must be both replicable and testable across cases, and the validity of the analysis will be evaluated accordingly. Usually hypotheses are generated and compared with other hypotheses, with an eye toward validity, explanatory power, and parsimony.

"What causes school shootings?" is a distinctly positivist question. Here we need to uncover the factual precursors of an event in order to develop and evaluate theories about its causes. If, for example, one explanation of the shootings is revenge because of school bullying, we need to ascertain whether the shooters were bullied and by whom. Did the shooters target those who bullied them?

Gathering accurate information to serve as the building blocks of any causal theory is complicated by a number of problems that are common to most retrospective research but are exaggerated when the highly charged nature of an event perpetuates divergent, and often contradictory, accounts of events. The controversial and highly publicized nature of the school shootings outside of Heath and Westside magnified these problems.

Perhaps the most obvious challenge to understanding an event that happened more than three years before the data collection is the problem of inadequate or inconsistent memory. Many respondents simply could not remember relevant information. For example, school personnel had trouble remembering whether programs to help freshman adjust to high school were implemented before or after the shooting—a crucial difference. The shootings were defining moments that brought about dramatic changes in school policy, school climate, and town image. It was difficult for respondents to remember clearly the different world that prevailed before this life-changing event.

The ability of interviewees to recall information may also be affected by the traumatic nature of the event. Many who were closely connected to the shooting—often those who should know the most about it—have been diagnosed with posttraumatic stress disorder, and it is likely that many more suffer from this condition but have not been diagnosed. The stress and emotional difficulty of reliving traumatic events such as a school shooting can cause respondents to block information about the events from their own memories.

On occasion, our interviewees substituted what they had read in the media or heard around town for what they actually knew, often subconsciously. These problems were exacerbated by the fact that, at least for some questions, much of the most important information was in the heads of the three shooters, whom we were not able to interview. Information about them had to come from family members, friends, teachers, neighbors, and other people who knew them well. Some of what respondents told us was contradictory or just plain untrue, a serious problem from the standpoint of positivist analysis of "objective truths."

Moreover, some of our respondents clearly had vested interests that affected the content of what they said. Given that there were past and pending lawsuits, those who were in some way implicated in the events were concerned with defending their own actions from future accusations of blame. At the extreme, some teachers, administrators, and fellow students simply refused to talk with us because of the potential implications for legal proceedings. Among those who did talk to us, their own practical interest in a certain account of events must be a consideration.

Moreover, the original purpose of our research—the fact that it was part of a congressional report that will have policy implications—may influence the content of the responses. In a few cases, we felt that a respondent's political beliefs were influencing what he or she told us. In other cases, the simple desire to be the center of attention or to tell a coherent story affected what respondents told us, akin to witnesses in court adding details in order to make their account sound more convincing.

There are no magical solutions to these problems. Our first line of defense is simply awareness of the various reasons why respondents may give incomplete, inaccurate, or contradictory information. If this awareness infuses the research design, the fieldwork itself, and the analysis of the data, some of these problems can be minimized and more accurate information can be obtained. We also conscientiously employed two broad strategies to improve the quality of our data: (1) *contextualizing* individual respondents' comments in light of everything known about the source of their knowledge, their personal or political agendas, and their social position; and (2) *triangulating* among various respondents and sources of data on the basis of this specific contextual knowledge.

Contextualizing means attempting to ascertain not only *what* a respondent knows, but *how* he or she knows it. Often this may be accomplished by including questions about the source of the knowledge in the interview. When nothing in the interview itself reveals the source of knowledge for a given fact or set of facts, the researcher should also be aware of how closely the respondent's comments correspond to accounts in the media or from those of others in the community. On numerous occasions respondents related details that were almost verbatim from media accounts, and therefore the fact that these accounts were reported by multiple people did not make a stronger case for this version of events. This pattern may also occur as a consequence of rumors, especially when numerous respondents had talked to one key respondent, and thus details that seemed to be supported by multiple "observations" are more properly considered multiple manifestations of a single observation. One example was the story that there was a third shooter involved in the Jonesboro case; although not reported by the media, this report spread quickly throughout the community. We traced the source of this account to the police investigation immediately after the shooting, where numerous children reported this account. This questioning took place after the traumatized students had spent several hours huddled together in the school gymnasium, discussing rumors that Mitchell had mentioned a third person prior to the shooting.

In addition to trying to assess the source of a respondent's knowledge, a respondent's comments should also be evaluated in light of everything else that can be discerned about them. This vital but peripheral information might include the respondent's political beliefs, occupational position, their position in the social structure of the community and relationships with other social groups, and their relationship to the shooters or the victims. Most obviously, this is a caution not to take at face value the football player's reports about bullying, or the principal's reports about school climate before the shooting. In these cases, it is obvious that the respondent likely has a personal or institutional agenda, which affects what he or she will say. But this attention to context can also explain subtler biases—for example, why a student whose mother has taken on an advocacy role over the dangers of Ritalin inferred that Andrew was taking Ritalin. On some occasions, such information did not come from the interview situation but from participant-observation and immersion in the setting. In other cases, the source of bias in an individual's account lay not in the their political beliefs or their occupational position but rather in their relationship to the shooter or victim. Questions that seek to probe these relationships were important in evaluating the data they provided.

Using multiple interviews and multiple sources of data (such as police interviews, psychological reports, primary documents, and so on) to triangulate the information— that is, to see if different sources agree on the same set of facts—is perhaps the most widely used approach in the social sciences, quantitative as well as qualitative.[5] In this sense, triangulation is similar to the common rule in journalism not to report anything that is ambiguous or controversial without at least two and preferably three sources to give it additional support.

However, when researchers discuss the use of triangulation to reconcile inconsistent data, they often use an implicit assumption that research should privilege the side that has "more" evidence. There is perhaps some positive weighting for "official" sources, such as newspapers and police reports, and a slight discounting of interview data that might be second- or third-hand.[6] Yet positivist analysis that is informed by a contextualized understanding of the positions and interests of respondents can triangulate in a way that is more consistent with the goals of uncovering causation.

Contextually informed triangulation takes this understanding into account during the process of triangulation and the subsequent "weighing" of evidence. Rather than adjudicating a particular question on the basis of which interpretation has "more" evidence, the goal is to differentiate between sources of evidence, privileging data that is likely to be less subject to the known sources of bias, and holding less reliable evidence to higher standards of support from triangulation. In data collection, this means being aware of the likely sources of contamination, and seeking out evidence that is more likely to be free of bias. In data analysis, it means understanding each piece of information within its context and tailoring the triangulation to the nature of the data, sometimes at the level of specific questions. There is also value in stratifying the structural positions of respondents whose responses were used for triangulation to counter bias stemming from the social positions of the observers, a technique we used in reconciling conflicting accounts about, for example, whether Michael was bullied.

Interpretivist Analysis of Contested Events

Our approach to interpretivism takes its inspiration from the Geertzian perspective and its successors in the sociological tradition, in which the primary focus of interpretivist research is the subjective meaning that events hold within a particular culture.[7] From an interpretivist perspective, multiple subjective "truths" or ways of understanding an event offer valuable insight into the social structures, group tensions and conflicting values in Heath and Westside. Rarely do these different accounts represent random variation; more often they reveal systematic differences in perspective based on the social status and position of the various community members as well as their relationships to the shooter and the victims. They may reveal the different stakes that community members have in the shooting and the way the shooting is interpreted by the wider society. The object of our inquiry in interpretivist approach is to seek not objective fact but the subjective interpretation that individuals in different social positions bring to objective facts. Thus we do not attempt to posit a causal argument when doing interpretive work.

School shootings provide an illuminating window into these normally hidden cleavages because they serve as a "breach" of the accepted understandings of how people usually behave in these communities.[8] Children in low-crime rural communities are not supposed to shoot their classmates. How were our respondents to make sense of this anomaly, which challenged some of their most strongly held assumptions about their communities? Given the shocking nature of the shooting and the lack of real information about its causes, residents were free to project their own interpretations on the events. As we discussed in chapter 8, moral debates revealed hidden class divisions in Heath.

Whereas hypothesis testing and causal theorizing provide a specified goal for the positivist researcher, the interpretive analyst has a no less important but much less clearly defined task. Interpretive analysis seeks to uncover the often competing sets of social meanings held by respondents. Contested events create a series of methodological problems for positivist researchers because of contradictory and inconsistent responses; yet for interpretive analysts, these same conflicting responses provide key data points that help us understand social meanings and underlying divisions within these communities.

Appendix C

QUANTITATIVE
DATA AND METHODS

THE CHAPTERS IN PART 3 ADVANCE SEVERAL ARGUMENTS ABOUT THE CAUSES OF RAM-
page school shootings in Heath and Westside, and in chapter 10 we present a general
theory of school shootings on the basis of these two cases and attempt to test the theory as best we can given the available data.[9] In this appendix we describe these data in
more detail and discuss how we test a theory involving multiple necessary but not sufficient conditions.

In chapter 10 we proposed a theory of five necessary but not sufficient conditions for
a rampage school shooting. A necessary condition is one that is required for the event to
occur; it cannot happen without it. A sufficient condition is one that always produces the
event. Thus, when we argue that there are five necessary but not sufficient conditions,
we mean that all five factors must be present for a shooting to occur, but that the presence of these five factors will not always produce a shooting. Such a formulation has
clear implications for prevention or reduction of rampage school shootings: eliminating
(or reducing the prevalence of) one or more of the five factors will reduce rampage
school shootings.

The theory also has other advantages over more typical social science models that
posit additive and independent effects of causes on the probability of an event's occurring. These advantages derive from the rarity of school shootings and the challenges involved in researching rare events. First, our theory implicitly contains an explanation for
the rarity of school shootings: school shootings occur only when all five factors converge
simultaneously. This also serves to move the debate away from the importance of any one
cause that might have the most predictive power. Second, it accounts for why some
clearly important causes are present in only some cases. Each of the five factors can be
satisfied in multiple ways. For example, some shooters are marginalized by bullying, but
others are marginalized in other ways. Third, it takes the individuality of each case seriously. Because each factor may be satisfied in multiple ways, the path or processes leading

to a school shooting need not be the same in every case, and we must take the individual paths and processes seriously in order to understand a particular case.

Nevertheless, the merit of a theory lies not in its analytical characteristics but in how well it accounts for real-world phenomena. In order to test whether our theory applies to other cases of rampage school shootings, we first need to define the population of cases to which it applies. Determining what a case *is* has generally been undertheorized in the social sciences.[10] Whereas some authors believe that one's case and population of cases should be determined at the outset of the research, others believe that determining what a particular event is a "case of" should be an inductive or iterative process. This split, perhaps not surprisingly, often follows the quantitative-qualitative or the variable oriented–case oriented methodological divides.[11] Sociologist Howard Becker falls squarely on the inductive side of this debate: "Researchers probably will not know what their cases are until the research, including the task of writing up the results, is virtually completed. What *it* is a *case of* will coalesce gradually, sometimes catalytically, and the final realization of the case's nature may be the most important part of the interaction between ideas and evidence."[12] In chapter 9, we develop our definition of rampage school shootings on the basis of what we believe are the essential aspects of the Heath and Westside cases. We then consider whether the information we have about the other cases that meet this definition also conforms to the five-factor theory.

DATA

In order to test whether the theory helps explain other rampage school shootings, we use data from three sources: the Centers for Disease Control and Prevention's School-Associated Violent Deaths database, the Secret Service's *Safe School Initiative* Report, and our own data set, which is based on available media accounts of rampage school shootings as well as case studies from the report on lethal school violence by the National Academy of Sciences and the Columbine Commission report.[13] The data sets have slightly different populations of interest and definitions of a school shooting, and they consider different time frames. Therefore the number of cases considered varies across the three sources.

Our Dataset of Rampage School Shootings

One of the advantages of constructing our own database from media accounts and case studies is that we are better able to consider only those cases that meet our definition of a rampage school shooting—that the incident occurred on a school-related public stage before an audience, is committed by a student or former student of the school, and involves multiple victims, some chosen for their symbolic significance or targeted at random.

We included in our database all cases that took place in the United States between 1974 and 2002 that meet this definition of a rampage school shooting (see chapter 10). To identify the population, we considered all school shootings previously identified by the Secret Service report and the National Academy of Sciences Report and then tried to determine whether the cases met our definition of a rampage school shooting. In all, we found twenty-five cases with twenty-seven offenders (see Table 10.2).[14]

For comparison, we also selected two cases in other countries (Canada and Germany) that meet our definition; however, these cases are not among the twenty-seven cases on which the majority of the findings in chapter 10 are based.

There are significant limitations to media accounts. First, as we learned when we began our research at Westside and Heath, media accounts are not always accurate and are often contradictory. Second, journalists are often concerned with certain core issues such as bullying and access to guns, but they do not conduct uniform surveys, and therefore data are often missing on key variables of interest. For example, when we find no reports of animal mistreatment in the media reports, it is often difficult to determine whether that is because the offender did not engage in such behaviors or whether reporters simply did not ask those questions. As a result, where we report *no evidence,* it implies that either the specific behavior or experience was not present *or* that the information was simply not available (or was not of interest to reporters). Third, the smaller number of media reports and the relative paucity of information on the earlier incidents made a fruitful comparison over time difficult at best. For these reasons, supplementing media accounts with the CDC data as well as the Secret Service report findings, even though those reports consider slightly different populations, greatly increases the reliability of our findings.

CDC Data Set of School-Associated Violent Deaths

The Centers for Disease Control and Prevention's Division of Violence Prevention, in collaboration with the U.S. Departments of Education and Justice, undertook a study of school-associated violent deaths in the United States.[15] The database includes all violent deaths on the campus of a functioning public or private elementary or secondary school in the United States, or while the victim was on the way to or from regular sessions at school, or while the victim was attending or traveling to or from an official school-sponsored event.[16] The data were collected from media databases, state and local agencies, and police and school officials on events that occurred between July 1, 1994, and June 30, 1999. This database includes 220 events involving 253 cases. Unlike our database, it omitted school shootings in which no death occurred and included acts of lethal violence in which no gun was used.

We were fortunate that the CDC allowed us to go to Atlanta and use their database, thereby enabling us to run our own analyses of their data and consider only those cases that best fit our population of interest. In our analysis of the CDC data, we include only homicides that involved a firearm, and we exclude homicides that are classified as legal interventions (death by a police officer in the line of duty) and unintentional firearm-related deaths. Because the database does not identify former students, we can include only offenders who were students at the school where the shooting occurred at time of their rampage. We limited our analysis further to multiple-victim events in which the shooting resulted in more than one death or a single death plus injuries that resulted in hospitalization. This leaves us with nineteen offenders[17] and twelve school shootings.

The CDC database has many important advantages. It employs a uniform survey instrument, facilitating comparability across cases and decreasing the risk of missing data. Because the CDC data were gathered to understand all school-associated violent deaths, we can also compare multiple-victim events and suicides to better understand in what ways rampage school shootings differ from other forms of lethal violence on school property.[18]

However, using a database that has been put together for other purposes can make it difficult to narrow the sample to fit our definition, and we are limited by the questions that other researchers asked. For example, the database did not identify former students of the school, so we were faced with the choice of either including all current students at the school where the crime occurred, any offender who was a student at the time of the shooting, or any offender under a certain age. The database excludes all nonfatal events, so it does not include shootings like those in Conyers, Georgia, or Stamps, Arkansas, in which no one died but which otherwise fit our definition. In addition, none of the questions allows us to determine whether there was an aspect of randomness to the attack, which is critical to our definition of rampage schools shootings. Because of confidentiality issues, we were not allowed to identify the individuals that were included in the CDC study, limiting our ability to consider only those cases that we know from our media analysis to fit our definition. Finally, the surveys were administered only to school and law enforcement officials familiar with the events. Although such individuals are often knowledgeable about many aspects of the case, they also may be less aware of issues such as bullying or teasing, in which peer or offender reports often diverge from adult perceptions.

Secret Service Report on Targeted School Shootings

The U.S. Secret Service's National Threat Assessment Center identified thirty-seven targeted school shootings involving forty-one attackers, that occurred in the United States between 1974 and 2000.[19] The data were collected from investigative, school, court, and mental health records. Secret Service researchers also conducted supplemental interviews with ten of the perpetrators of targeted school violence. They chose cases in which the assailants were current or recent students at the school and in which the attacker or attackers chose the school "for a particular purpose and not simply as a site of opportunity." The Secret Service report therefore excluded shootings that were related to drugs, gangs, or interpersonal disputes unrelated to school. Unlike rampage school shootings, targeted school shootings include incidents in which only one victim was targeted.

The Secret Service report adds to the CDC data in that it covers a greater time span, extending back to 1974. Furthermore, the report was especially useful because the Secret Service was given access to ten school shooters, allowing a rare inside perspective.

Because of issues of confidentiality, we were limited to the published findings in their report. The report provides results in terms of group averages or percentages, making it difficult for us to determine whether there are any systematic differences between targeted school shootings and rampage school shootings. It is also impossible to analyze the data in a person- or event-centered fashion, which is critical to assessing whether each shooting exhibited each of the five necessary but not sufficient conditions.

METHOD

Testing a theory that is based on five necessary but not sufficient conditions in a database of positive cases (those in which a shooting did occur) involves examining the prevalence of each factor in these cases. The theory predicts that each case will exhibit all five factors. For each of the three databases, we need only calculate the proportion of cases that exhibit each factor and the proportion of cases that exhibit all five factors. As noted, this last calculation is not possible with the Secret Service data because we must rely on published frequencies. Although a causal statement must be falsifiable—that is, able to be disproven—to be a theory, we do not interpret less than complete presence of all five factors in every case to be strong evidence against the theory. There are multiple sources of error in this analysis, including the downward biasing of measurement because of incomplete data and the need to dichotomize evidence into the presence or absence of the factor.[20]

Experienced researchers or regular readers of research reports will note that this simple "case-based" method differs dramatically from the most common form of quantitative analysis: a regression model that predicts an outcome (in this case, a binary outcome) on the basis of a set of independent variables thought to be causes of the outcome. The reason for the difference is that the underlying causal model is different in the two types of analyses. In contrast to our model of necessary and sufficient conditions, a regression model of a binary outcome most commonly assumes that the independent variables additively and individually increase the probability of the event occurring. A regression model also requires both positive cases and negative cases—in this case, students who are somehow potentially at risk of becoming school shooters but have not.[21]

NOTES

CHAPTER ONE

1. Michael may have been dissociating, one symptom of which is a change in bodily stance.

2. Although her injuries from the shooting prevented her from playing basketball again, her college honored her with a basketball scholarship, and after many months of physical therapy, she was able to play college soccer.

3. The others who died were not in this graduating class.

4. Elissa Benedek, M.D., et al., "Report of Psychiatric and Psychological Evaluation: Michael Alan Carneal," July 19, 1998, provided to the McCracken County Commonwealth Attorney in reference to Indictment No. 97-CR00350, dated December 12, 1997, p. 4.

5. Michael left three of the guns at Holt's house because he was afraid his father would discover them when he came to retrieve his son.

6. Benedek et al., "Report of Psychiatric and Psychological Evaluation: Michael Alan Carneal," p. 5.

7. Quoted from the Sheriff's Department investigative report.

8. They were Candice Porter (age eleven), who "dated" Mitchell for a few days before she broke up with him; Crystal Barnes (thirteen); Whitney Irving (eleven); Brittany Lambie (thirteen); Jennifer Jacobs (twelve), who reportedly dated Andrew and broke up with him before the shooting; Ashley Betts (twelve); Tristan McGowan (thirteen), who was Andrew's cousin; Christina Amer (twelve); Jenna Brooks (twelve), a cousin of the deceased Natalie Brooks; and Lynette Thetford, who taught Andrew in social studies.

9. Social critics have raised questions about what they see as the disproportionate amount of media attention given to rampage shootings since they are such rare events, while lethal violence is such a pressing problem in poor, minority neighborhoods in city centers. Michael Eric Dyson has argued that when killers are white, we see extensive profiles of perpetrators and victims, while black murderers and their victims are more anonymous, reflecting society's assumption that violence is not a white norm, but an exception requiring an explanation, whereas black violence is somehow to be expected. Michael Eric Dyson, "Uglier Than Meets the Eye," *Chicago Sun Times,* March 13, 2001. Orlando Patterson has suggested that we want to know what has gone wrong with "the nation's children" when murder happens in

bucolic communities like those of Westside Middle School or Heath High School, but we don't think in these broad, introspective terms when the victims or perpetrators are minorities. Orlando Patterson, "When 'They' Are 'Us'," *New York Times,* April 30, 1999.

10. Bono is the largest of these communities, with a population in 2001 of just over 1,000. Cash and Egypt count 280 and 112 residents, respectively.

11. This issue is discussed extensively in Wendy Roth and Jal Mehta, "The *Rashomon* Effect: Combining Positivist and Interpretivist Approaches in the Analysis of Contested Events," *Sociological Methods and Research* 31, no. 2 (2000): 131–173.

12. The first serious overview of the issue is to be found in a study conducted by the National Research Council and the Institute of Medicine: *Deadly Lessons: Understanding Lethal School Violence,* Mark H. Moore, Carol V. Petrie, Anthony A. Braga, and Brenda L. McLaughlin, eds. (Washington, DC: National Academies Press, 2003).

CHAPTER TWO

1. The WISC-III intelligence test was administered to Carneal on February 6, 1998, some months after the shooting. He performed at a high level on a consistent basis, reinforcing the view that Carneal is well above average in intelligence (e.g., his verbal comprehension score placed him in the 88th percentile). As Dr. Dewey Cornell noted in his psychiatric report, "Michael's intelligence test scores are generally consistent with the achievement test scores found in his school records; for example, his overall score on the Comprehensive Test of Basic Skills in the seventh grade placed him at the 91st percentile. Dewey G. Cornell, "Psychological Evaluation: Michael Adam Carneal," in the case of *Commonwealth v. Michael Carneal,* Indictment No. 97-CR–000350, 1998, p. 27.

2. Quoted in Elissa Benedek, M.D., et al., "Report of Psychiatric and Psychological Evaluation: Michael Alan Carneal," July 19, 1998, provided to the McCracken County Commonwealth Attorney in reference to Indictment No. 97-CR00350, dated December 12, 1997, p. 15

3. It is not possible to know how much of the material on Carneal's computer he actually read. Materials recovered from a hard drive are not necessarily intentionally stored there, since most Web browsers save temporary copies of online documents. Nevertheless, the range and amount of material on Carneal's machine suggests that our reliance on these data is justified.

4. We do not know who authored this story. It was on Carneal's hard drive, but it is not clear whether he wrote it himself, got it from a friend, or simply downloaded it from the Internet. Carneal told psychiatrist Dewey Cornell that Jered Parker had sent him this story but that he did not like it. Cornell, "Psychological Evaluation: Michael Adam Carneal," p. 19.

5. Cornell, "Psychological Evaluation: Michael Adam Carneal," (1998, p. 8).

6. In a national survey about bullying, males who were frequently bullied were asked about the specific types of bullying to which they were subjected; 19.8 percent report being teased about their looks or speech; 17.8 percent claim that they were physically hit, slapped, or pushed; 17.5 percent said they received sexual comments or gestures; 16.7 percent reported being the subject of rumors; and 8.8 percent reported that they were belittled about their religion or race. Tonja R. Nansel, Mary Overpeck, Ramani S. Pilla, W. June Ruan, Bruce Simons-Morton, and Peter Scheidt, "Bullying Behaviors Among U.S. Youth: Preva-

lence and Association with Psychosocial Adjustment," *Journal of the American Medical Association* 285, no. 16 (2001): 2094–2100, p. 2097.

7. Paper on self-esteem, found on Carneal's computer.

8. Cornell, "Psychological Evaluation: Michael Adam Carneal," p. 9.

9. Ibid., p. 18.

10. Ibid.

11. Ibid.

12. Margaret Bledson, the science teacher, encountered Jered Parker in her classroom minutes after the shooting, defended him, and claimed that he was not party to a conspiracy.

13. Deputy Hayden provided a sworn statement on December 4, 1997, in which he recalls a conversation he had with Michael Carneal during the time he was being transported back to the detention facility from the state police "post one." "He . . . said that he and [Jered Parker, Brian Mather, Bill Janson, Craig Holt] and another boy . . . had planned it. He said that plan was that he would start shooting, causing a distraction so that the other boys could pick up their guns and go to their points. . . . He said Wednesday he told all the boys that he would take the guns from Jered's house . . . [and] told them what kind of guns were available. He said that Brian requested a shotgun so he could hide it under his trench coat. He said Brian told him he thought it would be cool to have it under his trench coat and whip it out. . . . Matt then requested the other pistol. . . . He said that Jered wanted a knife." (Quoted from the official police statement of Deputy Mark Hayden, marked as exhibit 001255 in the civil suit.)

14. The transcript of this police interview is filled with "ums" and asides, which have been omitted here for readability.

15. The psychiatric reports are contradictory on this point. The team working at the request of the prosecution notes that Michael changed his story, at one point claiming that he never told anyone to avoid the lobby (Benedek et al. 1998, 7) and at another saying that he definitely told Jessica to stay away from the lobby (p. 8).

16. The Benedek report suggests that Michael got this impression because a boy who had gone to jail for stealing a car was very popular. Benedek et al., "Report of Psychiatric and Psychological Evaluation: Michael Alan Carneal," p. 6.

17. Ibid., p. 7.

18. Cornell, "Psychological Evaluation: Michael Adam Carneal," p. 19.

19. She has an older daughter, Angie, by her first husband.

20. This passage may suggest Chris's belief that Mitchell was responsible for the plot. The question of who played a leadership role was the subject of much debate. Chris admitted that he did not know who had the upper hand, and that sometimes he thought Andrew was the ringleader and Mitchell the follower. But he knew Mitchell better and that is at least partly responsible for the vantage point he had on this question.

21. The police discounted this theory, noting that by coincidence the boys were in gym together and the girls in music when the alarm sounded, and that this accounted for the pattern of who was exiting onto the playground when the alarm sounded, in range of the rifle fire. There is no evidence that the boys knew this would be the case.

22. In Jonesboro, students were divided over whether it would be worse if one were taunted for being black or gay.

23. These records are sealed because he was a juvenile. Our account of the incident is based on newspaper coverage subsequent to the shooting and Gretchen Woodard's reflections, offered during an interview with the authors.

24. Sandy Davis and Linda Satter, "Differing views depict character of suspect, 11," *Arkansas Democrat Gazette*, March 29, 1998, p. 1A.

25. Although Arkansas schools still make use of corporal punishment, parents can place their children on a "no paddle" list, and his did so.

26. Pat Golden had been married before and had two children by her first husband, but Dennis had not had children before. Andrew's mother, Pat Golden, had reversed a tubal ligation after she married Dennis so that she could conceive, and Andrew was the child they had waited for. Pat's children by her first husband did not get along well with Dennis or Dennis's parents and, after a time, they left the Golden home to live with other relatives.

27. Andrew's attorneys were rebuffed by the court on the grounds that juveniles are classified the way they are because the law assumes they are not capable of forming intent in the first place. The relevance of an insanity plea for adults is that it suggests that they are not capable of forming intent because of extreme mental incapacity.

28. Under Arkansas state law, juveniles must have an ombudsman assigned to them whose job it is to be sure that they are being fed, clothed, and housed appropriately and that they are not suffering verbal, emotional, sexual, or physical abuse. Juveniles are also required to receive an education even when they are behind bars, and this too is supervised by the ombudsman.

CHAPTER THREE

1. In chapter 10 we review in some detail all of the cases we have been able to locate since the 1970s.

2. Orlando Patterson, "When 'They' Are 'Us'," *New York Times,* April 30, 1999, p. A31; Michael Eric Dyson, "Uglier Than Meets the Eye," *Chicago Sun-Times,* March 13, 2001, p. 25.

3. Making generalizations about school shootings requires first a definition of the cases in which we are interested. There have been a number of studies of school deaths, rampage killings, or school shootings, each defining their sample differently. In chapter 10 we review two of them—one used by the Centers for Disease Control and Prevention (CDC) and the other by the U.S. Secret Service. Other relevant definitions include the following:

The National School Safety Center maintains a database of "school-associated violent deaths," which begins with the 1992–1993 school year and runs through to the most recently completed school year. It covers the same types of deaths as the CDC studies and also includes deaths that occurred "as an obvious direct result of school incident/s, function/s or activities, whether on or off school bus/vehicle or school property." This database, drawn from newspaper accounts, includes 322 deaths between 1992–1993 and 2000–2001. Seventy-eight of these deaths occurred in twenty-nine multiple-victim incidents. The database is available at www.nssc1.org.

Forensic psychologists James McGee and Caren DeBernardo studied twelve "nontraditional" school shooting incidents between 1993 and 1999 in an attempt to develop a behavioral profile of the "classroom avenger." By nontraditional they mean not apparently related to "juvenile gangs, inner-city problems, minority or ethnic status, turf warfare, drugs or more conventional criminal activity such as armed robbery or extortion." Their study is based on media accounts and includes incidents in Crayson, Kentucky, Redland, California, Blackville, South Carolina, Lynnville, Tennessee, Moses Lake, Washington, Bethel, Alaska, Pearl, Mississippi, West Paducah, Kentucky, Stamps, Arkansas, Jonesboro, Arkansas, Edinboro, Pennsylvania, and Springfield, Oregon. See James P. McGee and Caren R. DeBernardo, "The Classroom Avenger: A Behavioral Profile of School Based Shootings," *The Forensic Examiner* 8, no. 5/6 (1999): 16–18.

Clinical psychologists Stephanie Verlinden, Michael Hersen, and Jay Thomas studied nine incidents of "multiple victim homicide in American secondary schools" in school years 1995–1996, 1996–1997, and 1997–1998 in order to identify risk factors in school shootings. The study was based on media accounts and court records where available. It includes incidents in Moses Lake, Washington, Bethel, Alaska, Pearl, Mississippi, Paducah, Kentucky, Jonesboro, Arkansas, Edinboro, Pennsylvania, Springfield, Oregon, Littleton, Colorado, and Conyers, Georgia. See Stephanie Verlinden, Michael Hersen, and Jay Thomas, "Risk Factors in School Shootings," *Clinical Psychology Review* 29, no. 1 (2000): 3–56.

The Federal Bureau of Investigation investigated fourteen shooting incidents and four planned shootings that were prevented by law enforcement. These investigations were based on police and prosecution investigations and included offender interview transcripts, school materials and writings, witness statements, interviews with persons who knew the offenders, counseling and psychiatric reports, and other materials. The goal of the study was to develop a threat assessment system to help school officials and law enforcement personnel respond to threats of school shootings. See Mary Ellen O'Toole, "The School Shooter: A Threat Assessment Perspective," Federal Bureau of Investigation, 2000, available at http:www.fbi.gov/publications/school/school2.pdf.

The *New York Times* constructed a database of 100 "rampage" attacks by eighty-three adult and nineteen youth offenders between 1949 and 1999. The database included "multiple-victim homicides that were not primarily domestic or connected to a robbery or gang." Serial killers and political killings were also excluded. In all, 425 people were killed and 510 people wounded in the attacks studied. The database was constructed using media accounts, court records and interviews with police, victims, and offenders. See Ford Fessenden, "They Threaten, Seethe, and Unhinge, Then Kill in Quantity," *New York Times*, April 9, 2000, p. A1. Other articles based on this study also appeared on April 9, 10, and 11.

Child psychologist Reid Meloy and colleagues studied twenty-seven mass murders by thirty-four individuals involving three or more deaths and committed by attackers under the age of twenty between 1958 and 1999. They selected cases on the basis of a search of psychiatric, psychological, medical, social, and criminal databases and gathered data from court records and transcripts, scientific articles, academic books, video and audio tapes of offenders, family members, survivors, witnesses, and law enforcement officers as well as media accounts. See J. Reid Meloy et al., "Offender and Offense Characteristics of a Nonrandom Sample of Adolescent Mass Murderers," *Journal of the American Academy of Child and Adolescent Psychiatry* 40, no. 6 (2001): 719–728.

Unfortunately, none of these studies fits our purposes exactly. Ideally, we would like information on all cases of multiple-target shootings or planned shootings by youths in schools during a specified period, including those that succeeded in killing and those that did not as well as those that occurred and those that were planned but prevented. In this chapter we make reference to these studies as best we can where appropriate and where relevant.

In addition, we are skeptical of studies based in whole or relying substantially on media accounts for data. In our experience studying the Heath and Westside cases, we have discovered that media accounts of these cases are often incorrect or contradictory, and studies making claims about these cases sometimes come to incorrect conclusions when information is based on incorrect media accounts.

4. Based on the authors' search of newspaper articles on Dow Jones Interactive.

5. Sixteen months earlier, the day after the Columbine shooting, 50 percent of parents said they feared for their children's safety at school. Susan Gembrowski, "Life Goes on in a Troubled World: Well-Adjusted Teens Thrive Despite Violent Times," *The San Diego Union-Tribune,* November 11, 2001, p. A1.

6. There were 500 respondents in this survey. ABC News polls conducted March 11, 2001, and April 25, 1999. Available online at http:abcnews.go.com/sections/GMA/GoodMorningAmerica/GMA_School_Violence_POLL.html.

7. See note 29 for a discussion of various definitions of an "epidemic."

8. Elizabeth Donohue, Vincent Schiraldi, and Jason Ziedenberg, *School House Hype: School Shootings, and the Real Risks Kids Face in America* (Washington, DC: Justice Policy Institute, 1998); and *School House Hype: Two Years Later* (San Francisco: Center on Juvenile and Criminal Justice, 2000). For the CDC results on in-school deaths, see S. Patrick Kachur et al., "School-Associated Violent Deaths in the United States, 1992–1994," *Journal of the American Medical Association* 275, no. 22 (1996): 1729–1733, and Mark Anderson et al., "School-Associated Violent Deaths in the United States, 1994–1999," *Journal of the American Medical Association* 286, no. 21 (2001): 2695–2702. For the comparable number of out-of-school deaths, see Melissa Sickmund, Howard N. Snyder, and Eileen Poe-Yamagata, *Juvenile Offenders and Victims: 1997 Update on Violence* (Washington, DC: Office of Juvenile Justice and Delinquency Prevention, 1997).

9. For example, opponents of the epidemic hypothesis cite a 1998 proposal by Virginia Governor James Gilmore to "reduce the number of nighttime athletic events to prevent an increase in school violence" and to end after-school programs.

10. The definition and data are discussed in chapter 10.

11. Data for the near-miss plots are from Tatsha Robertson, "Across the Nation, School Attack Plots Pose Legal Challenge," *Boston Globe,* December 16, 2001, pp. A1, A26; and Associated Press State and Local Wire, "Police Say Students Planned to Bring Guns to School," December 19, 2001. We did not examine the data on near-miss plots that preceded the Columbine killings, but we recognize that there were many.

12. National Research Council and the Institute of Medicine. *Deadly Lessons: Understanding Lethal School Violence: Case Studies of School Violence Committee,* Mark H. Moore, Carol V. Petrie, Anthony A. Braga, and Brenda L. McLaughlin, eds. (Washington, DC: National Academies Press, 2003), Table 9-2, p. 295.

13. For example, on January 16, 2002, a student killed three and wounded three at the Appalachian School of Law in West Virginia, and on October 28, 2002, a student killed three and committed suicide at the University of Arizona nursing school. Frances X. Clines, "3 Slain at Law School; Student Is Held," *New York Times,* January 17, 2002, p. A18; John M. Broder, "Student Kills 3 Instructors and Himself at U. of Arizona," *New York Times,* October 29, 2002, p. A20.

14. See *Deadly Lessons.*

15. Fifty-two percent of those surveyed had heard of someone bringing a gun to school, and 52 percent had heard a weapons-related threat. Michael Healy, "Half of Teens Have Heard Gun Threat at School," *USA Today,* November 27, 2001, p. D6.

16. Robertson, "Across the Nation, School Attack Plots Pose Legal Challenge," lists twelve post-Columbine plots, of which seven appear to have been foiled after tips from peers.

17. Lois A. Fingerhut, Deborah D. Ingam, and Jacob J. Feldman, "Firearm and Non-firearm Homicide Among Persons 15 Through 19 Years of Age: Differences by Level of Urbanization, United States, 1979 Through 1989," *Journal of the American Medical Association* 267, no. 22 (1992): 3048–3053. These data refer to what the U.S. Census Bureau calls "core counties of metropolitan areas." Core counties are those that contain the primary central city of a metropolitan area with over 1 million residents in 1980. Firearm homicide was the leading cause of death of core county youths aged fifteen to nineteen in 1989.

18. Philip J. Cook and John H. Laub, "The Unprecedented Epidemic in Youth Violence," in Michael Tonry and Mark H. Moore, eds., *Youth Violence, Crime, and Justice: A Review of Research,* vol. 24 (Chicago: University of Chicago Press, 1998).

19. Delbert Elliott, John Hagan, and Joan McCord, *Youth Violence: Children at Risk* (Washington, DC: American Sociological Association, 1998). Black males are more likely than white males to be arrested for the same behavior.

20. Margaret A. Hamburg, "Youth Violence Is a Public Health Concern," in Delbert S. Elliott, Beatrix Hamburg, and Kirk R. Williams, eds., *Violence in American Schools* (New York: Cambridge University Press, 1998).

21. Jeffrey Fagan and Deanna L. Wilkinson, "Social Contexts and Functions of Adolescent Violence," in *Violence in American Schools.*

22. See William Julius Wilson, *The Truly Disadvantaged* (Chicago: University of Chicago Press, 1987), and William Julius Wilson, *When Work Disappears* (New York: Knopf, 1996).

23. Mark H. Moore, "Youth Violence in America," in Michael Tonry and Mark H. Moore, eds., *Youth Violence, Crime, and Justice.*

24. Mindy Thomson Fullilove et al., "What Did Ian Tell God? School Violence in East New York," and John Hagan, Paul Hirschfield, and Carla Shedd, "Shooting at Tilden High: Causes and Consequences," both in *Deadly Lessons.*

25. Figures based on the authors' analysis of data in the National School Safety Center's database on school-associated violent deaths (see note 3). In contrast, during the same period, an average of 5.7 students and 1.7 staff members were killed per year in violent attacks in non-city settings. Not surprisingly, in these areas student deaths peaked in the 1997–1998 and 1998–1999 school years, which saw fourteen and thirteen student deaths, respectively. The analysis excludes suicides, homicide victims unrelated to the school or found on school property, and accidental deaths due to firearm discharge, physical restraint of a student, or heart attack suffered by a staff member while breaking up a fight. Cities are defined as places with populations greater than 50,000. These figures somewhat distort the comparison of large cities with other areas by not taking into account differences in the total population of these two types of areas. Because larger cities have larger populations of students and teachers, the risk of death at school is probably lower in such areas.

26. These risks are vastly higher than national averages. In the country as a whole, only 9 percent of males and five percent of females report being injured *or* threatened while at

school. Delbert S. Elliott, Beatrix Hamburg, and Kirk R. Williams, "Violence in American Schools: An Overview," in *Violence in American Schools.*

27. See *Violence in American Schools,* especially pp. 6–7. Violence in urban schools is, however, a by-product of the violence in surrounding communities. The most accurate predictor of school violence in urban settings is the crime rate in the neighborhoods that surround the schools. See John H. Laub and Janet Lauritsen, "The Interdependence of School Violence with Neighborhood and Family Conditions," in Elliott et al., eds., *Violence in American Schools.* See also Hamburg, "Youth Violence Is a Public Health Concern," in the same volume.

28. James Garbarino, *Lost Boys: Why Our Sons Turn Violent and How We Can Save Them* (New York: Free Press, 1999).

29. The use of epidemic models for understanding violence has increased with the contributions of public health researchers, who see the injuries and death caused by violence as a public health problem. See Hamburg, "Youth Violence Is a Public Health Concern." There are, however, multiple meanings of the term epidemic. At the simplest level it refers to health problems that are above expected or previous levels. Yet, as Mark Moore notes, "whether there are contagious mechanisms at work is a matter to be investigated, not assumed." Moore, "Youth Violence in America," p. 6.

30. Garbarino writes, "What do the large numbers of anonymous killings have to do with the highly publicized killings in Jonesboro and Paducah and Springfield? What do they have in common? In this book we will find answers by moving beyond the surface differences between the two groups of violent boys—principally race and class—to see the profound emotional and psychological similarities that link them together. By getting to know the circumstances under which the epidemic of youth violence first took hold, among low-income minority youth in inner-city areas, we can begin to gain some insight into the lives of the boys in places like Jonesboro, Paducah, and Springfield." He goes on to argue that youth violence took hold among the most vulnerable populations first, disadvantaged inner-city youth, and then spread to the rest of society.

31. Diane L. Wilkinson and Jeffrey Fagan, "What We Know About Gun Use Among Adolescents," *Clinical Child and Family Psychology Review* 4, no. 2 (2001): 109–132.

32. The contrast between clustering and continuity could, however, be an artifact of the low number of incidents of nonurban shootings.

33. We should also recognize that if violence in schools is considered to be a product of violence in the surrounding communities, then lower levels of violence in nonurban communities would lead us to predict lower rates of violence in nonurban schools.

34. Wilkinson and Fagan, "What We Know About Gun Use Among Adolescents."

35. Ibid., p. 128.

36. Psychiatrist Mindi Fullilove and colleagues describe "beef" as "interpersonal problems that are at a boiling point. Beef can start over any apparent mistreatment, including a wrong look, a disrespectful action, or a move into personal space." Fullilove et al., "What Did Ian Tell God?" p. 225.

37. See Elijah Anderson, *Streetwise* (Chicago: University of Chicago Press, 1990), and Elijah Anderson, *Code of the Street* (New York: Norton, 1999).

38. A U.S. Secret Service study of thirty-seven school shootings between 1974 and 2000 involving forty-one shooters found that three-quarters of them planned their attacks and over one-half planned them at least two days before the attacks. See Bryan Vossekuil, Marisa

Reddy, Robert Fein, Randy Borum, and William Modzeleski, "Safe School Initiative: An Interim Report on the Prevention of Targeted Violence in Schools," U.S. Secret Service National Threat Assessment Center, U.S. Department of Education, and National Institute of Justice, 2000.

39. Fullilove et al., "What Did Ian Tell God?"

40. The study examined 418 officer-involved shootings recorded by the Los Angeles County Sheriff's Department between 1987 and 1997 and found that 11 percent of shootings and 13 percent of fatal shootings were cases of "suicide by cop." They met all of the following criteria: "(1) evidence of the individual's suicidal intent, (2) evidence they specifically wanted officers to shoot them, (3) evidence they possessed a lethal weapon or what appeared to be a lethal weapon, and (4) evidence they intentionally escalated the encounter and provoked officers to shoot them." H. R. Hutson, D. Anglin, J. Yarbrough, K. Hardaway, M. Russell, J. Strote, M. Cantor, and B. Blum, "Suicide by Cop," *Annals of Emergency Medicine* 32, no. 6 (1998): 665–669. None of the victims in this study were under eighteen years of age, however.

41. Alvin F. Poussaint and Amy Alexander. *Lay My Burden Down: Unraveling Suicide and the Mental Health Crisis Among African-Americans* (Boston: Beacon Press, 2000).

42. Criminologists James Alan Fox and Jack Levin define a mass murder as a single event involving four or more homicides. These incidents involved 697 offenders and 2,353 victims. James Alan Fox and Jack Levin, "Multiple Homicide: Patterns of Serial and Mass Murder," in *Crime and Justice: A Review of Research*, vol. 23, edited by Michael Tonry (Chicago: University of Chicago Press, 1998).

43. A smaller proportion of mass murders occur in the South than single-victim murders—31.3 percent for mass murders versus 42.1 percent for single murders. In all other regions, mass murders are either as common as or slightly more common than single murders. Fox and Levin, "Multiple Homicide"; see also Jack Levin and James Alan Fox, *Mass Murder: America's Growing Menace* (New York: Plenum, 1985), and James Alan Fox and Jack Levin, *Overkill: Mass Murder and Serial Killing Exposed* (New York: Plenum, 1994).

44. Fox and Levin argue that the causes of a mass murder episode can be classified into three categories: predisposers, precipitants, and facilitators. Predisposers are "long-term and stable preconditions that become incorporated into the personality of the killer," such as a long history of frustration and murder or blaming others for one's failures. Precipitants are "short-term and acute triggers," including a sudden loss, such as the end of a relationship or being fired from a job, or a catalyst such as the discovery of a model of mass murder, leading to a copycat crime. Facilitators are "conditions, usually situational, that increase the likelihood of a violent outburst," such as isolation from emotional support and the availability of firearms. Fox and Levin classify motives for mass murder as power, revenge, loyalty, profit, or terror. Fox and Levin, "Multiple Homicide."

45. The *New York Times* defined a rampage shooting as one in which at least one person died and the attack did not involve domestic conflict, robbery, or political terrorism.

46. Fessenden, "They Threaten, Seethe, and Unhinge, Then Kill in Quantity"; Ford Fessenden, "How Youngest Killers Differ: Peer Support," *New York Times,* April 9, 2000, p. 29.

47. James Alan Fox and Jack Levin, "Firing Back: The Growing Threat of Workplace Violence," *Annals of the American Academy of Political and Social Sciences* 536 (1994): 16–30.

48. Ibid.

49. Ibid.

50. A study of ten school shooters found that eight were depressed and six had made suicidal threats, but only two of the ten had ever received any mental health treatment. Verlinden et al., "Risk Factors in School Shootings."

51. Fessenden, "They Threaten, Seethe, and Unhinge, Then Kill in Quantity."

52. Michael Carneal was diagnosed with depression ("dysthymia") and schizotypal personality disorder, a mild and rare form of schizophrenia, by Dr. Dewey Cornell, and with dysthymia and "traits of schizotypal personality disorder with borderline and paranoid features" by Dr. Diane Schetky. See Dewey G. Cornell, "Psychological Evaluation: Michael Adam Carneal," September 3, 1998; Diane H. Schetky, "Forensic Evaluation of Michael Carneal," May 27, 1998; Diane H. Schetky, "Forensic Re-evaluation of Michael Carneal," September 8, 1998. Drs. Elissa Benedek, William Weitzel, and Charles Clark, hired by the prosecution, concluded that "Michael Carneal was not mentally ill nor mentally retarded at the time of the shootings." Elissa Benedek, William Weitzel, and Charles Clark, "Report of Psychiatric and Psychological Evaluation: Michael Adam Carneal," July 17, 1998, p. 26.

53. As we noted in chapter 2, Andrew and his parents were called in to the school counselor's office after another student heard him making suicidal remarks. However, access to his psychological evaluation would be needed to determine whether Andrew was really suicidal or was simply trying to get attention. We made three separate requests to examine these records, but were refused. The psychiatric evaluations of minors are sealed by the courts.

54. National Institute of Mental Health, *Depression Research Fact Sheet* and *Schizophrenia Research Fact Sheet* (Bethesda, MD: National Institute of Mental Health, 2000).

55. Representatives Jennifer Dunn and Martin Frost, "Bipartisan Working Group on Youth Violence Final Report," 1999. Available at www.house.gov/dunn/workinggroup/wkg.htm.

56. Vossekuil et al., "Safe School Initiative: An Interim Report on the Prevention of Targeted Violence in Schools," p. 5.

57. One study of ten shooters based on media accounts of eight incidents found that eight of the ten shooters lacked parental supervision and seven had troubled family relationships, but that only two perceived a lack of family support and only three had experienced abuse or neglect. Verlinden et al. 2000.

58. O'Toole, "The School Shooter: A Threat Assessment Perspective."

59. The portrait of the Carneal family that emerged from our interviews was almost unanimously positive (the exceptions came from the families of the victims).

60. Cited in William Pollack, *Real Boys* (New York: Henry Holt, 1998), p. 343.

61. Boys were most likely to report being teased about looks or speech (19.8 percent), followed by being hit, slapped, or pushed (17.5 percent), receiving sexual comments or gestures (17.5 percent), and being the subject of rumors (16.7 percent). Nansel et al., "Bullying Behaviors Among U.S. Youth: Prevalence and Association with Psychosocial Adjustment," *Journal of the American Medical Association* 285, no. 16 (2001): 2094–2100.

62. Ibid.

63. Fessenden, "How Youngest Killers Differ."

64. Vossekuil et al., "Safe School Initiative: An Interim Report on the Prevention of Targeted Violence in Schools," p. 6.

65. Fessenden, "How Youngest Killers Differ."

66. J. R. Moehringer, "Mastermind Allegedly Ordered High School Shooting Crime: Satan-Following Youth Is Called Ringleader of Teens Who Inspired Boy, 16, to Open Fire in Mississippi, Killing 2," *Los Angeles Times,* October 15, 1997, p. A25; *Dallas Morning News,* "Judge Drops Conspiracy Charges in Mississippi Shooting," July 23, 1998, p. 7A; Associated Press, "Sledge Says He Faced Isolation, Hatred After Arrest," December 24, 1998; *Milwaukee Journal Sentinel,* "Killer's Associate Gets 6 Months in Rehab," February 12, 2000, p. 4A.

67. Many in the Westside community believe that Mitchell and Andrew were helped by a third party, although the police investigation found no evidence to support the charge. Immediately after the shooting, several students who were huddled in the school gymnasium told teachers that they knew who had done this: Mitchell and Andrew had told them they were going to do "something big" with the help of an older boy who attended one of the Jonesboro city schools.

68. Vossekuil et al., "Safe School Initiative: An Interim Report on the Prevention of Targeted Violence in Schools."

69. William DeJong, Joel C. Epstein, and Thomas E. Hart, "Bad Things Happened in Good Communities: The Rampage Shooting in Edinboro, Pennsylvania, and Its Aftermath," *Deadly Lessons.*

70. Laura Vozzella, "School Killings Cast Shadow on Small Towns," *Fort Worth Star-Telegram,* March 29, 1998, p. 1. See also Mercer L. Sullivan and Rob T. Guerette, "The Copycat Factor: Mental Illness, Guns, and the Shooting Incident at Heritage High School, Rockdale County, Georgia," in *Deadly Lessons.*

71. Emile Durkheim, *Suicide: A Study in Sociology* (New York: Free Press, 1951).

72. Sylvia Ann Hewlett and Cornell West, *The War Against the Parents* (Boston: Houghton Mifflin, 1998); Arlie Russell Hochschild, *The Time Bind: When Work Becomes Home and Home Becomes Work* (New York: Metropolitan Books, 1997); Jody Heymann, *The Widening Gap: Why America's Families Are in Jeopardy and What Can Be Done About It* (New York: Basic Books, 2000).

73. Juliet B. Schor, *The Overworked American: The Unexpected Decline of Leisure* (New York: Basic Books, 1992).

74. On culture of violence, see Fox Butterfield *All God's children: The Bosket Family and the American Tradition of Violence* (New York: Bard, 1998).

75. The phrase "culture of honor" has been used to describe southern European, especially Italian and Spanish, cultures as well. Anthropologists have discussed a culture of honor, linking machismo to it. Eric Hobsbawm had a more structural argument: the Sicilian Mafia developed because of a weak state. The Mafia became its own law in the absence of anything else one might call state authority. Eric J. Hobsbawm, *Primitive Rebels: Studies in Archaic Forms of Social Movements in the 19th and 20th Centuries* (Manchester, England: Manchester University Press, 1959).

76. Richard E. Nisbett and Dov Cohen, *Culture of Honor: The Psychology of Violence in the South* (Boulder: Westview Press, 1996).

77. In a ranking of states by violent crime rate—a combination of the rates for murder and non-negligent manslaughter, forcible rape, robbery, and aggravated assault—the sixteen southern states and Washington, DC, had an average rank of 16.9 for 1999, whereas the other thirty-four states had an average rank of 30.6. The average violent crime rate in the sixteen southern states and Washington, DC, was 624 per 100,000 in 1999 (561 with Washington,

DC, excluded), compared with a national average of 524.7 (based on the authors' calculations from data in the *Sourcebook of Criminal Justice Statistics, 2000,* Kathleen Maguire and Ann L. Pastore, eds. (2001), p. 290. Available at http:www.albany.edu/sourcebook/). In *Culture of Honor,* Nisbett and Cohen also present evidence that the only types of homicide that are significantly more common in the South are those involving threats to property or self-image and that regional differences hold only for whites, which is consistent with the fact that most American black families have their origins in the South.

78. Nisbett and Cohen, *Culture of Honor.* Nisbett and Cohen also cite survey evidence that southerners are more likely to endorse violence for self-protection and social control. They are more likely to endorse spanking and to say that it is appropriate for a child to respond to a bully who hit him by fighting.

79. For example, see Lewis W. Diuguid. "Guns Are Way of Death in America," *Kansas City Star,* April 4, 1998, p. C1, or Robert L. Kaiser, "Kentucky Killings Shatter a Town's Sense of Innocence," *Fort Worth Star-Telegram,* December 7, 1997, p. 1.

80. Philip J. Cook, Mark H. Moore, and Anthony Braga, "Gun Control" in *Crime: Public Policies for Crime Control,* James Q. Wilson and Joan Petersilia, eds., (Oakland, CA: Institute for Contemporary Studies, 2001).

81. Wilkinson and Fagan, "What We Know About Gun Use Among Adolescents"; Josephson Institute of Ethics, "The Ethics of American Youth: 2000 Report Card," 2001, available at www.josephsoninstitute.org; Joseph F. Sheley and James D. Wright, "High School Youth, Weapons, and Violence: A National Survey," National Institute of Justice Research in Brief, 1998.

82. A few representative quotes: "There are a lot of guys at school who hunt, and I know they have at least a gun, if not several guns. But it's . . . shotguns and stuff for hunting. . . . I could get one if I needed it, I guess. If I just, ask the right person, but I've never touched one and I don't intend to." —Christine Olson, Westside student

"The only person I've seen that has one or that has many is my uncle, but I never go over there. Or my grandpa. So if I really wanted one, it really wouldn't be that difficult. Because he doesn't have it locked up or nothing. And they're loaded. But I don't even think I'd be, I don't think I would have enough courage to take it out of the house." —Jasper Andrews, Heath High student

"If you wanted to get a gun, how easy is it to get one?"

"Wicked easy."

"Why do you say that, what would you do?"

"I would sneak one. I would find one and sneak it out of the house."

"Do you know people who have guns in their house?"

"Yes, but I wouldn't get one." —Chuck Phillips, Heath High student

83. CNN Web site, "White House Summit Looks for Answers to Youth Violence, May 10, 1999," and "Transcript: Clinton Opens Youth Violence Summit." In addition, a major part of the 1999 Congressional Bipartisan Working Group on Youth Violence involved examining the media and popular culture. Representatives Jennifer Dunn and Martin Frost, "Bipartisan Working Group on Youth Violence Final Report."

84. J. Cantor, "Media Violence," *Journal of Adolescent Health* 27, no. 2 (2000): 30–34.

85. For a review of this evidence, see Brandon S. Centerwall, "Television and Violence: The Scale of the Problem and Where to Go From Here," *Journal of the American Medical Associ-*

ation 267, no. 22 (1992): 3059–3063, and M. B. Rothenberg, "Effect of Television on Children and Youth," *Journal of the American Medical Association* 234 (1975): 1043–1046.

86. Two representative quotes: "It doesn't affect me because I'm not that stupid that I see something on TV, I got to go do it. If, like little kids, it's, you know, if they're around it all the time, I'm pretty sure they'd pick up on it because they pick up on anything. . . . But I mean, but it doesn't affect me." —Jim Jacobs, Heath High student

"I think that maybe, it may put an idea in someone's head. But as far as it playing a major role, I don't think it does that much. I mean they may see it and say, well, okay I can do something like that if that's what their plan is, but I don't think that it plays a major role." —Rick Bowman, Heath High student

87. Cornell, "Psychological Evaluation: Michael Adam Carneal," p. 16.

88. Lyrics from Bone Thugz n Harmony's "Crept and We Came" include: "Cocking the 9 and ready to aim, Pulling the trigger, To blow out your brains, Bone got a gang, Man we crept and we came." A song by TuPac Shakur, "When We Ride," includes the lyrics: "I'll make you famous mother******, I'm talking about *Time* magazine, *Newsweek* and all that other good s***, My niggas make the paper, baby, My niggas make the front page." Ken Heard, "Teen Ambush Suspect in Jonesboro Shootings Loved Rap Music, Teacher Says," *Arkansas Democrat-Gazette,* June 16, 1998.

89. For a review, see Edward Donnerstein and Daniel Linz, "The Media," in *Crime: Public Policies for Crime Control,* edited by James Q. Wilson and Joan Petersilia (San Francisco: Institute for Contemporary Studies Press, 1995).

90. See David P. Phillips, "The Influence of Suggestion on Suicide: Substantive and Theoretical Implications of the Werther Effect," *American Sociological Review* 39, no. 3 (1974): 340–354; David P. Phillips and Kenneth A. Bollen, "Imitative Suicides: A National Study of the Effects of Television News Stories," *American Sociological Review* 47, no. 4 (1982): 802–809; Ira M. Wasserman, "Imitation and Suicide: A Reexamination of the Werther Effect," *American Sociological Review* 49 (1984): 427–436; James N. Baron and Peter C. Reiss, "Same Time, Next Year: Aggregate Analyses of the Mass Media and Violent Behavior," *American Sociological Review* 50, no. 3 (1985): 347–363; David P. Phillips and Kenneth A. Bollen, "Same Time, Last Year: Selective Data Dredging for Negative Findings," *American Sociological Review* 50, no. 3 (1985): 364–371; Madelyn S. Gould and David Shaffer, "The Impact of Suicide in Television Movies," *New England Journal of Medicine* 315, no. 11 (1986): 690–694; David Phillips and Lundie L. Carstensen, "Clustering of Teenage Suicides After Television-News Stories About Suicide," *New England Journal of Medicine* 315, no. 11 (1986): 685–689; David P. Phillips and Lundie L. Carstensen, "The Effect of Suicide Stories on Various Demographic Groups, 1968–1985," *Suicide and Life-Threatening Behavior* 18, no. 1 (1986): 100–114; Steven Stack, "The Media and Suicide: A Nonadditive Model, 1968–1980," *Suicide and Life-Threatening Behavior* 23, no. 1 (2000): 63–66; and Steven Stack, "Media Impacts on Suicide: A Quantitative Review of 293 Findings," *Social Science Quarterly* 81, no. 4 (2000): 957–971.

CHAPTER FOUR

1. Most of their neighbors came to the conclusion that the blame was misplaced. In fact, immediately after the shooting a local business donated T-shirts emblazoned with the phrase "We Believe in Heath" to show their support for the community and its high school.

2. According to a report from the Justice Policy Institute, as of spring 2000 the courts had yet to find schools legally liable in such cases. "In spite of compulsory attendance laws federal courts have routinely held that schools do not have a 'custodial' relationship over students that would give rise to Fourteenth Amendment Due Process rights arising from a duty to protect. In order for such a right, either a 'special relationship' must exist or there must be 'state created danger' sufficient to establish liability." Kim Brooks, Vincent Schiraldi, and Jason Ziedenberg, *School House Hype: Two Years Later* (Washington, DC: Justice Policy Institute, 2000).

3. Sociologists have long recognized the potentially negative consequences of the rise of bureaucratic organizations for the quality of social relations. But the rise of organizations also creates the possibility of new patterns of adverse social outcomes that occur as a result of bureaucratic error. Researchers working in particular areas such as medicine and technology have produced an enormous number of detailed case studies of specific incidents of organizational failure. For an excellent review of the literature in this field, see Diane Vaughan, "The Dark Side of Organizations: Mistake, Misconduct, and Disaster," *Annual Review of Sociology* 25 (1999): 271–305.

4. Diane Vaughan defines organizational deviance as "an event, activity, or circumstance, occurring in and/or produced by a formal organization, that deviates from both formal design goals and normative standards or expectations, either in the fact of its occurrence or in its consequences, and produces sub optimal outcomes." Vaughan, "The Dark Side of Organizations," p. 273.

5. The starting point for Vaughan's analysis, and indeed for the entire subfield, is Robert Merton's observation that any system of organized social action inevitably produces secondary consequences that run either perpendicular to or directly against its primary goals. In a 1936 article, Merton identified five broad factors responsible for the generation of these unintended consequences, two of which are particularly relevant to an understanding of school officials' lack of response. The first is simply a lack of sufficient knowledge; even when the likely adverse consequences of decisions are potentially identifiable, pressures within organizations to take immediate action often force officials to make decisions on the basis of limited information. And even if there is no need for immediate action, Merton pointed out, time and energy are costly resources that must be allocated among alternative wants, only one of which is the anticipation of consequences. A second factor contributing to the production of adverse outcomes is actual error in the appraisal of the relevant situation, in the process of making inferences to the future, in the selection of an appropriate course of action, or in its execution. Such errors are often attributable to an unwarranted assumption that the repetition of past actions will produce similar outcomes or to the allocation of attention to only one aspect of a situation because of simple neglect or of obsession. Robert K. Merton, "The Unanticipated Consequences of Purposive Social Action," *American Sociological Review* 1, no. 6 (1936): 900–901.

6. Vaughan, "The Dark Side of Organizations." The relevant characteristics of the system include: the structure of an organization, the environment in which it operates, and the normal "cognitive practices" of individual actors within organizations, that is, the ways in which information is regularly created, evaluated, and used.

7. Diane Vaughan, *The Challenger Launch Decision: Risky Technology, Culture, and Deviance at NASA* (Chicago: University of Chicago Press, 1996).

8. Vaughan, *The Challenger Launch Decision,* p. 273. See David W. Bella, "Organizations and Systematic Distortion of Information," *Journal of Professional Issues in Engineering* 113 (1987): 117–129.

9. An important exception, often used in middle schools, is team teaching, whereby a set of primary subject teachers all have the same students and meet regularly for discussions. Prior to the shooting, Westside Middle School teachers had the same students and had a common planning time where they could meet to discuss students, but teachers told us that such discussions were not expected or required and that they did not generally cover emotional adjustment. Heath Middle School had a similar structure, with all seven or eight teachers for each grade in a team, which met regularly to discuss planning and to discuss students who had problems. The high school had no such structure, however.

10. According to Vaughan, "structural secrecy refers to the way division of labor, hierarchy and specialization segregate knowledge about tasks and goals. Structural secrecy implies that a) information and knowledge will always be partial and incomplete, b) the potential for things to go wrong increases when tasks or information cross internal boundaries and c) segregated knowledge minimizes the ability to detect and stave off activities that deviate from normative standards and expectations." Vaughan, "The Dark Side of Organizations," p. 277.

11. Tables 4.1–4.3 illustrate how information about the shooters was not widely shared prior to the shootings. The tables include only information we gathered from interviews and from media and court reports and is not intended to be an exhaustive description of what was known about each of the boys. In addition, at one or more individuals specified in these tables have been given two identities in order to protect their privacy.

12. Howard Becker, whose work popularized labeling theory, argued that deviance is socially constructed and that deviant people are those to whom the "label has successfully been applied." Howard Becker, *Outsiders: Studies in the Sociology of Deviance* (New York: Free Press, 1963).

13. Nancy Gibbs and Timothy Roche, "Special Report: The Columbine Tapes," *Time,* December 20, 1999.

14. Robert Rosenthal and Lenore Jacobson, *Pygmalion in the Classroom: Teacher Expectation and Pupils' Intellectual Development* (New York: Holt, Rhinehart, and Winston, 1968); Robert K. Merton, "The Self-fulfilling Prophecy," *Antioch Review* 8 (1948): 193–210. For a review and meta-analysis of teacher expectancy experiments, see Stephen W. Raudenbush, "Magnitude of Teacher Expectancy Effects on Pupil IQ as a Function of the Credibility of Expectancy Induction: A Synthesis of Findings from 18 Experiments," *Journal of Educational Psychology* 76 (1984): 85–97.

15. The controversy is perhaps most strong for teacher expectancy effects on intelligence or IQ, the original claim of Rosenthal and Jacobson's research. For a review, see Herman H. Spitz, "Beleaguered Pygmalion: A History of the Controversy over Claims That Teacher Expectancy Raises Intelligence," *Intelligence* 27, no. 3 (1999): 199–234.

16. Both Kentucky and Arkansas state law and administrative regulations leave considerable discretion to local school districts or schools regarding privacy of student records and student discipline. Kara Anchrum is referring to a local school board policy regarding determining punishments based on "prior offenses" that prohibits considering discipline violations from previous school years. However, schools can still keep disciplinary records from year to year.

17. Karl Weick discusses the ways that offices in schools can operate quite autonomously. The principal's and counselor's offices are loosely coupled. "The image is that the principal and the counselor are somehow attached but that each retains some identity and separateness and that their attachment may be circumscribed, infrequent, weak in its mutual effects, unimportant and/or slow to respond." Karl E. Weick, "Educational Organizations as Loosely Coupled Systems," *Administrative Sciences Quarterly* 21 (1976): 1–19.

18. Bella, "Organizations and Systematic Distortion of Information."

19. Vaughan argues that action or inaction based on weak or mixed signals is an important cause of organizational deviance. Signals that analysts performing postlaunch investigations deemed glaring were actually weak or mixed prior to the launch. NASA engineers had seen O-ring erosion on a previous launch on a cold day, but they did not know that the low temperature was responsible for the O-ring erosion. In fact, there could have been a number of other causes, including brush hair, lint, and a defect in the putty used to seal the rings. The observation of O-ring erosion under cold temperatures was thus a weak signal. Similarly, in the past when engineers had found problems with the technology, they made changes. When, in subsequent flights, the problems seemed to have disappeared, it was a mixed signal. There had been problems but they now believed that they understood the technology and had corrected the faulty mechanism. Vaughan, *The Challenger Launch Decision*. For more on weak and mixed signals, see Michael Spence, *Market Signaling* (Cambridge, MA: Harvard University Press, 1974).

20. Sociologist Mitchell Duneier uses the concept of *segregation of audiences* to explain how individuals attempt to prevent being labeled as deviants by confining their deviant behavior to audiences that lack the power to label. See Mitchell Duneier, *Sidewalk* (New York: Farrar, Straus and Giroux, 1999).

21. Unlike the middle school, Heath High did have some formal structures established to help keep track of students and close the gaps produced by a fragmented day. The high school had an academic advising system that assigned a teacher to monitor the progress of a small group of students for their entire four years of high school. But before the shooting, advisers met only once a week with their students. Even with these measures in place, the school staff, including Michael's academic adviser, was generally unaware of his more unseemly behavior, even though much of it occurred on school grounds.

22. Julia Sampson went on to explain that middle school is a period of oscillation in what students look for in the way of emotional relations with teachers. "The way you treat elementary students is completely different than the way you treat junior high. It bridges the gap. It's a neat thing, but it's fragile, especially when you have fifth graders one period and seventh graders the next." She suggested that Mitchell was in an ambivalent period, one day more like an elementary student and the next like a high school student in his emotional needs. This is quite normal in her experience.

23. Excerpt of deposition of [Michael's English teacher] taken September 21, 1999:

Q . . . I have the story entitled "The Halloween Surprise." . . . Had you had a student write a paper like this for you, what would you have done?

A I would probably—let's see. Obviously, it sounds terrible. But there are kids who write things that are blood and gory. And they like to write in that style. Had I read that, I would probably ask him to change it, or just say, you know, this really isn't appropriate. That type of thing . . . Honestly, I don't have but the one year to compare it to. And it was two years ago.

I do know just if I had any concerns in anything that I would read, I would, first of all, talk to another teacher about it, share it with my resource teacher, who has taught English for many years, and then, certainly, talk to the individual and ask him to change it. But he did not write that for a grade in my class, I can tell you that, because I have not read that. . . .

Q You had other students in your eighth grade English class writing papers like this?

A No. I wouldn't have assigned it. But, I'm saying, has the other teacher read things that are, like, writing blood and guts, do they like to write scary stories and blood and guts— maybe not quite that violent. Don't get me wrong. But I guess it was out of the ordinary, which is what you want me to say. Right?

Q I just want you to answer my question. But not extreme. Okay? It was out of the ordinary, but not extreme, in your mind?

A I guess you could say that, yes. . . .

24. "The Halloween Surprise" was contained in the police investigative files that we were allowed to study. Michael Carneal explained in his deposition for the criminal case that he had submitted it to his eighth grade English teacher. However, as the deposition transcript makes clear, she had no memory of having seen the paper.

25. This information comes from a deposition of Bill Bond with the plaintiff's attorney Mike Breen on September 21, 1999. Bill Bond was made aware of Michael Carneal's writings only after the shooting.

26. Barbara McGinty, the current principal at Heath, made the point that it is very easy for kids to become a blur. "You all need to watch that movie sometime: 'Cipher in the Snow,'" she said. "It's just about a little boy who gets on the bus every morning, goes to school every day, and one morning or afternoon he gets off the bus and he dies, freezes to death in the snow, and when people are questioned about him, nobody really knew him. Nobody really knew anything about him. I really feel very guilty at this time of year that I truly do not know every freshman here. I know their faces, I know their names, but I'm not sure—and why? Because they are probably strong academic students that have no reason to be down here. We were going down the list for Awards Night tomorrow night with underclassmen, and I looked at the freshman list and like I say, the names I knew, but I tried to bring up the picture. When their name is called tomorrow night and he or she comes forward I'll say 'Oh, okay. I know this person.'"

27. According to the Centers for Disease Control and Prevention's Youth Risk Behavior Survey, 19.3 percent of youths seriously considered suicide in 1999, 20.5 percent in 1997; 8.3 percent of youths attempted suicide at least once in 1999, 7.7 percent in 1997. See Laura Kann et al., "Youth Risk Behavior Surveillance—United States, 1999," *Morbidity and Mortality Weekly Report* 49, SS05 (June 9, 2000): 1–96, and Laura Kann et al. 1998, "Youth Risk Behavior Surveillance—United States, 1997," *Morbidity and Mortality Weekly Report* 47 SS-3 (August 14, 1998): 1–89.

28. Dan Olweus has developed the concept of the "provocative victim" to describe the small minority of adolescents who exhibit high levels of both anxiety and aggressive behavior. He shows that individuals with this profile are often known for starting fights and engaging in other forms of disruptive behavior. See Dan Olweus, *Aggression in the Schools: Bullies and Whipping Boys* (Washington, DC: Hemisphere, 1978). Pellegrini et al. (1999) similarly suggest the idea of "aggressive victims," which they characterizes as youths who respond to bullying with reactive aggression. These individuals are distinguished by the fact that they don't

use aggression in a proactive or instrumental manner; rather they become aggressive only in retaliatory circumstances. See A. D. Pellegrini, M. Bartini, and F. Brooks, "School Bullies, Victims, and Aggressive Victims: Factors Relating Top Group Affiliation and Victimization in Early Adolescence," *Journal of Educational Psychology* 91 (1999): 216–224.

29. A national study of bullying in the United States found, in fact, that over half of those students who report bullying others are also at least occasionally the victims of bullying. Tonja R. Nansel et al., "Bullying Behaviors Among U.S. Youth: Prevalence and Association with Psychological Adjustment," *Journal of the American Medical Association* 285, no. 16 (2001): 2094–2100.

30. See G. M. Batsche and H. M. Knoff, "Bullies and Their Victims: Understanding a Pervasive Problem in the Schools," *School Psychology Review* 23, no. 2 (1994): 165–174; Dan Olweus, *Bullying at School: What We Know and What We Can Do* (Cambridge, MA: Blackwell, 1993).

31. We have far less information about Andrew and bullying. Many suggested that he may well have been bullied, given that he was small, which students told us was a common reason for being targeted. After the shooting, Andrew told one person we spoke with that he felt "put upon," but none of the staff we spoke with was aware that he was teased or even thought he was.

32. The description of schools as loosely coupled systems was first put forward in a 1976 article by Karl Weick now considered a classic work on the sociology of school organization.

33. Charles E. Bidwell, "The School as a Formal Organization," in *Handbook of Organizations,* James G. March, ed. (Chicago: Rand McNally, 1965).

34. In this sense, schools are what sociologist Amitai Etzioni calls "normative" organizations—organizations that rely on moral or normative power to control their members. In normative organizations, compliance with organizational goals and procedures is achieved because organization members understand them to be legitimate. In contrast, in what Etzioni calls "coercive" organizations, such as prisons and custodial mental institutions, members comply because of physical sanctions or the threat of physical sanctions, and in "remunerative" organizations, such as firms that employ blue- and white-collar workers, members comply because of material or economic incentives. Of course, no organization fits perfectly into one of these categories. See Amitai Eztioni, *A Comparative Analysis of Complex Organizations: On Power, Involvement, and Their Correlates,* revised and enlarged edition (New York: Free Press, 1975).

35. As Etzioni explains, "Normative organizations are organizations in which normative power is the major source of control over most lower participants, whose orientation to the organization is characterized by high commitment. Compliance in normative organizations rests principally on internalization of directives accepted as legitimate. Leadership, rituals, manipulation of social and prestige symbols, and resocialization are among the more important techniques used" (*A Comparative Analysis of Complex Organizations,* p. 40). Etzioni also notes that compliance in schools can be thought of in terms of teachers, but also in terms of students. Students also face primarily normative power in schools, but occasionally face coercive power, particularly in schools where corporal punishment is practiced (pp. 45, 127–130).

36. The technical details of a nuclear power plant's operation are, of course, quite complicated, but it is easy to understand the basic idea. These plants use nuclear fission to heat

water into steam, which turns an electric generator. There are actually two water systems, one that absorbs the heat from the nuclear "core" and another that is heated by the first and produces the steam that drives the generator. The two cannot mix because the first becomes radioactive when it is exposed to the core. The first water system also plays a key safety role because by removing heat from the core, it keeps it below the temperature at which a meltdown or radiation leak can occur. All of the many parts of the system must be kept at the correct temperature and pressure for the plant to work properly and safely. The operators of the plant work in a control room full of dials, lights, levers, and gauges that allow them to gather information about the functioning of the plant and to manipulate its various valves, pipes, and safety systems. A nuclear reactor is a good example of both a complex and a tightly coupled system. There are thousands of parts that interact with each other in many ways and that depend on one another closely for proper operation. Charles Perrow, *Normal Accidents: Living with High-Risk Technologies* (Princeton, NJ: Princeton University Press, 1999). This book was first published by Basic Books in 1984.

37. Ibid., p. 99.

38. Bryan Vossekuil, Robert A. Fein, Marisa Reddy, Randy Borum, and William Modzeleski, "The Final Report and Findings of the Safe School Initiative: Implications for the Prevention of School Attacks in the United States" (Washington, DC: U.S. Secret Service National Threat Assessment Center and U.S. Department of Education, May 2002).

39. "The following are objectives of the staff of Heath High School for each one of our students:

1. To develop students who understand and appreciate a democratic society and any limitations it may impose on the individual.
2. To develop students who respect themselves and can extend this respect to others and property both public and private.
3. To develop students who are proficient in all forms of written, oral, visual, and electronic communication.
4. To develop students who are self-reliant, productive, and responsible.
5. To develop students who cultivate the habit of thinking and reasoning with discernment and verve; who strive to be objective in their decisions.
6. To develop students who know their limitations and potential and respect these differences in others.
7. To develop students who promote an atmosphere of understanding and cooperation between school, community and all facets of society.
8. To develop students who will have a life-long love for education, knowledge, and the discovery of life.
9. To develop students who are mature without being somber; become adults without abstaining from childhood; and who love life despite its hardships."

40. According to Charles Bidwell, teachers "face two major role dilemmas" in their work. The first involves the maintenance of order. The second involves the "goals of teaching—whether the teacher's main aim is nurturance of students or emphasis on students' achievement." Bidwell, "The School as a Formal Organization."

41. Of course, many teachers believe that if they cannot connect with a student on their developmental needs, they will not be able to deliver the academic instruction in ways that will be effective.

42. Rebecca Morris confirms that none of the counselors at Westside were properly trained to handle the needs their students face. "Every counselor I've talked to who is honest—well, actually, even one of the elementary counselors at Westside who . . . [has] been there for years—she . . . admitted one time that . . . 'they didn't teach us this stuff in school.' The needs of kids these days are so different from when any of these counselors out here went to school."

43. Some referrals are required by law. For example, whenever a child speaks of being abused at home, the school must notify social services.

CHAPTER FIVE

1. For a review of this literature, see Robert Sampson, "What 'Community' Supplies," in Ronald F. Ferguson and William T. Dickens, eds., *Urban Problems and Community Development* (Washington, DC: Brookings, 1999), pp. 241–292. Classic works include Robert E. Park and Ernest W. Burgess, *The City* (Chicago: University of Chicago Press, 1925), and Clifford R. Shaw, *Delinquency Areas* (Chicago: University of Chicago Press, 1929). On social capital, see James S. Coleman, "Social Capital in the Creation of Human Capital," *American Journal of Sociology* 94 (1988): S95–S120; James S. Coleman, *Foundations of Social Theory* (Cambridge, MA: Harvard University Press, 1990); and Robert D. Putnam, *Bowling Alone: The Collapse and Revival of American Community* (New York: Simon and Schuster, 2000). On the relationship between social ties and social control, see Robert J. Sampson, Stephen W. Raudenbush, and Felton Earls, "Neighborhoods and Violent Crime: A Multilevel Study of Collective Efficacy," *Science* 227 (1997): 918–924.

2. Putnam, *Bowling Alone,* pp. 310–318. There is also evidence of an association between high social capital and lower crime in the United Kingdom. Robert J. Sampson and W. B. Groves, "Community Structure and Crime: Testing Social Disorganization Theory," *American Journal of Sociology* 94 (1989): 774–802.

3. While this is an extraordinarily widely held perception, in fact, residential mobility rates have not increased over the past century. See Claude S. Fischer, "Ever-More Rooted Americans," *City and Community* 1, no. 2 (2002): 175–194.

4. Francis Fukuyama, *The Great Disruption* (New York: Free Press, 1999).

5. Putnam is the only academic on President Bush's Council on Service and Civic Participation 2003, which is otherwise composed of politicians (John Glenn, Bob Dole), journalists (Cokie Roberts), athletes (Cal Ripken, Steve Young), business leaders, actors, and nonprofit leaders. See White House press release at http:www.whitehouse.gov/news/releases/2003/01/20030130-4.html.

6. For the leading work of this kind of social criticism, see Michael Sandel, *Democracy's Discontent* (Cambridge: Harvard University Press, 1996); for a range of interesting responses, see Anita L. Allen and Milton C. Regan, eds., *Debating Democracy's Discontent* (New York: Oxford University Press, 1998). For more social scientific treatments see, from the political left, Robert Bellah et al., *Habits of the Heart: Individualism and Commitment in American*

Life (Berkeley: University of California Press, 1985), and, from the political right, Gertrude Himmelfarb, *One Nation: Two Cultures* (New York: Knopf, 1999).

7. Richard Posner, in *Public Intellectuals: A Study of Decline* (Cambridge: Harvard University Press, 1999), pp. 281–319, provides a critical discussion of Putnam, Himmelfarb, and what he terms the "jeremiah school" of social science.

8. Residential stability is an important contributor in the development of social capital. Geographic mobility can disrupt social closure—that is, interlocking ties or networks— within communities and between families. See John Hagan, Ross MacMillan, and Blair Wheaton, "New Kid in Town: Social Capital and the Life Course Effects of Family Migration on Children," *American Sociological Review* 61 (1996): 368–385. See also Putnam, *Bowling Alone*.

9. In associational life outside the family (referred to as a "primary association"), Putnam distinguishes in *Bowling Alone* between "secondary associations," which provide face-to-face contact and enable members to meet one another, and "tertiary associations," in which membership may entail little more than carrying a card in one's wallet or sending in a membership fee. See also Theda Skocpol, "How Americans Became Civic," in *Civic Engagement in American Democracy,* Theda Skocpol and Morris P. Fiorina, eds. (New York: Russell Sage Foundation, 1999), pp. 27–80.

10. For the role of religious participation in building social capital, see Putnam, *Bowling Alone,* chapter 4, and Mark R. Warren, *Dry Bones Rattling: Community Building to Revitalize American Democracy* (Princeton, NJ: Princeton University Press, 2001).

11. On the impact of ties between adults and youth on children's welfare, see Putnam, *Bowling Alone,* chapter 17.

12. Clifford Geertz, "Deep Play: Notes on the Balinese Cockfight" in *The Interpretation of Cultures* (New York: Basic Books, 1973), p. 448.

13. The differences between rural and urban or between the heartland and the coasts have been widely discussed in the aftermath of the 2000 presidential election, which split between the more rural states won by Bush (colored "red" on the election maps), and the more cosmopolitan "blue" states won by Gore. These maps reignited popular interest in a long-running debate among scholars about the degree to which the United States is wracked by culture wars, or differences in lifestyle and outlook that can also be mapped onto geography. James Davidson Hunter initially advanced this thesis in his book, *Culture War: The Struggle to Define America* (New York: Basic Books, 1991). Others have since argued that he overstated the case (Paul DiMaggio et al., "Have Americans' Social Attitudes Become More Polarized?" *American Journal of Sociology* 102 (1996): 690–755; Alan Wolfe, *One Nation, After All* (New York: Penguin Books, 1998). For a witty and less data-driven look at the "blue and red states" question that also notes only moderate differences, see David Brooks, "One Nation, Slightly Divisible," *Atlantic Monthly,* December 2001. Although some analysts, such as Michael Kimmel, have noted that virtually all rampage shootings have taken place in "red" states, we argue in chapter 10, on the basis of information from thirty-seven cases, that a particular confluence of social, psychological, cultural, and material factors must come together for a shooting to occur and thus any kind of broad cultural "red state–blue state" differences will at best only provide a partial explanation.

14. Data from the 2000 show, for example, that the percentage of households with children that are married-couple families (including stepparents) in these areas do not differ

greatly from surrounding communities: Arkansas (71.9 percent), Jonesboro (71.1 percent), Bono (68.4 percent), Cash (64.9 percent), Egypt (63.65), Craighead County (73.9 percent), Craighead County except Jonesboro (79.3 percent), Kentucky (73.4 percent), Paducah (54.2 percent), McCracken County (68.4 percent), McCracken County except Paducah (76.8 percent). Calculations made by authors from Census 2000, SF3, Table P10.

15. There was a shooting during class in a nearby school in Jonesboro in 1987, though this particular incident was an attempted suicide—not a mass murder. According to a media account, students told police that "Bobby Emmons, a ninth-grader at MacArthur Junior High School in Jonesboro, pointed the pistol at a classmate with whom he had had a disagreement, said, 'This should be for you,' then turned the gun on himself Wednesday morning. He was wounded in the abdomen." *The Orange County Register,* evening edition, May 7, 1987, p. A27.

16. Vaughan, *The Challenger Launch Decision.*

17. Erving Goffman, *Frame Analysis: An Essay on the Organization of Experience* (Cambridge, MA: Harvard University Press, 1974).

18. Vaughan, *The Challenger Launch Decision,* p. 273.

19. Ibid., p. 122.

20. Over time, people formed an understanding of who Michael was that was shaped in part by his frequent talk of violence. Because his talk was so common, Michael was seen as someone who frequently bragged about committing violent acts, but it was seen as "just talk," and its frequency made it even easier to ignore.

21. James S. Coleman, "Social Capital in the Creation of Human Capital," *American Journal of Sociology* 94 (1988 supplement): S95–S120. These ideas were also articulated earlier by anthropologists Max Gluckman and Laura Nader: Max Gluckman, *The Judicial Process Among the Barotse of Northern Rhodesia,* 2nd ed. (Manchester, England: Manchester University Press, 1967), and Laura Nader, "Choices in Legal Procedure: Shia Moslem and Mexican Zapotec," *American Anthropologist* 67, no. 2 (1965): 394–399. Nader examines the role that simplex and multiplex ties play in settling legal disputes. Only when communities are dominated by simplex ties, she argues, do people have the luxury of suing or picking fights. The greater litigiousness of American society relative to others stems from the prevalence of simplex rather than multiplex relations. The fact that the victims' families in Paducah have been socially ostracized for suing illustrates the enforcement of this norm in a largely multiplex community.

22. Coleman, "Social Capital in the Creation of Human Capital."

23. James Coleman and Thomas Hoffer argue, in *Public and Private High Schools: The Impact of Communities* (New York: Basic Books, 1987), that shared beliefs are one reason why Catholic schools perform better than similar public schools. Normative closure is reinforced by social networks and by high rates of residential immobility in these communities, since some stability is needed for trust and commitment to shared norms to arise among the adults. See Rebecca Sandefur and Edward O. Laumann, "A Paradigm for Social Capital," *Rationality and Society* 10 (1998): 481–501, and Coleman, *Foundations of Social Theory.*

24. For more on gossip and the spread of information as a means of social control, see Sandefur and Laumann, "A Paradigm for Social Capital." See also Ronald S. Burt, *Structural Holes: The Social Structure of Competition* (Cambridge, MA: Harvard University Press, 1992); Coleman, *Foundations of Social Theory;* Edward O. Laumann and David Knoke, *The Organizational State: Social Choice in National Policy Domains* (Madison: University of Wisconsin Press,

1987); and Edward O. Laumann and Peter V. Marsden, "Microstructural Analysis in Interorganizational Systems," *Social Networks* 4 (1983): 329–348.

25. There is also some evidence pointing in the other direction, that some students confide more in teachers with whom they have a close family connection. One Heath teacher who was not originally from the Heath area told us that students did not confide in her as much as in the teachers who were from there:

I: Do they ever come to you about things that are not necessarily either going on in school or related to school? Either like things in the home or drug or alcohol problems or pregnancy or eating disorders?

R: No. They may tell me how much they partied on Friday or Saturday night, but I don't think they would ever admit to having a drug or alcohol problem to me. The students that I have been in contact with are pretty closed mouth about their family life, but even though I am from Paducah, I am not from Heath. We have several teachers out here who are from Heath, and they were born and raised in this area, and they know the students, they know the students' families, they know their grandparents, they know—I think they tend to go to those schools more than they do those that are new.—Audrey Shaw, Heath English teacher

It is important to remember that social capital does have the intended benefit for some, perhaps most, children in these communities; unfortunately, those for whom it has negative repercussions seem to have the greatest problems.

26. Diane Schetky, "Forensic Evaluation of Michael Carneal," May 27, 1998, p. 5.

27. Ibid., pp. 16–17.

28. Social psychologists point to another reason for a failure to act. In situations where there are many observers, individuals may all think that someone else will act first. Moreover, under tense and ambiguous circumstances, they look to others for cues. But since everyone else is doing the same, it can result in a failure to act altogether. Situations like this are called "pluralistic ignorance" by psychologists who study what happens when there is uncertainty about what is actually transpiring, which is not quite what happened in the speeding example given here. But the phenomena are related. Even if neighbors all suspect that someone else will act, they have reasons for letting those other people take the heat, namely, the social cost of bringing bad news to neighbors in a small community. For more on pluralistic ignorance, see B. Latane and J. M. Carley, *The Unresponsive Bystander: Why Doesn't He Help?* (New York: Appleton-Century-Crofts, 1968); B. Latane and J. M. Carley, "Group Inhibition of Bystander Intervention in Emergencies," *Journal of Personality and Social Psychology* 10 (1968): 215–221; and Robert Craldini, *Influence: Science and Practice,* 2nd ed. (New York: Harper Collins, 1988).

29. According to the principal of Heath High, Michael was caught looking at the *Playboy* website on the school library computer. This charge was vigorously contested by Michael and his mother, Ann. Ann complained that the library had ineffective filtering software. In this he-said, she-said situation, it is hard to determine the truth. But we do know that Ann requested that both Michael and his sister, Kelly, be barred from using the library computers thereafter. Psychiatric reports, compiled on the basis of interviews with Michael's friends, note that he downloaded pornography on his home computer, printed it, and tried to sell it and give it away to kids at school. These materials were on the hard drive of the computer the police confiscated from the Carneal home.

CHAPTER SIX

1. James Coleman was among the first to explore this puzzle in his classic work *The Adolescent Society* (New York: Free Press, 1961). Coleman argued that the movement from a primarily agricultural economy in the nineteenth century to an industrial economy in the twentieth century brought about a decisive shift in relations between youths and adults. Whereas before youths were essentially apprenticed to their parents and education was an extension of the process of socialization, in an industrial (and now postindustrial) society, students engage in ever longer periods of general training intended to prepare them for the much more differentiated and unpredictable occupational sphere. The result is that adolescents become more dependent on the opinions of their peers (hence the "adolescent society"), and thus adult influence on adolescent behavior is greatly diminished. For a less functional explanation of the same shift, see John Boli, *New Citizens for a New Society* (New York: Pergamon Press, 1989).

2. As students got older, and college seemed like a more immediate prospect, the status of those who did well in school rose, although never to the level of the *really* popular kids like the athletes and the cheerleaders.

3. Sociologist Stephanie Coontz has labeled this product of the modern economy "rolelessness," because it is a lengthy time during which youths are too old to listen mindlessly to the dictums of adults but not yet old enough to have firm identities rooted in established work and family patterns. Stephanie Coontz, *The Way We Really Are* (New York: Basic Books, 1997), esp. pp. 12–18.

4. This process of performing for one another, and the superficiality and conformity that it can produce, is not distinctive to adolescents—indeed modern adolescents are very similar to the "other-directed" adults that David Riesman powerfully critiqued as being symptomatic of the conformity of the 1950s in *The Lonely Crowd* (Garden City: Doubleday, 1953). But what differs is that (most) adults also have a more fully developed sense of personal identity, against which to balance the opinions of others. Adults also have concrete markers by which to differentiate status, primarily income and occupational status, whereas adolescents' status markers are much more ambiguous and dependent on perceived social standing. Absent an internally defined set of goals or life purpose—and with the primary externally defined marker of school success so seemingly disconnected from any real-life consequences—the opinions of others in the society become a primary good for which adolescents compete. In this competition for approval, what are from an adult perspective minute differences in dress, musical taste, and so forth become important ways of distinguishing oneself.

5. Patricia Adler and Peter Adler, "Preadolescent Clique Stratification and the Hierarchy of Identity," *Sociological Inquiry* 66, no. 2 (1996): 122.

6. Ibid., p. 123. This is somewhat parallel to Orlando Patterson's argument that racial integration leads to conflict because of greater day-to-day contact, in comparison to a more peaceful (but less desirable) segregated society. Orlando Patterson, *Ordeal of Integration* (Washington: Civitas, 1997).

7. Erik Erikson, *Identity Youth and Crisis* (New York: Norton, 1994), esp. pp. 135–142.

8. David Kinney, "From Nerds to Normals," *Sociology of Education* 66, no. 1 (1993): 21–40. Kinney reviews the survey research in support of this point (p. 34). For a more general review of the consequences of stigmatization, see Jennifer Crocker, Brenda Major, and

Claude Steele, "Social Stigma," in Daniel T. Gilbert, Susan T. Fiske, and Gardner Lindzey, eds., *The Handbook of Social Psychology,* 4th ed. (New York: Oxford University Press and McGraw Hill, 1998). There is also considerable evidence that sometimes individuals or groups are able *not* to internalize stigma and have a variety of protective responses to avoid doing so. See Jennifer Crocker and Brenda Major, "Social Stigma and Self-Esteem: The Self-Protective Properties of Stigma," *Psychological Review* 96 (1989): 608–630. Why junior high adolescents are less able to do this is not clear. Kinney suggests that there are developmental reasons, but it is also possible that within a closed social system with a single source of status, resistance is very difficult.

9. This is similar to what Charles Cooley described as the "looking glass self." See Charles Horton Cooley, *Human Nature and Social Order* (New York: Scribner's, 1902).

10. For an interesting modern read on this same process, see Garrett Epps, "Can Buffy's Brilliance Last?" *American Prospect,* January 28, 2002, 28–31.

11. This story was on Michael's computer hard drive. It appears to have been submitted to a teacher because it says, "sorry, messy writing."

12. This has been described in its most extreme form in H. G. Bissinger, *Friday Night Lights: A Town, a Team, and a Dream* (Cambridge, MA: DaCapo Press, 2000).

13. Coleman argued in *The Adolescent Society* that sports are accorded special respect in high schools because they bring status and esteem to the whole community, as opposed to academics, which are primarily a competition among individuals. The fact that academic *teams* still are much less well-respected than sports teams, particularly football and basketball, suggests that cultural notions of what activities are desirable are playing an important role as well.

14. Lorraine Adams and Dale Russakoff, "Dissecting Columbine's Cult of the Athlete" *Washington Post,* June 12, 1999, p. A1.

15. Jackson Katz and Sut Jhally, "The National Conversation in the Wake of Littleton Is Missing the Mark," *Boston Globe,* May 2, 1999, p. E1.

16. Mark Obmascik, "High School Massacre Columbine Bloodbath Leaves Up to 25 Dead," *Denver Post,* April 21, 1999.

17. Diane Schetky, "Forensic Evaluation of Michael Carneal," May 27, 1998, p. 16.

18. In *The Adolescent Society,* Coleman argued that the reason that sports has such high status in schools is that teams represent the school in competition against other schools, whereas academic competition took place *within* schools, and hence tended to set kids against each other. He suggested that by having debating teams and the like compete against other schools, it would raise the social status of these activities. Our evidence suggests that these assumptions, while plausible, do not take into account to the powerful forces that valorize athletic talent in our society. In a world where even poor kids in Africa are wearing Michael Jordan jerseys and band camp is the subject of never-ending sarcasm in movies like *American Pie,* there is little chance that band members will be on a par with athletes in the adolescent social tournament.

19. Interview of Matt Stone by Michael Moore in *Bowling for Columbine.*

20. Eric Harris, one of two shooters in the Columbine massacre was stuck: He had no college plans and had been rejected by the military when he tried to enlist. The social rejections he suffered in high school looked like they would become a staple of his reality for

some time to come. By contrast, Dylan Klebold had already been accepted at the University of Arizona and knew that he had a way out of Littleton.

21. Taken from a letter she wrote to Nicole Hadley after Nicole's death.

22. Even those who leave often find their way back when they are ready to settle down. There are no exact figures available, but many residents told us that a common pattern was to return either after college or, more rarely, to retire after spending one's career years in a bigger city.

23. Michael told Dr. Schetky, a psychiatrist who examined him in the course of the criminal trial, that he did not write this story, but that it had been downloaded from a Web site and given to him by a friend because Michael still liked Smurfs. Diane Schetky, "Forensic Evaluation of Michael Carneal," May 27, 1998, p. 16. Michael told Schetky that he thought the story was "weird," although it is not clear whether by this he was referring to the characters' deviant sexual acts or to its strange violence. The former seems more likely, because there were many other similarly violent materials on his hard drive, but he told his psychiatrists that he was very uncomfortable with his emerging sexuality. At the very least, this idea of a dissident moving to take over and then destroy a community whose harmonious lifestyle disgusts him clearly appealed to Michael. The parallels to the Goth conversations about taking over the mall or the school are unmistakable.

24. Because our focus is rampage school violence, our discussion of the negative consequences of social capital has been directed toward its implications for Michael Carneal. But even for those who do not take such drastic actions, there can be downsides to social capital, the most obvious of which is a lack of privacy and autonomy. See Alejandro Portes and Patricia Landolt, "The Downside of Social Capital," *American Prospect* 7, no. 26 (1996): 18–21; Alejandro Portes, "Social Capital: Its Origins and Applications in Modern Sociology," *Annual Review of Sociology* 24 (1998): 1–24; Jeremy Boissevain, *Friends of Friends: Networks, Manipulators, and Coalitions* (Oxford: Basil Blackwell, 1974); Georg Simmel, *The Sociology of Georg Simmel* (New York: Free Press, 1950), particularly "The Metropolis and Mental Life," pp. 409–426. Morgan and Sorenson (1999) argue that the kind of norm-enforcing social capital that is so pervasive in Paducah and Westside can also inhibit academic achievement, perhaps by promoting a more parochial or insular mind-set. This would explain why so few students leave either of the towns to go to college, and why the few students we talked to do who had said that they needed to make a clear break from their home communities. See Stephen L. Morgan and Aage Sorenson, "Parental Networks, Social Closure, and Mathematics Learning: A Test of Coleman's Social Capital Explanation of School Effects," *American Sociological Review* 64 (1999): 661–681.

25. See Mary Pipher, *Reviving Ophelia* (New York: Putnam, 1994), and Myra and David Sadker, *Failing at Fairness* (New York: Scribner's, 1994), on the troubles of girls, and Christina Hoff Summers, *The War Against Boys* (New York: Simon and Schuster, 2000), on the problems of boys.

26. For more on boys and masculinity, see William Pollock, *Real Boys* (New York: Henry Holt and Company, 1998).

27. Timothy Egan, "Body-Conscious Boys Adopt Athletes' Tastes for Steroids," *New York Times*, November 22, 2002, p. A1.

28. Eli Newberger, *The Men They Will Become* (Reading, MA: Perseus, 1999).

29. The KKK had a noticeable presence at Westside. In Heath, only the Future Farmers of America, a relatively small group of rural students, were thought by their peers to be racist.

30. This is somewhat similar to the nation as a whole. See Alan Wolfe, *One Nation, After All* (New York: Viking, 1998).

31. On scripts, see Naomi Quinn and Dorothy Holland, "Culture and Cognition," in *Cultural Models in Language and Thought,* Dorothy Holland and Naomi Quinn, eds. (Cambridge, England: Cambridge University Press, 1987), and Paul J. DiMaggio and Walter W. Powell, "Introduction," in *The New Institutionalism in Organizational Analysis,* Paul J. DiMaggio and Walter W. Powell, eds. (Chicago: University of Chicago Press, 1991). Powell and DiMaggio's primary context is organizational analysis, but their discussion of different notions of culture, particularly the primacy given to scripts and schema, is useful for our analysis. On strategies of action, see Ann Swidler, "Culture in Action: Symbols and Strategies," *American Sociological Review* 51 (1986): 273–286. More recently, Swidler has revisited the question of how culture affects action, in *Talk of Love* (Chicago: University of Chicago Press, 2001).

32. The campaign was created by the Harvard School of Public Health. The "squash it" script was featured on a variety of popular teen television shows, and a national survey in 1997 of high school junior and seniors revealed that 60 percent of African-American youths had used the phrase, and 29 percent had used the hand signal. Report available at http://www.hsph.harvard.edu/chc/squashit.html

33. William Pollack, *Real Boys: Rescuing Our Sons From the Myths of Boyhood* (New York: Random House, 1998).

34. Alvin Poussaint and Amy Alexander, *Lay My Burden Down* (Boston: Beacon Press, 2000), p. 114.

35. Steve Fainaru, "Alaska School Murders: A Window on Teen Rage," *Boston Globe* (October 18, 1998), p. A1.

36. When girls experience this kind of psychological distress, by contrast, they seem to turn their anger inward, sometimes cutting themselves or developing eating disorders. Thus far, a "feminine script" does not provide for lashing out violently toward others as much as an inward-turning self-destruction.

37. Again, the purpose of school shootings is to make a public statement. The other killers who commonly take public credit for their actions are terrorist groups, who similarly want to be known so that their killings carry a symbolic message.

38. Steve Fainaru, "A Tragedy Was Preceded by Many Overlooked Signals (Part 2 of 3)'" *Boston Globe,* October 19, 1998.

39. Both Mitchell and Andrew also somehow thought that after a time away they were going to be able to come back to enjoy their newfound status. Mitchell told a friend, "I'm gonna be running from the cops for a while" but that he planned to return in the not-too-distant future. This suggests that they thought that they were going to be able to cash in on their changing social status.

40. Katz and Jhally, "The National Conversation in the Wake of Littleton Is Missing the Mark."

41. Elisa P. Benedek, William D. Weitzel, and Charles R. Clark, "Report of Psychiatric and Psychological Evaluation," July 17, 1998, p. 6.

CHAPTER SEVEN

1. Steve Fainaru, "Alaska School Murders: A Window on Teen Rage," *Boston Globe,* October 18, 1998, p. A1.

2. Bryan Vossekuil, Robert A. Fein, Marisa Reddy, Randy Borum, and William Modzeleski, "The Final Report and Findings of the Safe School Initiative: Implications for the Prevention of School Attacks in the United States" (Washington, DC: U.S. Secret Service National Threat Assessment Center and U.S. Department of Education, May 2002), p. 25.

3. Stephanie Verlinden, Michel Hersen, and Jay Thomas, "Risk Factors in School Shootings," *Clinical Psychology Review* 20, no. 1 (2000): p. 43. It should be kept in mind that Verlinden et al.'s analysis is based primarily on media reports of the incidents, which are often unreliable and even contradictory. However, in the case of Columbine, the evidence appears overwhelming that there were in fact numerous warning signs prior to the attack that were essentially ignored; the extent to which this is true in other cases is subject to confirmation. Also see Vossekuil et al., 2002.

4. Of the two dozen or more students who heard threats from the three shooters, one student who heard a threat from Andrew did report it to the school, as we discussed in chapter 4.

5. Although for the most part it was other teens who heard specific threats, a variety of adults in both communities had seen threatening, violent, or odd behavior and did not report it to the school or the students' parents. We examined the reasons for this reluctance in chapter 5.

6. Kim Brooks, Vincent Schiraldi, Jason Ziedenberg, "School House Hype: Two Years Later," Justice Policy Institute, April 2000.

7. Michael Healy, "Half of Teens Have Heard Gun Threat at School," November 27, 2001, *USA Today,* p. D6.

8. Brian Hallett, "Overcoming Linguistic Violence," *Peace Review* 10, no. 4 (December 1998): 511–513. This entire issue of the *Peace Review* is on "linguistic violence."

9. Jim Clarke, "Teen Kills Principal, Student in Rural Shotgun Rampage," *Associated Press Newswires,* February 20, 1997.

10. Jim Clarke, "Alaska Boy Warned He'd Kill Principal, Student," *Associated Press Newswires,* February 21, 1997.

11. Quote from Joyce Canaan, "A Comparative Analysis of American Suburban Middle Class Middle School and High School Teenage Cliques," p. 386 in George Spindler and Louise Spindler, eds., *Interpretive Ethnography of Education: At Home and Abroad* (Hillsdale, NJ: Lawrence Erlbaum, 1987), pp. 385–406.

12. On rate-busters in the workplace, see David I. Levine, "Piece-rates, Output Restriction, and Conformism," *Journal of Economic Psychology* 13 (1992): 473–489. Many of the empirical findings in this literature on rate-busters in firms seem likely to be equally applicable to rate-busters in the classroom. For example, rate-busters in firms tend to be less affected by their opinions of their coworkers, much as rate-busters in classrooms must force themselves to be indifferent to the hostility directed at them by their classmates.

13. A similar kind of fantasizing took place among Evan Ramsey and two of his closest friends. In this case, though, authorities believe that the other students, James Randall and Matthew Charles, were convinced that the crime was going to happen, and they were even-

tually convicted of lesser charges. Both fantasized with Ramsey about the killings, making a hit list with him, and egging him on by telling him about the glory he could win through the shooting. Randall actually taught Evan how to use a gun, and Charles initially volunteered to act as a backup but eventually settled for simply videotaping the crime. Randall was convicted of two counts of second-degree murder; Charles pleaded guilty to criminally negligent homicide. Their situations are qualitatively different from that of the other students on the balcony or the other students in Heath and Westside, in that they were accomplices to the crime, not merely kids who heard threats and did not tell. Consequently, the actions of Randall and Charles need to be explained in a similar manner to the shooters themselves, and thus should be analytically separated from the other kids who heard threats and did not come forward. See Steve Fainaru, "A Tragedy Was Followed by Overlooked Signals," *Boston Globe,* October 18, 1999, p. A1; *Associated Press Newswires,* "Bethel Teen Convicted for Role in High School Shooting," October 19, 1998.

14. Some parenting experts have suggested emphasizing that "telling is not tattling." Young children in particular often like to tattle as a way of indicating that they know that a behavior is wrong. They are looking for adult approval for making this kind of moral judgment and for denying themselves the pleasure of doing what their friend did. These experts suggest that parents discourage "tattling" aimed to get someone in trouble, but encourage "telling" when the kid is in danger, uncomfortable, and so forth. See Kathryn M. Hammerseng, *Telling Isn't Tattling* (Seattle: Parenting Press, 1995). This approach might work for young children, but is unlikely to be effective with adolescents, because the threat of social sanctioning is unlikely to be overcome. Telling is often even further stigmatized as kids get older and are more expected to be able to handle problems without adult intervention. We discuss later the circumstances in which the kids we talked to did think that telling would be socially acceptable.

15. This is an example of the disqualification heuristic, discussed at more length in chapter 5. Students make a cognitive mistake in assessing the probability of future events by assuming that past events provide a reliable guide. See Amos Tversky and Daniel Kahneman, "Judgment Under Uncertainty: Heuristics and Biases," *Science* (1974) 185: 1124–1131.

16. Stan Mitchell, "Grandfather of Golden Shooter Out of Suit," *Jonesboro Sun,* May 9, 2000.

17. Of course, it is possible that specific threats were overheard by fewer students, making confidentiality harder to protect. Some school personnel that we talked to suggested that adults should say that a teacher overheard the conversation if necessary to protect student identity. Again, it is not always easy to do, but it must be an important priority.

CHAPTER EIGHT

1. Both repentance and public "performance" have long been part of the Christian traditions of conservative Protestants such as Evangelicals and Fundamentalists, whose numerical presence and cultural influence are strong in the small towns and rural areas of the South and play a large role in both Jonesboro and Heath. The importance of the church in all facets of community life was eloquently described by one teacher who compared it to a more urban area where she had previously lived:

If you go to a certain church the people in that church will support you. They don't necessarily support people of this other church. . . . They are like little islands not necessarily connected. And that's true in all ways. You're from my church I will help you out first. . . . If you went to this town and you don't have a home church, you don't have a community to hang out with.

Here we do not carefully distinguish between Evangelical and Fundamentalist beliefs and practices, because our interest is in understanding the local culture, which is influenced by them jointly rather than any particular individual's own interpretations. We are also not interested in detailed doctrinal distinctions. For analyses of the distinctions, see Randall Balmer, *Mine Eyes Have Seen the Glory: A Journey into the Evangelical Subculture in America*, 3rd ed. (New York: Oxford University Press, 2000), pp. xv–xviii, or Nancy Tatom Ammerman, *Bible Believers: Fundamentalists in the Modern World* (New Brunswick, NJ: Rutgers University Press, 1987), pp. 4–5.

2. Dennis Prager, "The Sin of Forgiveness," *Wall Street Journal,* December 15, 1997, section A, p. 22.

3. Pat Brockenborough, "Automatic Forgiveness Should Not Be Considered a Sin," *Paducah Sun,* December 21, 1997, p. D2.

4. Michael's plea was an "Alford plea" (in the jargon: "pursuant to *North Carolina v. Alford*"). This plea was especially disturbing to the victim families and others in the community because it allows the defendant to plead guilty without admitting guilt. The defendant is simply acknowledging that the state has sufficient evidence for a conviction. Michael's lawyers recommended that he submit an Alford plea to protect himself and his family in case of potential future civil litigation. In the event of a civil suit, having already *admitted* guilt in criminal court would help the plaintiffs suing Michael or his family, more so than if Michael had just been found guilty. Although technically the Alford plea is subsidiary to the guilty plea, the victims' families and the others were just as frustrated by the Alford aspect of the plea as the guilty but mentally ill plea itself.

5. Quoted in Bill Bartleman, "Heath: Fantasy Gone Too Far?" *Paducah Sun,* December 17, 1998.

6. Developmental psychologist Lawrence Steinberg argues that youths younger than thirteen should never be considered adults by criminal courts, because they are not developmentally advanced enough to truly understand the consequences of their actions or assist in their own defense. Similarly, he argues that youths over sixteen are not very different from adults developmentally and thus should always be considered adults. In between, determination should be made on a case-by-case basis by qualified developmental psychologists. See Lawrence Steinberg, "Should Juvenile Offenders Be Tried as Adults? A Developmental Perspective on Changing Legal Policies," Joint Center for Poverty Research Working Paper 147, 2000. Available at http:www.jcpr.org/wp/WPprofile.cfm?ID=151.

7. Martha Fields, a professor of constitutional law at Harvard Law School, has suggested that one reason for this trend may be the procedural safeguards that attend adult criminal cases. Juvenile court tends to be informal, with the requirement for an adversarial trial barely in evidence. She notes that just as public discomfort is growing with lenient sentences for heinous crimes committed by youthful offenders, so too may discontent be developing

among lawyers about the loose nature of procedure in criminal courts when young people can be sentenced for lengthy periods. Virtually no defense was mounted for any of the offenders we discuss here. (Martha Fields, personal communication).

8. A second suit followed on April 14, 1999, and the two suits were eventually consolidated.

9. Thus far the courts have found overwhelmingly against the victims' families. With the exception of a $42 million dollar judgment against Michael Carneal himself, all of the other cases were dismissed by the judge before trial and are on appeal. (Since Michael himself has no assets or income, the judgment against him can only be collected if the families win a suit against the Carneals' insurance company, a case that is still pending.) As of this writing, the appeals have been rejected by the Kentucky Court of Appeals and the U.S. Court of Appeals for the Sixth Circuit.

10. The civil suits against the gun manufacturer and against Andrew's grandfather have been dismissed. The court agreed that the parties could not have predicted the intervening proximate cause of the burglary and use of the guns by the boys. The suit against the Goldens was settled out of court and a settlement was paid by their homeowners' insurance. At the time of this writing, the suit against Mitchell's parents is still outstanding, but they have no money or insurance to cover a damage award anyway. The suits against Mitchell and Andrew are also outstanding. By Arkansas law, a minor must have a guardian *ad litem* to be sued, but the court is refusing to provide them with one and no one else has stepped forward to do so either. Except for the occasional article in the *Jonesboro Sun,* the civil suits in Westside are rarely discussed and have not created conflicts similar to those in Heath. The most controversy relates to the suit against the gun manufacturers because of the gun-control connotations. When asked, however, people express a wide range of not particularly strong views about the suits. Some see the plaintiffs as money hungry, others don't want to judge them because of the magnitude of their loss, still others think it's silly to try to blame anyone but Mitchell and Andrew since "they're the ones that pulled the trigger," and still others think the effort is futile.

11. As we explained in chapter 5, many people in the community perceived Michael as socially awkward. We were given many examples of his odd behavior in contexts that varied from band trips to gatherings at church to Halloween escapades with his friends. He was known to have trouble fitting in and to engage in antics designed to draw attention, which generally backfired. The victims' parents drew on this pattern of social incompetence to suggest that "everyone knew" what Michael's parents seemed unable or unwilling to recognize. However, few in the community thought of Michael as a troublemaker. Most thought of him as a good kid, even if he was a bit odd.

12. The need to recognize one's sins, repent and seek forgiveness is formalized in many world religions. Judeo-Christian rituals, such as Catholic confession and the Jewish tradition of atonement during Yom Kippur, are but two examples.

13. Historian Randall Balmer describes one of the core beliefs of Evangelicals as "spiritual rebirth," derived from John 3. True "born-again" Christians have had such an experience, an experience in which "one acknowledges personal sinfulness and Christ's atonement." Such an experience and commitment are necessary for salvation. Randall Balmer, *Mine Eyes Have Seen the Glory: A Journey into the Evangelical Subculture in America,* 3rd ed. (New

York: Oxford University Press, 2000), p. xvi. Sociologist Nancy Ammerman describes an "extreme separation" of believers and nonbelievers among members of one Fundamentalist congregation, for whom personal salvation is one's "most important identifying characteristic." Nancy Tatom Ammerman, *Bible Believers: Fundamentalists in the Modern World* (New Brunswick, NJ: Rutgers University Press, 1987), p. 72.

14. As anyone who has attended services at a Fundamentalist or Evangelical church knows, the acknowledgment of one sin's (and acceptance of Christ) is done in a particularly public manner. Often a portion of the service is reserved for those who wish to come forward and publicly proclaim their faith for the first time. The "performative" aspect of Christian services extends beyond this single moment, often structuring the entire Sunday service. Fundamentalists, Evangelicals, and particularly Pentacostals are known (and often derided by those of other faiths) for the intensity of emotions displayed by their pastors and embraced by church members. Sunday morning televangelists and faith healers are just two well-known examples. However, for many Evangelicals, the public aspect of their religion extends beyond the church doors. For Evangelicals, being a Christian means sharing one's faith with others, publicly "witnessing" to nonbelievers or those of other faiths in an effort to convert them. Balmer, *Mine Eyes Have Seen the Glory*, p. 4. Witnessing is an "oral performance" that relies on narrative and story, often the individual's own story of spiritual rebirth and "opening one's heart to Christ." Susan Friend Harding, *The Book of Jerry Falwell: Fundamentalist Language and Politics* (Princeton, NJ: Princeton University Press, 2000). Public performance and repentance are closely linked to the importance of a church-based community, of "fellowship" with those who share one's commitment to Christ. Church members constantly reinvigorate and resolidify their community through such public collective acts, which serve to draw people together through shared experiences. Nancy Ammerman describes her fundamentalist congregation as one that does not just come to church on Sunday for a once weekly private retreat from the secular world, but for engagement with a community that fulfills multiple needs in all aspects of daily life. Ammerman, *Bible Believers*, pp. 78–79.

15. Sociologist Amitai Etzioni points out that shaming is possible only in a community of shared values, where there is considerable agreement on evaluations of deviant actions. Accepting shame is as key as recognizing that we are all eligible for a dose of it. And that realization, in turn, depends upon a community of shared values that agrees about what constitutes deviant behavior. A violator must view the shame heaped upon him as legitimate in order for shaming to be effective both as a punishment and as a guardian of shared values. The process of shaming and forgiveness also has the potential to be a cleansing force, with the capacity to reintegrate the transgressor. Shame catalyzes rituals of reconciliation through which a community can repair the damage done to itself, usually through face-to-face encounters between offender and victim. See Amitai Etzioni, *The Monochrome Society*. (Princeton, N.J.: Princeton University Press, 2001) (see especially Chapter 2).

16. Taking responsibility for evil action and suffering the consequences must take place in a much wider public arena, where the central figure cannot shield himself from shame. This aspect of the culture in the Bible Belt has much in common with the ideas of conservative philosophers such as Gertrude Himmelfarb and William Bennett, who believe that the emphasis that traditional cultures gave to shame as a means of holding their members in check has evaporated. Disastrous consequences follow, Himmelfarb argues, for shame is a crucial force in curbing criminal behavior and deviance. It was once considered deeply embarrassing

to be pregnant out of wedlock; the disappearance of shame with the growth of moral relativism opened the floodgates to behavior that was ultimately damaging to the social fabric. The only way back, Himmelfarb argues, is to restore the limits of proper conduct and enforce them through public shame. See Gertrude Himmelfarb, *The De-Moralization of Society: From Victorian Virtues to Modern Values* (New York: Knopf, 1995), and John Braithwaite, *Crime, Shame, and Reintegration* (Cambridge, England: Cambridge University Press, 1989).

17. The same themes have dominated discussions of forgiveness in the aftermath of genocidal warfare. As Yugoslavia began to dissolve, Serbian paramilitaries engaged in ethnic cleansing, killing Roman Catholic Croats by the thousands. Pope John Paul II visited Vukovar, site of one of the worst episodes of genocide in the course of the war, in June 2003 to encourage reconciliation. Croats found it very hard to hear the Pope's message, as the *New York Times* coverage of his visit made clear: "'It's hard to forgive,' said Ivka Babaric, 50, as she paused before entering the church . . . as she recalled the day in November 1991 when Serbian soldiers burned down her home, killing her two sons, Mirko, 3, and Darko, 16 months old. . . . 'If I forgive them,' she added, . . . 'I would have to forget my sons. I can't do this. . . . The priest and the pope say you must forgive, but they don't understand. . . . ' . . . 'We still cannot understand why people who come to Vukovar go to the victims and ask why can't you forgive,' Father Spehar [the parish priest] said. 'You can't forgive if no one asks you to forgive him. We still did not get any request from the Serbian people or even from the Serbian Orthodox Church asking for forgiveness.'" Peter S. Green, "Forgive Pope Says, but Croats Find It Hard," *New York Times*, June 8, 2003, p. A10.

18. Gretchen Woodard, Mitchell's mother, explained the origins of his statement: "He had sat and written to the family how sorry he was, and he wanted the chance—he asked his lawyer, he said, 'Will I have a chance to turn around and tell the families how sorry I am?' And Mr. Hart said, 'Oh Mitchell, here's another one: They might spit on you.' He was trying real hard to prepare Mitchell and protect him. Mitchell looked at him and said, 'They can't say or do anything that's worse than what I thought about [my]self.' . . . At least he's never changed his story. Like I said, he wanted to say to the families that he was sorry. The judge allowed him to read it, he couldn't turn around and look at them anymore. But it was something that he had wrote, it wasn't something that Bill Howard or I or anyone else had said. It comes from the heart of Mitch."

Mitchell's defense attorney said that Mitchell had written the first draft of the statement and then the attorney had helped him revise it. "Those were his words, and not mine. I tried to help him put it together, but I mean that came from him and not me. And it would not have been my defense."

19. It is not clear how Wright knew about this incident or whether it actually occurred, but our interviews with those inside the jail did note that Andrew and Mitchell had laughed and bragged about the shooting and reenacted it for other inmates.

20. Writing on the conservative Protestant view of the family, sociologist W. Bradford Wilcox notes: "The family is afforded enormous social utility, both as an 'enclave of loving authority' amidst the discontents of modern life and as an institution where children learn the virtues required to become good citizens, parents, and workers. The family's symbolic power also is derived from its biblically mandated role in bringing children to Jesus Christ and its status as a fount of psychological well-being for parents and children alike." W. Bradford Wilcox, "Conservative Protestant Childrearing: Authoritarian or Authoritative?" *American Sociological*

Review 63 (1998): 796–809; quote at p. 798. It is no surprise, then, that conservative Protestants look first to the family for the explanation of a child's problems and judge adults by their success as parents.

21. The prosecutors accepted the plea because it was an agreement to the maximum sentence. But the victim families felt that Michael should have gone to trial and could not understand why he didn't. Most especially they couldn't fathom the prosecutor's concern that he might not get a conviction. Wayne Steger was incredulous on this point. "He truly did not even want a trial because he was not sure, even with more physical evidence than he's probably ever had . . . that he could get a conviction." More troubling to the victim families was their understanding that until just a few minutes before a trial was to begin, the prosecutors had assured them that they would never accept a plea bargain.

22. Joe James said, "[The Carneals] kept their computer three days after the shooting. The day of the shooting, that evening Kelly and about five or six kids she knew were over at the house having a cleaning computer party." We asked, "So they were taking files out, you think?" "Yes, without a doubt, he responded. "The sheriff had to be pushed to get the computer to look at it." Although James was not the only person to voice this suspicion, we have no independent evidence that anyone tampered with the computer.

23. Joe James told us that state attorneys had requested the records of phone calls made from the Carneal house. "We were told that [the records] would be there [on file] for six months. Six months and one day, the county prosecutor got around to asking for [them], . . . and they were gone."

24. The victim families believed that a month was too short a time to do a thorough investigation and were certain that had it been more probing, they would have reconsidered the wisdom of a civil suit. Wayne Steger said, "Realistically, if we felt like there had been a thorough investigation, I doubt there would have been civil suits against a lot of individuals. . . . We just felt like it was just so poorly done and there is a lot of questions that still need to be answered. . . . I want to know why the other kids knew. . . . I don't know why they're not in jail."

The view that investigations ended early was not universally shared. Prosecutors felt the investigations had been sufficiently thorough. While victims like to be consulted about criminal trial tactics and informed in advance about the state's plans, prosecutors represent the people of the state, not the victims, a point that is hard for victims to accept. Joe James complained about this point, paraphrasing what the prosecutors told him when he raised his objections: "I'm not your lawyer, I am the state lawyer. And I don't want you here but I have to have you here because the law says I have to talk to you. That [was] the high point of our relationship with him. . . . He didn't want to deal with us."

25. Louisiana governor Huey Long built a powerful political career on the back of exactly this kind of class-inflected populism. In a state riven with racial inequality, it was the "little guy" versus the big and powerful that made Long the larger-than-life politician that he was. It very nearly carried him into national office. (See Alan Brinkley, *Voices of Protest: Huey Long, Father Coughlin, and the Great Depression.* [New York : Vintage Books, 1982].)

26. Conservative Protestants have become increasingly uneasy about the worldly institution of criminal law. Spiritual life and moral rectitude seem to be taking a back seat to the secular institutions of our society, a contaminating force that should be regarded with some suspicion as a man-made enterprise, as opposed to a godly one. See Randall Balmer, *Mine*

Eyes Have Seen the Glory: A Journey into the Evangelical Subculture in America, 3rd ed. (New York: Oxford University Press, 2000). On the wider "culture wars" between religious conservatives and secular progressives, see James Davison Hunter, *Culture Wars: The Struggle to Define America*. (New York: Basic Books, 1991). Hunter sees the culture wars as a conflict between the orthodox and the progressive over the moral vision that will govern public life in the United States, and therefore as a struggle over national identity. It is fundamentally about which moral vision will dominate the other. The culture wars are manifested in both local and national conflicts over issues such as abortion, rights for homosexuals, women's rights, education, and the media.

CHAPTER NINE

1. Kai Erikson, in his *Everything in Its Path: The Destruction of Community in the Buffalo Creek Flood* (New York: Simon & Schuster, 1978), notes that in natural disasters that devastate entire regions, euphoric togetherness does not develop. In his study, the cleavages were evident from the very beginning, and no one was left untouched. In Jonesboro and Paducah, the fault lines took a while to surface, but eventually they erupted into divisions that match Erikson's description exactly.

2. Edward T. Linenthal, *The Unfinished Bombing: Oklahoma City in American Memory* (New York: Oxford University Press, 2001).

3. Freedom Forum, *Jonesboro: Were the Media Fair?* The Freedom Forum Report No. 98-W08 (Arlington, VA: Freedom Forum, 1998).

4. Monte's family told us that his moving to Minnesota to live with his father was not related to the shooting or the response he received afterward. His parents felt he would have better educational opportunities in Minnesota.

5. Emotional reactions do not line up perfectly with individual locations on the concentric circles of damage done. As the nation learned in the wake of the September 11 attacks, people far from the center of a disaster can be completely undone, even when the events did not touch them directly. Some of the students who were most upset at Westside were those who had been sheltered from the shooting because they exited out of the other side of the building. How sensitive people were and how well they coped with the stress affected the rate at which they healed. Psychologists who deal with posttraumatic stress disorder describe this as the type of resources that individuals have for dealing with trauma, either psychological skills and "self capacities" or social resources in the form of external support (see, for example, Beverly James, *Treating Traumatized Children: New Insights and Creative Interventions* (Lexington, MA: Lexington Books,1989), and I. Lisa McCann and Laurie Anne Pearlman, *Psychological Trauma and the Adult Survivor: Theory, Therapy, and Transformation*. Brunner/Mazel Psychological Stress Series No. 21 (New York: Brunner/Mazel, 1990).

6. Larry Fugate, "Westside Shooting Survivors Reflect as Anniversary Nears," *Jonesboro Sun,* March 22, 2003.

7. Ibid.

8. Jim Stockton, who drives a shuttle van from the Memphis airport to Jonesboro, picked us up when we first arrived in the community and quickly struck up a friendly conversation. Before long he asked why we were coming to town and we explained that we were doing research on school shootings and would be staying in Jonesboro. Jim immediately responded

that the shooting was not in Jonesboro (although we had only said we would be staying there). The shooting was in Westside, he said, although he thought that Jonesboro had "tried to take credit for it." Rather than trying to distance themselves from the shooting, he felt that most people in Jonesboro had tried to associate themselves with the shooting because they got more attention that way. He said, with a slightly critical tone, that when the Westside shooting happened, President Clinton was on a visit to Africa. As soon as he returned, he called to send his condolences, and Mayor Brodell of Jonesboro took the call, rather than the Mayor of Bono—the community closest to the school. When we spoke with Mayor Brodell, he spoke with pride about the attention he received after the shooting. He said, "We had callers from all over the United States. I did a lot of interviews." By contrast, Mayor Duncan of Bono had little to say on this subject.

9. At Westside, so many services were donated to the victims' families that the courts found that they did not have sufficient out-of-pocket expenses to justify an order of criminal restitution from the offenders.

10. In fact, more people in the Jonesboro community criticized the victims' fund for the opposite reason: for not distributing the money to the victims quickly enough. Initially, the victims' fund gave out only a portion of the money collected. Organizations that deal with emergency donations know that holding back is often fiscally responsible, because trauma victims have long-term needs that can be met only by creating a reserve fund. Several of the charities that distributed funds donated to victims of the September 11 attacks argued that disaster relief funds and similar charities typically work by investing some donations for long-term needs (Stephanie Strom, "Families Fret as Charities Hold a Billion Dollars in 9/11 Aid," New York Times, June 23, 2002, Metro pp. 29, 33). To the uninitiated, however, keeping rather than distributing donations appears to be contrary to the intentions of donors or an indication of corruption and mismanagement.

11. Raynaud's Syndrome is a physical disorder that may remain dormant for years and be brought on by nervous exhaustion. It is frequently considered a nervous condition.

12. Kay Danielson, "A Healing Place for Children Touched by Violence," Current Response, Presbyterian Disaster Assistance, Situation Report, Ferncliff Camp, August 4, 2000. Available at http:pcusa80.pcusa.org/pcusa/wmd/pda/response/USDisasters/FerncliffReport/shtml.

13. Russ Dixon, a clinical psychologist at Arkansas State University who was part of the immediate crisis response team after the Westside shooting, explained on a *Nightline* broadcast a year later that returning to the site of a trauma quickly is an important part of recovery. Although most of the research on returning to the site of a trauma comes from studies of the military, Dixon argued that the same rules apply for middle school students, who should return to the site of a school shooting as soon as they are able to. *Nightline* transcript, p. 10.

14. The stigmatization of mental health counseling and mental illness more generally is not unique to these communities. A large body of literature from around the world shows similar trends in many communities and cultures. For the United States, see, for example, Amy E. Cooper, Patrick W. Corrigan, and Amy C. Watson, "Mental Illness Stigma and Care Seeking," *Journal of Nervous and Mental Disease* 191, no. 5 (May 2003): 339–341; Bruce G. Link, Elmer L. Struening, Sheree Neese-Todd, Sara Asmussen, and Jo C. Phelan, "On Describing and Seeking to Change the Experience of Stigma," *Psychiatric Rehabilitation Skills* 6, no. 2, (Fall 2002): 201–231; Faith B. Dickerson, Jewel L. Sommerville, and Andrea E. Origoni, "Mental Illness Stigma: An Impediment to Psychiatric Rehabilitation," *Psychiatric Re-*

habilitation Skills 6, no.2 (Fall 2002), 186–200. For Europe, see Marion Freidl, T. Lang, and M. Scherer, "How Psychiatric Patients Perceive the Public's Stereotype of Mental Illness," *Social Psychiatry and Psychiatric Epidemiology* 38, no. 5 (May 2003): 269–275 (Germany); Joan Ablon, "The Nature of Stigma and Medical Conditions," *Epilepsy and Behavior* 3, no. 6 (Part 3 of 3) (December 2002): S2–S9 (UK).

15. Despite such views, held by many in these communities, the psychological literature on treatment of PTSD is consistent in advocating therapy or some other form of treatment that involves careful revisiting of traumatic memories. See James, *Treating Traumatized Children;* McCann and Pearlman, *Psychological Trauma and the Adult Survivor;* and Michael J. Scott and Stephen G. Stradling, *Counselling for Post-Traumatic Stress Disorder* (London: Sage Publications, 1992); David W. Foy, "Introduction and Description of the Disorder," in David W. Foy, ed., *Treating PTSD: Cognitive-Behavioral Strategies* (New York: Guilford Press, 1992); Edward M. Carroll and David W. Foy, "Assessment and Treatment of Combat-Related Post-Traumatic Stress Disorder in a Medical Center Setting," . in David W. Foy, ed., *Treating PTSD: Cognitive-Behavioral Strategies* (New York: Guilford Press, 1992), pp.39–68. Failing to do so will likely result in further psychological damage or distress. This is true for children as well as for adults. Beverly James writes: "Most adults, therapists included, are naturally inclined to shield a child from pain rather than help him confront it. To be clinically successful in the unnatural process of having the child examine hurtful experiences, the practitioner must understand and accept that the process is necessary for integration and mastery." James, *Treating Traumatized Children,* p. 5; see also Scott and Stradling 1992, p. 161.

16. Research shows that children's symptoms are no more likely to be transitory than adults'; children are not more likely to simply "bounce back." For example, W. Yule and O. Udwin, "Screening Child Survivors for Post-Traumatic Stress Disorders," *British Journal of Clinical Psychology* 30 (1991): 131–138, reported their findings in child survivors of the 1988 sinking of the cruise ship *Jupiter.* The children's anxiety levels, which were normal ten days after the sinking, had significantly increased five months later. At the initial assessment, the children's depression scores had been significantly greater than those of a normal sample, and by the 5-month assessment they had significantly deepened.

17. Although rehearsing a traumatic incident should not lead to retraumatization if proper guidelines are followed, those guidelines must be tailored to the individual patient and his or her particular coping resources and reactions to the events and to the counseling. This requires a considerable amount of human judgment, and there is potential for error or miscalculation. See Thom Spiers, "Introduction," in *Trauma: A Practitioner's Guide to Counselling* (New York: Brunner-Routledge, 2001); Scott and Stradling, *Counselling for Post-Traumatic Stress Disorder;* James, *Treating Traumatized Children,* p. 12.

18. School has not been in session on March 24 since then, either because the day fell on a weekend or because of flood days or other cancellations. People were quick to point out that school was not closed because the school was trying to memorialize the date.

19. A quiet dedication ceremony for the memorial garden was later held, with little media coverage.

20. Several years later, two survivors of the shooting told the *Jonesboro Sun* that "the memorial at the school is simply a reminder of a day filled with horror, and they refuse to visit the scene." Larry Fugate, "Westside Shooting Survivors Reflect as Anniversary Nears," *Jonesboro Sun,* March 22, 2003.

21. This teacher has subsequently submitted a workers' compensation claim, which had not been resolved at the time of the interview. She was initially advised by the school board not to submit a claim because Arkansas laws would cover teachers' physical injuries from a criminal violent act, but not mental health. It is unclear whether this initial advice was incorrect or if this provision was changed later to permit teachers to submit workers' compensation claims for mental health needs. However, this teacher claimed that the school board's attitude toward teachers trying to submit workers' compensation claims, at least in the period after the shooting, was decisively negative and discouraging. She told us that the workers' compensation papers were given out by the school, but when she inquired about submitting a claim, the school board president told her, "It kind of seems like you've got some personal problems. You need to get yourself together."

22. One teacher we spoke with took the opposite view, that the Westside school administration offered her all the support she could have wanted. She said, "Our administration, they were hurting too. [The school principal was a] saint. Superwoman. I have nothing bad to say about anyone." She felt that sufficient funds were available for counseling and therapy, and she gratefully noted the support she received from the Victims' Advocate, prosecuting attorneys, and law enforcement officials.

23. Erikson, *Everything in Its Path,* p. 233.

CHAPTER TEN

1. We mean necessary conditions in the probabilistic sense of the term. That is, the overwhelming majority of cases will share these five factors (in statistical terms, our theory explains much of the variation), but finding a case that does not should not be seen as an invalidation of our theory. See Douglas Dion, "Evidence and Inference in the Comparative Case Study," *Comparative Politics* 30 (1998): 127–146; David J. Harding, Cybelle Fox, and Jal Mehta, "Studying Rare Events Through Qualitative Case Studies: Lessons from a Study of Rampage School Shootings," *Sociological Methods and Research* 31, no. 2 (2002): 174–217.

2. We have not only posited a five-factor model; we have grouped phenomena that are distinct but may play roughly the same role in the creation of a shooting. For instance, we argue, social marginalization is a necessary factor in school violence, although exactly how a shooter is marginalized may vary from case to case. One kid may be physically bullied, whereas another is tortured by his inability to fit in the popular circle. We think that this has the advantage of not simply ruling out subfactors because they are not present in all the cases. For example, if "only" 60 percent of the shooters are bullied, it seems unwarranted to say bullying is unimportant. But what about the other 40 percent? Our theory suggests that they, too, must have been socially marginalized, but that this must have happened in a different fashion (they didn't have any extracurricular activities, they were loners, and so forth). We think this retains some theoretical parsimony, without ruling out factors simply because they were not present in all cases.

3. See the discussion of case definition in Harding et al., "Studying Rare Events Through Qualitative Case Studies."

4. We have excerpted from the CDC data only that subset of cases that comes closest to meeting our definition of rampage shootings. Hence, for example, we have eliminated shootings that were committed by individuals who were not students, knife attacks, or shootings with only one victim. Culling the CDC data for the cases that fit our definition of rampage

school shootings reduces this data set by about 95 percent, but what remains are the cases that we are genuinely interested in. In the discussion that follows, then, when we use the phrase "according to the CDC data," we are referring only to the "culled" database of rampage school shootings, with the exception of suicide cases, where we include only those cases in which a student committed suicide at school.

5. Bryan Vossekuil, Robert A. Fein, Marisa Reddy, Randy Borum, and William Modzeleski, "The Final Report and Findings of the Safe School Initiative: Implications for the Prevention of School Attacks in the United States" (Washington DC: U.S. Secret Service National Threat Assessment Center and U.S. Department of Education, May 2002).

6. For two of the shootings, those in Conyers, Georgia, and Edinboro, Pennsylvania, we were fortunate to be able to rely on case studies prepared for the National Research Council's report on lethal school violence. National Research Council and the Institute of Medicine. *Deadly Lessons: Understanding Lethal School Violence: Case Studies of School Violence Committee,* Mark H. Moore, Carol V. Petrie, Anthony A. Braga, and Brenda L. McLaughlin, eds. (Washington, DC: National Academies Press, 2003). For the Columbine case, we made use of the report by the Columbine Review Commission, "Report of Governor Bill Owens' Columbine Review Commission" (2002).

7. See Appendix B for a more in-depth description of the case selection and a discussion of the benefits and limitations of each data source.

8. Using media accounts or case studies also allows us to perform a person- or event-centered analysis as opposed to a variable-centered approach. Whereas the data from the Secret Service, taken from their published reports, only allow us to do counts (for example, X percent were bullied, Y percent were loners, and so on), our data allow us to examine a range of characteristics that describe individual shooters. We want to know, for each and every one of them, whether there is any indicator of social marginality (bullying, loner, etc.).

9. The studies are not perfectly congruent, in part because of differences in the years covered and the different definitions of school shootings employed. Indeed, the definition used to identify a school shooting can have a significant impact not only on our assessment of how rare the event is but also on the substance of the theory that is subsequently developed to explain the phenomenon.

10. There have been school shootings where the perpetrators were girls. However, to our knowledge none of these qualifies as a rampage school shooting. For example, on March 7, 2001, two days after the shooting at Santee, an eighth grade girl shot a female student at Bishop Neumann High School, a private school in Williamsport, Pennsylvania. This incident does not meet our definition of a rampage shooting because there was only one target.

11. Table A.1 in Appendix A summarizes the twenty-five cases and provides demographic data on the offenders and the communities where the shootings occurred.

12. Because there is no standard definition of rural and urban areas used in policy, research, and planning, we rely on national media descriptions of the environments as rural, suburban, and urban for our study. Had we used the Office of Management and Budget definition of an urban area, for example, the Westside shooting would be said to have occurred in an urban county, despite the fact that Westside was universally described as a rural area by local residents and the national media.

13. Jerry Adler and Karen Springen, with Pat Wingert, T. Trent Gegax, and Evan Halper, "How to Fight Back," *Newsweek,* May 3, 1999.

14. Only 11 percent of the offenders in the CDC data were considered by school or law enforcement officials to be loners, and only 12 percent of attackers in the Secret Service report had no close friends. But being a loner and *feeling* like one are very different things. The Secret Service researchers were therefore interested in knowing not only whether *other* students thought the offender was a loner but also whether the shooter himself felt that way. Looked at from this subjective perspective, roughly a third of all attackers (14 of 41 shooters in the Secret Service study) could be considered loners. Our own sample, drawn from media reports, reveals that at least a quarter of the shooters (7 of the 27) were described as loners: Patrick Lizotte, James Alan Kearbey, Nicholas Elliot, Scott Pennington, Jamie Rouse, T. J. Solomon, and Jason Hoffman. Wayne Lo and Kip Kinkel, who were somewhat marginalized, were borderline cases.

15. According to the media reports we examined, 52 percent (14 of 27) had friends: Anthony Barbaro, Wayne Lo, Toby Sincino, Barry Loukaitis, Evan Ramsey, Luke Woodham, Michael Carneal, Mitchell Johnson, Andrew Golden, Andrew Wurst, Kip Kinkel, Eric Harris, Dylan Klebold, and Charles Andrew Williams.

16. According to our media reports, 78 percent (21 of 27). The numbers are similar in the CDC data: 84 percent (16 of 19) were described by principals or law enforcement officials as "wannabes," "gothic," "geeks," members of a satanic cult, loners, or members of no particular group at school. The Secret Service data suggest that 41 percent of attackers generally "socialized with mainstream students or were considered mainstream students themselves" and 27 percent socialized with peers who were either disliked by mainstream students or were "considered part of a 'fringe'" group. We see "mainstream students" as too amorphous a category to be helpful—and so we focus on CDC and media report descriptions of what social clique the students fall into.

Participation in extracurricular activities is another measure of the degree to which students are integrated in the school. Although the majority of offenders were affiliated in some way with clubs, sports, or other extracurricular activities, 41 percent of offenders in the CDC study did not participate in *any* extracurricular activities. Only 16 percent (3 of 19) were involved in sports. Similarly, Secret Service data indicate that slightly more than half of all attackers (56 percent, or 23 or 41) were not known to be involved with any organized social activities *in or outside of* school.

17. In the CDC study, 53 percent were called names or bullied, 14 percent were physically threatened, 5 percent were physically assaulted, and 5 percent had their personal property damaged or stolen by their peers.

18. Using the media reports, which often include the perspectives of both knowledgeable adults and peers, we found indications of bullying and teasing in nearly two-thirds of the cases (63 percent, or 17 or 27): David Lawler, James Alan Kearbey, Nicholas Elliot, Scott Pennington, Toby Sincino, Barry Loukaitis, Evan Ramsey, Luke Woodham, Michael Carneal, Joseph "Colt" Todd, Mitchell Johnson, Andrew Golden, Kip Kinkel, Eric Harris, Dylan Klebold, T. J. Solomon, and Charles Andrew Williams. Not included are borderline cases such as Andrew Wurst, who was teased only by his brother for bedwetting.

19. Seventy-one percent (29 of 41). Although we do not have a representative national sample with which to compare these figures, 17 percent of sixth through tenth graders nationwide say that they have been bullied at least sometimes. A 1998 study of almost 16,000 sixth through tenth graders found that 10.6 percent of students in this age range are sub-

jected to this kind of torment at least "sometimes," 13 percent bully others at least "some-times," and an additional 6.3 percent both are bullied and bully others. Tonja R. Nansel and her colleagues at the National Institute of Child Health and Human Development define bullying as "a specific type of aggression in which (1) the behavior is intended to harm or disturb, (2) the behavior occurs repeatedly over time, and (3) there is an imbalance of power, with a more powerful individual or group attacking a less powerful one. This asymmetry of power may be physical or psychological, and the aggressive behavior may be verbal (e.g., name-calling, threats), physical (e.g., hitting), or psychological (e.g., rumors, shunning/exclusion)." Tonja R. Nansel et al., "Bullying Behaviors Among U.S. Youth: Prevalence and Association with Psychosocial Adjustment," *Journal of the American Medical Association* 285, no. 16 (2001): 2094–2100 (quote from p. 2094).

20. Scott Bowles and Martin Kasindorf, "Friends Tell of Picked on But Normal Kid," *USA Today,* March 6, 2001, p. A4.

21. Sarah Tippit, "Bullied Teen Faces Court Over Killings," *Daily Telegraph,* March 9, 2001, p. 27.

22. Alex Roth, "Dad Says Bullying Drove Son to Act," *San Diego Union Tribune,* September 6, 2001, p. A1.

23. One adult who knew Williams said "I know he gets picked on. I've seen it. But he laughs a lot. He's always hugging and saying, 'I love you.'" Bowles and Kasindorf, "Friends Tell of Picked on But Normal Kid."

24. David A. Fahrenthold, "Shooting Suspect Well-Liked," *Washington Post,* March 11, 2001.

25. Jason Hoffman was the only one described as physically large at 6-foot-1 and 210 pounds, and he had always been big for his age. However, Navy recruiters who had recently rejected Hoffman said that he had a serious skin condition. "His [face] was kind of bleeding. They can't let you in like that," the recruiter said. Karen Kucher and Alex Roth, "Teen's Motive Emerges: Suspect Blamed Dean for Rejection by Navy," *San Diego Union Tribune,* March 24, 2001, A1.

26. Our media data indicate 63 percent (17 of 27): James Alan Kearbey, Kristofer Hans, Nicholas Elliot, Eric Houston, Scott Pennington, Toby Sincino, Barry Loukaitis, Evan Ramsey, Luke Woodham, Michael Carneal, Joseph "Colt" Todd, Mitchell Johnson, Andrew Wurst, Eric Harris, Dylan Klebold, Charles Andrew Williams, and Jason Hoffman. Borderline cases, such as David Lawler (his brother was called a pussy, not him) and Jamie Rouse (whose father was obsessed with his son's masculinity for fear he might be gay like the father's brother) are not included in this category.

27. Andy Williams wasn't the only school shooter for whom the teasing took on a gay-baiting aspect, even though none of the shooters apparently identified themselves as gay. Michael Carneal was called a "faggot" by the kids at his school. So were Barry Loukaitis, Eric Harris, and Dylan Klebold. However, all nineteen of the offenders in the CDC study were perceived by school and law enforcement officials to be heterosexual.

28. There is, of course, a difference between feeling rejected and feeling emasculated after such rejection. Not all boys who are rejected by girls feel emasculated by the slight. Emasculation happens when a girl is seen in the boy's eyes primarily as a way of demonstrating his masculinity—so young men for whom masculinity has high salience in their self-conception are likely to be particularly wounded by female rejection. This was certainly the case for Mitchell Johnson.

29. In fact, according to our analysis of the media reports, there is evidence that at least two-thirds of all shooters (18 of 27) believed they were disliked, unwanted, or somehow abused by their peers. To determine whether there was any evidence that the shooters *felt* marginalized, we considered the shooter's own statements, their writings, and accounts of peers and adults who knew them well.

30. Only in the case of Eric Houston do we see no evidence of marginality. However, the evidence of marginality is weak in three cases—Anthony Barbaro, Kristofer Hans, and Shawn Cooper.

31. The Secret Service study found that 34 percent (14 of 41) of shooters received a mental health evaluation and 17 percent (7 of 41) had been diagnosed with a mental health or behavior disorder prior to the shooting.

32. This figure does not include Pat Lizotte, who feared that his teacher would institutionalize him, and Andrew Golden, who would have been classified as having a mental illness on the basis of the plea at trial had we not known more about the case. Including these two cases would increase the proportion to 59 percent.

33. Even in an era when many kids are diagnosed with mental problems, school shooters seem much more likely than the average child to have them. Between 12 and 15 percent of adolescents have psychosocial problems that warrant treatment, and one in five children and adolescents experiences the signs and symptoms of a diagnosable mental disorder—including anxiety, mood, disruptive, or substance disorders—during the course of a year. U.S. Congress, Office of Technology Assessment, *Adolescent Health* (Washington, DC: U.S. Government Printing Office. Diagnosable mental disorders are any serious deviations from expected cognitive, social, and emotional development. If we limit the definition to include only those disorders that require a significant functional impairment, the percentage drops to 11 percent. When we limit the definition to include only extreme functional impairment, the prevalence drops further to 5 percent. U.S. Surgeon General, *Mental Health: A Report of the Surgeon General* (Rockville, Md.: U.S. Department of Health and Human Services, Substance Abuse and Mental Health Services Administration, Center for Mental Health Services, National Institutes of Health, National Institute of Mental Health, 1991).

34. The CDC's National Center for Health Statistics defines suicidal ideation as "having thoughts of suicide or of taking action to end one's own life. Suicidal ideation includes all thoughts of suicide, both when the thoughts include a plan to commit suicide and when they do not include a plan." Suicidal ideation is measured in the Youth Risk Behavior Survey by the question "During the past 12 months, did you ever seriously consider attempting suicide?" National Center for Health Statistics, "NCHS Definitions," available at www.cdc.gov/nchs/datawh/nchsdefs/Suicidal%20Ideation.htm.

35. The proportion is 37 percent (7 of 19). Furthermore, 26 percent (5 of 19) had received school-sponsored psychological counseling prior to the incident.

36. The proportion reported in the Secret Service study is 78 percent (32 of 41. Sixty-one percent had a "documented history of feeling extremely depressed or desperate."

37. Seventy-four percent of offenders (20 of 27) in our own media database were reported to have been suicidal, depressed, or feeling desperate. This figure does not include Anthony Barbaro, who killed himself in his cell after being caught, and Luke Woodham, who left a will, figuring he wouldn't make it out of the shooting alive. They are not included be-

cause there is no specific evidence that they were depressed or suicidal prior to the shooting. If we include these two individuals, the figure increases to 81 percent.

38. School shooters appear far more likely than most youth to suffer from depression or consider suicide. Approximately one in five high school students surveyed in 1997 said they had seriously considered committing suicide in the past year. And according to the National Institute of Mental Health, 8.3 percent of adolescents suffer from depression. Laura Kann, Steven A. Kinchen, Barbara I. Williams, James G. Ross, Richard Lowry, Carl V. Hill, Jo Anne Grunbaum, Pamela Ş. Blumson, Janet L. Collins, Lloyd J. Kolbe, and State and Local YRBSS Coordinators, "Youth Risk Behavior Surveillance—United States, 1997," *Morbidity and Mortality Weekly Report* 47(SS-3) (1998): 1–89. National Institute of Mental Health, *Depression Research Fact Sheet* (Bethesda, Md.: National Institute of Mental Health, 2000).

39. The figure reported is 63 percent (26 of 41). The study also found that 44 percent lived with both biological parents, and 19 percent lived with one biological parent and a stepparent.

40. Only in a minority of cases were the "usual" structural features of family instability in evidence: approximately 20 percent of the shooters lived with only one biological parent, and 5 percent lived with either a foster parent or a legal guardian.

41. The proportion is 48 percent (13 of 27). The count includes Kristofer Hans, Scott Pennington, Jamie Rouse, Barry Loukaitis, Evan Ramsey, Luke Woodham, Joseph "Colt" Todd, Mitchell Johnson, Andrew Wurst, Shawn Cooper, T. J. Solomon, Charles Andrew Williams, and Jason Hoffman. It does not include Wayne Lo, whose family had "high expectations," and Eric Harris, who endured frequent moves because his father was in the military.

42. This account is based on Richard Meyer, "When the Shooting Stops," *Los Angeles Times,* April 22, 2000.

43. Rouse would later say that the anger in this music contributed to the murders by feeding and sustaining his own anger. It "didn't give him the idea," but it did "[make] him feel capable of it. . . . It takes the horror out of death." "Tennessee Killer, Now 22, Says 'Death-Metal' Music Was a Factor," *Associated Press Newswires,* June 4, 2000.

44. Meyer, "When the Shooting Stops."

45. Overall, 23 of 27 fit this category. Not included are Anthony Barbaro, Patrick Lizotte, James Alan Kearbey, and Nicholas Elliot.

46. School authorities dispute that teachers witnessed the incident. See footnote 204, Columbine Review Commission (2001).

47. Steve Fainaru, "Alaska School Murders: A Window on Teen Rage," *Boston Globe,* October 18, 1998, p. A1.

48. Just about all of the school shooters—98 percent (40 of 41), according to the Secret Service study—experienced or perceived some sort of loss before the attack. These are often the precipitating events—the loss of a loved one, rejection by a girlfriend, or a drop in social status—that drive shooters over the edge. According to the Secret Service study, "these losses included a perceived failure or loss of status (66%, n=27/41); loss of a loved one or of a significant relationship, including romantic relationship (51%, n=21/41); and a major mental illness experienced by the attacker or someone significant to him (15%, n=6/41)."

49. "Mother Testifies at Son's Hearing," *Associated Press,* September 27, 1996.

50. At school Barry Loukaitis was harassed and teased, called "dork" and "gaylord" by other students. According to one friend, Loukaitis never wore shorts because he didn't want others to see the bruises on his legs inflicted by bullies. Defense attorneys contended that Loukaitis suffered from a severe mental illness—mixed bipolar disorder with psychotic and delusional features—and met the legal standard for insanity at the time of the shootings. Prosecutors said that Loukaitis suffered from a less serious depressive illness and was not insane when he fired on the class. They argued that he was faking mental illness, pointing out that he had ordered information on bipolar illness shortly before his psychological examination. Alex Tizon, "Scarred by Killings, Moses Lake Asks: What Has This Town Become?" *Seattle Times*, February 23, 1997, p. A1.

51. According to the Secret Service study, 12 percent of attackers (5 of 41) killed themselves during the shooting.

52. Mercer L. Sullivan and Rob T. Guerette, "The Copycat Factor: Mental Illness, Guns, and the Shooting Incident at Heritage High School, Rockdale County, Georgia," in *Deadly Lessons*.

53. William DeJong, Joel C. Epstein, and Thomas E. Hart, "Bad Things Happen in Good Communities: Edinboro, Pennsylvania," in *Deadly Lessons*.

54. Dan Morain and Carl Ingram, "School Dropout Questioned as Town Agonizes Murders," *Los Angeles Times*, May 3, 1992.

55. Lisa Levitt Ryckman, "Demonic Plan Was Months in Making: Teens' Journals Show Hatred that Exploded in Columbine Killings," *Denver Rocky Mountain News*, May 16, 2000, p. A4.

56. Jerry Buckley, "The Tragedy in Room 108," *U.S. News & World Report*, November 8, 1993.

57. This quotation is pieced together from various news reports over time. The entire manifesto was not released, so the sequence of these fragments is not known.

58. John Bacon, "Teen Accused in Killings Wrote Note, Officials Say," *USA Today*, October 3, 1997.

59. J. R. Moehringer, "Tale of Teen Murder Plot Terrify Mississippi Town," *Los Angeles Times*, October 9, 1997, p. A1.

60. Sue Anne Presly, "A Bible Belt Town Searches for Answers," *Washington Post*, October 22, 1997.

61. Gina Holland, "Teen Outlines Anger in Note," *Associated Press Newswires*, October 3, 1997.

62. We have evidence for this sort of targeting in six cases: Columbine, West Paducah, Pearl, Moses Lake, Conyers, and maybe Edinboro.

63. Ginny Holbert, "A Shared Lust for Blood: 'Killers' Just as Guilty as Media," *Chicago Sun Times*, September 7, 1994, p. 49.

64. A year before the shooting, Klebold and Harris made entries into each other's 1998 yearbooks describing what was to come. The entries referred to "the holy April morning of NBK (*Natural Born Killers*)." Tom Kenworthy, "Killers Wrote of Alienation, Anger Prior to Rampage," *USA Today*, March 16, 2000, p. A3; Ryckman, "Demonic Plan Was Months in Making," p. A4. Barry Loukaitis watched *Natural Born Killers* seven times and told friends he wanted to go across the country killing people like in the movie. Tizon, "Scarred by Killings, Moses Lake Asks: What Has This Town Become?"

65. Sullivan and Guerette, "The Copycat Factor."

66. Steve Fainaru, "A Tragedy Was Preceded by Many Overlooked Signals" (part 2 of 3)," *Boston Globe,* October 19, 1998.

67. The proportion reported is 81 percent (30 of 37).

68. This includes Eric Houston, who warned people not at the school, and Toby Sincino, who threatened suicide. It does not include James Alan Kearbey, who was seen with the gun in the school minutes before opening fire.

69. Bowles and Kasindorf, "Friends Tell of Picked on but Normal Kid."

70. Sullivan and Guerette, "The Copycat Factor."

71. Overall, 44 percent (18 or 41) fit this category.

72. Tizon, "Scarred by Killings, Moses Lake Asks: What Has This Town Become?"

73. According to the Pew Research Center, in 1998 the news story that the public voiced the most interest in was the Jonesboro shooting. News coverage of that event was followed closely by 49 percent of their respondents. "What Americans Think: Top 10 News Stories of 1998," *Spectrum* 72, no. 2 (1999): 15. Available at stars.csg.org/spectrum/1999/spring/sp99spec15.pdf.

74. According to the Secret Service study, 59 percent of school shooters (24 of 41) had exhibited some interest in violent media.

75. There is convincing evidence that Jason Hoffman, T. J. Solomon, Seth Trickney, and Andrew Wurst were copycat shooters. We see this total of four cases as a lower-bound estimate, as it is often difficult to get reliable information about a shooter's thought processes. Associated Press, "Suspect in School Shooting Referred Earlier to Columbine, Classmates Said," *St. Louis Post-Dispatch,* March 24, 2001, p. 23; "Case File, Hearing Show Fort Gibson Shooter Influenced by Columbine," *Associated Press Newswires,* June 11, 2000. Also see DeJong et al., "Bad Things Happen in Good Communities."

76. A character in the movie says, "Movies don't create psychos: movies make psychos more creative!" See http:us.imdb.com/Quotes?0117571.

77. The following account is based on as series of articles by Steve Fainaru: "Alaska School Murders: A Window on Teen Rage" (part 1 of 3), *Boston Globe,* October 18, 1998; "A Tragedy Was Preceded by Many Overlooked Signals" (part 2 of 3), *Boston Globe,* October 19, 1998; "Many Struggle to Put Their World Together" (part 3 of 3), *Boston Globe,* October 20, 1998.

78. According to the Secret Service report, 63 percent of shooters (26 of 41) had never or rarely been in trouble at school, 27 percent (11 of 41) had ever been suspended, and 10 percent (4 of 41) had been expelled. Similarly, only 21 percent of the offenders in the CDC study (4/19) were known to have been suspended or expelled in the previous year.

79. In the CDC study, only 16 percent (3 of 19) had been reported for disobeying authority, and 58 percent (11 of 19) had never been reported for physical fighting, name-calling, teasing of peers, or damaging or stealing personal property. Seventeen percent (2 of 12, with data unavailable for the rest) had been reported for bringing weapons onto school grounds. In the rural and suburban cases, none of the shooters had ever been reported for carrying weapons on school grounds before the attack.

80. The four were Toby Sincino, Evan Ramsey, Kip Kinkel, and Jason Hoffman.

81. In the Secret Service study, 41 percent (17 of 41) were getting As and Bs, 15 percent (6 of 41) were getting Bs and Cs, and 22 percent were getting Cs and Ds (9 of 41).

82. No change in academic performance, 56 percent (23 of 41); in friendship patterns, 73 percent (30 of 41); in interest in school, 59 percent 24 of 41); in school disciplinary problems, 68 percent 28 of 41).

83. In the Secret Service study, 5 percent (2 of 41) showed improvements in academic performance and 7 percent (3 of 41) had declining disciplinary problems at school.

84. Our analysis of media reports indicates that although a third of the shooters (9 of 27) had received counseling before the shooting, almost all of them (7) were seeing counselors or therapists outside of school. It is not clear whether school authorities had any idea these kids were so troubled.

85. According to the Secret Service study, 37 percent (15 of 41) of "attackers exhibited an interest in violence in their own writings such as poems, essays or journal entries." According to our media reports data, 44 percent of school shooters (12 of 27) had written violent essays, notes, or journal entries. This includes Luke Woodham, for whom the only evidence is the manifesto he handed to a friend before the shooting. The only shooters who are known to have written violent essays that were not turned in to school authorities are T. J. Solomon, Luke Woodham, and Jason Hoffman.

86. The following account is based on Buckley, "The Tragedy in Room 108."

87. In the CDC study, 37 percent (7 of 19) had been previously charged with a crime. In the Secret Service study, 27 percent of the attackers (11 of 41) had a history of arrest and 31 percent (13 of 41) had a known history of violent behavior. In our analysis of the media reports, we found evidence of previous trouble with the law for 19 percent of the shooters (5 of 27).

88. Much of the this account of Klebold and Harris comes from the Columbine Review Commission (2001) and the Jefferson County Sheriff's Report, available at www.cnn.com/ SPECIALS/2000/columbine.cd/frameset.exclude.html.

89. The Columbine Review Commission report (2001) does not explicitly state that the school was unaware of Klebold and Harris's arrest, but it notes that before "the events at Columbine High School, school authorities, law enforcement officials, juvenile authorities and other persons with relevant information about a student were uncertain about whether they could share that information." It also states that school officials knew about the violent writings and about the disciplinary incident and that law enforcement officials knew about the arrests and the Web page. In a *Denver Post* article published soon after the shooting, at least one teacher was quoted who said she was unaware that Harris and Klebold had been in a diversion program. "'I absolutely knew nothing about either one of the boys,' said Judith M. Kelly, a creative-writing instructor at Columbine." Although the article also reported that "principals are normally notified when a student enters the diversion program," given the Columbine Commission Report, it appears that the principal was not notified. See "Harris' Life Described as 'In Shambles,'" *Denver Post,* April 23, 1999.

Diversion officers were also privy to warning signs. Harris told his probation officer that he suffered from homicidal and suicidal thoughts; these admissions led his probation officer to put him in the anger management class. "Eric said he has problems with anxiety and allows his anger to build up until he explodes," a counselor wrote, adding that Harris said he "punches walls" and has "thoughts about suicide." After he finished the anger management class, Harris wrote a letter saying: "I learned that the thousands of suggestions are worthless if you still believe in violence." This information was not made public until two and a half years after the shooting. "Columbine Killer Told of Violent Thoughts," *Associated Press,* October 6, 2002.

90. The threat read: "I'm coming for EVERYONE soon and I WILL be armed to the f____ing teeth and I WILL shoot to kill. . . . God, I can't wait til I can kill you people. Feel no remorse, no sense of shame, I don't care if I live or die in the shoot-out. All I want to do is kill and injure as many of you . . . as I can especially a few people. Like brooks brown." Columbine Review Commission (2001).

91. According to the Columbine Review Commission (2001), "information about the threat was forwarded to Jefferson County Deputy Neal Gardner, Columbine High's school resource officer. Gardner noted no untoward behavior by Klebold and Harris at school and commented that the pair had 'treated him with appropriate respect.' A television interview with Gardner taped sometime later made clear that Gardner did not know and thus could not identify Harris."

92. Charley Able and Lynn Bartels, "Bill to Help Police Alert Schools," *Denver Rocky Mountain News,* December 20, 1999.

93. In the CDC study, 82 percent (9 of 11); in the Secret Service study, 81 percent (30 of 37); in our media analysis, 72 percent (18 of 25).

94. In the Secret Service, others had some knowledge in 59 percent of the cases (22 of 37). In the vast majority of these cases (93 percent, 28 of 30), the information was shared with a peer—a friend, a schoolmate, or a sibling. "Some peers knew exactly what the attacker planned to do; others knew something 'big' or 'bad' was going to happen, and in several cases knew the time and date it was to occur."

95. Jeff McDonald, "Terror Hits Home," *San Diego Union Tribune,* March 6, 2001, p. A1.

96. Scott Bowles, "Two Shot Dead at School: 15 Year Old Arrested in California Shooting that Also Injures 13," *USA Today,* March 6 2001, p. A1.

97. McDonald, "Terror Hits Home."

98. Bowles and Kasindorf, "Friends Tell of Picked on but Normal Kid."

99. According to the Secret Service study, almost all (93 percent, 38 of 41) of the "attackers engaged in some behavior prior to the attack that caused others—school officials, parents, teachers, police, fellow students—to be concerned." "In most cases, at least one adult was concerned by the attackers' behavior (88%, n=36/41)." "In three-quarters of the cases, at least three people—adults and other children—were concerned by the attacker's behavior (76%, n=31/41)."

100. Jim Hughes and Jason Blevins, "Father Had Hunch Son Was Involved," *Denver Post,* April 22, 1999.

101. In court later, a child neurologist testified that Kinkel had brain abnormalities that could impair functions such as memory, emotional control, and the ability to plan and prioritize. Defense lawyers argued that Kinkel had paranoid schizophrenia and had been fighting voices in his head telling him to kill from the time he was twelve; they also cited a family history of depression and schizophrenia. The family psychologist, however, had found no indication that Kinkel was suffering from delusions or any kind of psychosis.

102. Christopher Reed, "Teen Charged in Killing Bragged of Violent Ways," *Globe and Mail,* May 23, 1998.

103. In our media analysis, the shooters had access to a weapon at home or a relative's home in 67 percent of the cases (18 of 27). In the CDC study, at least 42 percent (8 of 19)

got their weapons at home. (We use the qualifier "at least" because in two cases this variable is unknown.)

104. In another 11 percent of the cases we studied (3 of 27), the shooters purchased the weapons themselves. In two cases (7 percent) the shooter got access to the gun through a friend.

105. According to the Secret Service study, "Nearly two-thirds of the attackers had a known history of weapon use, including knives, guns and bombs (63%, n=26/41). Over half of the attackers had some experience specifically with a gun prior to the incident (59%, n=24/41), while others had experience with bombs or explosives (15%, n=6/41)." About 44 percent (18 of 41) of the shooters in the Secret Service study also displayed fascination or excessive interest with weapons.

106. Phillip J. Cook, Mark H. Moore, and Anthony A. Braga, "Gun Control," in *Crime: Public Policies for Crime Control,* James Q. Wilson and Joan Petersilia, eds. (Oakland: Institute for Contemporary Studies Press, 2002).

107. Yvon Dandurand, *Firearms, Accidental Deaths, Suicides, and Violent Crime: An Updated Review of the Literature with Special Reference to the Canadian Situation,* Working Document (Vancouver, Canada: International Centre for Criminal Law Reform and Criminal Justice Policy, 1998). Available at http:canada.justice.gc.ca/en/ps/rs/rep/wd98-4a-e.html.

108. Acquaintances described the 14-year-old shooter in Taber as smart but shy, a perpetual misfit with few friends who was ostracized by other students at school. He drew insults because of his greasy, disheveled hair, his chronic acne, and his tendency to mumble when he spoke. The boy had been bullied for years. When he was six, his schoolmates doused him with lighter fluid and threatened to torch him. Once, as he was receiving a particularly savage beating, a girl snapped pictures for fun. That attack left him with a hole in his lower lip that was so large he could put his tongue through it. A schoolmate said that "people picked on him and bullied him and called him a nerd, idiot, and faggot." For weeks leading up to the shooting, the boy had been scared to leave his home for fear of yet another beating.

His mother said that her son had psychological problems, that he was depressed, but that there was nothing that seemed dangerous. "He did have his troubles," his mother said. "They weren't criminal type of troubles. They were dealing with his inadequacies and teenage stuff like that." The boy was clearly obsessed with the Columbine massacre. But even before Columbine, he talked about getting revenge and started threatening to shoot kids in his class. After Columbine, his mother later said, "he got into a fantasy that he just could not get out of." Carol Harrington, "Alberta Teen to Admit Shootings at School," *Gazette,* August 28, 1999, p. A7; Gary Dimmock, "Teenage Killer Wrote Out Hit List," *Ottawa Citizen,* April 30, 1999, p. A1; *Canadian Press Newswire,* "Taber Shooter a Brainy Pinball Wizard Picked on by Peers as Shy Cyber Geek," November 18, 2000.

109. A few school shootings, such as those in Grayson, Blackville, and Lewiston, fall at the margins of this typology. In the Grayson case, Scott Pennington was a loner who was bullied and teased by classmates for, among other things, his stuttering problem. In his rampage shooting, he shot a teacher who had given him a bad grade and a custodian who came to investigate the noise, and then held the class hostage, taunting the students for forty minutes.

In Blackville, Toby Sincino apparently randomly shot two math teachers before he fatally shot himself. He had had discipline problems at school, and his mother claimed that racism at the school may have contributed to the problem: Sincino was black, and some in the community contended that black students were disciplined more harshly than white students.

However, at under five feet, Sincino was small for his age and was tormented by other students as well. His cousin reported that he was often stuffed into lockers and thrown into garbage cans. Clif LeBlanc and Christine Crumbo, "Rumors, Racism Allegations Creating a Stir in Blackville," *The State,* October 17, 1995.

Because the Lewiston shooting occurred in 1986, we have far less information about Kristofer Hans. There is little evidence that he was marginalized, and his primary target was a teacher who had flunked him. Although he injured two students, he may have hit them while firing wildly as he was attempting to flee the school.

110. Toby Helm, "Double Life of Massacre Gunman," *Daily Telegraph,* April 29, 2002, p. 11.

111. "Dropout Kills Four at School in California," *Houston Chronicle,* May 3, 1992, p. A1.

112. Caitlin Lovinger, "Carnage in Colorado: Youthful Killers in America Not a Recent Phenomenon," *Milwaukee Journal Sentinel,* April 25, 1999.

113. In discussing the near-miss cases, we have included cases identified by the Boston Globe and the Associated Press. (Tatsha Robertson, "Across the Nation, School Attack Plots Pose Legal Challenge," *Boston Globe,* December 16, 2001, pp. A1, A26; *Associated Press State and Local Wire*, "Police Say Students Planned to Bring Guns to School," December 19, 2001). Not all cases resulted in indictments, and some who were indicted were not convicted. We have refrained from using the names in cases where no charges were brought.

114. This synopsis of the original investigation comes from the police report, available at http:www.thesmokinggun.com/archive/nbedford1.shtml.

115. "Plea Deal for Suspect in School Plot Case," *Associated Press,* May 30, 2002.

116. "Student in Elmira Arrested After Bringing Bombs, Guns into School," *Associated Press,* February 14, 2001; Carolyn Thompson, "'What If?'" Haunts Students, Parents After School Bomb Scare," *Associated Press,* February 17, 2001.

117. Rik Stevens, "School Officer Credits DARE with Helping Thwart Possible Attack," *Associated Press State and Local Wire,* February 21, 2001.

CHAPTER ELEVEN

1. One such conference, held in September 1999 in Quantico, Virginia, was called "School Violence: Investigative, Preventive, and Predictive Strategies." See also Robert A. Fein, Bryan Vossekuil, William S. Pollack, Randy Borum, William Modzeleski, and Marisa Reddy, "Threat Assessment in Schools: A Guide to Managing Threatening Situations and to Creating Safe School Climates," (Washington, DC: U.S. Secret Service and U.S. Department of Education, 2002). Available at http:www.ed.gov/offices/OESE/SDFS/threatassessment-guide.pdf.

2. Freedom Forum, *Jonesboro: Were the Media Fair?* (Washington, DC: Freedom Forum, 1998).

3. The psychological literature on treatment of PTSD is consistent in advocating therapy or some other form of treatment that involves careful revisiting of traumatic memories. See Beverly James, *Treating Traumatized Children: New Insights and Creative Interventions* (Lexington, Mass.: Lexington Books, 1989); I. Lisa McCann, and Laurie Anne Pearlman, *Psychological Trauma and the Adult Survivor: Theory, Therapy and Transformation* (New York: Brunner/Mazel, Psychological Stress Series No. 21, 1990); Michael J. Scott and Stephen G. Stradling, "Group

Cognitive Therapy for Depression Produces Clinically Significant Reliable Change in Community-Based Settings," *Behavioural Psychotherapy* 18: 1–19; David W. Foy, "Introduction and Description of the Disorder," in David W. Foy, ed., *Treating PTSD: Cognitive-Behavioral Strategies* (New York: Guilford Press, 1992); Edward M. Carroll and David W. Foy, "Assessment and Treatment of Combat-Related Post-Traumatic Stress Disorder in a Medical Center Setting," in David W. Foy, ed., *Treating PTSD: Cognitive-Behavioral Strategies* (New York: Guilford Press, 1992), pp. 39–68. Failing to do so will likely result in further psychological damage or distress. This is true for children as well as for adults.

Treatment strategies should be closely tailored to individuals, based on the counselor's assessment of their reactions and coping strategies. Counselors need to "assess the degree to which memories are repressed or within conscious awareness and the degree to which they are fragmented or whole, as these are clues to how painful this material will be for the client." I. Lisa McCann and Laurie Anne Pearlman, *Psychological Trauma and the Adult Survivor: Theory, Therapy and Transformation* (New York: Brunner/Mazel, Psychological Stress Series No. 21, 1990), p. 85.

Treatment strategies for children attempt to "guide and assist the child through the painful process whereby the event is carefully unwrapped, gone over in slow motion to gain some developmentally appropriate understanding and acceptance of what happened, and then put away." Beverly James, *Treating Traumatized Children: New Insights and Creative Interventions* (Lexington, Mass.: Lexington Books, 1989), p. 4. Treatment of children should actively involve parents or caregivers, as they will be important resources in children's recovery processes.

4. In principle, the schools were supposed to be closed campuses even before the shootings. At Westside, individuals were only supposed to enter through the main entrance and all other doors were supposed to be locked. In practice, one Westside parent told us, the other doors were usually open.

5. "Fully Loaded Machine Pistol Seized from Teen at High School," *Associated Press State and Local Wire,* May 23, 2003.

6. One way to initiate these discussions is through a video and a set of classroom exercises explicitly designed for this purpose. One well-known program, "Tough Guise," developed by Jackson Katz, an expert on issues related to masculinity, can be found online at http:mediaed.org/videos/MediaGenderAndDiversity/ToughGuise/studyguide/html.

7. C. McNeeley, J. Nonnemaker, and R. Blum, "Promoting School Connectedness: Evidence from the National Longitudinal Study of Adolescent Health," *Journal of School Health* 72 (2002): 138–146; and R. Matthew Gladden, "Reducing School Violence: Strengthening Student Programs and Addressing the Role of School Organizations," in *Review of Research in Education,* vol. 26, Walter G. Secada, ed. (Washington, DC: American Educational Research Association, 2002), pp. 263–299.

8. Gladden, "Reducing School Violence," and M. Small, S. Everett, L. Dahlberg, M. Albuquerque, D. Sleet, B. Greene, and E. Schmidt, "School Policy and Environment: Results from the School Health Policies and Programs Study 2000," *Journal of School Health* 71 (2001): 325–334.

9. G. D. Gottfredson, D. C. Gottfredson, and E. R. Czeh, *National Study of Delinquency Prevention in Schools* (Ellicott City, MD: Gottfredson Associates, 2000); R. Skiba, *Zero Tolerance, Zero Evidence: An Analysis of School Disciplinary Practice* (Bloomington: Indiana Education Policy Center, 2000); and R. Skiba, and R. Peterson, "School Discipline at a Crossroads: From Zero Tolerance to Early Response, *Exceptional Children* 66 (2000): 335–347.

10. S. Heaviside, C. Rowand, C. Williams, E. Farris, S. Burns, and E. McArthur, *Violence and Discipline Problems in U.S. Public Schools: 1996–97* (Washington, DC: National Center for Education Statistics, 1998); M. Mayer, and P. Leone, "A Structural Analysis of School Violence and Disruption: Implications for Creating Safer Schools," *Education and Treatment of Children* 22 (1999): 333–356.

11. R. Matthew Gladden, "Reducing School Violence"; K. Dwyer, D. Osher, and C. Warger, *Early Warning, Timely Response: A Guide to Safe Schools* (Washington, DC: U.S. Department of Education, 1998).

12. "Announcing SPEAK-UP: Groundbreaking National Campaign to Prevent School Violence," *Business Wire,* October 16, 2002.

13. Mark Acosta and C. J. Schexnayder, "Teen Charged as Adult; Inland Threats Revealed: Campus Officials Are Taking Local Students' Menacing Words Seriously," *Press Enterprise* (Riverside, CA), March 8, 2001, p. A1.

14. Robert A. Fein, Bryan Vossekuil, William S. Pollack, Randy Borum, William Modzeleski, and Marisa Reddy, "Threat Assessment in Schools: A Guide to Managing Threatening Situations and to Creating Safe School Climates," (Washington, DC: U.S. Secret Service and U.S. Department of Education, 2002). Available at http:www.ed.gov/offices/OESE/SDFS/threatassessmentguide.pdf.

15. G. Roy Mayer, William J. Ybarra, and Holly Fogliatti. "Addressing Bullying in Schools," (Los Angeles: Los Angeles County Office of Education Safe Schools Center, 2001). Available at http:156.3.254.236/lacoeweb/docsforms/20011023084343_bullying102201.pdf.

16. Sarah Goddard and Jenny Cross, "A Social Skills Training Approach to Dealing with Disruptive Behavior in a Primary School," *Maladjustment and Therapeutic Education* 5 (1987): 24–29; Ludwig Lowenstein, "The Study, Diagnosis, and Treatment of Bullying in a Therapeutic Community," in *Bullying: A Practical Guide to Coping in Schools,* Michele Elliot, ed. (Harlow, England: Longman, 1991); and David P. Farrington, "Understanding and Preventing Bullying," in *Crime and Justice,* vol. 17, M. Tonry, ed. (Chicago: University of Chicago Press, 1993).

17. The Second Step Violence Prevention program, a time-limited, curriculum-based social skills and anger management program taught in the classroom by specially trained teachers, is aimed at elementary school students. An evaluation of the program found a decrease in physical aggression as measured by direct behavioral observation, but not by parent and teacher-reported behavioral measures (D. Grossman, H. Neckerman, T. Koepsell, P. Liu, K. Asher, K. Beland, K. Frey, F. Rivara, "Effectiveness of a Violence Prevention Curriculum Among Children in Elementary School," *Journal of the American Medical Association* 277 (1997): 1605–1611.

18. Stuart Twemlow, Peter Fonagy, and Frank Sacco, "A Social Systems–Power Dynamics Approach to Preventing School Violence," in *School Violence: Assessment, Management, and Prevention,* Mohammed Shafii and Sharon Lee Shafii, eds. (Washington, DC: American Psychiatric Press, 2001).

19. Dan Olweus, *Bullying at School: What We Know and What We Can Do* (Oxford, England: Blackwell, 1993); and Dan Olweus, "Victimization by Peers: Antecedents and Long-Term Outcomes," in *Social Withdrawal, Inhibition, and Shyness in Childhood,* K. H. Rubin and J. B. Asendorf, eds. (Hillsdale, NJ: Erlbaum, 1992).

20. One teacher we spoke with in Westside tried a survey like this in the classroom after the shooting and was amazed to find that bullying was widespread.

21. Laura Kann, Steven A. Kinchen, Barbara I. Williams, James G. Ross, Richard Lowry, Carl V. Hill, Jo Anne Grunbaum, Pamela S. Blumson, Janet L. Collins, Lloyd J. Kolbe, and State and Local YRBSS Coordinators, "Youth Risk Behavior Surveillance—United States, 1997," *Morbidity and Mortality Weekly Report* 47(SS-3) (August 14, 1998): 1–89. August 14, 1998. (Available online at http:www.cdc.gov/mmwr/preview/mmwrhtml/00054432.htm.)

22. See William Pollack, *Real Boys: Rescuing Our Sons from the Myths of Boyhood* (New York: Henry Holt, 1998), pp. 322–327. Pollack notes that the formal criteria that clinicians use to diagnose depression are heavily informed by the way we would expect depressed adult women to behave, and that professionals also must adjust their expectations to meet the needs of younger boys.

23. William Glasser, "School Violence from the Perspective of William Glasser," *Professional School Counseling* 4, no. 2 (2000): 77–80.

24. Institute of Medicine, *Reducing Suicide: A National Imperative,* S. K. Goldsmith, T. C. Pellmar, A. M. Kleinman, and W. E. Bunney, eds. (Washington, DC: National Academies Press, 2002); and National Mental Health Association Fact Sheet on Teen Suicide, available at http:www.nmha.org/infoctr/factsheets/82.cfm.

25. Resources can be found at the UCLA School Mental Health Project, available at http:smhp.psych.ucla.edu; at the Center for School Mental Health Assistance of the University of Maryland, available at http:csmha.umaryland.edu/csmha2001/main.php3; and at the Comer School Development Program, Yale Child Study Center, Yale Medical School, available at http:info.med.yale.edu/comer/index.html. See also Mark D. Weist, Steven Evans, and Nancy Lever, eds., *Handbook of School Mental Health Programs* (New York: Kluwer Academic/Plenum Publishers, 2002).

26. "Four out of five teens who attempt suicide have given clear warnings, including: (1) Suicide threats, direct and indirect; (2) Obsession with death; (3) Poems, essays and drawings that refer to death; (4) Dramatic change in personality or appearance; (5) Irrational, bizarre behavior; (6) Overwhelming sense of guilt, shame or reflection; (7) Changed eating or sleeping patterns; (8) Severe drop in school performance; (9) Giving away belongings." National Mental Health Association Fact Sheet on Teen Suicide, online at http:www. nmha.org/infoctr/factsheets/82.cfm.

27. Laura Mansnerus, "'Smart Gun' Measure Wins Approval in New Jersey Senate," *New York Times,* December 17, 2002, p. B8, and Laura Mansnerus, "Gun Billed Signed," *New York Times,* section 14NJ, December 29, 2002, p. 2

EPILOGUE

1. *Jonesboro Sun,* September 29, 2002.

2. Because Mitchell Johnson and Andrew Golden are under the age of eighteen, they are not allowed to make decisions of this sort.

APPENDIX B AND APPENDIX C

1. National Research Council and the Institute of Medicine, *Deadly Lessons: Understanding Lethal School Violence: Case Studies of School Violence Committee,* Mark H. Moore, Carol V. Petrie, Anthony A. Braga, and Brenda L. McLaughlin, eds. (Washington, DC: National Academies

Press, 2003). The Heath and Westside cases were assigned to us by the Case Studies of School Violence Committee. The other cases were those of Edinboro, Pennsylvania, Conyers, Georgia, East New York, New York, and Chicago, Illinois.

2. In this section we draw on Wendy D. Roth and Jal D. Mehta, "The *Rashomon* Effect: Combining Positivist and Interpretivist Approaches in the Analysis of Contested Events," *Sociological Methods and Research* 31, no. 2 (2002): j131173.

3. Lawrence B. Angus, "Developments in Ethnographic Research in Education: From Interpretive to Critical Ethnography," *Journal of Research and Development in Education* 20, no. 1 (1986): 59–67. Gordon Marshall, ed., *The Concise Oxford Dictionary of Sociology* (Oxford: Oxford University Press, 1994).

4. Paul Shankman, "The Thick and the Thin: On the Interpretive Theoretical Program of Clifford Geertz," *Current Anthropology* 25, no. 3 (1984): 261–280; Ann Chih Lin, "Bridging Positivist and Interpretivist Approaches to Qualitative Methods," *Policy Studies Journal* 26, no. 1 (1998): 162–180.

5. Gary King, Robert O. Keohane, and Sidney Verba, *Designing Social Inquiry: Scientific Inference in Qualitative Research* (Princeton, NJ: Princeton University Press, 1994); Gary King, Robert O. Keohane, and Sidney Verba, "The Importance of Research Design in Political Science," *American Political Science Review* 89, no. 2 (1995): 475–481.

6. Hans L. Zetterberg, *On Theory and Verification in Sociology,* 3rd enlarged ed. Totowa, NJ: Bedminster Press, 1966); Bernard Phillips, *Social Research: Strategy and Tactics,* 3rd ed. (New York: Macmillan, 1976); Robert MacKay, "How Teachers Know: A Case of Epistemological Conflict," *Sociology of Education* 51 (1978): 177–187; Todd D. Jick, "Mixing Qualitative and Quantitative Methods: Triangulation in Action," *Administrative Science Quarterly* 24 (1979): 602–611; Jerome Kirk and Marc L. Miller, *Reliability and Validity in Qualitative Research* (Beverly Hills, CA: Sage Publications, 1986).

7. The comparison to journalism is instructive, because the newspaper's job is not to discover truth but rather to present the best truth it can find in a limited time frame, in a way that is responsible enough to protect the paper from libel lawsuits.

8. Clifford Geertz, "Thick Description: Toward an Interpretive Theory of Culture," in *The Interpretation of Cultures* (New York: Basic Books, 1973), pp. 3–30.

9. On interpreting such breaches, see Martha S. Feldman, *Strategies for Interpreting Qualitative Data* (Thousand Oaks, CA: Sage Publications, 1995).

10. On qualitative case studies, causality, and theory development, see David J. Harding, Cybelle Fox, and Jal Mehta, "Studying Rare Events Through Qualitative Case Studies: Lessons from a Study of Rampage School Shootings,"*Sociological Methods and Research* 31, no. 2 (2002): 174–217.

11. Charles C. Ragin and Howard S. Becker, *What Is a Case? Exploring the Foundations of Social Inquiry* (Cambridge, England: Cambridge University Press, 1992).

12. Charles C. Ragin, "Turning the Tables: How Case-Oriented Research Challenges Variable-Oriented Research," *Comparative Social Research* 16 (1997): 27–42; Charles C. Ragin, "Case-Oriented Research and the Study of Social Action," in *Rational Choice Theory and Large-Scale Data Analysis*, Hans-Peter Blossfeld and Gerald Prein, eds. (Boulder, Colo.: Westview Press, 1998), pp. 158–168; and Charles C. Ragin, "The Distinctiveness of Case-Oriented Research," *Health Services Research* 34, no. 5 (1999): 1137–1151.

13. Ragin and Becker, *What Is a Case?* p. 6.

14. National Research Council and the Institute of Medicine. 2003. *Deadly Lessons: Understanding Lethal School Violence: Case Studies of School Violence Committee,* Mark H. Moore, Carol V. Petrie, Anthony A. Braga, and Brenda L. McLaughlin, eds. (Washington, DC: National Academies Press, 2003; State of Colorado, *Report of Governor Bill Owens' Columbine Review Commission* (Denver, 2001).

15. There were many incidents in which only scant information on the shootings was available in the media accounts, particularly among those that took place in the 1970s through the early 1990s, when school shootings were extremely uncommon events. It is possible, therefore, that we have excluded other cases that would meet our definition had we been able to gather more information about the event.

16. Mark Anderson, Joanne Kaufman, Thomas R. Simon, Lisa Barrios, Len Paulozzi, George Ryan, Rodney Hammond, William Modzeleski, Thomas Feucht, Lloyd Potter, and the School-Associated Violent Deaths Study Group, "School-Associated Violent Deaths in the United States, 1994–1999," *Journal of the American Medical Association* 286, no. 21 (2001): 2695–2702.

17. The CDC specifically defined a case "as a homicide, suicide, legal intervention, or unintentional firearm-related death of a student or non-student in which the fatal injury occurred 1) on the campus of a public or private elementary or secondary school, 2) while the victim was on the way to or from such a school, or 3) while the victim was attending or traveling to or from an official school-sponsored event." Anderson et al., "School-Associated Violent Deaths," p. 2695.

18. The CDC defined offenders liberally as any individual charged with a crime related to the event. This includes individuals who were not found guilty of the crimes.

19. There are a total of twenty-four suicides (that were not associated with homicides) of students on school property. Nine of them took place in urban areas, eleven in suburban areas, and four in rural areas. Eighteen of the victims were male and six were female. The victim's ages ran from thirteen to nineteen. Nineteen were white non-Hispanic, two were black non-Hispanic, three were Hispanic, and one was listed as "other race." Two of victims were students at another school, one event was a multiple-victim suicide.

Twenty-one of these suicides involved a firearm, two involved a rope, and one a blanket and lighter fluid.

20. Bryan Vossekuil, Marisa Reddy, and Robert Fein, "Safe School Initiative: An Interim Report on the Prevention of Targeted Violence in Schools" (Washington, DC: U.S. Secret Service National Threat Assessment Center, U.S. Department of Education, and National Institute of Justice, 2000).

21. On probabilistic models of necessary conditions, see Douglas Dion, "Evidence and Inference in the Comparative Case Study," *Comparative Politics* 30 (1998): 127–146.

INDEX

athletes
    failure to discipline for bullying, 284
    harrassment by, 286
attacks on institutions, 261–263

Barbaro, Anthony, 263
behavior following shooting
    at Alexander Juvenile facility, 45–46
    Andrew Golden's silence, 42
    Michael Carneal's confession of regret,
        33
    Mitchell Johnson, questions of remorse,
        42–43, 44
Bella, David, 81
Bethel Regional School, Alaska
    description of shooting, 155–156
    Evan Ramsey, 150, 151
Bible Belt reaction
    compassion for victim's families,
        189–190
    requisites for forgiveness, 187–189
blame, school staff and, 77–79
Bond, Bill
    on information loss, 85–86
    on Michael Carneal as non-disruptive
        student, 95, 103–104
    on parental involvement, 135–136
    role as principal at Heath High School,
        6–7
Bowling Alone (Putnam), 112
Bowman, Amylee, 266–267
Brazill, Nathaniel, 184
Brooks, Natalie, 40
bullying
    adolescent masculinity and, 144
    Dan Olweus program, 293–294
    Michael Carneal's endurance of, 98–99,
        150
    as missed signal, 96–100
    as normalization, 97
    overreaction response and, 99
    prevention programs, 293
    as problem in U.S. schools, 63–64,
        292
    social harrassment and, 97–98

social marginality factor, 241–242
teachers role in preventing, 100,
    293–294

Canaan, Joyce, 165
Carleton, Liz, 9, 13
Carneal, Ann, 7, 23, 304–305
Carneal, John, 7, 23, 304–305
Carneal, Kelly, 3, 4, 22–24
Carneal, Michael, 22–33
    adolescent masculinity and, 146
    confession of regret, 33
    family of, 22–24
    finding sense of purpose, 305–306
    gay label, 145–146
    gun acquisitions, 30
    Heath High School shooting, 3–5
    overlooked signs of trouble, 17
    in prison, 304–305
    psychological disintegration, 24–26
    response to small-town life, 142–143
    seeking peer acceptance, 29–33
    sibling tension, 22–24
    social failure of, 132–135
    suicide attempts, 48, 304
    threats issued, 157
    as victim of peer harassment, 26–28
    at Youth Correctional facility, 303–304
CDC (Centers for Disease Control and
        Prevention) data
    gun availability, 260
    individual vulnerabilities, 243, 244, 245
    overview of, 232–235
    school-associated violent deaths, 231
    social marginality, 235, 241
    undetected signals, 254–256
The Challenger Launch Decision: Risky
        Technology, Culture, and Deviance at
        NASA, 80
Challenger space shuttle explosion, 80–81,
        117
civil suits, 185–186
Cohen, Dov, 67–68
Coleman, James, 120
Collins, Michelle, 42–43, 77